Strategic Theories

Admiral Raoul Castex
(1878–1968) in 1938

ADMIRAL
RAOUL CASTEX
FRENCH NAVY

Strategic
Theories

Selections translated and edited,
with an introduction,
by
Eugenia C. Kiesling

NAVAL INSTITUTE PRESS   Annapolis, Maryland

These essays by Raoul Castex were originally published in *Théories stratégiques*, volumes 1–5, 1931–39, by the Société d' Editions Géographiques, Maritimes et Coloniales.

Naval Institute Press
291 Wood Road
Annapolis, MD 21402

First Naval Institute Press paperback edition published in 2017.
ISBN: 978-1-59114-594-3 (paperback)
ISBN: 978-1-68247-278-1 (eBook)

The Library of Congress has cataloged the hardcover edition as follows:
Castex, Raoul, 1878–1968
    [Théories stratégiques.   English.   Selections]
    Strategic theories / Raoul Castex ; selections, translated and edited with an introduction by Eugenia C. Kiesling.
        p.   cm.—(Classics of sea power)
    Includes Bibliographical references.
    ISBN 1-55750-100-9 (alk. paper)
Naval strategy.   I. Kiesling, Eugenia C.   II. Title.
III. Series.
V163.C37   1993
359.4—dc20

♾ Print editions meet the requirements of ANSI/NISO z39.48-1992 (Permanence of Paper).
Printed in the United States of America.

25 24 23 22 21 20 19 18 17   9 8 7 6 5 4 3 2 1
First printing

CONTENTS

PART III: EXTERNAL FACTORS

PART IV: INTERNAL FACTORS

PART V: THE SEA VERSUS THE LAND

PREFACE

Probably only one person in the world knew both that my dissertation touched upon the career of Admiral Raoul Castex and that the Naval Institute Press was seeking an editor for Castex's major work. Thus, my first debt is to my old teacher Steven T. Ross of the Naval War College, who often manages to put two facts together. Special thanks to series editor John Hattendorf for offering me the project and for valiant efforts to prevent me from botching it. Co-editor Wayne Hughes and Castex expert Hervé Coutau-Bégarie offered useful criticism of an early draft of the introduction. I am responsible for the errors that remain.

Castex's broad erudition is a challenge to the editor, and I am grateful to at least a dozen friends and colleagues for explanations of points of history, philosophy, naval architecture, geography, and French translation. Special thanks go to Peter Law, who, though he finds living with the French army taxing enough, tolerated the intrusion of naval affairs into our marriage and provided professional interpretations of Castex's beloved mathematical analogies.

I would like to thank the Service Historique de la Marine in Paris for access to Castex's papers back in 1985, when I had no idea how profitable that diversion in my research would prove to be.

Though accomplished mostly during an academic year at

the University of Alabama, the task was begun while I was a Ford Fellow in European Society and Western Security at Harvard's Center for International Affairs and completed during a research year at Southampton University funded by a Leverhulme Commonwealth/U.S.A. Fellowship.

No editor deserves to be confronted simultaneously with Castex's style and Kiesling's spelling, but Carol Swartz's sharp eye and tactful pen protected both the manuscript and the author's pride. Equal thanks to Linda O'Doughda, who inherited the project from Carol and guided it in the anxious final weeks. Whatever errors escaped their vigilance are my responsibility alone.

If that very private man Raoul Castex had intended *Théories stratégiques* to have a dedication, he would have given it one. Whatever in this volume is not the admiral's, however, but mine, I offer to George Forrest and Peter Derow, ancient historians of Wadham College, Oxford, in thanks for the priceless gift of confidence.

INTRODUCTION

I F PROLIFIC writing alone could ensure enduring influence,
then Admiral Raoul Victor Patrice Castex would be second in importance among naval theorists only to Alfred
Thayer Mahan. The author of eighteen major works and
more than fifty journal articles as well as the five-volume
Théories stratégiques,[1] this "greatest of the classical strategists" is now forgotten, his biography aptly subtitled *Le
stratège inconnu.*[2] Superficially, Castex's disappearance was
a natural consequence of his time and place. He wrote in a
day when major navies did not look to France for inspiration and on the eve of a pivotal conflict, after which war
would be very different and the wisdom of the past would
seem obsolete. Doubtless, too, the work's sheer bulk de-

1. Raoul Castex, *Théories stratégiques* (Paris: Société d'Editions Géographiques, Maritimes et Coloniales, 1929–1935). A sixth volume was
published posthumously as Raoul Castex, *Mélanges stratégiques,* Hervé
Coutau-Bégarie, ed. (Paris, 1976) (cited hereafter as Castex, *Mélanges*).
2. Hervé Coutau-Bégarie, *Castex: Le stratège inconnu* (Paris, 1985).
The assessment comes from Coutau-Bégarie, *La puissance maritime*
(Paris, 1985). Coutau-Bégarie's studies of the life and work of Admiral
Castex are the most important source for what follows and will be cited
hereafter respectively as *Castex* and *Puissance maritime*. The other important source for the admiral's life and work are the fifty-three cartons
of his papers deposited at the Service Historique de la Marine in Paris.

terred postwar readers from too close an investigation of *Théories stratégiques*.[3]

Though such considerations would justify the relegation of the French admiral's books to the lower library shelves, they do not explain their vanishing altogether while lesser books by less-distinguished authors survive to gather dust and bibliographical citations.[4] Indeed, Castex deserves to be more than a mere survivor; his prescient observations about matters ranging from French decolonization to the future Soviet threat, his emphasis on naval cooperation with land forces, his nuanced insistence on combining the search for fleet action with pursuit of the *guerre des communications,* and, most important, his introduction of the notion of *stratégie générale* might have put him in the forefront of postwar naval thought. What condemned Castex to virtual oblivion was less the substance of his work than his analytical approach. Not content to prescribe action for the present, he sought to understand the essence of strategy and to investigate the intellectual methods that can justify claims about it.

A world that faced the urgent material fact of the atomic bomb had little time for Castex. What passed for strategy became the province of physicists who measured explosive yields, engineers who understood payloads, and social scien-

3. The first edition contained 2,493 pages, the second an additional 159.

4. Brief references to Castex's work appear in Theodore Ropp, "Continental Doctrines of Sea Power," in Edward Meade Earle, ed., *Makers of Modern Strategy* (Princeton, 1943, 1971): 446–56 (Ropp's piece is omitted from Peter Paret's third edition of Earle's classic); in Geoffrey Till, *Maritime Strategy and the Nuclear Age* (London, 1982); in Phillipe Masson, "La pensée navale française de 1871 à 1940," *Revue historique des armées* 30 (1982): 43–51; and in Phillipe Masson, *De la mer et de sa stratégie* (Paris, 1984).

tists willing to reduce enemy response to calculations of probability. In this scientific world there was little room for generalship and none at all for a strategic analysis that assumed of its readers a philosophical bent and a working understanding of epistemology.[5]

Within thirty years of Hiroshima, however, a combination of defeat by the Democratic Republic of Vietnam and dismay at the implications of putatively rational strategies for the use of nuclear weapons had undermined confidence in strategy as a science and revealed the danger of allowing its degeneration into mere seizure of every technological possibility. Since the early 1970s, the study of strategy in the United States has looked to the scholarship of an earlier age. Pride of place at institutions of higher military study now goes to Thucydides' account of the Second Peloponnesian War, with its emphasis on human nature rather than technology; to Carl von Clausewitz, who explains that military effort is meaningless when devoid of political purpose; and to Alfred Thayer Mahan's historical arguments for the existence of universal strategic principles. Shared by these very different works is the premise that strategy contains elements independent of contemporary material conditions and common therefore to every time and place. In this era of revived interest in the nature of strategic thought, *Théories stratégiques* can be profitably reread, for no author has wrestled more earnestly than Castex with the methodological questions that ought to underpin the study of strategy.

The navy that Castex entered in 1896 had been for two

5. Even his contemporaries could find Castex's approach uncongenial. Upon reading *Théories stratégiques,* one British naval theorist observed that "the habit of the French mind is to think out its problems in a manner different from our own," Admiral Sir Herbert Richmond, "*Théories stratégiques,* vol. 4," *The Naval Review* 21 (1933): 621.

decades in a state of doctrinal turmoil. Subsumed within a vocal public conflict between advocates of a battleship fleet and advocates of coastal defense torpedo boats were antagonisms between blue-water and inshore strategies, historical and materialist strategists,[6] and, within the materialist camp, two rival factions whose competing icons were the torpedo and the naval gun. Best known in the French navy and easiest to locate in the tangle of doctrinal debates was a minority faction known as the *Jeune Ecole*.[7] Explicitly materialist in elevating contemporary technological imperatives over strategic principles, these advocates of the torpedo boat flotilla offered a coherent argument extending from the alleged capabilities of the torpedo to the primacy of a strategy of coastal defense.

In contrast to the solidly materialist *Jeune Ecole,* the battleship camp included members of both the historical and the materialist schools. For the former, the "French School" of Mahanian strategy,[8] the capital ship reified the Mahanian

6. The former, exemplified by Mahan, argued that, since strategic principles were unchanging, they could be distilled from the records of the past; the latter argued that strategy changed constantly as the weapons and other material conditions of warfare changed.

7. The *Jeune Ecole* came into existence in 1884 with the publication of Admiral Hyacinthe-Laurent-Théophile Aube's *A Terre et à bord, notes d'un marin.* It united naval advocates of torpedo boats and fast commerce raiders with those left-wing politicians who favored a small-ship navy for financial, political, and diplomatic reasons. See Theodore Ropp, *The Development of a Modern French Navy 1871–1904* (Annapolis, 1987): chapter 10; Ropp, "Continental Doctrines"; Masson, "Pensée"; and Castex, *Théories,* vol. 1, 50–52.

8. The leading French interpreters of Mahan were Admirals Pierre-Joseph-Gabriel-Georges Darrieus (1859–1931), author of *La guerre sur mer,* and René Daveluy (1863–1939), who wrote *Les lèçons de la guerre russo-japonaise* (1906), *L'esprit de la guerre navale* (1909), and *Les enseignements maritimes de la guerre anti-germanique* (1919). Discussions of the French School are in Castex, *Théories,* vol. 1, 46–49; Hervé Coutau-Bégarie, "Reflexions sur l'école française de stratégie navale," in H.

ideal of struggle for command of the sea; the latter merely judged it the best platform for the big gun, which was their weapon of choice. Their apparently shared emphasis on command of the sea was a contingent one; the French School favored the battleship as the centerpiece of a blue-water strategy, the materialists favored a blue-water strategy only because it suited the gun-carrying battleship.

Not that the proponents of the French School simply parroted Mahan's gospel of capital ships and fleet actions; in interpreting the American admiral for a French audience, they had to tack skillfully against the contrary winds of their national history and geography. Great Britain and the United States could seek command of the sea, but naval building in France would always take second place to continental military requirements. Thus, proponents of Mahan's historical method had to separate what was feasible for France—the building of a moderate-sized force of capital ships—from what was not—challenging the Royal Navy in a winner-take-all battle for naval supremacy. To be relevant to French naval possibilities, Mahan would have to be reinterpreted for what could never be other than a second-place fleet.

For Castex, these abstract distinctions had substantial consequences; the navy had not only to adopt the correct policies but to do so for the right reasons. Although, for example, authorization of a battleship building program in 1905 and promulgation in 1910 of tactical regulations emphasizing the big gun marked the victory of the naval cannon over the torpedo and of the blue-water strategy over the *Jeune Ecole,* he remained unsatisfied with decisions reflecting a methodological marriage of convenience between the materialism of the gunners and the historically based

---

Coutau-Bégarie, ed., *L'évolution de la pensée navale* (Paris, 1990): 31–56; and Masson, "Pensée."

analysis of the French School. Not only might the materialists prove ephemeral allies, shifting allegiances with any
change in technology, but their obsession with tactical fire-
power diverted attention from such indispensable strategic
lessons of historical analysis as the role of *manoeuvre*[9] and
the importance of combined arms in naval war.[10]

Castex believed that the absence of a coherent, historically grounded understanding of strategy prevented the
smooth assimilation during the Great War of events that,
instead, "created in many minds a profound and unnecessary upset." Of the postwar situation, Castex complained
that "we live in a confusion of ideas, in an undeniable doctrinal crisis, in a constant controversy over the lessons to be
drawn from the last conflict. . . ."[11]

Heir to the French School, Castex combined passionate
belief in the historical method with recognition that Mahan's prescriptions required modification to fit specific national circumstances and material conditions. Historical
principle was the best, but not the only, source of truth. If
materialists erred in their single-minded focus on a single
technological element, they offered a useful corrective to the
historians' tendency to operate at a level of abstraction that
evaded discussion of the actual conduct of war. Strategy had
to acknowledge both historical principles and material conditions as "one must apply with today's tools the stable lessons of the past."[12] Thus, Castex saw the schism between
historical and material schools as an unnecessary misunderstanding that could and had to be bridged in order to end

9. See page 101, note 1, for Castex's use of this term.

10. Castex, *Mélanges*, 301.

11. Raoul Castex, preface to Lt. de Vaisseau de Rivoyre, *Histoire de
la guerre navale 1914–1918* (Paris: L. Fournier, 1921): 6. Nowhere does
Castex better describe his own method than in this preface to another's
work.

12. Rivoyre, 8; Castex describes his method below, 24–25.

the wasteful struggles between the rival materialist factions within the navy.[13] Furthermore, giving heed to historically valid principles would inoculate the navy not only against obsession with any single weapon but also against strategic heresies like the *guerre de course* and the "fleet in being." Thus had the navy survived the challenge of the *Jeune Ecole,* spreader of "the morbid germs that would have poisoned us had we not eliminated them through judgment, good sense, and the historical method."[14]

Though called the synthesizer of the historical and material schools,[15] Castex does not simply combine the conclusions offered by two schools of naval thought nor extract elements from each, but instead he replaces the question "what is the right naval strategy for the moment?" with the more difficult "what methods for determining the appropriate strategy for the moment can be justified logically and generalized to other times and places?" The result he achieves does not give equal weight to its two elements. For all that Castex's historical emphasis is diluted by materialist considerations, historical conclusions are the final arbiters in any dispute.[16]

Castex's contribution to the naval thought of his own day urges upon his successors the duty to reevaluate constantly the foundations of received strategic wisdom. He recognized

13. Castex, *Mélanges,* 299; Raoul Castex, *La Liaison des armes sur mer,* ed. Hervé Coutau-Bégarie (Paris, 1991): 23.

14. Castex, *Théories,* vol. 1 (Paris, 1927): 51–52. For a discussion of the French army's version of the debate between historical and material schools, see Ladislas Mysyrowicz, *Anatomie d'une défaite: Cinq études sur les origines profondes de l'effondrement militaire français 1919–1939* (Lusanne: Editions de l'age d'homme, 1973).

15. See discussion in Coutau-Bégarie, *Puissance maritime,* 85.

16. Coutau-Bégarie's analysis understates Castex's subordination of material to historical principles. See below, 77–78, and Ropp, "Continental Doctrines," 455–56.

that, as a writer on a very different subject has observed, "the greatest problems of our time arise from the need to get our premises as well as our priorities right."[17] Behind the strategy chosen to meet the needs of the moment must be a transparent and resilient conceptual foundation—transparent so that its validity can be challenged and reaffirmed, resilient so as to endure as conditions change.

Admiral Castex's major work can be read in three different ways: as a prescriptive strategic handbook, as a text in the history of strategic thought, and as a source of insight into French military policy in the years between the costly victory of 1918 and the wrenching defeat of 1940. These three possibilities complicate both the editor's task of abridging the five volumes and the manner of their translation, but, fundamentally, the question resolves itself into a choice between looking to Castex for substance or for method. If substance is the aim, then *Théories stratégiques* has to be presented as a coherent strategic analysis. To do so would require culling the irrelevant and the anachronistic passages, expanding the project to include material from the posthumous sixth volume, and casting the remaining nuggets of insight in modern prose far removed from Castex's pedantry. However valuable to the strategist, the resulting distillation of Castexian wisdom would be deceiving to the historian and would deprive the work of the emphasis on method that is its greatest intellectual interest.

Stricter treatment of Castex as a historical figure and of his magnum opus as a historical document would demand that the edition be representative of the work as a whole, that it include some material tedious, irrelevant, and, to the modern reader, even absurd and do so in a style evocative

17. Elizabeth Fox-Genovese, *Feminism without Illusions* (Chapel Hill, 1991): 10.

of the author's own. The result would be unreadable and, in subjecting an early twentieth-century Frenchman to judgment by the vastly different intellectual and literary conventions of the late twentieth century, unfair.

Neither approach promises to be satisfactory, and 428 pages cannot capture the contents of 2,660, but this edition seeks to emphasize Castex's method of strategic analysis while omitting most of the chapters of historical narrative. Included are chapters defining strategy and relating it to policy and geography, analyzing the role of maritime forces and the significance of command of the sea, prescribing a theory of the conduct of operations, and introducing Castex's favorite themes: strategic *manoeuvre,* "*stratégie générale,*" and the theory of "perturbation." Two narrative chapters, on German operations in the North Sea from 1914 to 1916, remain as examples of the author's historical style. Most of the chapters have been abridged to eliminate lengthy and repetitive historical examples.

Castex's prose, though readable and clear almost to excess, sometimes defies literal translation. Much of the following translation approaches paraphrase, but, if the authentic voice of Castex the prolific pedagogue is lost in the process, perhaps his ideas will not share the same fate. Translation always involves interpretation, and while individual instances of difficulty are discussed in the footnotes, several repeatedly employed phrases deserve preliminary comment. *Sûreté,* described in a contemporary British review as "everything—patrols, intelligence, defensive organization—that secures and assures against surprise" appears throughout as "security."[18] *Servitudes,* used by Castex for the nonmilitary factors—political, social, financial, economic, moral, and psychological—that impinge on strategy,

18. The reviewer, Sir Herbert Richmond, preferred "surety," "*Théories stratégiques* vol. 2," *Naval Review* (1931): 361.

is translated "constraints." More problematic are *la force organisée*, rendered here in Mahanian style simply as "the fleet,"[19] and the untranslatable *manoeuvre*, which Castex himself defines as "to move intelligently in order to create a favorable situation," but uses in a variety of ways. Also left in the original French is *perturbateur*, Castex's label for a country with an insatiable appetite for expansion.[20]

Born in 1878, Raoul Castex entered the *Ecole Navale* for aspiring naval officers first in his class in 1896 and graduated first with a spectacular academic record two years later. Posted to Indochina, he inaugurated his long writing career with the publication in 1904 and 1905 of three books on Indochina.[21] As titles like *Jaunes contre Blancs: Le problème militaire indo-chinois* suggest, Castex had already adopted the set of racial categories fundamental to his later theory that the history of the world can be seen as an ongoing struggle between West and East.

Although he hoped to continue serving in Indochina, illness brought Castex back to France where he served from 1907 to 1908 as an ordnance officer in the Ministry of the Navy. In this period of upheaval in the French navy, Lieutenant Castex offered his own prescriptions for reform in a new book, *Le Grand état-major naval: Question militaire d'actualité*, that played a direct role in the reorganization of the naval staff in 1910.[22] *Le Grand état-major naval* is also

19. If "the fleet" perhaps exaggerates the Mahanian component of Castex's thought, Till's "the main concentration of the particular fighting forces of the time" (*Maritime Strategy,* 50) leans too far in the materialist direction.

20. See page 101, note 1. For the theory of perturbation, see chapter 19.

21. See pages 429–35 for a list of Castex's publications.

22. For subalterns to comment on naval policy was perhaps less strange in a navy where, as of 1894, the average lieutenant was 52.3 years of age, Ropp, *The Development of a Modern French Navy,* 40.

noteworthy as the work in which Castex, influenced by the distinction between the historical and material schools of naval strategy introduced by Sir Reginald Custance in *Naval Policy*, first defined his theoretical approach to naval strategy and proclaimed his allegiance to the historical school.[23] Moreover, his emphasis on the navy's role in an overall plan of national defense foreshadows Castex's later notions of *stratégie générale* and his emphasis on the importance of coherent national planning for the new era of total war. Among his suggestions was the creation of a shared course in strategy for officers of the navy and army, an idea that received no great attention at the time but presaged his appointment more than twenty-five years later as the first director of the *Collège des Hautes Etudes de Défense Nationale.*

While pursuing his literary career, Castex was also furthering his professional education as a professor at the *Ecole de Pilotage* and as a pupil at the *Ecole des Officers Cannoniers*, from which he characteristically graduated at the top of his class. At the former he wrote *Les Idées militaires de la marine au XVIIIe siècle: de Ruyter à Suffren,* which won a prize from the *Académie des Sciences Morales et Politiques* in 1913.[24] Suffren is Castex's ideal, a fighting sailor who, while cautious contemporaries eschewed fleet action in favor of the *guerre de course,* took as his target the enemy fleet.

During his next assignment, as chief gunnery officer

Castex applied his analysis of the general staff to the United States Navy in "Functions of the Office of Naval Operations," trans. Allan Westcott, U.S. Naval Institute *Proceedings* 46, no. 214 (December, 1920): 1987–99.

23. Coutau-Bégarie, *Castex*, 30. Custance published *Naval Policy: A Plea for the Study of War* (London: Blackwood, 1907) under the pseudonym "Barfleur."

24. Coutau-Bégarie, *Castex*, 43.

aboard the *Danton*-class battleship *Condorcet*,[25] Castex continued to produce historical studies at a stunning rate.[26] Nor did Castex allow his scholarly pursuits to detract from his professional performance, which received a glowing report from the *Condorcet*'s commander. The year 1912 also offers us a rare glimpse of Castex's image among his peers, for in that year another French lieutenant attributed to Castex the exhortation "*Tout le monde à la grande bataille!*", which he took as an epigram for his own book.[27]

In 1913, Castex was again posted to the Ministry of Marine, where he met one of the formative influences on his thought, the minister's chef de cabinet, Rear Admiral Darrieus, from whom he adopted his definition of strategy, the theory of "servitudes," and the notion that France should divest herself of unprofitable colonial possessions.[28] With Darrieus's enthusiastic support, Castex received a coveted appointment to the 1914 class of the naval staff college, the *Ecole Supérieure de la Marine*. Though his studies terminated abruptly with the outbreak of the war, Castex had used his short stay at the college to enter into the ongoing debate over the tactical implications of the conflict between the material and historical schools of naval theory by beginning a new study—*La liaison des armes sur mer*. The book,

---

25. Though commissioned in 1911, *Condorcet* was a pre-dreadnought battleship of 18,000 tons displacement, *Brassey's Naval Annual*, 1915.

26. Coutau-Bégarie, *Castex*, 41.

27. A. Baudry, *La bataille navale. Etude sur les facteurs tactiques* (Paris, 1912). Baudry, killed in action in 1914, was engaged in extending the historical method to the tactical realm (Castex, *Liaison*, Introduction, 7), and his emphasis on the importance of *manoeuvre* in tactics foreshadows Castex's later focus on strategic *manoeuvre* in *Théories stratégiques*. "*Tout le monde à la bataille*" would be Marshal Foch's battle cry in 1918.

28. For Darrieus's mentorship, see Coutau-Bégarie, *Castex*, 45, 126.

whose title promises an argument for combining the efforts of the gun and the torpedo and implicitly denies that any single weapon should dominate the strategic thought of its day, was Castex's most direct challenge to the material school.[29]

The war that interrupted his course at the staff college proved a series of disappointments for the energetic young officer, who chafed at the high command's refusal to release French ships to fight a decisive battle in seas teeming, at least in their imagination, with German torpedo boats and submarines. Unable to come to grips with the Germans, he vented his frustrations in his journal. "The brilliant successes of our army render even more painful the inaction we endure here. We must do something. The prestige of the French navy demands it. Better serious damage to our ships than the grave harm done to our honor and our reputation as we do nothing. Better ten ships sunk than such a disgrace."[30]

When the navy finally participated in a major campaign, in the Dardanelles in 1915, Castex vehemently denounced what he considered to be a weak and ineffective naval contribution to an operation that he thought, in any case, to be a strategic mistake. It was, he thought, "strange and humiliating that in spite of their vast resources the four great allied powers appear to have to beg the alliance of eastern upstarts. This dishonesty will be interpreted as a sign of weakness and will have pernicious political consequences."[31]

29. Though abandoned unfinished at the beginning of the war, sections of *La liaison des armes* appeared in *Revue maritime,* and Coutau-Bégarie published the whole work in 1991.

30. Journal entry of 11 September 1914, quoted in *Castex,* 71.

31. *Castex,* 76. The passage adumbrates Castex's belief that the real strategic problem for France and all of western Europe was, in the long run, the danger from Asia.

His own comprehensive, and personal, plan for an operation directed against Constantinople[32] was the product of a thwarted energy that received no suitable outlet until his appointment in the summer of 1916 to command the newly commissioned sloop *Altair*.[33] Much as Castex had eagerly awaited a return to sea duty, *Altair*'s antisubmarine patrols in the Mediterranean ultimately produced only a further round of bitter journal entries. "I have seen nothing of the submarines I was sent out to 'chase.' I have no orders, no intelligence. I do not even know whether other ships are participating in this chase or where they are. . . . It is difficult to show enthusiasm for these idiotic operations."[34]

For all his dislike of a duty he found "stultifying, pointless, unpleasant, and dull," Castex believed, however, that the struggle between submarine and submarine hunter would be the war's decisive battle.[35] The deadlock on the Western Front had become so firm, he argued, that no conceivable alteration of the military balance could create a breakthrough for either side. "The entry of the Americans into the front will not change the situation at all. One could bring the Chinese there and the Eskimo, and all of the inhabitants of the planet Mars, but no one will break through." The war could only be won behind the front, by Germany if she could strangle Allied commerce or by the Allied blockade should the German submarine war fail. In

32. Coutau-Bégarie, *Castex*, 77.
33. *Altair* was an *Etoile*-class sloop of 1,200 tons displacement carrying two 5.5-inch guns and a 3-pdr antiaircraft gun. The class was built in England from 1916 to 1918 and was virtually identical to the Royal Navy's Flower-class sloops, Frederick Jane, *Fighting Ships 1918* (London, 1918): 252.
34. Castex, "Journal," 25 November 1916, quoted in Coutau-Bégarie, *Castex*, 83.
35. Castex, "Journal," 11 December 1916, quoted in Coutau-Bégarie, *Castex*, 84.

any case, "the sea would decide the issue."[36] Castex objected to antisubmarine patrols not because he denied the importance of the submarine menace, far from it, but because he deemed them a wholly ineffectual response to a serious enemy threat. His own experience led him to argue in his postwar writings that submarines were best dealt with by heavily armed convoys rather than by dispersed and apparently aimless patrols.[37] In his own nine months of antisubmarine patrol, Castex located, and failed to sink, one German submarine.

The French eventually adopted the convoy system, but not before the commander of the Mediterranean antisubmarine patrols had convinced the Ministry of the Navy to find a more challenging assignment for his exceptional and exceptionally unhappy subordinate. On 1 July 1917, the thirty-nine-year-old Castex was promoted to lieutenant commander and became the Ministry's liaison with the Navy Commission of the Chamber of Deputies, an ironic posting in view of his hostility towards politics. Frank as ever, his journal laments the "good first six months of the war when there was no parliament."[38] Castex served out the war in command of antisubmarine air patrols over the western Mediterranean.

As the most active historian among serving naval officers, Castex was the obvious choice to head the naval staff's new Service Historique de la Marine created in January 1919 to

36. Journal entry of 2 January 1917, quoted in Coutau-Bégarie, *Castex*, 84–85. Masson identifies this theory of the "arrières," a central theme of *Mélanges*, as one of Castex's major contributions to strategic thought, Masson, "Pensée," 51.

37. See Raoul Castex, *Synthèse de guerre sous-marine. De Pontchartrain à Tirpitz* (Paris, 1920). (Hereafter referred to as *Synthèse*.) Chapters 1–4 were published in *Revue maritime*.

38. Journal entry of 25 November 1917, quoted in Coutau-Bégarie, *Castex*, 87.

study the lessons of the recent conflict. He was also editor of the revived *Revue maritime,* and, from 1921, taught at the *Ecole de Guerre Navale.* His first postwar book, *Synthèse de guerre sous-marine,* a product of his frustrating period in the *Altair,* brought Castex some rather unpleasant international attention for criticizing not German submarine warfare but German failure to coordinate the submarines' depredations with the actions of the High Seas Fleet. While contemporary writers condemned attacks on civilian shipping on moral grounds, Castex implied that Germany had been not so much criminal as inefficient in exercising her "right and duty" to use every means to defend her existence. So far was Castex from challenging the propriety of the submarine war against commerce, that he claimed the idea to have been borrowed by the Germans from *Jeune Ecole* theorists Charmes and Aube.[39]

The opening chapters of *Synthèse* appeared in *Revue maritime* in time to undermine the position of the French delegation at the Washington Naval Conference of 1921. While the dominant naval powers, Britain and the United States, favored abolishing the submarine, France, now merely fourth among naval powers, quietly opposed eliminating this inexpensive means of compensating for her inferiority in capital ships. French demurrers on a submarine ban met, however, an attack by Britain's civilian First Lord of the Admiralty, who unexpectedly introduced as evidence of French intentions Castex's observation that "thanks to the submarine we now possess the instrument once and for all to reverse the naval power of the British empire"[40] and who proposed that France could best demonstrate her rejection of Castex's thesis by signing the Root Resolutions designed

39. Castex, *Synthèse,* 26, 28.
40. Castex, *Synthèse,* quoted in Coutau-Bégarie, *Castex,* 98.

to shackle the submarine.[41] Though Admiral Bon of the French delegation claimed that Castex's views in the *Revue maritime* were his alone and that his "monstrous theories" were rejected by the French navy, the uproar continued until the embarrassed French delegation in Washington grudgingly accepted the Root Resolutions.[42] Castex, who claimed at the time that Lord Lee had misconstrued his argument, later admitted with obvious amusement that, while the Englishman had chosen the wrong passages, the book offered ample ammunition for his case.[43]

Nothing suggests that the incident discouraged Captain Castex from expressing unpopular opinions, and he set out in his new *Questions d'état major* once again to influence French naval organization. In challenging the army's four-bureau staff organization, *Questions d'état-major*[44] contained the material for a possible interservice spat, and there was inflammatory political analysis as well. Discussing proper arrangements for wartime government, Castex underscores the importance of the executive and answers his own question "what do we do with the legislature?" with the wish that it would go on holiday for the duration. Conceding, however, that wartime suppression of the legislature would be detrimental to public morale, Castex argues that

41. The Root Resolutions required the submarine to conform to the same procedures as surface raiders when attacking civilian ships, but submarines could not safely warn a merchant ship's crew of impending attack nor carry crew and passengers to safety.

42. Coutau-Bégarie, *Castex*, 98.

43. Coutau-Bégarie, *Castex*, 99. Castex gloats in chapter 17, 373, at having tricked the Englishman.

44. The navy tactfully refused to publish Castex's hostile evaluation of the four-bureau organization in *Revue maritime*. The United States Naval War College translated the first volume of *Questions d'état-major* in 1924.

a patriotic and decisive executive can "conquer [the legislature's] independence and freedom of action, as Bonaparte conquered those representatives sent to control him through charm and enchantment."[45]

In the meantime, Castex had requested sea duty and been assigned on 16 July 1921 to Rear Admiral Levavasseur's staff on the battleship *Jean Bart*.[46] He spent six months' leave in 1923 finishing *Questions d'état-major* and successfully badgering the naval staff for command of the *Jean Bart*, which he left regretfully in December 1925 to head the third bureau of the general staff in the expectation that Chief of Staff Admiral Salaün would soon appoint him deputy chief of staff.[47] Within eight months, however, Castex had come to see the staff as singularly unresponsive to his ideas, especially to his conviction that Italy, not Germany, was the paramount threat to France and that naval dispositions should place less emphasis on the Atlantic theater, and he left to become deputy director under Vice-Admiral Durand-Viel[48] of the *Ecole de Guerre Navale* and the *Cen-*

45. *Questions d'état-major*, vol. 1, 291, quoted in R. Chalmers Hood, *Royal Republicans: The French Naval Dynasties between the Wars*, 143. By connecting the passage to peacetime political turmoil rather than to the special exigencies of war, Hood exaggerates the authoritarian streak in Castex's politics.

46. The *Jean Bart* was a battleship of 23,100 tons displacement completed in 1913, *Brassey's Naval Annual, 1915*.

47. Henri Salaün (1866–1936) was navy chief of staff and vice-president of the *Conseil Supérieur de la Marine* from July 1924 until his retirement in January 1928. He and Admiral Violette led a progressive movement within the navy that favored an expansion of the officer corps to include more middle-class officers and equality of status for officers in the technical branches. Their left-wing political affiliations were unusual in a largely conservative service, Hood, 114.

48. Coutau-Bégarie, *Castex*, 113. Durand-Viel (1875–1959) served as naval chief of staff and vice-president of the *Conseil Supérieur de la Marine* from May 1931 until March 1937.

tre des Hautes Etudes Navale. Now engaged in teaching a course on naval strategy, he began writing *Théories stratégiques.*

Castex had mixed success as a teacher. Himself thoughtful and broadly educated, he did not necessarily encourage these traits in his students, but expected them instead to absorb official doctrine without cluttering their minds with the abstract or theoretical. An American naval attaché's report on Castex noted that "his mind may be so logical that when he has overestimated the value of one of his premises, he will stubbornly go on to an obviously unsound conclusion," while a historian notes his "exclusion of material which did not offer predigested conclusions for the officer students."[49]

On 25 August 1928, after two years at the *Centre des Hautes Etudes Navales,* Castex was promoted to rear admiral and posted briefly to command the naval forces at Marseille before being recalled to Paris as first deputy chief of the naval staff under the new chief of staff, Admiral Violette. Given his expressed antipathy to staff work, Castex was understandably miffed by the new assignment, but it was only a year before he raised his admiral's pennant on his beloved *Condorcet* as commander of the First Squadron's training division in the Mediterranean.[50] On 25 November 1932, Castex returned, as director, to the *Ecole de Guerre Navale* and the *Centre des Hautes Etudes Navale.* Durand-Viel had been appointed chief of staff, and Castex exploited his relationship with his former boss to encourage direct collaboration between the naval schools and the staff.

Upon attaining the rank of vice-admiral on 1 November

49. Hood, 82–83.
50. Though a good posting, this was not a great one. The aged *Condorcet* was one of the three surviving pre-dreadnoughts in the French navy, and Castex was still short of achieving squadron command, a virtual prerequisite for the pinnacle of the naval hierarchy.

1934, Castex became one of the highest ranking officers in the French navy and, with Darlan, one of two possible successors to Durand-Viel upon his retirement in early 1937. Although younger than Castex, Darlan had two years' seniority in grade and was also blessed with connections in the Radical Socialist Party.[51] Against Castex were his not having commanded a squadron and his reputation for outspokenness, and Darlan received the coveted appointment after a competition that left lingering hostility between the two admirals.[52]

Between 1927 and 1935 Castex published his huge *Théories stratégiques*.[53] While borrowing from Mahan the historical method, insistence on the centrality of sea power in human history, and the primacy of the battleship fleet, Castex sought to offer a more comprehensive theory. The American had prescribed for nations suited for the pursuit of naval power; Castex wrote as well for those for whom command of the sea was impossible or irrelevant and with the understanding that, for some nations, naval affairs would rightly occupy a minor place in strategy as a whole. Because naval power is merely one of many components of an over-arching structure that Castex calls "stratégie générale," *Théories*

51. For the role of politics in the French navy, see Hood, 114–16. Castex shared Darlan's party affiliation but hardly his good relationships with politicians.

52. Absence of political deference and a pointed sense of humor combined when Castex chose the occasion of the navy minister's attendance at the *Ecole de Guerre Navale* in 1934 to lecture on "La stratégie et la tactique du budget de la marine" and to argue that superior strategy had brought the navy victory over both the ministry and the parliament in the "battle" for funds, "Hommage à l'amiral Castex," *Revue maritime* (1968): 1157.

53. Although *Théories stratégiques* does contain much new material, one explanation of Castex's tremendous productivity is his willingness to recycle entire sections and chapters of earlier writings.

stratégiques addresses strategy as a whole, not naval strategy alone.

Though Castex accepts fleet action as the goal of naval warfare, he gives it scant attention as both uncommon and unproblematic. Any navy capable of forcing battle has its strategic situation well under control. His interest is in the plight of the weaker navy, that of France, for example, which must assert itself in other ways, accepting battle only after having used *manoeuvre* to create a favorable shift in the naval balance. Strategic *manoeuvre*, therefore, not battle, is the centerpiece of *Théories stratégiques.* Involving forms of war—attacks on commerce, blockade, naval raids, mine warfare, and amphibious operations—dismissed by Mahan as distractions from the battle fleet's struggle for sea mastery, the notion of *manoeuvre* distances Castex from the American admiral and fits him into the French School, which could never hope to craft strategy for a navy of the first rank.

Though the five volumes of *Théories stratégiques* range over a surprising number of sometimes equally surprising topics, the work draws cohesion not only from the author's methodological consistency but from the existence of the single theme—the importance of navies even for states unable to pursue a Mahanian strategy of naval mastery. For, although Castex's thesis that naval power is only one element of *"stratégie générale,"* and his endlessly repeated observations about the implications of the different geographical situations of states superficially appear to undermine the centrality of sea power, Castex exploits the notion of the limits of sea power subtly to reinforce its importance. In showing what navies cannot do, he underscores what they can and must, especially given the facility of *manoeuvre* to compensate for numerical disadvantage. The argument reaches a crescendo in the fifth volume, where sea power is shown to be both the peaceful Europeans' best weapon against the continental *perturbateur* and the West's only defense against the barbarian East. In this presentation of the importance of sea power, each of the five volumes has its special part to play.[54]

Volume One, *Generalities About Strategy—The Mission of Maritime Forces—The Conduct of Operations* (1927, 1937),[55] reiterates, but in more nuanced language, the Mahanian theses of command of the sea and the centrality of the surface. The volume then integrates its modified Mahanian ideas into a theory of operations that stresses the primacy of the battleship fleet while listing the wide range of missions that a navy may be called upon to perform. Volume Two, *Strategic Manoeuvre* (1930, 1939), introduces *manoeuvre,* the tool that makes battle possible by allowing the weaker navy to force an engagement on competitive terms and, in a series of chapter-length historical studies, presents strategic *manoeuvre,* not the fleet action that is its ultimate purpose, as the key to naval warfare.[56] Volume Three, *External Factors in Strategy* (1931), introduces the "servitudes" of strategy, the notion that military strategy does not operate independently but is constrained by political concerns, by geography, and by the requirements of coalition war, public opinion, and international law.[57] It also

54. The five parts of this edition reflect the five volumes of the original.

55. Two of the chapters ("Mise au point [suite]. Le mode de recherche du combat" and "Deuxième approximation d'une théorie de la conduite des opérations") were substantially expanded for the second edition, and many received addenda bringing the argument up-to-date, with the longest, not surprisingly, attached to the chapter on airpower.

56. The main addition to the 1935 edition is an appendix reprinting Castex's 1935 analysis of Russia's history of expansion, *De Gengis-Khan à Staline.*

57. The reification of abstractions, thus "strategy" rather than "strategists" is characteristic of Castex. Slow sales of the first edition of this volume precluded publication of a second.

discusses *"stratégie générale,"* Castex's signal innovation in strategic theory.[58] Though ostensibly devoted to the impact of policy on strategy, the book gives equal attention to its opposite, strategy's influence on policy, and seeks to describe, in a chapter pessimistically entitled "The Least Bad Compromise," the optimal relationship between the two. Volume Four, *Internal Factors in Strategy* (1933), identifies and analyzes such elements of strategy as concentration and dispersion, economy of force, the offensive, the defensive. He applies the results to certain specific problems: the attack and defense of communications and plans of operations.

Each of the first four volumes has a single obvious theme. The fifth, *The Sea Against the Land* (1935), presents three superficially disconnected subjects that cohere, however, in an agenda very dear to the author's heart. The first part discusses minor naval operations: raids, mining, blockades, raids against the land, to show the effect that even the lesser manifestations of sea power can have against continental adversaries if part of a coherent plan. The second introduces the theory of perturbation, which describes European history as a series of wars fought in defense of order against the depredations of a single conquering state and argues that, in each case, sea power was vital to the success of the resisting coalition. Finally, Castex moves beyond the European *perturbateur* to describe the importance of sea power in the defense of Europe as a whole against a recur-

---

58. Coutau-Bégarie, *Puissance maritime,* 85. For a brief discussion of *"stratégie générale,"* see Rear Admiral Lepotier, "Les vues prospectives de l'amiral Castex," *Revue de défense nationale* 24 (1968): 836–48. Though easily conflated with the *nation armée,* that repository of French strength and trusted panacea for apparent national military weakness, Castex's *stratégie générale* represented a reversal of the traditional concept. Where the theory of the nation in arms aimed to concentrate resources on the battlefield, *stratégie générale* involved not armed might alone, but every aspect of national strength.

rent threat from Asia. It is this special naval role in the protection of Europe that provides the volume's unifying theme.

The chapters on perturbation also fulfill another function. With his classical liberal belief that humans naturally craved peace and progress, Castex felt the need to explain the apparent anomaly of war's existence. His answer was that every century sees the existence of one ambitious state, the *perturbateur,* whose designs on its neighbors produce a life and death struggle that the intended victims survive only by fighting, usually at sea. Forced to defend against the current *perturbateur,* a peaceful state wanting only "a little calm, the rare honest and peaceful pleasures which dot the ephemeral earthly existence, the tranquility of a future that no storm threatens . . . a little taste of happiness, of a blue sky, of a soft breeze, of the charm of nature, of a moment of repose . . ."[59] unwittingly arms itself only to appropriate its defeated rival's place as the new aggressive force in Europe. Usually forced to ally with others to check the aggressor, the peaceful state sacrifices itself for the common good: "Happy are those whose destiny was to do battle, so often painful and unhappy, finally victorious, always glorious, against the power unleashed against the rights of man and the liberty of the world! What finer and grander role than that of savior of peoples?"[60]

Though his theory points to Germany as the next *perturbateur,* anticommunism, racism, and geopolitical calculation combine to draw Castex's attention inexorably towards the Soviet Union.[61] He attributes to the Soviets the inheritance of an earlier Russian plan "for European and Asiatic

59. Below, 404.
60. Below, 418.
61. Other passages emphasize the threat posed by a revanchist Germany. See *Théories,* vol. 2, 355–56, and below, 264.

hegemony, camouflaged by communism, which haunts Judeo-Slavic brains in Moscow," and proposes the enlistment of Germany as a partner in the defense of European civilization against "that human cancer" ("*ce néoplasm humain*"), the Soviet regime.[62]

In the succeeding chapter, Castex describes world history from the battle of Salamis in 480 B.C. to the growth of Japan and China in the twentieth century as a perpetual struggle between Europe and the barbarians. Viewing Asian aggression against the white race and European civilization as the most important issue of his day, Castex argued that Europe must give up internecine war and focus her combined energies to defend the white race.

Claiming to offer one explanation for the existence of war, Castex now has two, for two different kinds of war. Conflict between Asia and Europe stems from Eastern ambitions that flourished unchecked in the absence of a liberal ideology. Within the liberal West, however, wars reflect the existence of adventurer-states whose ambitions reject liberal bounds.

Superficially compatible when they refer to two different arenas of conflict, the two theories of the origins of war can clash when applied simultaneously. After World War II, when the Soviet Union seemed the obvious heir to National Socialist Germany as the *perturbateur* of Europe, Castex set aside the whole concept, and his ideological concerns as well, to argue that Russia, Soviet or not, would fulfill her historic role as protector of the West. For Castex, the Cold War was already over in 1955, "eclipsed by the still more gigantic struggle" between East and West.[63]

While most of Castex's arguments rest either on logical

62. Below, 425, and for the metaphor, 283, note 24.
63. Raoul Castex, "Moscou: rampart de l'occident?" *Revue de défense nationale* 20 (1955): 129–43, 141.

deduction or historical example, he is willing when it suits him to adduce expert testimony as well. *Théories stratégiques* owes much to Mahan but also borrows from the geopoliticians' argument that a nation's relationship with the sea will depend on its physical configuration[64] and the French strategic tradition of naval subordination to the army. Although Castex disparages Sir Julian Corbett's challenges to Mahan as serving only as a check on and reaffirmation of Mahanian principles,[65] he tacitly adopts so many of Corbett's principles as to be deemed by Coutau-Bégarie a secret follower.[66] Perhaps Castex believed that dismissing Corbett's notion of limited war as "dada,"[67] would hide his own tacit, and very Corbettian, qualifications to Mahan's notions of decisive battle and command of the sea. Coutau-Bégarie attributes Castex's refusal to acknowledge his debt to Corbett to a professional officer's disdain for civilian critics and a blue-water sailor's dislike for the pure theoretician,[68] but one also suspects defensiveness about a career more marked by literary than naval achievement and, even less charitably, a competitive dislike for contemporaries. Surely only the last can explain Castex's disparagement of Admiral Sir Herbert Richmond, whose "quite curious and picturesque works" he declines even to discuss.[69]

64. See Derwent Whittlesey, "The Geopoliticians" in Edward Mead Earle, *Makers of Modern Strategy*, 2nd ed. (Princeton, 1943): 388–414.

65. Castex, *Théories*, vol. 1, 56–59.

66. Coutau-Bégarie, *Puissance*, 153–56.

67. Castex, *Théories*, vol. 1, 57.

68. Coutau-Bégarie, *Castex*, 128.

69. Castex, *Théories*, vol. 1, 62. It is tempting to believe that the two were simply too similar to get along. Richmond (1860–1946) was Britain's foremost sailor-historian, director of the Naval War Course at Greenwich, co-founder of the *Naval Review* and promoter of the creation of a Naval War Staff. A strong believer in interservice cooperation, he proved the natural choice as first director of the Imperial Defence College in 1927 as Castex would be for the French equivalent in 1936. Also like

If Castex is warm towards Mahan, critical of Corbett, and disdainful of Richmond, he treats Carl von Clausewitz, whose arguments he often finds it convenient to borrow, with calculated discourtesy. Both in *Théories stratégiques* and in his annual lecture on policy and strategy at the *Collège des Hautes Etudes de Défense Nationale* Castex follows the remark that "war is nothing other than policy continued in arms," with a grudging admission that "it is, I believe, Clausewitz who said this or something similar."[70]

Castex's treatment of a reference to Clausewitz in Corbett's *Some Principles of Maritime Strategy* confirms the impression. Castex attributes to Corbett the following justification for the theoretical study of war: "At first sight nothing appears more unpractical, less promising of useful result than to approach the study of war with a theory. . . . The truth is that mistrust of theory comes from a misconception of what it is that theory claims to do. It does not pretend to give the power of conduct in the field; it

---

Castex, his career fell short of his ambitions. Though command of HMS *Dreadnought* was a plum, his tendency to offer unwanted advice to his superiors relegated him thereafter to relics of the pre-*Dreadnought* era. Promoted a full admiral in 1929, Richmond was soon forced to retire for having publicly advocated the construction of smaller battleships, a view Castex had himself already championed. Richmond offered a thoughtful and positive review of *Théories stratégiques*, vol. 4, in the *Naval Review* 21 (1933): 614–21, and referred to Castex in his *Seapower in the Modern World*. The two met only once, in 1933, Coutau-Bégarie, *Castex*, 128. See D.M. Schurman, *The Education of a Navy: The Development of British Strategic Thought, 1867–1914* (London, 1965): 126–27; Arthur J. Marder, *Portrait of an Admiral* (London, 1952): 29–30; and Barry D. Hunt, *Sailor-Scholar: Admiral Sir Herbert Richmond* (Waterloo, Ontario, 1982).

70. See below, 205. For a better translation of *On War*, book 8, chapter 6B, see Carl von Clausewitz, *On War*, Michael E. Howard and Peter Paret, eds. (Princeton, 1976): 605. All references to *On War* are cited by book and chapter as well as by page number in the Howard-Paret edition.

claims no more than to increase the effective power of conduct. It is only education and judgment that the great authorities pretend to obtain by means of theory." The first three sentences of what Castex offers as a direct quotation are actually a compression of almost two paragraphs from *Some Principles of Maritime Strategy,* while the fourth sentence very loosely paraphrases a sentence that could not accurately be translated without homage to Clausewitz: "The greatest of the theorists himself puts the matter quite frankly. Of theoretical study he says, 'It should educate the mind of the man who is to lead in war, or rather guide him to self-education, but it should not accompany him on the field of battle.' "[71] Nothing better summarizes Castex's attitude to the German thinker than the following "quotation" from *Synthèse de la guerre sous-marine:* "The forces acting in war are the material forces of which one disposes and the force of will. For victory, it is necessary to extend these forces to the extreme." In attributing these lines to "Clausevitz, *Le droit des gens à la guerre,*" Castex misspells Clausewitz's name, ignores *On War* in favor of what appears to be a derivative French work, and disseminates a superficial interpretation of Clausewitz's notion of absolute war.[72]

Though written and revised during the course of a decade when any thoughtful observer would feel increasingly anxious about France's diplomatic and military situation, *Théories stratégiques* remains dispassionately theoretical in tone and offers remarkably few prescriptions for current policy. Rare exceptions are a recipe for rationalizing the French colonial empire, his insistence that geography renders Spanish

71. In similar fashion, Castex excises a reference to Clausewitz from the passage of Marshal Foch's *Principes des guerre* quoted below, 68.

72. The passage is a crude distillation of Carl von Clausewitz, *On War,* book 1, chapter 1, paras. 2–5 (Howard, 75–78).

neutrality a minimal aim of French foreign policy, and concerns about French relations with Italy.

The reluctance to advocate specific courses of action contrasts with a willingness, at least, to talk about how policy ought to be made. For example, the chapter on the "least bad compromise" between foreign policy and military strategy identifies the government's failure to make plans in peacetime as a major obstacle to rational national defense. "The phrase 'government war plan' often appears in the treatises of specialists but rarely corresponds to anything real. Like the great sea serpent, many people speak of the government war plan, but no one has ever seen it, and one is not very confident of its existence."[73]

Though Castex treads relatively lightly in the minefield of civil-military relations, he cautiously admits the possibility that a civilian government might fail to provide the necessary national defense leadership. Warning first that "soldiers must not play at politics, a profession that is not his and for which others are better qualified," he adds, however, that failure to act in the absence of government policy represents "laziness, inertia, and abdication of responsibility," while misguided policies must be corrected by informed military advice. Specifically, "the soldiers will have to call upon their own political understanding, which serves as an emergency reserve and is not employed in normal times but saved for such eventualities."[74]

Far from rendering *Théories stratégiques* tangential to the study of French national defense arrangements of the 1930s, Castex's reticence about urgent national defense issues constitutes evidence in itself about a major weakness in French national defense planning. If a few mavericks publicly wondered how an army dependent on short-service conscripts

73. See below, 250.
74. See below, 262, 264.

and the fortifications of the Maginot Line could sustain a foreign policy based on reciprocal military alliances with the states of Eastern Europe, such unanswerable questions were rarely expressed, especially not by active-service officers inhibited by the strict boundaries that separated the military and civilian spheres under the Third Republic. Since the inadequacies of French defense policy could not be discussed in public, politicians took refuge in platitudes, and scholar-officers like Castex in theoretical abstraction.

The immediate impact of *Théories stratégiques* in France was not great. Rarely cited at the *Ecole de Guerre Navale*, the work was generally dismissed as "a maritime history covering the period from the Renaissance to 1939."[75] In other countries, however, especially in Latin America and the Mediterranean, *Théories stratégiques* was widely read. The entire work was translated by the Argentine navy into Spanish, and selections were rendered into Serbo-Croat, Greek, and Russian, though proposals for English, Japanese, and Italian translations all came to naught.[76] Reports from American naval attachés indicate a continuing interest in the activities of a man described in 1930 as "probably the best French writer on naval strategy and tactics and . . . one of the most successful and well thought of French officers."[77]

The publication of *Théories stratégiques* made Castex the best-known strategic thinker in France just as the nation's leaders had discovered a use for one. Recognition that the

75. Capitaine de Corvette Mariaux, "L'enseignement de l'amiral Castex est-il encore valable?" *Revue maritime* (June 1958): 801.

76. Coutau-Bégarie, *Castex*, 132–33. Nine chapters were translated at the United States Naval War College in 1936. For Soviet interest, see Robert W. Herrick, *Soviet Naval Theory and Policy* (Newport, RI, 1988): 83.

77. Attaché's report in Naval War College files appended to a translation of his "La guerre sous-marine allemande," *Revue de Paris* (15 September 1930).

French long-war strategy required mechanisms for coordinating the national effort led in 1936 to the creation of a new *Collège des Hautes Etudes de Défense Nationale*, whose curriculum would be nothing other than Castex's own *"stratégie générale."*[78] Castex's suitability for the post on academic grounds was reinforced by his published views on interservice cooperation. Though an advocate of collaboration, particularly between the air force and each of the other two services, Castex dismissed unified command over the armed forces as a whole as "an imaginary state of affairs, a myth, a seductive dream far removed from reality. It is usually as unrealizable in practice as it is advantageous in theory."[79] Only in this narrow position between service separatism and unification could be found a director for the college palatable to the junior services, which feared that the army would use the new college to impose upon them its particular interpretation of national strategy.

Director of the *Collège des Hautes Etudes de Défense Nationale* from September 1936, Castex was posted in 1939 to Dunkirk as commander of French naval forces in the Channel. This, the least important of the wartime commands, manifested Chief of Staff Darlan's continuing enmity.[80] Charged with defending the coast of northern France, Castex began to bombard Paris with his own heated

78. For the history of the institution, see E. C. Kiesling, *A Staff College for the Nation in Arms: Le Collège des Hautes Etudes de Défense Nationale, 1936–1939* (Unpublished Ph.D. Dissertation, Stanford University, 1988). The assertion that Castex founded the college, though confidently made by Admiral Lepotier in Castex, *Mélanges,* xiv, and J. Essig, "Aspects civils et militaires," in T. Albord, ed., *La défense nationale* (Paris, 1958): 211, is incredible, given that his list of mechanisms for improved civil-military coordination (*Mélanges,* 285) ignores the college he is alleged to have invented to address just that problem.

79. Raoul Castex, "Les Hautes Etudes de Défense Nationale," *Revue militaire générale* 1(1937): 45.

80. Coutau-Bégarie, *Castex,* 186.

analyses of the strategic situation. In letters to Darlan, to the local army command, and once, in a significant violation of protocol, directly to Prime Minister Daladier, Castex insisted that the real threat was from the land and proposed that the French army create a coastal redoubt at Dunkirk. Annoyed by the criticism of French military dispositions, Darlan instructed his subordinate to confine his attentions to purely naval matters and to cease communicating directly with the army. The frustrated Castex promised to obey his orders but asked for a transfer to a different assignment and hinted at his own poor state of health. Darlan exploited that admission for his own purposes by ordering Castex to undergo a medical examination. Castex rightly believed the doctor's report to reflect the wishes of higher authority; the decree of 21 November 1939 placing Castex on the reserve list was promulgated a mere three days after the examination.[81] Thus, Castex, whose World War I service had proved professionally disappointing, found no opportunities at all during World War II. Without his premature retirement, he, not Admiral Abrial,[82] would have had the thankless task of commanding the defense of Dunkirk during the evacuation.

His skepticism about parliament notwithstanding, Castex was no follower of Pétain and Darlan.[83] Retiring to the country, he held himself aloof from the Vichy regime, whose existence he acknowledged only in complaints about the censorship of some of the 105 articles on strategic subjects he submitted to La Dépêche during the war.[84] Though his

81. Coutau-Bégarie, Castex, 196–203.

82. Admiral Jean-Marie Charles Abrial (1879–1962).

83. Castex's opinion of Pétain comes through clearly in his marginal notations on a copy of Pétain's scathing memorandum "Collège des Hautes Etudes de Défense Nationale," 2 July 1937, 2–3, cited in Coutau-Bégarie, Castex, 179.

84. Coutau-Bégarie, Castex, 208.

anti-Vichy credentials earned him an offer of the presidency of his community's *Comité de libération*, he refused, however, to participate in what he deemed vigilante activities.[85]

After the war, Castex continued to be a valued lecturer at the *Institut des Hautes Etudes de Défense Nationale* that superseded the *Collège des Hautes Etudes de Défense Nationale*. Recipient of the Grand Cross of the *Légion d'honneur* in 1959, he wrote on strategic subjects until the early 1960s and died on 10 January 1968.[86]

The contrast between the magnitude of Castex's intellectual effort and its contemporary repercussions is a stark one. For all that Castex offered, "arguably the most complete theoretical survey of maritime strategy to appear so far," his impact had been described as limited to raising overall naval confidence after the depressing events of World War I and educating the smaller naval powers about the proper use of a second-class fleet.[87]

Whether or not noise made by a falling tree strikes a con-

85. Coutau-Bégarie, *Castex*, 213. Castex's biographer is disappointingly reticent on the subject of Castex's politics. Although *Théories* praises national socialism for "the domestic cleansing process which freed [Germany] from communism and certain undesirable elements" and asserts that "If fascism understands its place in a defensive union with its western neighbors, then one can only commend its birth and prosperity," there is no reason to believe that Castex would have proposed for France the measures he approved for Germany and Italy.

86. Coutau-Bégarie, *Castex*, 214–16.

87. Till, 49–50. An anecdote, however, makes Castex a favorite resource of the commander of one first-class navy—Fleet Admiral King of the United States. When French Admiral Battet remarked upon seeing *Théories stratégiques* on King's desk in 1944, the latter insisted that the volumes' presence reflected the regularity with which he consulted them rather than a courtesy towards his visitor, Castex, *Mélanges*, xiii. King's autobiography, Ernest J. King and William M. Whitehill, *Fleet Admiral King: A Naval Record* (London, 1953) contains no reference, however, to the French theorist.

temporary ear, the physical evidence remains to benefit future scavengers. Castex's immediate audience was smaller than his admirers imply or his work deserved, but his method, which tempers the enthusiasm to know "what" with the discipline to ask "why," can fruitfully be appropriated by a new generation of naval thinkers.

Théories stratégiques offers much of substantive interest as well. Castex wrote to remind France of the vital importance of naval power while cautioning her to take Mahan seriously, but not too literally. Though unable to rule the waves, France could not, however, abjure the battle fleet for less expensive methods of naval defense. Today, as modern technology undermines the very notion of command of the sea, all navies share the need, once faced by only those of the second rank, to vindicate their expensive existence in terms more Castexian than Mahanian. Moreover, navies have to define themselves for the twenty-first century in the context of Castex's other major discovery—that war is a whole of which military and naval strategy comprise only one facet. Demonstrated by the Allied victory through national mobilization in World War II, the importance of *"stratégie générale"* has been a salient lesson of the postwar world.

Strategic Theories

PART I

GENERALITIES ABOUT STRATEGY

CHAPTER 1

GENERALITIES ABOUT STRATEGY[1]

GENERAL CONSIDERATIONS

FIRST, WHAT is strategy? Where does it fit in the ensemble of military studies? What preliminary questions must be resolved so as to have an idea of what one is talking about?

The intellectual or physical actions of war are generally considered to belong to the realm either of strategy or tactics. It remains to establish the essential difference between the two. Etymology provides us with a useful approximation of the distinction. "Strategy" comes from the Greek word meaning "a military expedition, a campaign," "tactics" from a Greek adjective meaning "ordered, regular."[2] Strategy treats the totality of war, embracing war as a *whole* and, especially, its directing principles. Tactics evokes the idea of clearly defined, regular movements that occur (if at all) only on the battlefield. Tactics is the world of *detail;* it governs combat, itself a detail of the greatest importance.

---

1. Raoul Castex, *Théories stratégiques*, 2nd ed., vol. 1 (Paris: Société d'Editions Géographiques, Maritimes et Coloniales, 1937): 3–27.
2. More directly, "tactics" derives from "$\tau\acute{\alpha}\xi\iota\varsigma$" (an arrangement of troops) and "$\tau\acute{\alpha}\sigma\sigma\theta$" (to draw up troops).

3

Earlier authors, happily, offer clear and vivid reinforcement for this distinction.

At the end of the eighteenth century, an active period of military thought that heralded the grand transformations to come, Guibert wrote: "*grand tactics* is properly the science of the generals in chief, because it is the compilation of all military knowledge."[3] In Guibert's day, the term "grand tactics" was commonly used for what we today call strategy. Napoleon never used the word "strategy," preferring "grand tactics" or, his particular favorite, "the higher parts of war." For Archduke Charles, "Strategy is the science of war. It sketches plans, it includes and determines the course of military enterprise; it is, properly speaking, the science of the generals in chief."[4] Marshal Marmont thought that strategy was "the part of the art of war that applies to the overall movement of armies."[5]

The commentators on the wars of the Revolution and the Empire better expressed the distinction between strategy and

3. Jacques Antoine Hippolyte Comte de Guibert (1743–1790), author of *Essai générale de tactique* (1772) and *Défense du système de guerre moderne* (1779). Although the *Essai* divides tactics into "elementary" and "grand," coinciding roughly with distinctions between tactics and strategy, Guibert's general thrust was not to narrow the scope of "tactics" but to expand it to encompass everything related to military activities. See R. R. Palmer, "Frederick the Great, Guibert, Bülow: From Dynastic to National War," in P. Paret, ed., *Makers of Modern Strategy.* 3rd ed., 91–119, 107.

4. Archduke Charles (1771–1847), son of Emperor Leopold of Austria and author of *Principles of the Higher Art of War* and *Principles of Strategy* (1814) is best known for his notion that certain geographical points constituted the "keys to the country." For a survey of eighteenth-century strategic thought, see Azar Gat, *The Origins of Military Thought* (Oxford, 1989).

5. Auguste Frédéric Louis Viesse de Marmont (1774–1852), Duke of Ragusa, marshal of France from 12 July 1809.

tactics. "There exist," said Clausewitz, "two absolutely distinct activities: tactics and strategy. The first orders and directs the action of combats while the second relates the combats to one another in order to arrive at the objects of the war." This led the creator of modern military theory to two compressed and very expressive definitions: "strategy is the employment of battle for the object of the war; tactics the employment of troops in battle."[6] Jomini did not veer far from Clausewitz in noting that strategy encompasses everything that happens in the theater of war while tactics concerns fighting on the battlefield. Thiers,[7] a layman whose intimate experience of the military events of his era makes him worth consulting, said that "strategy ought to conceive of the plan of campaign, embrace the whole theatre of the war with a single *coup d'oeil,* trace the lines of operations, and direct the mass against the decisive points." Field Marshal von Moltke, whose functions in the course of the wars of the nineteenth century called upon him to operate exclusively in the strategic domain, expressed his concept in these terms: "Strategy indicates the best way to conduct battle; it dictates *where* and *when* one ought to fight. Tactics teaches how to make use of the different arms in combat; it says *how* one ought to fight."[8]

6. An uncharacteristically positive reference to the German thinker. Clausewitz's distinction between strategy and tactics appears in *On War,* book 2, chapter 1 (Howard, 128) and book 3, chapter 1 (Howard, 177).

7. Orleanist in 1830, Bonapartist in 1848, leader of the provisional Republic's bloody suppression of the Commune in 1871, and president of the Republic from 1871 to 1873, Louis Adolphe Thiers (1797–1877) remained throughout these political twists a stalwart supporter of the professional over the conscript army.

8. As Chief of the Prussian General Staff from 1857 to 1888, Helmuth Karl von Moltke (1800–1891) masterminded the three wars of German unification. Rejecting the notion that war could be scientific and its operations predictable ("no plan survives the first clash with the enemy"), he

More contemporary authors have maintained this distinction. Captain Gilbert[9] addresses the problem in his *Essais de critique militaire* from the point of view of concentration and calls strategy "the art of moving forces in the theater of operations in order to concentrate them on the battlefield while tactics is the art of concentrating forces at the decisive point on the battlefield itself." Von der Goltz[10] holds an analogous view: "One defines strategy as the theory according to which one conducts and directs armies, tactics as how one conducts and directs troops."

Bernhardi[11] gives the following complete and satisfying formula: "Strategy is the art of leading troops to combat in the decisive direction and in the most favorable conditions." For General Mordacq, strategy is the art of directing armies in the theater of war and tactics the art of conducting a unit on the ground.[12] Captain de Vaisseau Darrieus extends this concept to naval war. "Strategy," he says, "evokes the idea

---

emphasized staff training to ensure that the actions of subordinate officers would conform to the commander's will even after he had lost the ability to control events directly.

9. French army captain Jean-François-Georges Gilbert (1851–1901).

10. Freiherr Colmar von der Goltz (1843–1916) argued that the offensive continued to be possible in spite of contemporary technological developments. His *Das Volk im Waffen* (1884) (translated as *The Nation in Arms*, London, 1906) advocated universal conscription on the French model.

11. Head of the military history section of the German General Staff, Friedrich Adam von Bernhardi (1849–1940) contributed to the "cult of the offensive" by arguing that decisive victory remained possible if contemporary nations were willing to absorb large losses. For Bernhardi's fluence on German policy, see Loren K. Campion, *As Bismarck Fell: The Restive Mind of the German Military* (Greenville, NC, 1976).

12. *La Stratégie. Historique. Evolution* (Paris: Fournier, 1912): 15. Clemenceau's military adviser during World War I, Jean Jules Henri Mordacq (born 1868) wrote over twenty books on strategy including *Etudes stratégiques* (1910), *Essais stratégiques* (1912), *Politique et stratégie dans une démocratie* (1912), and *La guerre au XXe siècle* (1914).

of preparation for which the end is battle, and tactics the execution of battle."[13] Let us finally note that Admiral Mahan[14] placed the separation between strategy and tactics at the point and the moment when the opposing forces enter into combat.

These authors all agree on a single, generally accepted approach to defining strategy and distinguishing it from tactics, but dissidents exist. For example, General Bonnal's[15] lectures at the French army's *Ecole de Guerre* in 1892–1893, while purporting to sum up the preceding definitions, actually offered the altogether new thesis that "strategy is the art of conception, tactics the science of execution." Italian authors like Bonamico,[16] General Marselli,[17] Sechi,[18] and Corticelli[19] have established a similar distinction. For Sechi, "The conduct of maritime war belongs to maritime strategy, the execution of strategic conceptions falls into the realm of logistics when one is not in

---

13. *La guerre sur mer* (Paris: Challamel, 1907): 11. Captain Gabriel Darrieus (1859–1931) was Castex's mentor. See introduction, 22, and Coutau-Bégarie, *Castex*, 45, 126.

14. Alfred Thayer Mahan (1840–1914) remains America's most influential naval writer. His distinction between strategy and tactics, found in *The Influence of Sea Power upon History 1660–1783* (New York, 1957): 6, reflects Jomini's *Précis*.

15. General Henri Bonnal (1844–1917).

16. Dominico Bonamico was the leading Italian naval writer of the 1880s and 1890s. See Castex, *Théories*, vol. 1, 53.

17. Nicolo Marselli, *La guerra e la sua storia*, 3 vols. (Rome, 1904).

18. Professor at the naval academy at La Spezia and author of *Elementi di arte militare marittima*, 2 vols. (Livorno, 1903, 1906). Admiral Giovanni Sechi retired from the Italian navy in 1920, Castex, *Théories*, vol. 1, 53.

19. Lt. Colonel Carlo Corticelli, author of *Manuale di organica militare: eserciti italiano, germanico, austro-ungarico, francese e svizzero* (Torino, 1892).

the presence of the enemy and of tactics when cannons thunder. . . . Thus we can say that strategy is the mind that thinks, logistics and tactics the arms that act."[20] Recently, Captain Laurent revived this idea. For him, "One means by strategy everything that addresses the conception and general conduct of operations. One means by tactics everything involved in execution."[21] Laurent's approach has the important and controversial consequence that "everyone, at every level of the hierarchy, is at the same time commander and subordinate. In planning an operation, one is a chief; in carrying one out, a subordinate."[22] Marselli agrees. "Strategy," he writes, "is not a princess marriageable only to a single commander-in-chief, but every soldier commanding a platoon applies, or ought to apply, strategy appropriate to the operation to be accomplished."

. . . I cannot accept this novel thesis that strategy and tactics should be seen respectively as conception and execution. By this definition, a commander is acting strategically when he conceives of an operation, but since his orders must also prescribe the dispositions for the execution of these orders, he is performing tactically at the same time. Similarly, the subordinate who acts tactically in executing orders must also act strategically in conceiving of their execution. Thus the definition leads in practice to the unworkable thesis that everyone, at every level of command, is simultaneously strategist and tactician. In envisaging dispositions for executing his plan, the supreme commander does tactics; in making a fire plan to suit a particular case, a vessel's gunnery officer thinks strategically. The idea is an original one.

20. *Elementi di arte militare marittima*, Livorno, 1905, vol. 1, 74 (author's note).

21. *Introduction aux études de stratégie* (Paris: Challamel, 1927): 5 (author's note).

22. Compare Clausewitz's distinction of ends and means in war, *On War*, book 3, chapter 1 (Howard, 177).

Strategy is everywhere, at every level. It cannot be isolated as governing certain particular parts but is intermingled in the totality of war itself. There are no longer strategic operations since all military activity qualifies.[23]

A geometric diagram may help to depict the differences between the two schools of thought and show how the revisionists do retain a certain sort of distinction between strategy and tactics. Drawing the various levels of command on a vertical scale, one sees that the first set of writers place strategy on the higher rungs and tactics on the lower. Between strategy and tactics they place a horizontal separation. Within each of these two fields—strategic and tactical—operations retain their unity; conception and execution are never separated from one another.

The revisionists would bisect all of the levels of command with a vertical line constituting the frontier between strategy and tactics. Strategy, or conception, is on the left; tactics, or execution, lies to the right. The result is that, for any given operation undertaken by an echelon of command, the conception remains separated from the execution. Conception is deprived of its base, of its substance, of the shape that it assumes in execution. The whole left side, strategy or conception, is nothing but a collection of theoretical principles, an accumulation of abstract precepts—nebulous, obviously easy to formulate, but disconnected from the real, from the concrete, from everything that would give them force and strength.

I cannot therefore place myself among the proponents of this notion of vertical separation between strategy and tactics. They have, I think, wrongly charged the school that limits strategy making to the higher echelons with establish-

23. This is essentially the opinion of Corticelli, who, in his *Manuale di Organica* (Turin, Bertolero, 1900), thinks that strategy is not simply a part of military science but rather its synthesis (author's note).

ing a hierarchy to the disadvantage of tactics. Not at all. There is no more sense of superiority between strategy and tactics than between doctor and financier, architect and lawyer, industrialist and functionary. All operate in equally important areas. Without good strategy, the best tactics bring a feeble return; without tactical superiority, the best strategy fails.

I, more than anyone, have a horror of Byzantine arguments over words, of all the petty distinctions of the sterile scholasticism of the Middle Ages, of the pedantry of Molière's doctors. I have repeated the arguments solely to illuminate the premises of the subject and to define the object of the speculations that follow, and I hasten to end this introduction with a firm conclusion.

I remain, for my part, faithful to the system of the "horizontal separation," that is, to the tradition accepted by the majority of the writers we have cited. In effect, there is already a sort of customary law, to oppose which is to upset the whole system without any compensatory benefit. . . . For me, strategy is nothing other than the general conduct of operations, the supreme art of leaders at a certain level in the hierarchy and of the general staff that serves them. Strategy prepares the battles, striving to bring them about under the best of conditions and to make them bring about the best results. Strategy links the battles together, controlling and coordinating them in accordance with the general inspiration of the campaign while reacting also to events. Guiding tactics, strategy gives it its head at the proper time. Strategy before and after battle, tactics during battle—from the beginning to the end of the clash of arms—that is the formula to which I rally.

The frontiers of strategy are not, of course, as well defined as the theory implies. . . . On the one hand, as we will see later, strategy has intimate, undissolvable links with policy. Some operations are so much half strategic and half political that they exist in a neutral region in which these two forms of activity cannot be disentangled. . . . [24]

Strategy's neighbor at the other extreme is tactics, and the horizontal line that we have drawn between the two is only a symbol and cannot be a rigid barrier. Theoretically, tactics ought to begin only at the firing of the first cannon or torpedo, but one can hardly subtract from tactics all of the movements preliminary to battle on the pretext that they still belong to strategy. The moment of "contact" defined by Admiral Mahan as the threshold of the tactical realm is rather that after which close proximity renders an encounter inevitable. Also logically abandoned to the sphere of tactics are such operations as scouting and the navigation of naval forces which, by strict consideration of their distance from the enemy, ought to belong to strategy. Here again, there is a neutral zone disputed between strategy and tactics and constituting a territory of meeting and union rather than an isolating wall. Leaders of intermediate rank can alternate indifferently between tactical and strategic action.

In sum, strategy is like the solar spectrum. It has an infrared, which is the realm of policy, and an ultra-violet, that of tactics. And just as the bands of the spectrum merge by invisible gradations, strategy also flows gradually into policy and into tactics. Policy, strategy, and tactics form an ensemble, a whole, rather than a triptych of clearly separated parts.

Characteristics of modern naval war have shifted the boundary between strategy and tactics to the benefit of the latter and thereby accentuated the imprecision of the earlier

24. The interaction of policy and strategy is the subject of chapters 10–12.

distinction.[25] In an earlier day, before the appearance of submarines and aircraft, tactics was limited to areas where it was possible to encounter the enemy on the surface. Each belligerent tended to group his forces together, and the effect of this concentration on both sides was to reduce the possibility of their meeting and, in consequence, the number of zones of contact. Between these tactical arenas, islands speckling the liquid expanse touched by the war, were vast "blank spots" where no naval action took place and strategy held sway.

Belligerents could hardly do otherwise than concentrate their forces since to disperse them to cover the entire sea would result in certain destruction. Moreover, with the appearance of engines independent of the wind, considerations of range of action and resupply have intervened to circumscribe each side's ability to manifest his power.

This aspect of former naval warfare at first seems to affect only the fleets[26] and not to apply to forces employed to attack communications. Privateers' actions rested on different principles, manifested in their dispersal and in the extent of their enterprises. Thus, the enemy threatened by commerce war could protect his merchant ships only by the ordinarily ineffectual methods of free navigation and patrolling routes or focal regions, and the number of points of contact was very great. But resorting to escorted convoys produced a situation analogous to that of the fleets. The raiders had then either to resign themselves to individual destruction or to unite in their turn into groups to attack and to protect themselves, whereby the vast and fluid expanse of the tactical field was again compressed into a few separate points. . . .

Dispersed operations do not, however, trouble the sub-

25. Note the addition of material considerations to a theoretical discussion.

26. "*Les forces organisées.*"

marines. They do not fear isolation and can be left to themselves. Invisibility and the ability to make a safe retreat into the depths permits the submarine to contemplate with equanimity the solo counteroffensive that is the death warrant of the isolated surface vessel. Less hampered than surface ships by supply problems, the submarine can undertake very long cruises and has a noticeably increased field of operations.[27]

These two properties make available to the submarine forms and spheres of action forbidden to surface vessels. The submarine will almost always fight as a single cavalier.[28] Though it is no more able than any other ship to cover the entire sea, it will, however, do so in the mind of the enemy, in whose imagination the submarine's invisibility confers the gift of omnipresence. Fear therefore leads the enemy to take constant antisubmarine measures, just as if there were one to be found in every mile of sea. . . .

The influence of aviation is less marked but nonetheless real. Though visible, airplanes are extremely mobile and capable of rapid intervention in a situation. In defending against other airplanes, they are handicapped by the length of time necessary to leave the ground and gain the necessary altitude. Nor can defensive air units remain aloft forever. An aerial attack always has a good chance of passing through the defensive mesh. These are the inherent particularities of the air arm. The airplane's rapidity of action parallels the submarine's ability to dive and permits, although to a lesser degree, individual operations that are impossible for isolated surface ships.

27. In this regard, the German cruisers *Moewe, Wolf,* and *Seeadler,* ships with a very great range of action, marked an intermediate step between the surface steam cruiser and the submarine (author's note).

28. In fact, German submarines proved far more effective in World War II when operating in packs rather than alone. This paragraph surely reflects Castex's remembered frustration with France's exaggerated fear of German submarines in 1914.

Aviation, moreover, works in an entirely new sphere of action. Since it is able to attack points situated in the interior of the country (arsenals, airfields, important communications, urban centers, etc.) or to bomb or torpedo a fleet placed in a fortified base and protected against action by surface or submarine vessels, its presence greatly expands the theater of the war beyond the coasts. It can, moreover, be employed by either side, so both attacker and defender must concern themselves with it. In sum, the new tools of war have increased the area of the principal act of war—combat—and therefore the relative weight of tactics.

Accompanying the transformation of space is another transformation relating to time. When only surface fleets existed, their geographical separation created a parallel temporal separation between periods of combat. One did not meet the enemy every morning. Between two engagements there were often long delays for redeployment. By preventing surprise, reconnaissance gave fleets a sense of security and eliminated pressure for precipitate action. Nothing sudden was to be expected during these intervals of tactical ceasefire and mental rest. . . .

All this has changed. The submarine has the capacity for continuous action, at least where it matters, which is in the opponent's mind. The enemy can be expected to appear anywhere and at any time, and such is the danger from submarines that one must react instantly to any hint of their presence. Aviation presents the same problem, though less intensely because the defender has somewhat more time to react. Still, within the range of operations of enemy aircraft, the periods of complete rest at anchor can be nothing but a distant memory. The tension of action is never relaxed completely. . . .

Combat has thus been extended in time, as well as in space. The line of demarcation between strategy and tactics, fluid enough in the past, moves discernibly to the advantage of the latter. . . . Those who execute strategy at sea will always experience tactical problems and must be ready to react at this level. Only the highest military leaders, theater commanders, for example, remain wholly in the strategic domain. . . .[29]

Moving to another order of ideas, one finds that some authors have described strategy in ways that trespass not only on the realm of tactics but also beyond the events of war itself. Admiral Mahan's broad definition—"Naval strategy has as its goal to create, to favor, and to increase the maritime power of a nation in peacetime as well as in war,"[30]—introduces a "peacetime strategy," composed of all measures serving to augment naval force. These measures undeniably are strategic, for they have the effect, in Bernhardi's expression, of leading to battle under the most favorable conditions. The most important element of peacetime naval strategy is the acquisition, creation, development, and organization of naval bases. Great Britain's occupation for naval purposes of Cyprus, Egypt, Aden, Weï-Haï-Weï, and so many other places illustrates the point admirably. Similarly, the preparation of Rosyth before the 1914 war and the creation of Singapore thereafter were essentially strategic acts. France with Bizerte, Germany with Jiao-Tcheou, the United States with the Hawaiian Islands, have proceeded no differently.

The strong roots in the American navy of this concept implanted by Admiral Mahan are evident from a lecture by

29. For the intrusion into British strategy during the Falklands War of the cruiser *Belgrano*, see Sandy Woodward, *One Hundred Days: The Memoirs of the Falklands Battle Group Commander* (London, 1992). Omitted here are three paragraphs describing parallel developments in land war.

30. *Influence* (author's note).

Admiral Schofield[31] to the press during the American maneuvers of 1924. Like Mahan, Schofield naturally included naval bases and new construction in peacetime strategy, but he offered a new and striking ingredient—international conferences—that he doubtless saw as a means of using treaties to clip the wings of annoying rivals—totally disarming those unable to defend themselves around a green table. The Washington Conference in 1922 taught us, and it would be unforgivable to forget, that disarmament and other conferences can be strategic moves on the part of our rivals or adversaries.[32]

Admiral Sir Reginald Bacon[33] distinguishes the strategy of peace, which prepares for war, from wartime strategy, which conducts it.[34] In *The Art of Naval Warfare*,[35] British Admiral Sir Cyprian Bridge[36] expands at length on what he also calls the "strategy of peace." He places under that rubric a very large and varied set of measures including the simplification of administration, the establishment of naval programs and the characteristics of ships, the constitution of supplies and stores, the establishment of naval bases, the functioning of services, training of personnel, preparation of plans of operations, and organization of the intelligence and mobilization services. Clearly, every preparation for war is included. "The action of strategy never stops," says Bridge, and he shows its effect in the considerable development of United States naval power, which has not participated in a

---

31. Frank Herman Schofield (1869–1942).

32. Similarly, one must be alert to the grave dangers for France implied in many League of Nations transactions in Geneva and must resist them resolutely when necessary (author's note). Personal reasons for Castex's antipathy to peace conferences are revealed in chapter 16.

33. Sir Reginald Hugh Spencer Bacon (1863–1947).

34. *Some Notes on Naval Strategy* (London, 1901) (author's note).

35. London, 1907 (author's note).

36. (1839–1924).

naval war since that of the Secession.[37] Properly speaking, preparations of this sort constitute naval policy, and their realm borders that of policy as a whole; this is the "infrared" of strategy.

To achieve its ends, strategy calls upon two elements—principles upon which to base its conceptions and methods for their execution.[38] The principles of strategy form a collection of evident truths derived from the experience of the past and from relations of cause and effect that one observes in the manifestations of military activity across the ages. These principles are independent of the instruments of action and, consequently, of the two variables, time and milieu, of which those instruments are a function. They form a permanent body of doctrine, or as close to such as anything in human affairs can be. Few in number and easily surveyed, the principles are limited to some major rules of action and common-sense guidelines.

The methods are the means, the fundamentals of employment, the technical factors that one utilizes to apply the principles. Their study is of special interest because, without methods of execution, the principle remains in a philosophical state—an abstract word, a pure affirmation without tangible form, in sum, a dead thing. The crux of military problems lies in the use of appropriate methods to achieve a satisfactory application of the principles to each particular case. The method is so strictly governed by material things that combinations seemingly inferior from the point of view of principle, theory, and art prove necessary, given the technical conditions and one's circumstances. The conception must suit the realities. "As real circumstances enter the pic-

37. Castex offers no explanation for omitting the Spanish-American War.
38. Here Castex integrates the historical and material approaches.

ture, the conception increasingly loses its artistic elements; above all, the progress of armaments compresses the range of conception. . . . Conception exists only in relation to execution."[39] It is because of this troublesome difficulty that many writers on strategy say nothing about methods of execution and instead remaining safely encamped in a sententious enunciation of principles.[40]

Strategic methods obviously depend on tools and, consequently, on the times and the milieu. The importance of the latter ought to be kept constantly in mind by those who try to transpose to naval warfare certain modes of conducting land war. That they depend on the times should lead us to adopt for our own use the systems that have proved useful in the past only after intense scrutiny.[41] We are in an essentially changing realm. Certainly, strategic methods are less contingent on changes in armament than are tactical methods. Though functions of time, they have small coefficients.[42] Nonetheless, one must not forget that they do change.

Strategy as a whole, as an ensemble of principles and methods, varies because the latter component is not constant. Those who defended the once-favored dogma of the immutability of strategy apparently considered only one aspect of the question and failed to pass beyond the realm of

39. General Debeney, *The Chef. Centre des Hautes Etudes Militaires,* 1925 (author's note). Commander of the French First Army in 1918, Marie Eugène Debeney (1864–1943) was commandant of the *Ecole Supérieure de Guerre* (1919–1924) and Chief of General Staff (1925–1930).

40. Castex's objection to much of the output of the historical school.

41. Castex, however, goes so far in criticizing the "unjustified" eclipse of weapons in *La liaison des armes sur mer* as to suggest that the fireship and the ram were both abandoned prematurely.

42. In spite of his denial that strategy is a science (below, 21–22), Castex loves analogies, however awkward, from mathematics and physics.

principle. Of course, faith in this semi-permanence is such a soft cushion, it so well serves the natural human taste for minimizing effort, that one can hardly wonder at its advocates. "The extreme generality of the principles of strategy is an accomplice to mental laziness. It relies on eternal and self-evident truths to produce results whenever necessary."[43]

For example, British strategy has often been praised for imperturbability and immutability. Political and military at the same time, this strategy has permitted brilliant and continuous successes against whatever nation—Spain, France, or Germany—threatened the European equilibrium and British naval superiority. The salient features of that strategy are well known. Britain distracted the *perturbateur*[44] on the continent in order to lead him to a major land effort that would diminish his resources for naval action. Britain would then sweep him from the sea and tighten the pressure by interrupting his maritime communications. What remains of this strategy today given the existence of new machines and new situations?

A maritime rival, the United States, has appeared on the horizon. Against her, the method of continental diversion is completely inoperable. She had nothing to fear on her land frontiers, especially given her strong affinities with Canada. Against the United States, Britain must have recourse, as in Washington in 1922 and Geneva in 1927, to the fragile and uncertain system of arms limitation conferences.

A material effort on land no longer absolutely bars a na-

---

43. Commandant Z. and H. Montéchant, *Essai de stratégie navale* (1893): 6. This passage represents, as we will see, one of the work's rare judicious observations (author's note). A major formulation of the theories of the *Jeune Ecole, Essai de stratégie navale*, was written pseudonymously by Paul Fontin and J. H. Vignon.

44. For the theory of "perturbation," see chapter 19.

tion from simultaneous naval competition with Britain because the airplane can be involved in land and sea war simultaneously. The resources that the adversary devotes to aviation in order to increase his land forces can be fully utilized in the maritime struggle and thereby modify the balance of surface naval forces. Moreover, the advent of the submarine has virtually nullified the notion of sweeping the enemy from the sea because it remains able to act in the face of superior surface forces. As for maritime communications, they cease to be important when the adversary is none other than Russia supported by the Asian continent, a block that threatens Britain while laughing at sea lanes because it has everything that it needs. Against Russia, it is necessary to act on land either through foreign mercenaries or with one's own forces, in spite of horrific memories of the pill that had to be swallowed in Wellington's day and during the 1914 war.

The existence of rivals or enemies against whom the ancient methods are impotent, the diminished predominance of surface units, and the unaccustomed dangers represented by the airplane and the submarine are the new elements of Britain's strategic problem and explain the unhappiness, anxiety, and malaise that manifests itself there. Such feelings are to be expected in minds that, having had faith in the permanent efficacy of a particular strategy, have just been awakened to its obsolescence and the imperious necessity for change.

To avoid such serious difficulties, one must abjure the illusion of invariable principles and remain ever attentive to the evolution of strategy and, especially, of its methods. Having studied analogous past situations in order to illuminate a question and to identify the appropriate doctrine, one must ask whether the conclusions remain correct in our day and what modifications are required in view of the day's technology or that of the foreseeable future. Every discussion of strategy requires that an effort be made to understand the actual conditions and to eschew the mental laziness that leads one to treat strategy as purely abstract. Otherwise, one cannot do useful work. Because they have forgotten this truth, so many of the strategic analyses produced in recent years have had only limited and antiquarian interest. They declaim general principles from the safe high ground of empty formulas while changes occurring all around them demand novel ideas and original applications.

Is strategy an art or a science? A good subject for those with the mentalities of the Blues and Greens of Byzantium and for those with time to waste but one that I cannot avoid touching lightly upon in passing. Personally, I believe that strategy, like war itself, of which strategy is only one face, is an art. The expression "science" evokes an element of absolute certainty, of relations of cause and effect crystallized into rules so invariable and rigid that they become veritable laws, governing everything and impossible to escape. A scientific law asserts that the same scientific observation will always give rise to the same result, just as a mathematical formula generates the same answer whenever the same numbers are used. War is not at all like this, and strategy less so than tactics. Instead, strategy is, at least for the most part, an art. One sees the intervention of individuality, of personality, in a word, of psychological and moral factors, which play no role in science.

The simple principles that govern strategy are not chains but flexible guides leaving free play to the creative imagination and to the human spirit in situations that are themselves enormously variable. Precisely here lies the essential character of art, which never entirely breaks free of principles nor, even, of rules but still manifests itself in an unlimited variety of ways.[45]

If strategy has a scientific side in its methods of implementation, which depends on machines whose construction and operations are the creations of science, so too, for the same reason, does art. The painter also employs materials—brushes, fabrics, or colors—of known physical properties and susceptible to chemical analysis and fabrication. Similarly, the painter observes the laws of perspective, which are absolutely mathematical in their essence. If he stops there, however, in contemplating his tools, creation never happens; art manifests itself only in their manipulation. It is the same in music. Musical notes obey perfectly understood physical and mathematical laws, but a physicist, however expert in acoustics, is not a composer because he does not achieve the artistic creation that is the marriage of those sounds whose elementary structure he knows so completely. In summary, in strategy as in art, science furnishes the materials and the methods. To accomplish the definitive creation, however, requires their composition by means of an intellectual effort that is free and powerful but respectful of certain principles—art.

Art has no country, and the artistic point of view allows us to behold the great strategic writings, regardless of their time or place of origin, with admiration and envy. Just as international finance and religion have no boundaries, just as there is a workers' international and an international diplomatic fraternity, so there is an international world of art and a military international, itself a branch of the artistic international.[46]

45. Castex ignores Clausewitz's important suggestion that war is neither an art nor a science, *On War*, book 2, chapter 3 (Howard, 148–50).
46. Castex takes this unpromising metaphor to extreme lengths in chapter 4.

Strategy, like all human activity and art itself, rests on theory. If inspiration and imagination reign there, they acknowledge the principles that form their underlying technique. The theory of strategy can be learned. It is learned in a special manner, half through books, half through practice, when, as is generally the case, it is not possible to learn through personal military experience. Such experience is rare enough and only brings strategic illumination to those on the highest rungs of the hierarchy or in their entourage. It does not prepare others for the strategic tasks that might be in the future. For these, theory is the only path and study an obligation. The doctrine of innate ideas, fashionable at a certain epoch, has long since yielded to general disbelief. "The adage," said Archduke Charles, "that one is born a general and that one has no need of study to become one, is one of the most dazzling errors of our century, an offspring whose parents are laziness and pusillanimity."

In the introduction to *Some Principles of Maritime Strategy*, Corbett pleaded the case of theoretical study of strategy in particularly happy terms. "At first sight nothing appears more unpractical, less promising of useful result than to approach the study of war with a theory. . . . The truth is that mistrust of theory comes from a misconception of what it is that theory claims to do. It does not pretend to give the power of conduct in the field; it claims no more than to increase the effective power of conduct. It is only education and judgment that the great authorities pretend to obtain by means of theory."[47]

Shared theoretical study ought to create between commanders and subordinates an intellectual solidarity or, as we

---

47. Sir Julian Corbett, *Some Principles of Maritime Strategy*, Eric J. Grove, ed. (Annapolis, 1988), 3–4, cited hereafter as Corbett, *Principles*. See above, *xxxvii* for a discussion of the attitude towards Clausewitz evidenced in this misquotation.

say in France, unity of doctrine. Certainly, Corbett, like all students of the question, was not unaware that the value of theoretical study is limited by the infinite variety of things that can happen in war. There is always the danger of asking more from a theory than it can give. But theory at least allows one to establish the "normal case," a gauge against which one can compare other situations so as to temper one's original conclusions to specific circumstances. For Corbett, strategy is like meteorology. Meteorology's laws are subject to considerable variation from the norm, but one cannot deny that the sailor's art demands study and knowledge of its laws. It is an element, not in itself sufficient, but absolutely necessary to the seaman's education.

The study of strategy includes both principles and means of execution. The latter study is based on the positive method, on examining the material premises that, not being particular to strategy, in themselves exercise a considerable influence on tactics. We need not review those technical matters here as long as we remember that they affect strategy as well as tactics.

The study of principles ought to be conducted in a certain manner and with certain precautions. The results that one reaches through theory are almost exclusively approximations of principles verified by observation of a large number of cases. That is to say, theory rests in large part on the historical method, which works only when employed with critical acumen. In deriving lessons from history, one must distinguish general truths from ephemeral ones and retain only the former so as not to commit the dangerous error of brutally transplanting ideas from one period to another to which they are entirely alien.

Since the historical method will not serve us in treating machines known only in our own time, we will have to call upon the positive method to fill the gap. Outmoded methods can be distinguished from those valid today by means of intellectual exercises in which one imagines a strategic problem from the past and asks how to resolve it using the material means of our own day and whether the method once recognized as good or bad remains so at present.[48] Finally, above all, one attempts to integrate the *application* of today's weapons with the stable part of the lessons of the past and, if possible, to extend this application to the immediate future. All of this naturally requires numerous exercises, on the map and in reality, that permit not only the application of known theoretical notions but also the acquisition of new ones.

In a word, the study of the interaction between principles and contemporary practice is a particularly important and obligatory part of strategic theory, without which the subject is an empty one. Moreover, the study of naval strategy ought to be accompanied by that of land strategy. Many maritime authors have insisted on this point, and I, recalling to mind everything that the study of war on land has taught me, am of their opinion. The method is fruitful as long as one takes account of the change of milieu, just as the employment of the historical method requires acknowledgment of changes over time. But, if this reservation is very important for strategic methods, it is less so in matters of principle. Here, the transpositions are more appropriate, and they offer an valuable contribution to the sailor's military education. . . .

48. For an example of the method, see chapter 9.

CHAPTER 2

MARITIME
COMMUNICATIONS[1]

MARITIME TRANSPORT IN TIME OF PEACE

WHILE FOR most people in the past and many today the sea is a line of demarcation, the frontier of the known world, others view the sea as a productive terrain that they compete to monopolize, and some as a road that unites the farthest and most diverse regions. This is the true conception, the only one that permits an exact understanding of the role of the liquid element in human affairs. As Mahan has already said, "The fundamental truth about the sea—perhaps we ought to say water—is that it is nature's great means of communication."[2]

Such is the value of seaborne communications in peace-

---

1. Raoul Castex, *Théories stratégiques*, 2nd ed., vol. 1 (Paris: Société d'Editions Géographiques, Maritimes et Coloniales, 1937): 65–85.

2. *Le salut de la race blanche*, trans. Izoulet, 102 (author's note). The provocative title of Izoulet's translation of Mahan's *The Interest of America in Sea Power* (Boston, 1898), admitted by Castex to be *"un peu approximatif"* (Castex, *Théories*, vol. 3, 178, and chapter 13, 286), disguises the book's true purpose but not the author's underlying assumptions. The better-known formulation of Mahan's thesis is "the first and most obvious light in which the sea presents itself from the political and social point of view is that of a great highway; or better, perhaps, a wide common over which men may pass in all directions . . ." *Influence*, 22.

time that those able to exploit them have often achieved wealth belying the mediocrity of their political power or territorial extent. The Phoenicians, Genoa, Venice, the Hanseatic League, Holland, and Portugal are characteristic examples from various epochs. The sea's economic importance also explains the pressure to pursue maritime activities among peoples whose situation and political destiny does not drive them towards the ocean. Richelieu[3] in France, Peter the Great[4] in Russia, Cavour[5] in Italy, and Germany under Wilhelm II[6] all created navies and developed their nations' relationships with the sea. All were more or less inspired by the famous aphorism of Walter Raleigh that "Who commands the sea commands commerce, who commands commerce disposes of the riches of the world and thereby dominates the world itself."

Maritime commerce did not, however, have the same character in each historical period. The national products of the Phoenicians, the Genoese, the Pisans, the Venetians, and the Hanseatic cities comprised only a tiny part of the goods that they transported. Carters rather than manufacturers, they maintained the flow of international trade in merchandise that was precious, expensive, and rare. The first change occurred in the seventeenth century, when the rise of industry stimulated states to build ships in order to transport their new domestic production. Maritime traffic linked itself to traffic on land and supported itself from the hinterland.

3. Armand Jean du Plessis, Cardinal and Duc du Richelieu (1585–1642) was Louis XIII's chief minister and the architect of French foreign policy during the Thirty Years War.

4. The first Russian tsar to promote naval expansion, Peter (1672–1725) led his country through the eighteen-year Great Northern War against Sweden.

5. Camillo Benso, Conte di Cavour (1810–1861). Premier of Sardinia and architect of Italian unification under King Victor Emmanuel.

6. (1859–1941), emperor of Germany 1888–1918.

27

The commerce of the Hanseatic League, Genoa, and Venice declined and disappeared. The newcomers—Holland, Britain, and France—were not international traders in the old manner but tended, through policies like the British Navigation Act[7] and Colbert's customs rights, to reserve both their exports and their imports for their own national flag. Until the French Revolution, however, transoceanic commerce remained a luxury trade, and the high cost of transportation forced nations to be virtually self-sufficient in the essential commodities.

It took the great industrial revolution of the nineteenth century to upset these old principles, and Britain was the first to profit from the new economic phenomenon. Her foreign trade rose from 1.682 million pounds sterling in 1800 to 4.225 million in 1850, from 13.685 million in 1870 to 17.100 million in 1873, and to 33.750 million pounds in 1913. To a lesser degree, the other European countries and certain countries of America and Asia have had parallel success. With industrial growth came increases in population; Europe's rose from 175 million in 1801 to almost 400 million in 1900.

But this transformation created a new problem. Vast productive agglomerations demanded, on the one hand, food and raw materials and, on the other, markets for their products. States no longer able to live on their own resources required a strong flow of trade with the outside world, generally overseas. Survival meant not only foreign trade but colonial expansion. . . . Hence, there was a corresponding

---

7. A direct attack upon trading states like the Netherlands, the Navigation Acts were a series of British regulations from 1381 to 1854 designed to bar third parties from participating in Britain's trade with her colonies.

development of maritime traffic, and the European commercial fleet, though smaller in numbers of ships, became much larger in tonnage than it had been in the seventeenth century.[8]

Several characteristics of modern maritime commerce explain its important in the world economy. First, the nature of the merchandise has changed. No longer limited to rare items of great cost and little weight, ships now transport heavy materials: fuel, minerals, grains, fertilizers, and foodstuffs. The increase in ship dimensions and the improvement of nautical engines has led to a continuous and considerable decrease in transport costs. In consequence, the relative cost of maritime and terrestrial transportation has come strongly to favor the former. Finally, the price advantages, the new conditions of maritime transport, and industries' demands for transport of primary materials and finished products have rendered the world's ever-growing population increasingly and more strictly dependent on sea communications.[9]

Parallel to this economic and colonial revolution has come another, political and social, which, by bringing self-government to peoples, has increased the influence of material concerns on the thinking of their elected leaders and, consequently, the repercussions of such concerns on the foreign policies of nations. Thus, commercial, industrial, and colonial rivalries have profoundly influenced the conflicts that have occurred between nations. . . . Since the sea supports the economies of the majority of nations, "in a general sense, all of the great modern wars are naval wars."[10]

8. The larger size of steel hulls allowed tonnage to increase even as ship numbers declined.

9. A compression of a much longer presentation.

10. Tramond et Reussner, *Eléments d'histoire maritime et coloniale contemporaine*, 277 (author's note).

29

MARITIME TRANSPORT IN TIMES OF WAR

An important cause of conflict, the sea also greatly influences the course of the war, although the exact nature of the maritime communications available to the antagonists has changed considerably over time. Generally, maritime communications have a threefold duty in warfare: they sustain the economy, allow the movement of military forces, and, where geography requires, form part of the nation's internal communications. . . . [11]

Maritime communications retain their great economic value in war because it is extremely important to maintain the nation's commercial and industrial activity at the highest level that its diminished facilities permit so as to eliminate the need for expensive intermediaries. . . . Exacerbating the problem of maintaining the economic activity so vital to modern warfare was the appearance, also during this period of great commercial and industrial development, of the nation in arms.[12] Thus, even as a nation's economic requirements increased, its production was half-paralyzed by the incorporation of a large part of the available manpower into the armed forces. The result has been an even greater recourse to foreign sources for needs ranging from war material to foodstuffs. Finally, the last stage in this evolution, the advent of "total war" caused questions that had seemed both economic and military to take on an entirely military form because the privations of the civilian population were now understood to diminish its capacity to fight. Attacks on the rear threaten the front as well. The transformations of the economic and military organizations of the state had rendered society more vulnerable. . . .

11. Compression.
12. First proclaimed by the Constituent Assembly in France on 23 August 1793.

In addition to their economic role, maritime communications must in wartime also meet abnormal demands stemming from the army's transportation requirements. First, there is the matter of moving the armies, or the personnel destined for the armies, between different parts of the same nation, for example, between the mainland France and her colonies. This is pure transportation, differing from trade only in that its cargo is more precious. Armies must also, however, move to new theaters of war accessible by sea and, finally, be transported for seaborne assault against enemy territory.

With this kind of transport, we move into that very important domain that certain writers, the Italians in particular (Sechi, Bernotti, etc.), call the "corrélation maritime et continentale" in order to express the enormous influence of maritime communications on terrestrial operations. History furnishes a vast and convincing set of examples of this correlation going all the way back to the campaigns marked by the battles of Salamis[13] and Actium.[14] The impact of maritime communications on the outcome of the Punic Wars is well known. Only possession of the sea, finally acquired after huge efforts including the battles of Mount Ecnomus and the Aegate Islands, allowed the Romans to conquer Sicily, to force Hannibal on his long detour, and to crush Carthage definitively at Zama.[15] Sea power also served Rome against Philip of Macedon[16] and Mithrid-

13. Greek naval victory over Xerxes' Persians in 480 B.C.

14. At Actium in 31 B.C. Octavianus (later Emperor Augustus) secured his Principate by defeating the fleet of Marcus Antonius and his Egyptian ally Cleopatra.

15. Castex leaps from Roman naval victories over Carthage at Mount Ecnomus (256 B.C.) and the Aegate Islands (241 B.C.) in the First Punic War (264–241 B.C.) to the conclusion of the Second Punic War in 202 B.C.

16. Carthaginian ally Philip V lost to Rome in the First (214–205 B.C.) and Second (200–197 B.C.) Macedonian Wars.

ates[17] and aided Caesar in wars against the Gauls and against Gaius Pompeius.[18]

The progress of the barbarians—that, for example, of the Genseric's[19] Vandals to North Africa and Rome— depended on their possessing sea routes. The sea also aided Belisarius's[20] Byzantine counter-offensives in Africa and Italy. Sea power determined the rise and decline of Arab power in the islands of the western Mediterranean and the outcome of the war between Sicily and Aragon. Losing sea control after Lepanto spelled the end of Arab progress on land.[21]

Modern events confirm the *"corrélation maritime et continentale."* The Mediterranean campaigns against Spain under Louis XIII[22] and Louis XIV,[23] in particular the Sicilian campaign in the course of the Dutch War, are examples.[24]

17. Rome fought three wars against Mithridates of Pontus in 89–84 B.C., 83–79 B.C., and 75–65 B.C.

18. The struggle has been better described as one between the strengths of Caesar on land and of Pompeius at sea, Clark G. Reynolds, *Command of the Sea* (London, 1976): 66–67.

19. King of the Vandals 428–477.

20. Emperor Justinian's General Belisarius's (c. 505–565) campaigns against the Vandals and Ostrogoths gained breathing space for the Eastern Roman empire.

21. Lepanto (1571), the last galley battle, saw the defeat of the Ottoman Turkish fleet under Ali Paşa a Christian alliance of Venice, Spain, and the Papacy commanded by Don John of Austria.

22. Louis XIII (1601–1678) was king of France throughout most of the Thirty Years War.

23. In addition to inheriting the struggle against Spain that ended in the Peace of the Pyrenees in 1659, Louis XIV (1638–1715) led France in four conflicts of his own making: the War of Devolution against Spain (1667–1668), the Dutch War (1672–1678), the War of the League of Augsburg (1688–1697), and the War of the Spanish Succession (1702–1714).

24. Engaged alone against Spain and Holland after Britain withdrew from the Dutch War, France supported Sicily's rebellion against Spain, E. H. Jenkins, *A History of the French Navy* (London, 1973): 55–59.

French efforts to land in Ireland and Britain during the War of the League of Augsburg depended on mastery of the Channel.[25] Similarly, under Louis XV,[26] the conquest of Minorca and the invasion of Britain succeeded or failed in response to naval fortunes.[27] The attack and defense of the colonies under the ancient monarchy, the Republic, and the Empire were governed by the need for communications. The United States achieved its independence because the operations of d'Estaing, Ternay, and de Grasse gave them the control of maritime communications from which Yorktown was the prize.[28]

British control of the sea made possible their operations against our coasts and their landings in Holland, the Dardanelles, Egypt, Copenhagen, the Escaut, and Spain during the Wars of the Revolution and Empire. What is the story of

25. Although Louis XIV's best strategy was to use his superior fleet to reinforce James II's efforts in Ireland, his exclusive concentration on the continent led to the decay of French naval power, Mahan, *Influence,* 159, and Geoffrey Symcox, *The Crisis of French Seapower* (The Hague, 1974).

26. (1710–1774).

27. In the Seven Years War (1756–1763).

28. In 1778 Comte d'Estaing brought the first naval help to the rebellious American colonists, but his hesitant operations proved disappointing to his allies. Charles Louis Chevalier de Ternay convoyed Rochambeau's French troops to Rhode Island in the late spring of 1780, where they remained for a year before marching to Virginia. Later, a second French admiral, the Comte de Grasse, brought more French troops from Santo Domingo to Virginia in August 1781 and cooperated with George Washington in transporting his troops and those of Rochambeau to besiege Yorktown. After this notably successful exercise in combined and coalition operations, de Grasse returned to the West Indies where he was outmaneuvered by Admiral Hood in a series of actions around St. Kitts and defeated by Admiral Rodney at the Battle of the Saints on 12 April 1782, Mahan, *Influence,* 417ff., and Don Higginbotham, *The War of American Independence* (Boston, 1983): 241–251, 379.

the Boulogne Flotilla but a vain and futile wait for the freedom of a tiny piece of sea?[29]

More recently, Navarino[30] solved the question of Turko-Egyptian possession of the Greek Peleponnesus, while the Crimean War and the Turko-Russian Wars of 1828 and 1878 demonstrated the possibilities implied by possession of sea routes; Federal strategy in the American Civil War illustrated the exploitation of maritime superiority to aid land armies. There would have been no Sino-Japanese or Russo-Japanese land wars had the Japanese not acquired mastery of the routes to the Asian continent. Cuba would still be Spanish if the route leading there had been barred to the Americans.

It is almost superfluous to mention the sea's importance for land armies in the 1914 war. The Dardanelles, Salonica, Mesopotamia, Palestine, the German seizure of the islands in the Gulf of Riga, the rescue of the Serbian army, the transport of American troops to France, the conquest of the German colonies all demonstrate the military value of maritime communications in that war. France alone transported 2,365,000 soldiers during the war, while 1,142 ship loads bearing 2,079,880 troops crossed from the United States to Europe. . . .

Finally, maritime communications in wartime sometimes have a military and political importance as *internal* communications between the political center and overseas territories that are not colonies but true parts of the national soil. Such was the case in the past with Genoa and Corsica, Ara-

29. Commonly called the "Boulogne Flotilla" after its principal base, the Flottille Nationale was the huge fleet of armed transports prepared by Napoleon for an invasion of Britain in 1801 and in 1803–1805; John Elting, *Swords Around a Throne* (New York, 1988): 304.

30. The Battle of Navarino Bay (Pylos) on 20 October 1827 pitted British, French, and Russian against Egyptian and Turkish fleets.

gon and its Neapolitan and Sicilian dominions, Venice and its foreign dependencies, and Piedmont and Sardinia.[31] It is now the position of France towards North Africa, which one can no longer consider as a colony, of Greece with the islands, and of the Japanese archipelago with Formosa, Sakhalin,[32] and Korea.[33] Maritime communications are the framework of that modern economic and political edifice that one calls the British "Empire" and that unites the enormous agglomerations of population and territories of Canada, the Indies, Australia, and Southern Africa. . . .[34]

THE MISSION OF MARITIME FORCES[35]

In general, maritime communications have played an important role during war and to have control over them is a priceless advantage. . . . This control has offensive and defensive aspects. Defensively, whoever controls communications preserves his overseas relations and virtually all of his peacetime trade routes while his coast is protected against major enemy action. Offensively, the master of the sea can paralyze or at least restrict enemy relations with foreign countries. He can attack enemy coasts, exploit the advantages offered by combined operations, and dictate the enemy's intercourse with seagoing neutrals.

31. Mediterranean communications played a very important role in the internal liaison of Charles V's empire (author's note).

32. Japan ceded the island of Sakhalin in the Sea of Okhotsk to Russia in 1875 but recovered the southern half in the Treaty of Portsmouth ending the Russo-Japanese War in 1905.

33. Japan moved troops into Korea in 1894 and governed the peninsula from 1910 to 1945

34. See M. Jean Brunhes: *La structure nouvelle de l'Empire brittanique. Illustration,* 26 November 1927 (author's note).

35. By the very general title "maritime forces" we refer to the totality of forces participating in war at sea, that is, not only surface and subma-

The mission of maritime forces is simply to dominate lines of communications, and the achievement of that situation is normally described as having *sea mastery*.[36] This inexact and inappropriate phrase engenders erroneous ideas, but, for the sake of simplicity, we will employ it until we have time to improve upon it. . . . [37]

FREEDOM OF THE SEAS

Those who reject the doctrine of domination of maritime communications advance the theory of "freedom of the seas," an old phrase exhumed from past polemics and implying a new and unsettling idea on which it is impossible not to comment here.

Certain people in the past have claimed to have monopolies of navigation and commerce—even on seas not touching their coast and in peace as well as war. Genoa, for example, had at one time exclusive commercial rights on the coasts of Provence and Naples, and Venice exercised them in the Adriatic. Spain and Portugal disputed each other's claims for mastery and were separated geographically by Pope Alexander VI's Bull of 1493.[38] Later, the British claimed sovereignty over the "British seas" from Cape Finisterre (Portugal) to Norway in a case defended by Seldon's *Mare*

---

rine naval forces but also air forces and even land units assigned to coastal defense (author's note).

36. This deserves a nod to Corbett, who defines command of the sea as "control of the communications in which the belligerents are adversely concerned," Corbett, "Green Pamphlet," in *Principles*, 317.

37. See chapter 3.

38. A series of bulls promulgated in 1493 granted all lands discovered by Columbus to Spain and the 1494 Treaty of Tordesillas divided the New World between Spain and Portugal along a line running north-south in the mid-Atlantic.

Clausum and opposed by Grotius in his *Mare Liberum* of 1609.[39] Criticized by later legal experts like Mably and Beccaria,[40] archaic ideas of sea dominance fell into disuse, and the principle of freedom of the seas received common acceptance in the nineteenth century.

Except for territorial waters, over which states maintain certain rights, and ignoring certain limitations imposed by international regulation, the peacetime sea is at present free and open to the commerce of all.

In our day, during the 1914 war, the old formula of freedom of the seas reappeared but with an entirely new sense. Some now claimed freedom of the seas to be valid in wartime, that commercial navigation should be free both to belligerents and to neutrals and that adversaries could make war only against armed forces; enemy merchants and neutrals were to be respected, regardless of destination, origin, or the nature of the cargo. In short, all private property being sacrosanct, contraband of war no longer existed and blockade ceased to be legitimate.

The United States was always strongly attached to this thesis, which it promoted in 1812, under Monroe in 1823, and in refusing to adhere to the Declaration of Paris of 1856.[41] At the Hague Conferences of 1899 and 1907 the

39. Dutch jurist Hugo Grotius's (1583–1645) book first proposed the principle of freedom of the high seas that John Seldon (1584–1654) attacked in his *Mare Clausum Seu Dominum Maris* of 1635.

40. The contributions of French philosopher Abbé Gabriel Bonnot de Mably (1709–1785) and of Cesare Beccaria (1735–1794), a Milanese utilitarian criminologist and economist, to maritime law are obscure.

41. The United States went to war against Britain in 1812 in part over neutral rights to trade with a blockaded France. The Declaration of Paris signed by representatives of Great Britain, Austria, France, Prussia, Russia, Sardinia, and Turkey abolished privateering and protected neutral goods, except contraband of war, even when carried under the enemy's flag. The United States could not sign the Declaration of Paris without

United States continued to advocate freedom of the sea with modifications to allow the notions of contraband and blockade. During the 1914 war, President Wilson aligned himself with the neutrals in demanding freedom of the seas in this extended sense.[42] Dropping the subject for a time after the United States entered the war, Wilson revived it in the famous Fourteen Points of 8 January 1918.[43] In the hopes of stirring up a quarrel between the United States and Britain, Germany became a last-minute convert to the new interpretation.

To interpret freedom of the seas to include the invulnerability of private property in wartime remains unacceptable on general principles. To eschew the possibility of capturing, seizing, or stopping (for those who prefer not to speak of "destroying") the enemy ships or merchandise, to respect the property of neutrals even when composed of contraband destined for the enemy, is to reject all of the benefits expected from the control of maritime communications. Such restrictions would strip that control of its double purpose—economic and military—whose redoubtable efficacy we have already seen. Freedom of the seas would leave fleets no function but to joust with enemy warships in a sterile battle whose outcome would affect only coastal operations. One might as well disarm, as is, in fact, the intention of some

---

first amending the Constitution, which granted to Congress the right to arm privateers. In practice, however, the U.S. has recognized the Declaration as part of international law.

42. Freedom of the seas found a passionate advocate in the person of Colonel House, President Wilson's *eminence grise*. . . . One finds in every line of House's papers a specifically American imperialism. . . . (author's note).

43. The second point was "absolute freedom of navigation upon the seas, outside territorial waters, alike in peace and in war, except as the seas may be closed in whole or part by international action for the enforcement of international agreements."

proponents of this interpretation of freedom of the seas. Such denial of all means of effective maritime pressure against the enemy can never be welcome in our epoch of total war.[44]

As practiced in earlier naval conflicts, commerce war was often stimulated by greed and, degenerating into piracy, was accompanied by inhuman acts parallel to the ravaging, pillaging, and endless destruction characteristic of contemporary land warfare. If both realms of warfare have seen the end of such excesses, however, at least in theory and law, land armies, however, retain effective methods of forcing a settlement upon the enemy. Occupation of territory or cities, seizure of wealth and resources, and forced contributions and requisition are all perfectly legal fruits of victory obtained from the clash of arms. Since nothing similar exists at sea, naval powers must be allowed to seize or to choke the enemy's private trade. Such actions are logical and less barbarous than the bombardment of coastal cities and ports, to which one would have to turn were there no other means of exploiting naval superiority. One can reasonably claim that the prospect of property losses will encourage the leading citizens of states to prefer peaceful actions since, otherwise, they could look with favor upon the prospect of hostilities without diminishing their profits. In short, naval war has no point if enemy property can travel without hindrance and if neutrals can supply the enemy or conduct his trade. Therefore, the notions of seizure of private property, contraband, and blockade must remain intact, though modified to meet contemporary sensibilities.[45]

These lessons must not be separated, however, from the circumstances of particular cases; the behavior of the belligerents towards neutrals must reflect the latter's importance.

---

44. The argument reappears in chapter 17.
45. *Théories* omits pages 82–84.

In wars during which there are many powerful neutrals, one cannot proceed in the same manner. Still, belligerents have always tended and will always tend to violate the sanctity of private property at sea and cannot do otherwise without losing sight of their own interest in controlling communications.

I admit that I never understood the point of the great debate some years ago on the subject of freedom of the sea. The phrase evoked nothing in me, and I still attribute to it no practical value. In peacetime, the sea is free for everyone. In war, it belongs to the strongest, who will chase both his enemy and any unfriendly neutrals from it as far as he is militarily and politically able. Such is the purpose of the navy, and that is the end of the argument. We can conclude with Richelieu's observation that "of all the sovereigns' domains, it is the sea on which they make the greatest claims, but the place which the rights of each are least clear. The true title to naval domination is force, not reason."[46]

46. And can we be sure that, in the next war, the Americans, ready to fight to defend the freedom of their own commerce when they are neutral, will brutally uphold the other point of view when they are belligerents. Humanitarian imperialism is always problematic (author's note).

CHAPTER 3

REVISION OF THE NOTION OF MASTERY OF THE SEA[1]

EXPLOITATION OF SEA MASTERY

As we have seen,[2] domination of maritime communications permits a double action, economic and military, against the enemy. It allows one, relatively, to protect one's transports and, again relatively, to paralyze those of the enemy. Virtually free use of the sea confers opportunities for coastal raids, seizures on the high seas, and, conditions permitting, old-fashioned blockade. . . . Traditionalists boast of the brilliant profits to be reaped by the master of the sea. Certainly incontestable, are they decisive? Do they offer the possibility of rapidly breaking the will of the adversary? Everything depends on the nature of the enemy.

There is an extreme case, that of an island or semi-insular belligerent unable to survive if deprived of maritime communications.[3] England is a rare example. At the beginning of this century, she consumed ninety million hectoliters of

---

1. Raoul Castex, *Théories stratégiques*, 2nd ed., vol. 1 (Paris: Société d'Editions Géographiques, Maritimes et Coloniales, 1937): 86–117.

2. Above, page 30.

3. Castex several times repeats this typology of island, coastal, and continental states.

41

grain and produced only eighteen million. Every week she imported three million pounds worth of foodstuffs divided among six hundred ships. Her maritime commerce represented four-fifths of her resources. The speedy result of any interruption of this commerce is obvious. Britain's obvious vulnerability to any interruption of her sea communications stimulated at the time an outpouring of pessimism by British military and naval writers, but their fears proved to have been excessive. During the last war even the submarine failed to bring about the predicted nightmares. One can make the same observation for Japan.[4]

Italy, a long and over-populated peninsula, badly provided with economic links to the continent and inadequately endowed with mineral and agricultural resources, would suffer noticeably from a loss of sea routes. Paralysis of her coastal trade, in particular, would be a serious problem. Ultimately, however, her situation would be less desperate than Britain's. During the American Civil War the Federal blockade, although very rigorous, was not able in and of itself to defeat the South, which was an economic island.

When the adversary has a respectable length of frontier and confines his foreign trade at least partially to neutral countries, one cannot hope to win simply by cutting him off from the sea. Germany and Austria remained unaffected by economic warfare throughout most of the 1914 war.[5] Neutrals, especially Holland and the Scandinavian countries,

---

4. Japan's vulnerability to submarine blockade would be demonstrated in World War II, and Castex rather quickly dismisses the German submarine offensive that led Admiral Jellicoe to predict in March 1917 that "they will win, unless we can stop these losses—and stop them soon" and United States Admiral Sims to report that Britain had grain supplies for only three weeks, William Sims, *The Victory at Sea*, David Trask, ed. (Annapolis, 1984): 376.

5. But Castex refers in chapter 8 to German economic difficulties as early as 1916.

supplied sufficient contraband to defer the decision indefinitely. It was only after the United States entered the war that the blockade tightened sufficiently to exclude neutral commerce. While Allied pressure on sea traffic hindered the Central Powers throughout the war and contributed to their defeat, it would never in itself have led to a definite break in the balance.

Against a continental adversary, purely economic exploitation of sea mastery will do no better than this and often even worse. British sea power was aided in the 1914–1918 war by the Central Powers' position within a ring of hostile states. They had, after all, but a half-open window on the outside. It is quite possible that the last war will prove to have demonstrated the very most that economic warfare can achieve.

Thus, in most conflicts, static mastery of the sea brings only incomplete results. Victory very frequently requires forcing a decision by more dynamic exploitation of sea power, by attacking or even invading the enemy's coasts. These operations draw military, not merely economic, profit from mastery of the sea.

Obviously the military side of sea power includes cooperation with land operations. The conclusion is hardly surprising; the success of land operations is after all what matters the most.[6] Only victory on land permits the occupation of the enemy's territory and forces him to acknowledge himself beaten. Sea power is important to the extent that it contributes to victory on land; only in exceptional cases does it achieve complete victory by itself.

England herself, though completely imbued with naval prejudices and convinced that naval mastery suffices to govern all the world, had to envision exploiting that mastery on

---

6. The French School of naval strategy acknowledges the primacy of French concerns on land.

land when she was engaged against a continental adversary. She experienced the impotence of a sea power that remains inactive on land and limits itself to halting the enemy's maritime traffic, paralyzing his commerce, and cutting off distant colonies. Nelson, who in 1796 found himself in the Gulf of Geneva when Bonaparte reported his brilliant victories in Italy, wrote bitterly: "It is regrettable, for us Englishmen, that the fate of nations is not decided on the sea." In our own day, Corbett did not hesitate to declare that "because men live on the earth and not on the sea, the outcome of great wars among nations has always resulted, except in very rare cases, either from what one army could do against the territory or national life of the enemy or from fear of the possibilities that a fleet could give to the army for undertakings against that same territory and that same national life."[7] Thus, England participated vigorously in struggles on land: in Spain, from Anvers to Waterloo under the First Empire; in France, from the Dardanelles to Salonika; in Mesopotamia, and in Palestine during the 1914 war. In these circumstances, her sea power served principally to facilitate the judicious application of the land effort with which she had, however reluctantly, to come to the aid of her continental allies.

The cooperation of the army and the navy is a manifestation of the principle of the *unity of war*. Unity of war implies the existence not only of land strategy and naval strategy but also of a *stratégie générale,* which transcends and coordinates them.[8] General strategy unites the actions of the

7. Corbett, *Principles,* 16.

8. It is this "general strategy" that Corbett, who sees things with the eyes of an Englishman, calls "maritime strategy" (author's note). Castex himself introduces the label *"stratégie générale"* to describe strategy made at the national level, which Anglo-American writers call "grand strategy," and defines it as "the art of managing the totality of the forces and resources of a nation in war and in peace. It unites them into a homoge-

armies and fleets whenever the two types of forces must work together.

From this point of view, the relations that should exist between the army and the navy strongly resemble those between infantry and artillery within the army. Just as the infantry is the "queen of battles," the army is the queen of general strategy. Everything has to be subordinated to it because its success means the success of the general strategy. The navy is often to the army as the artillery is to the infantry—an indispensable support that permits it to conquer its objectives.

In strategy there ought to be no more particularism between army and navy than there is in tactics between infantry and artillery. Each ought to be able, depending on the situation, to make the demands upon the other required by the general interest. They will support one another. Priorities will be established in accordance with the overall objective. If the situation demands that everything be sacrificed to the demands of the army, the navy will efface itself and vice versa.

The siege of Port Arthur by the Japanese illustrates the compromise. Because it began before the enemy's field armies had been put out of action, several authors have treated the siege as a mistake in terms of land strategy, but it was required by the navy as a means of destroying the Russian squadron shut up in port. Appearing to sacrifice itself in response to the navy's call, the army actually acted to further the overall strategy. The destruction of the Russian squadron meant not a private success for the navy but con-

neous whole at the service of a single will. It transcends, coordinates, and disciplines the individual strategies of the various components of the struggle: political, military, naval, air, economic, colonial, psychological, and others." The more natural term "national strategy" was already used in French military parlance for the army's highest level of strategy.

trol of the sea so as to safeguard the army's lines of communications and ensure the final victory. Thus, a healthy appreciation of general strategy led to effective army-navy collaboration.

General strategy requires the army and navy to develop the habit of working together as closely as infantry and artillery. Each of the two arms must sufficiently understand the other's organization, technique, requirements, possibilities, and means of combat.[9]

It is necessary finally to mention one last instance diametrically opposite to that of England; that of a struggle against an adversary like Russia who, with her vast land mass and resources, makes little use of the sea and can survive on her own resources for an indefinite period of time. The United States, a continent in itself, is in virtually the same situation. Against such an enemy, it is obvious that command of the sea, in a purely economic sense, is even more futile than it is against an ordinary continental power such as one finds in Europe.

The case merits analysis because one of the interesting novelties of our day is the inability of the master of the sea, in spite of his privileged position, to guarantee absolutely his maritime communications. Since even his sea transport will be threatened by surface ships, submarines, and aircraft, the future master of the sea will acknowledge the value of terrestrial communications and avoid sole reliance on maritime transport. The railway will not entirely be replaced by the ship. Large continental nations will thus be placed in the very favorable position of being able to threaten the communications of a maritime enemy while their own internal lines of communications remain secure.

---

9. With the air force, there are three liaisons to ensure instead of one. This is not the least of the arguments against this very contentious inno-

This strategic fact, more pronounced today than in the past, has not escaped those contemporary Germans who predict a brilliant future for their country under a policy of friendship with Russia.[10] Thus, Professor Oswald Spengler proclaimed in a lecture at Würzburg in February 1924 that the diminishing role of naval power in future conflicts spelled the end of British power.[11] Captivated by visions of a Russo-German-Asian coalition, Spengler predicted the conquest of India, China, and Persia, the end of Britain's claims to world power, and even the stifling of Britain through a revived continental system.

The thesis contains some exaggerations and recent British policy has aimed to mitigate the threat, but Spengler offers a valid reminder that command of the sea is impotent against continental powers if by command of the sea we mean only the ability to interrupt maritime communications. Continental powers, especially, must be fought on land, and naval power will primarily support the armies.

VARIABLE IMPORTANCE OF MASTERY OF THE SEA

Even assuming the complete and rational use of sea mastery, both economic and military, one cannot say that the command of maritime communications plays the same role and has the same weight in all conflicts. When the belligerents are separated by the sea (Crimean War, Spanish-American

---

vation (author's note). See page 350 for the same argument used to support an independent air force.

10. See especially the work of Professor Werner Daya: *Der Aufmarsh im Osten* (Munich, Eichorn Verlag, 1919), which heralds a Russo-German-Japanese alliance (author's note).

11. Oswald Spengler's (1880–1936) multivolume *Der Untergang des Abendlandes*, published from 1918 to 1922 (English translation *The Decline of the West*, 1926–1928) argued that cultures grow and decay by almost biological laws.

War, Sino-Japanese and Russo-Japanese Wars, etc.), its mastery is obviously a necessary condition for complete victory, but it is a sufficient one only in the extremely rare case of war against an island state.

When the nations at war have common land frontiers, mastery of the sea is, at least in theory, no longer even a necessary condition, since the issue of the hostilities will finally depend on the result of the combat between the land armies. But the command of the sea will most often have a serious effect on the operations of these armies and it will be useful to the power that holds it. . . . [12]

In spite of examples to the contrary, one cannot assert as a general thesis that the mastery of the sea is unnecessary but merely useful to the outcome in a conflict between adversaries with a common land frontier. Armies equipped with modern technology can find themselves locked in a stalemate breakable only by a flank operation or an operation overseas. In these two cases, the command of the sea again becomes a necessary condition for victory. It will also be essential if the stalemate on the principal front cannot be broken without deploying there personnel and matériel from overseas, in which case the combatants will seek to control the sea both to benefit from reinforcements and to deprive his adversary of them. Such was the situation during the 1914 war.

History only furnishes us with the spectacle of *what happened*; the mind is irresistibly drawn, however, to ask *what would have happened had one factor or another been changed? Alongside the actual case, there is the hypothetical case or rather the hypothetical cases*, since there are as many

---

12. Examples of the occasional impotence of sea power, including two Russo-Turkish wars, the Italian War of 1859, and the Franco-Prussian War, are omitted (pages 94–95).

combinations as there are parameters to vary, whose examination is as educational as the study of historical events.

Let us build upon a hypothesis. Let us take ourselves to the already faraway days of 1914 and suppose that Germany found herself engaged alone against England because France, emulating the policy of Louis XVI and his minister Vergennes[13] at the beginning of the American Revolution, averted threats to her frontiers by maintaining excellent relations with her continental neighbors. How would the British take advantage of their command of the sea?

Absolutely incapable of invading a militarily stronger Germany, they could simply attempt some aerial bombardments and bar Germany from her colonies. German maritime communications would be completely cut. Though speedy retirement to harbor would mitigate the destruction of shipping, *direct* German commerce would be interrupted. This would be a major blow, but German intercourse with the rest of the world would not be stopped at all. Coming to her aid with touching alacrity, her large and small continental neighbors would supply everything she needed. The Baltic would remain open to the Germans. . . . The neutrals would be too many and too powerful for British edicts to be enforceable.

On the defensive side, British coasts would be safe from invasion and only suffer occasional raids by surface ships or periodic aerial bombardment.[14] Protected by traditional surface means, British naval communications would con-

13. As foreign minister Charles Gravier, Count de Vergennes (1717–1787) aided the American rebels to avenge French losses to Britain during the Seven Years War.

14. Aerial operations will perhaps later have an entirely different amplitude. We will address this later, but we are now discussing 1914–1918 (author's note).

tinue to function, which is not to say that her merchant fleet would be exempt from loss. The Germans would concentrate their submarine effort against the coasts. Because the effort at protection would be concentrated and the neutrals numerous, the submarine war would prove less effective than in 1914–1918. Still, the British would have to deploy major resources for patrols, escorts, and minesweeping. Their traffic, though not blocked, would take place under disagreeably slow and abnormal conditions.

On one side, then, loss of colonies and a mere interruption of maritime commerce. On the other, continual submarine and aerial harassment. Who will lose under these conditions? Whoever gives up first. But neither of the two adversaries is touched in his vitals, and the situation may remain indefinitely indecisive in spite of British naval preponderance.

If this is not what happened in 1914–1918, it is because in the beginning Germany roused the ire of the continent against her and because Britain, operating adroitly, worked to increase the number of Germany's enemies on land. It was the good old method that had succeeded against so many other adversaries. It was the triumph of British policy, hugely abetted, as always, by the stupidity of the opposing policy. As a result, the victory of 1918 appears as much one of policy as one of pure naval power. In a conflict of another sort, mastery of the sea would have had infinitely less weight.

Thus, there can be no inflexible law on this matter but only specific cases, and each of them has to be considered carefully, those of the past as much as those of the future. One must distrust the formulas, the clichés passed from generation to generation without concern for their degree of truth.

"Whoever commands the sea commands the land." Yes,

but only if he is able to utilize his command of the sea to act effectively against the land.

"The trident of Neptune is the scepter of the world." Certainly, but with the reservation of knowing when and how to plant it on the coast.

"Waterloo was only the coup de grâce; Trafalgar had really been the mortal blow."[15] The final assertion deserves explanation.

After Trafalgar, before the suppression of her maritime communications, France was in very good shape. Though prices were inflated, supplies of necessary grains were adequate. Development of continental resources produced a great industrial and commercial expansion. Exports flourished. The exposition of 1806 gathered 1,422 exhibitors. Immense public works were undertaken everywhere: road building, canal digging, and harbor improvements. The regular budget, managed with economy, sufficed for expenses, while foreign war fed off foreign soil.

French economic success is easily explained. Her territorial acquisitions had given the French empire the use of almost all of the resources of Europe. The occupied countries being barely industrialized, the balance between industry and agriculture was infinitely better than today. The problem of raw materials was almost entirely resolved by local supplies; overproduction was not a concern. The newborn overseas countries occupied a far smaller place in the European economy than they have held since. For essentials, at least, continental Europe was largely self-sufficient. Though almost completely deprived of the sea, the French empire was able until 1814 to support the war and virtually feed huge armies and populations.

Thus, England faced an adversary of the continental type

---

15. Capitaine de Vaisseau Darrieus: *La Guerre sur Mer*, 77 (author's note).

against whom simple domination of maritime communications was of modest effect. Her own condition, moreover, was in no way bright. Austerlitz soon followed Trafalgar and when Pitt died[16] on 23 January 1806, his final utterance was the bleak exclamation, "Oh! my country! In what state I leave my country." Though Britain was mistress of the sea, her situation justified Pitt's dismay. The country was heading for a very serious crisis. With the continent closed to her, the stocks of manufactured goods and colonial crops accumulating in her ports found no buyers. The merchandise of the terra firma, foodstuffs in particular, increased considerably in price. The restoration of certain foreign markets and exports from overseas only slightly remedied this double problem. The English government would be led to accept enormous financial sacrifices, as much to support the factories and to allow them to produce without sales as to alleviate, by legal arrangements like the poor law, the awful misery. These expenses, added to those necessary for the maintenance of the armed forces and for subsidies to allies, imposed formidable demands on the treasury. Recourse had already been made to paper money and to the income tax. Repeated public loans would come to devour 74 percent of the total budget. By 1810 and 1811, Britain appeared to have reached her economic limit.

Such was the situation, the symptoms of which Pitt clearly perceived at the time of his death. Thus, in January 1806, three months after Trafalgar, Fox was led to enter into peace negotiations with France.[17] The master of the sea felt compelled, as in 1796 and again during the peace of

16. William Pitt the Younger (1759–1806), the architect of the Third Coalition, was prime minister 1783–1801 and 1804–1806.

17. A bitter enemy of Pitt and opponent of the war with France, Charles James Fox (1749–1806) was foreign secretary in the Grenville coalition government that came to power after Pitt's death in 1806. He proposed negotiations with France but died within the year.

Amiens,[18] to deal with the master of the land. Only Napoleon's excessive demands prevented a settlement.

Thus, Trafalgar and the sea mastery it brought were not mortal blows to France but only became so later when they were combined with ten years of struggle on the continent. Trafalgar was a necessary but not a sufficient condition for success. Only its intelligent exploitation could decide the victory and constitute a truly mortal blow. But would it have proved sufficient for victory if the monumental mistakes called the War in Spain and the Russian Campaign had not been committed?

RELATIVITY OF COMMAND OF THE SEA

The very term "command of the sea" gives the impression that its beneficiary enjoys the marvelous privilege of having to himself the immense expanse of the oceans, of building a sort of barricade whose key he puts in his pocket, thus totally banning its peacetime users. Many uninitiated persons harbor this infinitely misleading conception.

Such a situation is obviously utopian. All of the world's united fleets would not suffice to achieve it everywhere. Nor would the neutrals easily allow themselves to be cut off from trade. The maritime theater of operations, unlike the area of land operations, is constantly traveled by strangers to the conflict.

The mastery of the sea is not absolute but relative, incomplete, and imperfect. In spite of a sometimes crushing superiority, the dominator of communications has never completely prevented his enemy from appearing on the water. . . . After the battle of the Cardinal Islands,[19] privateers

18. 1802.

19. In English history, Admiral (later Lord) Edward Hawke's defeat of Admiral Conflans on 19 November 1759 is known as the Battle of Quiberon Bay.

continued to seize British merchant ships even at the coasts of Britain. After Aboukir,[20] Bruix made his voyage in the Mediterranean,[21] which, although without great result, nevertheless caused much alarm and confusion among the English. Trafalgar, Willaumez, Leissègues, and Leduc[22] did not keep our ships from remaining for years in the Indian Ocean in spite of the British preponderance of force. During the war in Spain, Wellington complained bitterly to the Admiralty of the insecurity of his communications along the coasts of the peninsula. The Allies' very solid maritime situation in the second half of 1914 did not impede the activities of the German cruisers. . . .

Naturally, the incompleteness of mastery of the sea is even more obvious when naval preponderance, although leaning clearly in favor of one side, has not yet been decided by battle. In the Seven Years War, three years were necessary before the balance fell definitely in favor of Britain. The situation remained similarly indecisive during the entire American Revolution. From 1793 to 1796, the French and the British fought over the regions around Toulon, Genoa, and Corsica. It was the same, as a whole, for the Allies and their enemies during the war of 1914; the fleets of the Central Powers, not destroyed or even seriously reduced, re-

20. The Battle of the Nile, 1 August 1798, saw Nelson's stunning destruction of de Brueys's fleet.

21. Details in Castex, *Théories*, vol. 2.

22. Castex refers here to a string of French defeats beginning with Trafalgar on 21 October 1805. On 13 December 1805 Comte Jean-Baptiste-Philibert Willaumez (1761–1845) and Corentin de Leissègues (1758–1832) sailed from Brest with two separate squadrons whose cruises ended disastrously. Leissègues's force was destroyed by Admiral Sir John Duckworth at Santo Domingo on 16 February 1806, while Willaumez took only seventeen merchant ships before his squadron was dispersed and most of its ships crippled by storms, Jenkins 266–67. Armand Leduc (1764–1832) attempted to relieve Martinique and was captured on 15 April 1809.

mained of the same order of magnitude as those of the Entente. Blockaded, they remained a threat. . . . Given its imperfection and relative nature, the word "master" of the sea appears a bit ambitious. Perhaps it would be more precise to speak, as do the British, of "control of communications," an expression coming closer to reality and having the advantage of encompassing the arrangements that it is necessary to take with regard to neutrals.[23]

Moreover, even relative mastery of the sea cannot be exercised at all points of the globe at the same time, because even the strongest power lacks sufficient force. There has never been general control of communications, but only *local control* over specific regions, many or few in number, greater or smaller in extent, depending on one's resources. Sometimes geography and the distribution of fleets has even shifted local control of the sea to the benefit of the weaker navy. In 1796, for example, after Bonaparte's conquest of northern Italy, Corsica's change of attitude and the Franco-Spanish alliance deprived Britain of her bases and led her to abandon the Mediterranean to the French. During the 1914 war, the Germans dominated the Baltic whenever they were able to move forces there from the North Sea, while the Sea of Marmara remained under Turkish power. Although without great effect on the overall course of events, these particular cases had a real impact on the local operations.

There is also *temporary control* due to special circumstances, to the distance of the enemy forces, for example. A local control can be no more than temporary if the enemy, though momentarily absent, is able to make his actions felt again.[24]

Notions of local control and temporary control take on

23. Corbett, not the generic "British," deserves acknowledgment here.
24. For Corbett's version of local and temporary control of communications, see *Principles*, 338.

concrete value in the context of strategic objectives. Particular actions require control over specific regions at specific times, while the rest does not matter. The Boulogne Flotilla wanted to be master of the Eastern Channel only for periods of time reflecting its specific plan. The Americans needed to be masters of the northern Caribbean Sea during their operations against Cuba; they did not seek control of the Gulf of Gascony. The mastery of the Yellow Sea was indispensable to the Japanese during their entire war with Russia, but they never cared to dispute the Baltic with the Russians. And so on. Everything depends on the interest of the moment. Perhaps one can summarize by saying that command of the sea is, bearing in mind its relativity, its imperfections, and its local price, the *control of essential maritime communications.*[25]

Of course, one constantly seeks to increase this minimum advantage by extending local control and making temporary control more permanent. Though obviously never arriving at the theoretical ideal of general, permanent, and perfect mastery of the sea—an ideal that is a purely mental creation—one approaches it as if it were a mathematical limit. At the same time, one resists similar enemy efforts and, especially, strives to profit by imperfections in his control of the sea.

This analysis reflects the conditions of old-fashioned surface warfare and must be extended to meet present conditions. What is the expression "mastery of the sea" worth today? Less than in the past, as pessimists never miss the opportunity to point out, since one cannot claim mastery of the sea as long as enemy submarines move at ease in the depths and enemy aircraft fly over the oceans with impunity and laugh at the self-proclaimed dominator of the sea.

25. Compare Corbett, *Principles*, 94, 316–17.

Thus English Admiral Bacon qualified the term mastery of the sea as an "enigmatic expression."[26] American Admiral Sims[27] also expressed his concern and uncertainty in the presence of new engines: "Great Britain did not have mastery of the sea. This mastery existed only in the old Nelsonian sense. . . . When submarines are able to operate as they like, it is ridiculous to say that there is a mastery of the sea. The submarines . . . take away from surface ships the advantages which had a decisive character in earlier wars. The surface forces are no longer able to protect communications as they were in a position to do in the times of Nelson and Farragut."[28] Admiral Sims could have made the same observations regarding aircraft.

Later we will evaluate these assertions, but let us simply note for the moment that the expression "mastery of the sea" is less meaningful than in the past and that it will be more precise and less pretentious to speak henceforth only of the *mastery of the surface,* this being itself understood in the same restricted sense we have already assigned to mastery of the sea. It is a new dilution, another step on the road to relativity.

Furthermore, one cannot embrace enthusiastically the neologism "submarine mastery" as an improvement over the old term "mastery of the sea." The new term has even less value than the old, none at all in fact. If I had ten submarines and my adversary fifty, he would not exercise any degree of control, since his submarines would not in the least prevent mine from circling around his.[29]

26. Admiral Sir Reginald Bacon, *The Dover Patrol 1915–1917* (New York, 1919) (author's note).

27. William Snowden Sims (1858–1936) commanded United States naval forces in Europe during World War I and was president of the Naval War College, 1917, 1919–1922.

28. Sims, *The Victory at Sea* (author's note).

29. This was true of submarine technology when Castex was writing.

Similarly, one hardly dares to utter the phrase "air mastery." What is more fleeting and more uncertain than this superiority? It is even more relative than mastery of the sea. The master of the air cannot hope to forbid it completely to his enemy by any permanent occupation of its three dimensions. He is even further disadvantaged in this regard than the master of the sea. He can never prevent the airplanes of even the weakest adversary from carrying out reconnaissances or even bombardments and then disappearing as quickly as they came. But he will be capable, when he has the initiative in operations, of having superiority at a desired point and at a desired time and of employing an irresistible mass of aircraft to sweep the skies. In the air much more than at sea, local and temporary control is the key. This is sufficient, after all, because it implies control of essential communications and has vital consequences for operations. Still, in the presence of the inherent peculiarities of this type of warfare, how can one not be struck by the incomplete and imperfect character of the mastery of the air?

The term "free usage" has also been proposed to replace the old term mastery of the sea, because this better describes the state of affairs since the appearance of modern weapons. The phrase is even more defective, in my opinion, than what it pretends to replace. Failing by default where the other failed by excess, it is too far from the desired goal. The combatant is concerned not merely with gaining free use of the sea but, necessarily, with denying it to his enemy. Free use is much less than control. . . . These observations lead us to examine the merits of the submarine and the airplane as means of transportation and communication.

SUBMARINE AND AERIAL TRANSPORT

Transport, or commercial, submarines first appeared during the 1914 war. The *Deutschland* (later transformed into the submarine-cruiser *U-155*) was the prototype. She displaced 1,750 tons on the surface and 2,100 tons submerged and had speeds of eleven and seven knots respectively.[30] Her submerged range was fifty miles at seven knots, and she could dive in two or three minutes. Her cargo capacity was 450 tons inside the hull and she could carry a certain amount of material impervious to water damage outside the hull. . . .

The *Deutschland* sailed from Bremen on 14 June 1916 and reached Baltimore on 16 July with a cargo of 200 tons of dyes and pharmaceutical products. Leaving again on 2 August, she reached Germany again with a cargo of nickel and rubber on 23 August, having traveled 4,200 miles, of which 100 were submerged. She made a second voyage to the United States in November 1916. Her luckless sister ship, the *Bremen*, disappeared during her first voyage to America. In spite of the delirious enthusiasm provoked in Germany by the *Deutschland*'s first voyage, these attempts were not continued. The commercial submarines were transformed into submarine cruisers and constituted the first series of this type, which went from *U-151* to *U-157*.

The idea of the commercial submarine was revived towards the end of the war, this time by the Allies. In France, at the beginning of 1918, following a lively press campaign in favor of the idea, navy Engineer in Chief Simonot introduced a proposal for a cargo-carrying submarine. The vessel displaced 10,020 tons on the surface and 10,520 submerged and had top speeds, respectively, of eight and five knots. Her range of action submerged was seventy miles at three and a half knots. Her cargo capacity was to be 7,000 tons. Attractive at first glance, the design raised lively criticisms. Skeptics questioned the maneuvering and diving capabilities of such a large vessel and noted that the increased cargo

30. All tonnages are metric.

capacity had been obtained at the expense of a reduced range of submerged operations, an absolutely unacceptable compromise for a ship conceived solely to avoid the enemy by traveling long distances under water. On the other hand, the weight of the hull was to be only 18 percent, which seemed exaggeratedly optimistic in comparison to the 33 percent generally attained. To remedy these faults, however, would considerably reduce her capacity.

Another more practical and more rational project also occurred in France. For a displacement of 3,950 tons (4,350 submerged), a speed of ten knots (seven submerged), a submerged range of 500 miles at four and a half knots, the proposed vessel could carry about 1,000 tons or 1,000 men with the necessary regeneration of air.

It is a big jump, however, from technical feasibility to practical employment. The submarine cargo vessel has prohibitive commercial limitations. Requiring a very specialized crew, it has an infinitely smaller carrying capacity, and it costs much more than a surface ship of the same tonnage.[31] Financially, it promises immediate ruin. Profitable in wartime, when one transatlantic crossing by the *Deutschland* carrying a full load of rubber paid three times the cost of the vessel, a submarine transport could not be built under peacetime market conditions. . . . To have cargo-carrying submarines in time of war, the state must build them in peacetime, a proposal of no interest to the navy.

In any case, submarines could satisfy a very minimal part of the enormous transport requirements of wartime. In view of its particular traits and inadequate means of loading and unloading, the submarine can only be used in a special manner. It cannot transport horses, cannons, automobiles, heavy

31. The freight comprises only 25 percent of the total mass of a submarine but an average of 70 percent of a contemporary surface ship (author's note).

munitions, or large material, but only infantry and only from one friendly port to another. It is useful to remember here that in the course of the last war 247,000 men were transported to France from North Africa and 134,000 from West Africa.

Let us move on to aerial transport, beginning by settling the matter of the dirigible. This pioneer in the conquest of the air has now been dethroned by the airplane, and but a few examples remain in the entire world. Its very high price, the ground installations that it demands, its small numbers, and its extreme vulnerability to ordinary risks as well as those of war mandated its disappearance. Eventually, perhaps, it will belong to the paleontology of the air. But, since its advocates continue to insist upon its virtues as a means of transport, some figures are in order.

The English dirigible *R-100*, built on the Air Ministry's account by the Airship Guarantee Company for communication between England, India, and Australia has a volume of 185,000 cubic meters, more than three times the volume of the zeppelin of the last war. At a ceiling of 5,000 feet, it has a lifting force of 150 tons. If one subtracts from this figure the weight of the hull, machinery, fuel, and crew, the vessel can carry a cargo of *eight and one-half tons.* The American dirigible *Shenandoah,* destroyed after a short career, displaced 78,000 cubic meters. Filled with helium, it had a lifting force of forty-nine tons. Subtracting thirty-six and one-half tons for the hull and engines, nine tons for the fuel, and three and a half tons for the crew leaves no cargo capacity whatsoever.

German calculations on the commercial cost of a cargo-shipping service connecting Europe and America using such means give a freight price (for passengers, merchandise, or post) of 700 pounds per ton simply to cover the cost and 1,200 pounds per ton if one adds the interest on the capital and the depreciation of the material. By boat, the cost averages five pounds for merchandise. Normally, therefore, the dirigible is a deplorable means of transport.

As for airplanes, one can make a useful evaluation of the transport capability of, for example, the best of the genre, the Dornier-Super-Wal seaplane, by hypothesizing on the France-Algeria line.[32] The Dornier could, in theory, do a round trip every two days, perhaps fifteen per month. Reducing this number to ten crossings to allow for bad weather, it would transport twenty tons a month from Algeria to France. For the sum of 140 million francs, one could purchase one hundred airplanes of this type and transport 20,000 tons a month, that is to say, the load of a small cargo ship.

The extremely small return from air transport stems from the fact that it needs four-fifths of its power to keep it airborne, and only one-fifth remains available for carrying cargo. Adding to the calculation the difference in the cost of fuels, one arrives at the impressive result that, for a given distance and weight of cargo, aerial transport costs 2,240 times as much as transport by railroad. With the airplane, we return to the times of the Phoenicians, transporting incense, purple dye, and aromatics.

Thus, in spite of the abundant optimistic predictions made since the end of the last war, commercial aviation is used for little other than carrying the mail, which benefits from more favorable conditions. Moreover, psychological reasons support the technical. Due to the discomfort and insecurity of air travel, the ordinary person, despite his lively enthusiasm for aerial spectacles, prefers to entrust his person or merchandise to vehicles that do not leave the land or the water. Thus, in every country, civil aviation survives only through large state subsidies.

32. Two pages of airplane specifications are omitted.

As for using aviation for purely military transport, one sees, taking the Dornier-Super-Wal as the best existing model, that an airplane can transport about twenty passengers. By making the considerable effort to gather up a hundred of these craft, one could move about 2,000 men at once—and only infantry relieved of their equipment. For the rest, recourse would have to be made to ordinary transport. The seaplane, like the submarine, can only accomplish such transport from friendly port to friendly port. The airplane can land directly on enemy soil and has a certain autonomy in combined operations, but we will reserve until later the examination of that side of the issue.

In sum, the preceding argument shows clearly that aerial transport, even less efficient than submarine, can manage in wartime only a tiny part of the commercial and military traffic vital to the nations and armies. Let us not misunderstand, however. They can render excellent service in certain special cases where the cargo is suitable (valuable, light-weight merchandise, couriers, small units of men, liaison agents, military leaders, etc.). Finally, let us remember that it may be necessary to resort to aerial transport when the circumstances prevent the use of other forms of communication or if one desires very rapid movement.

Of course, statistics furnished here concerning submarines and aircraft must not be assigned any permanent value. True today, they will probably be false tomorrow. The purpose of the purely material treatment of the problem of submarine and air transport—which may have appeared unusual in a study like this one—is to indicate a *method* of approach, to show how strategy must periodically revise its claims to take into account the evolution of technology. In any epoch, a similar evaluation of material factors is absolutely necessary. Otherwise, one risks being trapped in the past, a representative of a bygone age.

CONCLUSION

For the present, however, the study of submarine and aerial transport shows us that maritime transport, whose exceptional importance for most people we have previously indicated, can only be achieved by surface vessels. The old situation has only changed very slightly, and now, as in the past, the sea can only be completely and fruitfully exploited on its surface. . . . The mastery of the surface, the smaller heir of its brilliant forerunner, mastery of the sea, will have a decisive influence on events. The fundamental objective is its conquest.

But this mastery of the surface, just like the ancient mastery of the sea, is incomplete, relative, imperfect, local, and temporary. Everything depends on the concerns of the moment. . . . In our time, the mastery of the sea signifies *the control of the essential surface communications.* The mission of the maritime forces is to obtain this control and cooperate with land forces to exploit it economically and militarily within the framework of the overall war.

ADDENDUM 1937: REPARTITION—LAND-SEA-AIR[33]

The variable importance of the sea poses for continental nations the question of apportioning resources among the three armed forces—the army, navy, and air force. The three share one common denominator—money—and the problem is to determine which arm should receive the largest peacetime allocation of funds.

Reason obviously suggests that France should not go too far in any direction. She must not reduce her weapons for

---

33. Though much had happened, especially in aircraft design, between 1929 and 1937, the addendum to the second edition does little but rehash "the variable importance of sea mastery." See *Théories*, vol. 1, 129–31.

short wars—the army and the air force—in order to strengthen the navy—a weapon for long war—nor do the reverse. It is necessary to find a judicious balance. But this conclusion is more philosophical than useful. The problem remains shockingly difficult. . . .

On the one hand, not knowing whether the war will be short or long, one must arm for both. On another, once taken, decisions cannot readily be altered. They commit one for years. Extra ships, however useless, continue to exist. One cannot install wheels on them and send them to reinforce the army. Lack of sufficient ships cannot, however, be redressed in time. Above all, it is very difficult to shift material between the land, air, and sea fronts.

Actually, there have been some exceptions to the principle of rigid and permanent separation of the three arms. Sailors have sometimes reinforced the army (the siege of Paris of 1870 and the navy's rifle brigade in 1914), and soldiers used to be placed on ships to complete their crews. Naval reservists have been transferred to the army, and the navy arsenals produced munitions, vehicles, and equipment for the soldiers. Many naval guns have been sent to the front and, on the other hand, land guns have been placed on ships, especially merchant ships. The air force can participate in naval operations, and naval aviation can, within a certain range, reciprocate. One can *manoeuvre*[34] to a very limited extent, but, once the war has begun, it is too late to undertake anything important of this nature.

Finally, certain political premises are uncertain, such as, for example, the attitude of Britain, which has major implications for France's distribution of forces among the army, navy, and air force. Though the matter is of great importance, we are completely unable to come to a decision here.

One must have the courage to admit that the problem is

34. See below, 101, note 1, for Castex's use of *manoeuvre*.

terribly complex. It is brutal because the leaders of the three arms make equal financial demands. The solution is unstable. It changes with the situation and can never be solved on the basis of *a priori* rules. Still, in my opinion, one can say in principle that the air force ought to have priority because it can participate very effectively in the activities of both the army and the navy while the reverse is not true, at least tactically. Of the three, the air force is, if one can use such expressions, the more "reversible" and "omnibus." It, particularly, must be reinforced.

CHAPTER 4

FIRST APPROXIMATION OF A THEORY FOR THE CONDUCT OF OPERATIONS[1]

SINCE THE fleet is the *ultima ratio* in both the attack and defense of communications and the attack and defense of coasts,[2] our primary aim in both peace and war ought to be to bring our fleet to its maximum effectiveness, and the primary objective of our wartime operations ought to be to destroy the enemy's fleet by combat or at least to paralyze it so as to obtain mastery of the sea. This truth, that combat is the primary element of naval war, is nothing but the perfectly valid extension to naval war of a principle always recognized as valid for land warfare. For Clausewitz, "Combat constitutes the entire activity of war. In combat, the destruction of the opposing force is the means of attaining the goal. In war, the *destruction of the enemy's armed force* is the keystone of every combination. . . . Combat is the strategy's instrument for reaching the war's goal."[3] Rüstow is no less clear in observing that "the armies are the principal instrument and principal objective of strategy, for his own army to act as freely as possible and to impede the action of the enemy is the dominating thought that ought to guide

1. Raoul Castex, *Théories stratégiques*, 2nd ed., vol. 1 (Paris: Société d'Editions Géographiques, Maritimes et Coloniales, 1937): 199–213.
2. Attack and defense of communications and attack and defense of coasts and territories are the subjects of the two preceding chapters.
3. A loose précis of *On War* vol. 4, chapter 3 (Howard, 227–28).

67

the general in chief. The action of war is concentrated in battle. *It commands and determines all other operations of war."* Von de Goltz credits Napoleon with having reminded soldiers of "a thing that Frederick already knew but they had forgotten, the importance above all of *annihilating the enemy* forces, that it is battle that decides war." And in his own name the German author adds that "the first and principal goal to which the movements of armies tend is the enemy army." Similarly, Field Marshal Foch[4] once said, "The adversary will only concede himself beaten when he no longer can or will fight, that is to say when one has destroyed his army either physically or psychologically. . . . *To seek out the enemy armies,* the center of the opposing strength, *in order to defeat and destroy them,* . . . to choose the course and the tactic that leads to it soonest and most surely, that is the essence of modern war."[5] This view, reinforced by contemporary military studies, is still unanimously accepted as the rule for land warfare. Naval theoreticians have come to the same conclusion not only through the tenuous process of analogy but also by direct observation of the naval events discussed in the preceding two chapters.

Admiral Mahan's principal thesis was the preponderance of the fleet in maritime operations and that its destruction constituted a far more urgent and important objective than the conquest of territory or attacks on commerce. Speaking of the actions that took place in the West Indies during the American Revolution, he underlined that "the key to the situation in the Antilles was the fleet" and directed cold sar-

4. Ferdinand Foch (1851–1929) was a prominent advocate of the offensive and was appointed supreme commander of the Allied armies from 26 March 1918.

5. Ferdinand Foch, *Les principes de la guerre* (Paris, 1905): 40–41 (author's note). Castex cuts two sentences from Foch's argument, one of them a quotation from *On War.* In the original, "essence" is *"toute la morale."*

casm, disdainful and exasperated, at "the naval policy of the French," which was based on contrary views in which the famous "ulterior projects" played such a pernicious part.

Admiral Colomb declared formally that "the goal of naval war is control of the sea or 'mastery of the sea.'" A power that exerts itself elsewhere by attacking ports or territories or acting to protect commerce accepts an inferior status and will never be able to hope to cause his adversary serious damage. . . . It is pointless to try to obtain mastery of the sea through other means than battle, and the enterprise is so important that no other objective can be compared with it."[6]

The French School before 1914 clearly accepted the preceding affirmations. Admiral Daveluy expressed himself as follows:

> To reduce the enemy to impotence, it is necessary to disarm him, that is to say *to destroy the constituted forces* that are the guarantee of his power. The necessity to attack the constituted forces leads directly to combat. . . .
>
> The failure of many maritime writers is to see in naval war only specific cases. Some believe that the purpose of the navy is to assure the inviolability of the coasts and to attack those of the adversary. Others assure us that its role is to destroy commerce. Others finally want to devote it to assuring the success of an invasion. Well then! Destroy the enemy and you will have all of these results at once; the protection of coasts will be assured and you will be able successfully to carry out whatever operation the circumstances demand. . . . The role of the squadrons is to fight the enemy to win empire over the sea. Light vessels can then safely attack commerce without prejudicing all the other advantages that come from suppressing the military forces of the adversary.[7]

6. *Naval Warfare*, 24 and 202 (author's note).
7. *Etude sur la stratégie navale*, 7, 8, and 328 (author's note).

Admiral Darrieus's insistence on the same idea is the distinctive trait of his original and vigorous work. He says in various places:

> To consider the enemy fleets as the principal force that it is necessary to destroy, to render powerless, to more surely fulfill the object of the war . . .
>
> Mastery of the sea, which plays a preponderant role in the development of every naval war, can only be attained by two means: blockade of the enemy forces in their ports or their annihilation in battle.
>
> The goal, as the principal objective of the war, the surest means of satisfying its ends is and always will be combat and *the destruction of the enemy fleet.*[8]

Admiral Amet, who succeeded Darrieus in 1907 as professor of strategy at the *Ecole de Guerre Navale,* developed the same thesis while adding to it a new element of urgency.

> To seek out the fleet that the enemy sets at sea, to meet it in conditions advantageous to its destruction, such ought to be the primary, the principal objective for our naval forces, since the decisive combat comprises every activity useful to war at sea. . . .
>
> Attempt nothing at sea, neither against the coast nor against the adversary's commerce, before you are assured of maritime supremacy, before having acquired the mastery of the sea.[9]

The Italian school reasons similarly but with certain easily noticeable nuances. "The strategic offensive, " Sechi says,

> proposes to acquire in the briefest possible time absolute or almost absolute mastery of the sea and to proceed from there to vigorous and methodical attack on the coast and commerce of the enemy.

8. *La guerre sur mer, la doctrine,* 96, 300, and 358 (author's note).
9. *Ecole de Guerre Navale,* 1908 (author's note).

To attain mastery of the sea more quickly and more completely, it is usually appropriate to attack at the beginning of hostilities. But the *principal objective always remains the destruction of the enemy force,* and it is necessary to conduct these aggressions with prudence and circumspection so as to avoid serious and irreparable disasters.[10]

The Italian version implies a slight relaxation of the order of events to which we will return later. Captain Bernotti wrote in 1911: "It is indispensable that the fleet consider its essential objective to be conquest of the mastery of the sea or, when the relative conditions of the two forces do not allow the drive for mastery through decisive battle, at least an effective dispute of that mastery."[11] I shall end the list myself, humbly, entirely intimidated at finding myself in such imposing company. But one must accept one's responsibilities. *Scripta manent.*[12] And I wrote, I believe, that "we will first seek battle so as to suppress the enemy fleet and free ourselves to do *afterwards* what we desire. And in other terms, to follow the enemy fleet unrelentingly, to defeat it in a great battle, to fight with all of one's forces united, this is the goal of a rational strategy."[13] It is said that ten of a person's lines suffice to hang him. I ask to escape that unhappy fate by furnishing further clarifications that will perhaps mitigate the first impression.

This exposé of the facts and of expert conclusions has prepared us to establish the major rules for the conduct of

10. *Elementi di arta militare marittima,* vol. 2, 300 (author's note).

11. *Fondamenti di strategia navale,* 14 (author's note). An English translation of Romeo Bernotti's *Fundamentals of Naval Strategies* will be published in 1994 by the Naval Institute Press.

12. "What is written abides."

13. Raoul Castex, *La bataille du XVIe siècle. Lepante et ses enseignements d'actualité* (Paris, 1914): 30 (author's note).

hostilities at sea, that is to say somewhat ambitiously, the strategic doctrine of naval war.[14]

The enemy's organized mobile force, his fleet, will be primary in our thoughts. We will direct all of our actions against it because its suppression will resolve all of our problems. If it is divided into several sections of unequal weight, we will direct our greatest efforts at the largest of them, because its destruction will very probably irreparably compromise the rest of the enemy's organization.

Thus, we will attempt before everything, in one way or another, to put the principal enemy fleet out of action. The best method is obviously to destroy it in battle. If the enemy avoids this by shutting himself up in port, we will blockade him there more or less tightly to prevent his emergence or to force him to battle as soon as possible if he does.

The elimination of the fleet is then the first objective and the search for battle its necessary corollary. All aspirations, all dispositions must be directed towards this single end. The effort will be constant and active, manifesting itself in movement and pursuit, in chasing down the enemy whom we wish to dominate. Behind all of our plans will be a dynamic and vigorous drive.

For the time being, until we have achieved the necessary reduction of the enemy fleet, we will give up all other preoccupations. Before the battle we so much desire, which must determine everything, we will not hamper ourselves with ancillary concerns, notably, with defending coasts and communications, which would negate the principal objective by dis-

14. In what follows we have deliberately reproduced some of the excessive traits of an imperfect doctrine in order to achieve the promised first approximation. Let the reader be assured that he will find the necessary refinement later on (author's note).

persing our forces and effort.[15] Moreover, will our own threat to the enemy fleet not prove the best protection of all for our coasts and communications? Similarly, before accomplishing our primary goal of annihilating the enemy fleet, we will not undertake our own operations against coasts or commerce. This path, however attractive, would compromise everything. Nor, above all, will we seek geographical objectives, which count for little or nothing in this business. The fleet decides everything, and its fate determines the fate of everything else.

After having dealt with the enemy fleet, one is free to profit from mastery of the sea with other operations, but, undertaken prematurely, these will undermine the freedom of action essential to the destruction of the enemy fleet. We will be weighed down and paralyzed by contradictory needs, thinking about the coast, commerce, transports, and convoys in lieu of the real adversary or about everything at the same time to the detriment of singleness of aim. Chasing several hares simultaneously is the best way to catch none.

The same line of thought requires that we free ourselves as quickly as possible from any constraints foreign to strategy that the situation will tend to impose upon us. What is important is to be the victor in the naval theater itself. The military action must develop unshackled, and factors having to do with politics, economics, land war, morale, etc., must be demoted to the second level.[16]

Whoever wants to defeat the fleet by combat must neces-

15. The second approximation, chapter 5, adds an element of defense while chapter 17 reveals that the war over communications happens simultaneously with the struggle between the principal fleets.

16. Castex continues tongue in cheek. Even for a "first approximation," this is very far from his own theory that naval action must always be integrated into *stratégie générale*. The second approximation gives proper weight to non-naval considerations.

sarily take the offensive without concern for its inherent risks. To obtain by battle the desired decision requires engagement under the most favorable conditions and with the maximum of resources. We will concentrate as many forces as possible on the principal objective so as to have every possible advantage. And if fortune smiles on us in battle, we will not rest upon a half-success but will render the victory as complete as possible through the most energetic pursuit that our means allows. The whole program, finally, will be achieved by animating both the leader and his agents with the well-known elements of moral drive—ardor, activity, faith, will to win, etc.

The principle of annihilating the enemy fleet applies not only to the much-desired but not always achieved general battle but also to every encounter with even the smallest enemy force. No opportunity should be neglected to destroy anything that floats, dives, or flies, for anything accomplished now is one less task for the future. History offers many examples of men who neglected such opportunities and how they later repented of their mistakes.[17]

We have thus arrived at a doctrine of which the fleet and the battle constitute the cornerstone, the foundation upon which we will construct our plans. But is this doctrine irreproachable? Is it perfect? Though what follows will illuminate us further, we can be certain from the beginning that it encompasses a great part of the truth.

Reason alone brings the same result through the following intellectual exercise: What hinders us if we want to attack the enemy coasts or communications? The enemy fleet. Who threatens our own coasts or communications? The enemy

---

17. Castex's examples from the Lepanto Campaign, the War of the Austrian Succession, the American Revolution, the Wars of the French Revolution, and World War I, *Théories*, 206–8, are omitted.

fleet. Therefore, eliminating the fleet provides us unequalled freedom of action and security while its survival leaves us vulnerable to everything.

Since it is so simple to derive this common-sense rule from theoretical reflection, why did it have to be addressed in two meticulous chapters on the attack and defense of communications? In the first place, showing that practice confirms the theory is not superfluous, because it reinforces faith in the notion of naval mastery, but there is another reason. Two schools of thought—the "empirical" and the "dogmatic" or "doctrinaire"—exist about the objective of naval operations.[18] The former treats the four problems of the attack and defense of coasts and communications in terms of means alone without taking into consideration the fleet. This is the approach of the *Jeune Ecole*. The latter, whose opinions we have just cited, prefer to attain their goal by a prickly but surer path. Thus, we have a division into two schools, recalling that which in the first half of the nineteenth century split theorists of land strategy between the "doctrinaires," of whom Jomini was the most eminent, and the "ideologues," of whom Clausewitz was the brilliant example. These, however, disagreed with one another only on secondary points, agreeing about the objective of operations, while, in the modern navy, the divergence is infinitely sharper because it concerns absolutely vital matters.

Empiricism, as one knows, is the use of experience alone as the unique source of knowledge without any theory or reasoning. Locke and Condillac were its apostles.[19] Empiri-

18. These are the kindest labels for the latter. Some of the harsher ones go so far as to charge them with financial or industrial complicity with the manufacturers of one weapon or another (author's note). The charge seems more apt to the materialists, but *"ceux-ci"* must be "the latter."

19. More accurately, modern empiricism is a philosophical theory about the use of experience as a source of knowledge. John Locke

cism deals only with facts without trying to interpret them or to reduce them to principles. This is what distinguishes it sharply from the experimental method. It is therefore difficult to speak of the "empirical system," an expression that couples two irreconcilable terms.[20]

The doctrinaire, on the contrary, espouses a tight system of opinions, dogmas, or ideas. Dogmatism is a philosophy that admits certainty, a system of knowledge that attempts through reason alone to achieve absolute truth.[21] The distinction above is the same that separated the two medical camps of antiquity—the empiricists led by Heraclides of Tarentum and the dogmatics led by Hippocrates of Gallien.[22]

Is the distinction as deep as is claimed? The most vehement empiricist allows himself to be led fatally to extending facts beyond experience and creating a systematic work. On the other hand, not all dogmatics are positive. Some are negative, the positivists for example (ironic label), who, criticiz-

---

(1632–1704) and his French follower Etienne Bonnot de Condillac (1715–1780) are important from Castex's point of view, because they refused to generalize principles from separate phenomena.

20. To the modern reader, for whom the words "empirical" and "experimental" are virtual synonyms, this paragraph is likely to prove baffling. Locke and his fellows explored the limits of human ability to attain knowledge and argued that, while experimentalism could contribute to understanding about the world, it fell short of producing knowledge of it.

21. And is thereby opposed both to experimentalism, which denies that reason alone can produce certainty, and to classical empiricism.

22. The terms "empiricists" and "dogmatics" leap to the mind of one's own accord in this instance in part because military science bears a great resemblance to the natural sciences in its emphasis on experience and observation (author's note). They are more likely to occur to a Frenchman in the 1920s than an American of the 1990s. The most important empirical physician of antiquity, Heraclides (*floruit* c.75 B.C.) studied medicine by dissecting cadavers. Little is known about his fourth century predecessor, Hippocrates of Cos, who is credited with a rationalist effort to create an overall concept of the human body.

ing the empiricists, denounce the search for first principles as empty and useless.[23] One should not attribute too much importance to these grand words.

In the navy, however, the views of the empiricists and those of the dogmatics differ utterly in their qualities and their mistakes because each of them addresses only one part of the subject. Taking a prudently eclectic approach, it is less useful to criticize the errors of the two schools than to retain what each offers of value.

If I had to choose, however, between these two kinds of theory, I would incline, I believe, towards the dogmatic or at least towards the doctrinaire.[24] I confess my penchant for them. A question of temperament perhaps. I have a constructive, even systemizing, bent. My natural propensity is to consider facts as of little importance in themselves and to seek to discover what explains and connects them. Loving to build, I have an instinctive horror of "negativism," of negatives, of sterilizers, of demolishers. One cannot be other than what one is.

The doctrinaire approach, cultivated in moderation, is moreover perfectly explicable intellectually. The human spirit always wants to escape the murky depths, to thrust itself towards knowledge, to elevate itself from the particular to the general and from the fact to the law that regulates it. "There is knowledge only of the general," said the ancient philosophers.[25] Were it not for the doctrinaires, for the seekers of causes and laws, science would have remained in

23. It is not clear why Castex affiliates "dogmatics" with positivists, since the latter, believing sensory data to be our only source of knowledge about the external world, reject the rational approach that defines the "doctrinaire."

24. A distinction Castex has not clarified.

25. Presumably a reference to the Platonist doctrine that one has opinions about individual things but true knowledge only about the more real "idea" behind them.

its earliest wanderings, and we would still have plasters and unguents in place of modern serums and curative methods. The doctrinaire turn of mind is also morally praiseworthy. Noble, pure, and elevated, it aspires to improvement, to progress, to the ideal. In addition, the navy owes a special debt to the doctrinaires, without whom we would have come to nothing, or almost. They brought something into being where only an absolute void existed before.

For that matter, is the label "doctrinaires" well-chosen to describe them? Have they ever claimed to seek the total truth about strategy through reason alone? The two preceding chapters—and I finally touch upon their principal importance—refute the suggestion. Everything said about the attack and defense of coasts and communications demonstrates that the doctrinaires pay significant heed to experience inasmuch as their thesis depends fundamentally on historical cases. Far from being the fruit of a wandering imagination, their theory has a certain empirical basis. . . . But, if the doctrinaires have incontestably grounded their opinions in reality, have they taken account of *the whole reality*? Have they not been led to simplify excessively, to schematize too much an extremely complex whole—and this in analyzing surface war alone, the only form they knew? This remains to be seen. Finally, it is certainly necessary to bring their system up-to-date by incorporating the novelties of our epoch, the submarine, aviation, and modern communications.

CHAPTER 5

SECOND APPROXIMATION OF A THEORY FOR THE CONDUCT OF OPERATIONS

To DEVELOP a doctrine of operations valid for the contemporary world requires correcting our first approximation with the ideas developed in our analyses of specific aspects.[1] But it would be both deceptive and dull to do such a work abstractly and better to use as an explanatory tool a hypothetical conflict involving two parties, Red and Blue, facing one another in the situation depicted by Map 1.[2] Let us add interest to the affair by identifying ourselves with Blue's high command before studying our plan according to the general method described above.[3]

First, what is our objective?[4] Obviously, what we have defined for the maritime forces of a nation at war—to conserve and control the essential surface communications and

1. The first approximation is the sketch of naval doctrine in chapter 4. The specific discussions in Raoul Castex, *Théories stratégiques,* 2nd ed., vol. 1 (Paris: Société d'Editions Géographiques, Maritimes et Coloniales, 1937), part 3, chapters 4 through 7 ("Classification of Operations," "The Method of Seeking Combat," "The Submarine Factor," and "The Aerial Factor") are omitted from this edition.

2. *Ibid.,* 374–94.

3. See the chapter entitled "Plans of Operations" (author's note). Not in this edition.

4. Castex asks Foch's celebrated question—"*De quoi s'agit-il?*"

79

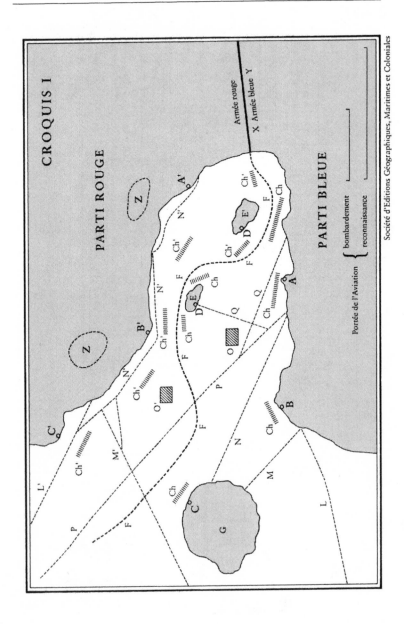

CROQUIS I

PARTI ROUGE

PARTI BLEUE

Armée rouge

X Armée bleue Y

Portée de l'Aviation { bombardement
                       reconnaissance

Société d'Editions Géographiques, Maritimes et Coloniales

to make use of them to attain the goals of the war. Aided by the army if necessary and dominating the opposing Red forces, we must acquire and exploit free use of the sea in order to attain our military, economic, and political ends and so deprive the Reds of the same possibilities. Defined thus, the Blue commander's mission is as simple to state as it is difficult to fulfill. To see how it should be done, let us begin by examining our situation.

For simplicity, let us suppose that the two camps are equal and mark the surface forces, which will play the greatest role in the conflict as O and O', like pawns on a chess board. Let us next examine the nature of the terrain, an important detail which, with beautiful disdain for geography, we neglected altogether in our first approximation. The shores whose contours are drawn on the map offer nothing remarkable except their symmetry with regard to the common land frontier XY. The island E is fairly well placed to threaten the Red coast, but, unhappily, the enemy can reciprocate from island E', which is disagreeably close to our shore. A vast overseas territory G, which we have made an island because of the small size of the map, belongs to us and plays a major role as a source of supplies and reinforcements for our armies.

We have at our disposal two principal bases A and B and two secondary bases C and D for our fleets; the Reds have the same situation: principal bases A' and B' and secondary bases C' and D'. The water depth increases evenly from the shoreline, and mines can be used up to a certain distance from the coast. The so-important aerial distances are easily determined on the map and indicate that almost the entire theater of operations can be traversed by the reconnaissance aircraft of both sides. A significant part of the Red coast can be reached by our bombers based on island E, while enemy bombers from A' can reach our coast from A to X.

Our maritime communications consist of lines M and N, which are very important in linking us with territory G, and lines L, P, and Q, which connect us with neutrals overseas and with island E. Lines L, P, and Q are particularly exposed to enemy attack—surface, submarine, and air. On the other side, the Red communications with neutrals are represented by lines L' and M', while arteries like N' allow important coastal commerce. Both parties establish mine fields and obstructions represented as Ch and Ch'.

In sum, the terrain offers a rough state of equilibrium. Each side commands a part of the theater of operation, but "command" is a manner of speaking. Positions command nothing at all, the fleet always remains preponderant. Positions, however, incontestably aid the fleet in occupying, surveying, and controlling a given region of the war zone. Such is the situation here. When their fleet operates along their coast and in the vicinity of island E', the Reds are favored because they have the support of the surface and submarine elements that normally operate only there. They will also have major air support and be close to bases for resupply and repair after battle, while their obstructions will serve them both defensively and offensively. On the other hand, we will have the same advantages in the southern part of the theater and in our advanced ground around island E.

Roughly separating the zones of respective Blue and Red strength is the line represented on the chart as FFF. By analogy with land war, especially the 1914–1918 war, this line has sometimes been called the "front," an appropriate label if we make allowances for the fact that naval war more closely resembles the open warfare of the past than it does the 1914 war. First, the front is neither continuous nor impenetrable. Largely insubstantial, it is easily crossed by submarine and air forces and sufficiently strong surface forces. Thus, the line FFF is not a barrier but only, as it were, the "line of equality of conditions" of the surface forces.

In addition, the front is not static but, like all imaginable land fronts, it changes with the military successes and failures of the two parties and the movements of forces within the fixed geographical framework. . . .

Finally, the contact between ourselves and the Red forces along the line FFF will not be a permanent one. *For surface forces* at least, the line is rather the axis of a more or less broad zone that neither they nor we will permanently dominate— a disputed field into which each side will venture in turn. Because of the advancements in armament since antiquity, the size of this zone has steadily increased; the torpedo, the submarine, and the airplane have reduced the contact between surface forces, which exists now only during those phases of activity that end in tactical encounters.[5]

Examples from the past confirm how the notions of permeability, mobility, and intermittent contact modify our notions of a front. During the wars of the Revolution and the Empire, a sort of Anglo-French front was established by the strength of Britain's fleet and her ability to operate freely from good positions acquired on our very coasts. Nonetheless, favorable circumstances sometimes brought about changes in the front, as in 1796, for example, when the British had to evacuate the Mediterranean after its banks fell into our hands.[6] Moreover, the stability of the front was never uncontested, but was challenged by local crises (the

5. But in chapter 9 Castex argues that the greater speed of modern ships and communications has essentially reduced the size of the naval theater, and chapter 1 argues that the tactical realm has grown at the expense of the strategic.

6. See *Théories*, vol. 1, chapter 3 (author's note).

battles of Prairial,[7] Noli,[8] Groix,[9] Saint Vincent,[10] and Camperdown,[11] and the expeditions to Ireland and Egypt) and by more general ones (Bruix's campaign in the Mediterranean in 1799 and the campaign of 1805). We also attacked the enemy's rear through the *guerre de course*.

The Russo-Japanese War offers an analogous case. By blockading Port Arthur and acquiring positional advantages (Korea, the Elliott Islands, etc.), the Japanese used their mastery of the sea to fix the front on the Russian coast of Asia. The stability they achieved allowed them almost completely to control and exploit the maritime communications behind the front. Again, however, there were moderate crises (23 June 1904[12]), more serious ones (10 August 1904[13]

7. Known to the victors as "The Glorious First of June," Prairial was fought on 1 June 1794 between the British under Lord Howe and the French under Admiral Villaret-Joyeuse. Though the revolutionary navy suffered a major tactical defeat, a major French convoy safely reached Brest with supplies.

8. Rear Admiral Martin was defeated at Noli in the Mediterranean on 13 March 1795.

9. The Ile de Groix was the site of a humiliating defeat, the *"débandage de Groix,"* of Villaret-Joyeuse's Brest fleet on 23 June 1795 by British forces under Admiral Hood (Alexander Lord Bridport) supporting an otherwise disastrous Anglo-*emigré* landing at Quiberon Bay.

10. Outnumbered fifteen to twenty-eight, Admiral Sir John Jervis captured four Spanish ships at Cape St. Vincent on 14 February 1797 and was created Earl St. Vincent in consequence.

11. Fighting in the North Sea off the coast of Holland against an equal Dutch force under de Winter, Admiral Adam Duncan of the Royal Navy captured eleven ships on 11 October 1797 and prevented the Dutch from supporting a planned French invasion of Britain.

12. When Russian admiral Vilgelm Vitgeft sortied from Port Arthur but withdrew without engaging.

13. A second sortie by Vitgeft produced the defeat at the Battle of the Yellow Sea in which the admiral himself was killed.

and Tsushima[14]), and, finally, operations by the Russians behind the lines (cruisers from Vladivostok).

The 1914 war closes the series for the moment. The front that the Allies succeeded in establishing in the North Sea, at the entrance of the Adriatic, and on the Turkish coasts was only solid when they had the use of the necessary positions at Scapa Flow, Moudros, Argostoli, Corfu, Salonika, etc. The enemy did as much as he could in the rear through the *guerre de course* of 1914 and the submarine war. There were serious crises, sometimes on the front itself (Jutland), sometimes in the rear (Coronel,[15] Falklands,[16] the submarine war of the spring of 1917). In the Baltic, where they themselves were free, the Germans operated in a similar fashion but on a smaller scale. . . .

Our examination of the situation will be incomplete if we do not consider the neighboring forces and the thousand diverse circumstances that can influence our strategy and impose extraneous operations upon it.[17] The only relevant neighboring force—and it is infinitely so—is the land army. In the conflict under consideration, the Red and Blue armies are very probably at grips along the length of the frontiers XY, each with one flank resting on the sea at X. The other "various circumstances" appear in the constraints[18] that remind us once again that war is a unified whole and that

14. At Tsushima Strait (27–29 May 1905), Admiral Togo Heihachirio destroyed or scattered Admiral Rozhestuevnsky's Russian Baltic Fleet in the most complete naval victory of the twentieth century.

15. Von Spee's defeat of Admiral Christopher Cradock on 1 November 1914.

16. Admiral Sir Frederick Charles Doveton Sturdee's defeat of von Spee on 8 December 1914.

17. Extraneous means relevant to general rather than to naval strategy.

18. The French is *servitudes.*

naval strategy is never independent. Military constraints will be primary. The Blue army will doubtless call for our aid in undertaking operations around the enemy's flank and protecting our own against similar enemy undertakings. It may demand even more from us if the land war has reached a complete stalemate that can be broken only by means of a combined operation against another part of the enemy territory. Moreover, the army will certainly expect us from the very beginning to transport indispensable troops from territory G along routes M and N.

The navy must also expect political constraints on its dispositions, reflecting the need to conciliate neutrals or gain allies, while economic constraints will push us into a struggle over communications. To fight, we must survive economically by protecting our trade along routes L and P as well as M and N. The latter two routes also have great political value as internal communications. Economic constraints may also manifest themselves in our government's decision to wage economic warfare against the Reds by attacking their communications L' and M' and their coastal trade N'.

We must also pay attention to the attack and defense of coasts and territories. As mentioned above, the army is likely to request our participation in combined operations intended to achieve a purely military decision. Such operations can also be demanded by the government if it thinks that an enterprise against the enemy's vital zones, Z for example, could end the war at a single blow. Island E' and its base D' might prove so constraining to our operations, communications, and coastal activities that we would have to seize them. Conversely, the Reds will calculate in the same way and decide to take our island E, a salient dangerously implanted in their front. An attack against E is written on the map, and we must look to its defense. The Reds are less likely to strike directly at our coast but might well threaten territory G. All of these possibilities will lead us to allot a significant proportion of our forces to the direct protection of our communications and coasts, and we cannot simply devote everything to maximizing the strength of our fleet O.[19]

Constraints may also arise in the sphere of morale. The supreme command may order the execution of operations that, though of no apparent military value, promise major psychological gains. These may happen at a critical moment when the enemy nerve is at the point of breaking, at the beginning of the war if he is particularly sensitive to initial events, or if our own people are susceptible to such influences.

What makes these external demands true constraints for naval strategy is that they can arise from the very beginning of the conflict without waiting to be satisfied after we have gained mastery of the sea and control of essential surface communications. Exploitation of sea power will necessarily interfere with the attempts made to secure it. While we will expect that these demands not be so tyrannical as to impose pernicious lines of action or the violation of fundamental principles, we will have to compromise the ideal defined in our first approximation of doctrine.

In this chaos of competing factors pushing in every direction, one idea ought to serve as our directing beacon. Guiding our *decision* and our conduct of operations is the notion of the primacy of the fleet and particularly the surface fleet. This premise has survived every analysis—historical or material—to which we have subjected it and remains the foundation of our action. . . .

19. Here Castex relaxes chapter 4's strictures against diverting resources from the main objective, the enemy fleet.

Our *general manoeuvre idea*,[20] which inspires us in the vicissitudes of changing situations, will be to put out of action the Red fleet O'. The best means to this goal is obviously to destroy it, either by surprise attacks with our technical weapons or by battle on the high seas, if possible, a single decisive battle under favorable conditions. If destroying O' in battle is not feasible, we will instead attempt to immobilize, paralyze, and annihilate it by pushing our own forces as far forward as possible, by supporting ourselves properly, and by coordinating all of our mobile forces in order to confine fleet O' by blockade.

Spiritually and psychologically, the enterprise will require zeal, energy, the will to win, an offensive mentality, a constant search for the initiative, and tenacity. Fighting for a just cause, seeking only the preservation of possessions threatened by the enemy's inexorable expansion, we will struggle to the end with all of our energy and resources.[21]

If the conservative spirit excludes all aggressive policy, it is far from incompatible with the ferocious determination to take the offensive or with the resolution to perish rather than yield. Illustrious examples prove that the defense of interests imperiled by others can be as powerful a motive as is the spirit of conquest. Look at Holland in the Anglo-Dutch wars, the British during the First Empire, the Confederacy, and ourselves during the 1914 war.

Passing now to the question of *execution,* we must first learn the location of force O' and seek all possible information about its movements. As well as using extra-maritime

20. For definition, see page 101.
21. Castex's first reference to what many would have put first—the political objective of the war. His answer—achievement of command of the sea—to the question *"de quoi s'agit-t-il?"* does not admit to the possibility that a small-scale political objective might require a lesser naval effort.

sources like neutrals, the press, the secret service, etc., we will employ such military means as surface and submarine patrols and the surveillance of enemy bases. Our aviation can render us a great service in reconnaissance because of the relatively limited dimensions of the theater of operations and the placement of the bases from which we can dispatch them.

Aviation will also be employed from the very beginning to bomb fleet O' at sea or in port in order to reduce it to a condition of inferiority and to impede Red's mobilization of personnel and material. Defensively, our air force will protect us against reciprocal enemy actions, especially by raiding enemy airfields from bases on our coastline between A and X and on island E. Submarine attacks can also help tilt the surface balance to our advantage.

Though we will undertake an offensive against fleet O' as soon as possible, we cannot simply lower our heads and charge blindly forward. An encounter requires favorable conditions, and we can expect reality to impose a large gap between our hopes and actual events. Obstacles like distance, obstructed terrain, unfavorable weather, shallow water, and the enemy's unwillingness to fight can impede the search for battle. We may have to defer our effort because the necessary detachment of units or damage to vessels has rendered our forces temporarily inferior in number or because external constraints impose more immediate, if fundamentally less important, objectives.

Though one cannot always take the offensive when and where one wants, one ought to aim for it absolutely and to struggle constantly to overcome the accumulated hindrances and even, where external constraints are concerned, to use them in pursuit of our principal and permanent offensive designs against fleet O'.

How shall we conduct this offensive? Because the relatively confined theater allows us to track the movement of

O' or any of its components, it will be based on movement. It is to be feared that the enemy will be able to take advantage of the small size of the field of action and the speed of his ships to escape us, perhaps under cover of night, and that he will be able to continue for a long time the game of threatening our interests with repeated attacks followed by rapid disappearances. To attack such an enemy will probably require recourse to the second form of offensive, that of the "channeled direction." Taking advantage of the enemy's attacks against our coasts or undertaking something against his own, we will impose a more or less known direction of attack or riposte. To the same end, we can also use our most exposed communications, lines P, Q, and N, as bait and organize our traffic along them so as to *manoeuvre* and to avoid being *manoeuvred* against. The attack on communications M' and N' could bring a similarly profitable return in attracting fleet O' towards us. The choice of method will depend on the situation at the moment.

When good fortune offers us reasonable chances of battle, we must prepare so as to employ all of our arms. The submarines will cooperate with the surface vessels, perhaps not in exactly the same action but in related engagements forming part of the whole *manoeuvre* and situated on the enemy's probable routes. It will also be desirable to deploy the maximum number of airplanes both offensively and defensively. This goal will be difficult to achieve for land-based planes, at least in some sectors. The liaison of arms and the coordination of resources are fully possible only when one has the initiative by undertaking a preconceived *manoeuvre*.

Air superiority, in default of an unachievable air mastery, must be sought at any price. Large numbers of Red airplanes must be destroyed in battles forced upon them in conditions of our choice. Assistance from army aviation will be very useful in such battles, as in air actions in general, and we will return the favor when the situation demands.

If fleet O' refuses to do battle, we will put it out of action by means of a blockade by fleet O and its satellites, by redoubling our offensive surveillance, and by sowing obstructions and mines around the Red bases, but efforts to initiate combat must not be abandoned. Battle can be forced by offering unacceptable threats to enemy interests (his communications or his territory) or by baiting a trap with the promise of an easy success. In either case, the objective is to lead him to do battle in a place where he has no support. Promising more than mere blockade, the method serves the idea of *manoeuvre* better because it aims at the destruction of force O'. Other possible ways of achieving this include the difficult and rather old-fashioned land-based siege of the enemy base and the more modern and effective aerial attack by bomb or torpedo. In our time, maintaining an expectant posture in harbor may suffice to avoid decisive battle but not serious losses.

Operations involving communications can be conducted directly in conjunction with fleet operations. Although continual in defense of our own communications, these operations will probably be intermittent against those of the enemy. Since the front FFF is in no sense a perfect obstacle, our communications will always be exposed to attack by Red submarines and also, though less so as long as the balance of forces is not too much against us, to raids by surface elements. Air attacks are also to be feared. To defend our rear areas, we must assign a significant portion of our forces directly to protecting our lines of communication and escorting convoys.

But not all of our arteries are equally at risk. Relatively weak escort units will suffice on line L and perhaps on line

M, where conditions will not differ greatly from those of peace except for the constraints imposed by travel in convoy. Matters will be very different on line N and, especially, on lines P and Q, where surface and air attacks are to be expected. Traffic will be at grave risk, and the need for more escorts and for aerial protection argues for fewer and larger convoys. It may prove impossible to safeguard a convoy on routes P and Q except by fleet operations involving O.

The attack on Red communications, probably less frequent and more circumstantial than the defense of our own,[22] must be considered not only in terms of economic pressure, but also as an aid to the force O, for whose actions it is necessary to seek the most favorable conditions. Attacks against communications will be part of a general system of operations and often contribute to strategic *manoeuvre* by diverting O'. Avoiding mistaken reliance on commerce war alone, we will respect the intimate link that ought to exist between attacks on enemy communications and fleet operations.

Thanks to the resources offered by territory G, we will undoubtedly be able to attack line M' by surface and air units, but against lines L' and N' we will be restricted to using submarines. The large submarine[23] will be especially useful for attacking those parts of routes M' and L' that are on the high seas. We will, of course, conduct this submarine war according to the rules of law and with all possible regard for human life, but it represents too good an opportunity to be neglected. The submarine campaign will immobilize major enemy surface and air forces by forcing them to protect communications and to handle the tasks of patrol-

22. For the priority of defense over offense in the struggle over communications, see below, 357.
23. The interwar French navy experimented with a big-gun submarine.

ling, providing escorts, and minesweeping, and one must not fail to benefit from such diversion. Since the attack against communications provides the most economical use of all of our means against the enemy who provoked us, we will, while respecting every consideration of humanity, go as far down this road as foreign policy considerations permit.[24]

Though undoubtedly less frequent than those concerning communications, operations against coasts and territories will also be undertaken by both sides in conjunction with those of their respective fleets. They will also create a permanent problem for the defender and impose a considerable sacrifice of force so as to provide direct protection. Indirect cover by force O alone will prove illusory, especially in view of the threats posed by modern machines.

But the fleet, while occasionally bringing its weight to bear to protect the coast, cannot confine itself to this role without losing its indispensable freedom of action. The coast, at least the important positions, must be rendered in some measure self-sufficient through a solid coastal defense. Island E, in particular, will certainly be the target of major attacks and ought to be prepared to resist them to a certain degree by using its own resources.

As defenders, we must also concern ourselves with the placement of our bases with respect to enemy air attack. Our principle base A and secondary base D are badly situated from this point of view because of their proximity to island E'. Perhaps it will be necessary to forgo the use of A for resupply and rest, shifting these functions and that of mobilization to bases like B and even C, which we would look upon with disdain in time of peace. The enemy is in the same situation with B', which he will doubtless abandon for A'.

---

24. Chapter 17 argues that opportunity offered by the submarine overrides any concern for the laws of war, but Castex's uncharacteristi-

Attack on the enemy coast, whether by raids or deeper combined operations, can only be occasionally contemplated. The latter cannot be foreseen in advance in the case under examination. Raids cannot be rejected *a priori,* as a certain school once recommended. In spite of their generally unimpressive material effect, these, like bombardments and *coups de main,* could have a great impact on Red morale and lead him to redistribute his forces so as to further our projects and improve the conditions of the struggle between O and O'. When they thus contribute to our strategic *manoeuvre,* these operations are not to be despised. In the regions where the surface units cannot operate, one can advantageously employ the big-gun submarine.

Naturally, the air force will contribute by bombarding the land as far inland as its range allows. Its normally great zeal for such enterprises will have to be restrained and its effort directed instead against the enemy fleet, whose destruction is more important even than that of its supporting bases and arsenals. Other targets (cities, industrial centers, etc.) come only later unless some special necessity gives them unexpected priority and adds them to the constraints on strategy.

The principal contingencies to foresee are precisely those represented by these constraints, that is to say, the imposition in the course of the struggle between O and O' of objectives foreign to that struggle. Some, like the defense of our lines of communications, island E, and territory G, are permanent concerns because they remain at the enemy's initiative. There are also temporary constraints resulting from our own offensive undertakings. We have mentioned, for example, the flanking operations or combined operations demanded by the army, the transport of troops from terri-

cally defensive reference to the enemy's role in starting the war adumbrates his awareness of the need to justify submarine warfare.

tory G, attacks on the Red lines of communication L', M', and N', attack on island E', and the combined operations that the government orders against zone Z. Generally, when such eventualities present themselves before the struggle between O and O' is settled and when O must participate in such actions, O must take up positions suitable to handling the possible intervention of O'. In each case, we must remain aware that our actions are outside of the normal sequence of events and weigh the value of the compromise we are obliged to make. So long as force O' exists, it retains its primordial importance and everything ought to be organized with reference to it.

It is possible that these constraints, ordinarily so painful to bear, will permit us to satisfy our desire for battle and to achieve it even earlier than we had hoped. It is necessary not only to endure what one cannot avoid but even to exploit it as an element of strategic *manoeuvre*.

There are two possible final outcomes. If we manage to put O' out of action, either by inflicting grave losses in several battles or by means of blockade, we will have acquired mastery of the sea, that is to say the control of the essential surface communications. While we then have every interest in improving the effectiveness of our blockade against the remnants of the Red force and in achieving its total destruction by the means already mentioned, we ought also to exploit our sea mastery economically and militarily.

If the clash of arms goes against us, if the series of confrontations between O and O' turns out to our disadvantage and, reducing us to a serious inferiority of surface means, places us in the situation that we have just described for the enemy, then we must continue the struggle no less ardently with the resources remaining to us. We will employ our surviving forces to hinder the consolidation of Red's forces, always watching for opportunities to even up the balance by destroying isolated contingents. We will undertake minor counterattacks,[25] at first with submarines and aircraft in order to alter the surface balance to our advantage and later through raids into enemy-controlled territory. We will wage a constant harassment, especially of his communications, with every resource, both surface and, especially, submarine and air. Starting with a very solidly organized coastal defense, we will make it an absolute rule, above all, to avoid inaction and to make our defense as active as possible.

Fighting tenaciously to the end we will inspire ourselves, even if there is no hope of ultimate success, with the idea that the effort and energy so manifested not only affect the immediate conflict but may have future moral and political repercussions of the greatest importance. In the material realm, we will not lose sight of the fact that submarines and aircraft offer possibilities hitherto unknown and that we ought to make all possible use of them. Thanks to them, the difference that formerly existed between the offensive and the defensive has been attenuated and is limited to events on the surface of the sea. Even though the final decision will always be determined by the surface forces, one can at least take advantage of the material circumstances to retain certain external appearances and moral elements.

The scheme of action must be completed by considering the organization and equipment of the future theater of operations. We must treat the supporting elements: resupply, the collection of provisions at appropriate points, the transmissions network, coastal defense, the arrangement of the terrain (mines, obstruction), the organization and functioning of lines of communications, an intelligence plan, etc.—in a word, all of the usual components of a rationally ordered campaign plan.

25. "Minor counterattacks" appear in Corbett, *Principles*, 227ff.

Such is our "second approximation" of the doctrine of war. The specific details depend upon each individual case, but the theory sketches the general lines according to which operations ought to be conceived, prepared, and conducted. One cannot ask more of theory, which cannot offer original recipes, clever formulas, or secret systems but only principles and rules of action based on experience, on judgment, and on the actual material situation. Everything will then depend on what one is able to do with these truths. In this chapter we have limited ourselves to summarizing the entire mechanism, which we will disassemble later in order to examine its constituent parts.

PART II

STRATEGIC
MANOEUVRE

CHAPTER 6

GENERALITIES ABOUT STRATEGIC *MANOEUVRE*[1]

S TRATEGIC *MANOEUVRE* is a key element in the conduct of operations. It is a *method* used by strategy to improve the conditions of the struggle, to multiply the return on her efforts, and to obtain the greatest results, whether in the duel between the principal forces themselves or to the benefit of particularly important nonmaritime requirements.[2] It is therefore necessary to devote a special study to this method.

1. Raoul Castex, *Théories stratégiques*, 2nd ed., vol. 2 (Paris: Société d'Editions Géographiques, Maritimes et Coloniales, 1939): 1–26. The use of the word *manoeuvre* in interwar French military writing is a study in itself. Although it sometimes carries the modern connotation of movement, *manoeuvre* often means something closer to "plan of action" or "scheme," and the army's distinction between "*manoeuvre* by movement" and "*manoeuvre* by fire" denied that movement was a necessary element of *manoeuvre*. See Robert A. Doughty, "The French Armed Forces, 1918–40," in Allan R. Millett and Williamson Murray, *Military Effectiveness*, vol. 2: *The Interwar Period* (Boston, 1988): 55. Castex uses the word in both senses, sometimes so abstractly as to argue that ship designers *manoeuvre* with tonnage. To avoid any equation of Castex's *manoeuvre* with our own "maneuver," the word is left untranslated.

2. "The character of strategy is to utilize weak resources or at least to draw from these resources their maximum return," Daveluy, *Etude sur la stratégie navale*, 4 (author's note).

Military writers have characterized *manoeuvre* in various ways. Some describe it as achieving numerical advantage, some as bringing strength against weakness. Another version makes it an operation in strength against the decisive point, while still another view is that *manoeuvre* is organizing one's effort.

I suggest the following formula: *to manoeuvre is to move intelligently in order to create a favorable situation.* This definition subsumes the earlier ones while going beyond them; it is complete. It applies not only to strategy but by extension to politics, business, and every activity in which humans struggle to overcome obstacles and achieve a goal.

Thus presented, *manoeuvre* becomes the pinnacle of the art. It is the divine part of the profession, that which calls upon all of the treasures of spirit, intelligence, imagination, will, and knowledge.

Manoeuvre must now be explained and its constituent elements identified.

Strategic *manoeuvre* happens any way but naturally. One's first instinct when on the attack is not to *manoeuvre* but to attack the enemy wherever he has forces and interests, dividing one's forces proportionately to his. On the defensive, one is similarly tempted to protect everything that the enemy threatens, distributing one's resources, again, in response to the enemy's dispositions. Past wars demonstrate the generally unimpressive payoff of this dispersion.

For things to turn out differently requires a superiority of force everywhere at once, which implies an improbable degree of overall superiority. In the normal case where resources are comparable, a uniform distribution of effort cannot produce a decision. Instead, the result is reached after the brutal addition of individual encounters, themselves decided by chance, by the strength of the combatants, and by local conditions. Reverses sustained at one point will frequently cancel out successes elsewhere. In the case of general inferiority, the effect of such dispersal of resources will probably be defeat everywhere.

To obtain a decision, especially on the offensive, it is necessary to improve upon the homogeneous distribution of forces, to avoid their being spread out in an impotent cordon, whose symmetry and uniform density represent a lack of inspiration, creative faculties, and intelligence in the commander.

One observes, however, that it is extremely rare that all of the points in the enemy's dispositions are equally vital to him and that there usually is one of particular importance to him, either because it is the center of his power and resources or because its loss would put him in a seriously inferior position and compromise the outcome of the campaign. There, where a successful action would promptly place the enemy in a critical situation, one can upset the balance. One must concentrate one's effort against this point, which is the key to all of the others. This point, which commands our attention, is the *principal objective.*

Determining the *principal objective,* though vitally important to the outcome of the war, is not always easy. It involves many elements that must be carefully weighed. One can begin by asking whether to attack a position of strength or one of weakness. There are good arguments for attacking a strong, even the strongest, position. If it should yield, the entire system will probably collapse, while if one ignores the strong point in favor of operations elsewhere, nothing has been accomplished. Certainly the most redoubtable tack, the attack against strength, yields the highest return. One application of this point of view is the oft-expressed theory of putting out of action the enemy's *principal fleet.* The concept is valid, although proponents of a contrary view object to it, saying that generalship is to exert the greatest effort against the sector offering least resistance.

The discussion is truly Byzantine, especially when, as here, it occurs in the cloudy realm of principle. Fundamentally, the decision depends on the individual circumstances of the situation. There is no general rule. The principal object can be either a strong or a weak point, but it must be one whose fall will lead to a vital result. There is no other criterion than that of *decisive direction* for choosing between several options.

It may be, moreover, that the fleets will not be the only factors in the decision. One may wish, for various reasons usually foreign to naval operations per se, to be strongest in one particular *region* rather than in another and to make the maximum effort there. In such cases, the principal objective will be derived not from the idea of a clash of forces but from that of a *principal theater,* that is to say, a physical zone. The principal objective will thus be either the principal fleet or the fleet in the principal theater, which need not be the same.

Naval strategy is never autonomous but must obey concerns and constraints imposed by nonmaritime forces and interests. . . . The favorable situation that one attempts to create by *manoeuvre* must conform to one's strategic goal, which may, however, be not only naval, but also political, military (combined operations, transport of troops), aerial, economic (resupply, communications, etc.) or psychological (effect on friendly or enemy morale). The choice of the principal objective will naturally be influenced at every moment by such considerations, which tend to give importance to one region or another and thereby generate the geographical idea of the principal theater.

Alongside the principal objective, there will be *secondary objectives,* which will be either the less important enemy forces or those placed in *secondary theaters.* The secondary objectives or secondary theaters can be more or less numerous, although the principal objective or principal theater is necessarily unique at any given time. The label "secondary" reflects only initial intentions and may be belied by events one cannot control. Operations in secondary theaters may exceed expectations and bring a success having major repercussions upon the principal theater, where all remains in doubt, even though the plan of *manoeuvre* has foreseen exactly the opposite. These sometimes pleasant surprises underscore the interdependence of diverse theaters of which one should never lose sight.

Manoeuvre is quintessentially a creative activity. "To create a favorable situation" is the proposed definition. *Manoeuvre* attempts to alter or control the course of events, to dominate fate rather than yield to it, to conceive and bring forth action. But the creation can not take place entirely alone. The enemy is far from cooperative, and it is up to us to create the conditions that we desire. It is imperative that we immediately take the *initiative of operations.* One cannot conduct a *manoeuvre* if one yields either to the enemy's will or to the laws of chance.

To achieve success against the principal objective or in the principal theater requires resources. The group charged with this work must be concentrated. To this end, we will combine all arms and assemble the largest possible forces in every category. "Too strong has never failed" says an old sailor's maxim.[3] And this concentration must extend in the broadest sense, embracing not only military forces, the elements of combat, but also general resources intended to ful-

3. Superficially compelling, the maxim ignores logistical problems stemming from excess numbers.

fill the forces' every requirement (resupply, repair, communication, etc.). That supply provides the basis of action has been the experience of ages. It determines the organization of the theater of operations, which rests largely on the permanent or temporary bases that one finds in the region or can create there. Its worth depends on the position of these bases, hence on the geography.

The *assembly of forces* is obviously the most urgent operation, the preliminary requisite for *manoeuvre*. Without gathering our resources, we will be impotent to undertake anything. Moreover, the enemy may strongly oppose our mobilization from the beginning, so that we have to execute it at a distance. Assembly can be facilitated or severely hampered by geographical peculiarities.

However desirable, an infinite increase in the strength of our principal force is impossible. Since our strength is finite, we can increase the main force only by reducing resources allocated to secondary objects or situated in secondary theaters. We will economize on these in order to increase our shock force. The maximum here, the minimum there. To arrive at our ends, we will employ *economy of force*.[4]

Though the search for an appropriate definition of economy of force has given rise to much writing and discussion, we will not experience any difficulty because our point of view leads us to a perfectly clear understanding. For us, the economy of force seems quite simply to be the economy realized at the expense of the secondary objectives and to the profit of the principal object.

Economy of force is an aspect of *manoeuvre;* it implies, it presupposes, it demands *manoeuvre.* One would not at-

4. One will find later, in volume 4 of this work, a more detailed study of these important questions of economy of force, interior lines, liberty of action, etc. (author's note).

tempt and cannot hope to economize upon one's forces unless one has in mind a willingness to *manoeuvre,* while *manoeuvre* imperiously demands the economy of force, which is an indispensable element in its achievement.

The value of the economy diminishes proportionately to the forces assigned to secondary objectives and increases in proportion to those devoted to the principal object. In other words, one can characterize the economy of force by a coefficient that is the ratio between the means devoted to the principle objective and those devoted to the secondary objective—the larger the ratio, the better the economy obtained.

To increase this ratio, it is necessary to decrease the denominator and increase the numerator (the one implies the other, given a fixed amount of resources). To diminish the denominator is to reduce the quantity of forces assigned to secondary objectives or placed in secondary theaters. How far can one go on this path? Not as far, certainly, as one would like. The size of those forces depends on a number of factors. First of all on the enemy: on his strength, on the attitude that he will take towards the secondary theaters, on the forces that he himself will put there, on the interests that he has in these areas, etc. We must similarly calculate our interests in the secondary theaters, the risks that we run there, the sacrifices which we are willing to accept. In certain regions, one is willing to tolerate retreats, sometimes even defeats, as a necessary contribution to the hoped-for victory in the principal theater. At other points, it will, on the contrary, be necessary to resist at any price.

Many elements affect the economical division of forces. We have here the delicate problem of the distribution of forces[5] among the missions, a particularly thorny problem

---

5. Castex's word *dosage* is a technical military term.

that demands all of the commander's experience and judgment. The optimal economy, moreover, is not necessarily the same for all categories of force. It can differ according to whether one is dealing with capital ships, light vessels, submarines, aircraft, or other types and is a function of the particular properties of the different arms.

Finally, the principle of economy applies not only to forces but also to the very diverse means that accompany the forces and give them their efficacy. One pursues economy in matters of supply, equipping bases, material for resupply and repair, communications, etc. It applies to the armament and distribution of the fleet, to programs of new construction, and to determining the proportion of various types of ships that one would like to acquire. In all of these domains, one ought to direct resources towards primary concerns and away from secondary ones.

Of course, neither the principal object nor the principal theater necessarily remains unchanged throughout the entire course of a war. The importance of a force or a region can vary with the evolution of the general situation or according to the will of the one who *manoeuvres*. He can, after having eliminated an adversary, turn against another, then against a third, and so on. He can operate successively against several forces or in several regions. He will go thus from one to another, and, at each turn, he ought to modify, sometimes profoundly, the distribution of his forces. The economy adopted at the beginning will be changed whenever the principal objective or theater shifts.

If these modifications take place between two objectives or two theaters only, with periodic reversals, a constant oscillation results, a sort of balancing, marked by an alternation of the economy of force between two solutions that are, if not entirely symmetrical, at least inverse. Each of the two objects or theaters will in turn be principal or secondary according to the progress of events, the commander's will, or both.[6]

One recognizes here the well-known *manoeuvre* on *interior lines* and sees how it relates to the notion of economy of force. It is truly the supreme art. But its achievement is far from always being easy, because of the new conditions imposed upon land war by modern technology and, more so, because of the properties specific to naval war. In addition, it is very necessary to say that one will often find oneself dealing with regions too important for many reasons to be demoted, even momentarily, to the rank of secondary theaters and that circumstances can give such a force or zone an absolutely permanent value. If the principal object remains static, all *manoeuvre* by interior lines becomes, if not impossible, at least very difficult.[7]

When one reaches this point in the organization of the *manoeuvre,* that is, when one has chosen a principal object, disposed of one's resources appropriately, consolidated a force, divided the missions, and all the rest, one has instigated a radical transformation of the initial situation. In place of a gelatinous whole, boneless and without form, in place of an initially homogeneous, symmetrical, and uninspired deployment appears an asymmetrical and unbalanced arrangement oriented in a direction chosen by the directing intelligence. . . . It is this asymmetry that is the essential trait of *manoeuvre.*

Now the *manoeuvre* begins to reveal itself. The creation takes form; the work of art is sketched. The product of the intelligence and the imagination that guides the technique in complete awareness of both its possibilities and its limits is

6. The passage exemplifies Castex's tendency to systematize.
7. That "interior lines" offer a strategic advantage is one of Jomini's central principles.

very indeed a work of art. Certain *manoeuvres,* those of a Suffren, a de Ruyter,[8] a Nelson, a Napoleon, a Schlieffen,[9] or a Foch, arouse the same emotions as do proper works of art—a Rembrandt painting, Notre Dame, or the Arc de Triomphe. One feels the same sentiments, the same artistic reaction. Viewed in this light, one can say that there is indeed—I believe this and I have written it elsewhere—in the military realm a *maneuverers'* international that is a branch of the artists' international.[10]

Manoeuvre is an essentially intellectual factor that transforms a physical situation. . . .

Movement is the primary element of *manoeuvre.* In our definition, *manoeuvre* is to *"move intelligently."* First it is movement to achieve the desired dispositions, then it is movement of the principal and secondary forces to exploit the situation thus created and to execute the *manoeuvre.* The *manoeuvre* can originate simply in a sudden movement of troops from one region or theater of operations to another. Favorable geographical conditions, convenient communications between the operating areas of the various forces, for example, can greatly ease these movements, while contrary geographical conditions can prevent them altogether.

Movement above all demands space. Because the advent of new machines has compressed both linear dimensions and time, *manoeuvre* now encounters new obstacles. The war of movement, where the strategic *manoeuvre* flowers

8. Michael Adriaanszoon de Ruyter (1607–1676) was Holland's premier naval commander in the Second and Third Anglo-Dutch Wars.

9. Chief of the German General Staff (1891–1905) Alfred von Schlieffen (1833–1913) conceived the plan for a two-front war against France and Russia that hamstrung German policy in 1914.

10. See chapter 1 for another version of this infelicitous image.

fully, is only fully possible in areas where there are the necessary distances. Elsewhere, *manoeuvre* is notably more limited, though not absolutely impossible.

Movement ought to be managed with a care not to waste time, another precious factor, and, on the contrary, to exploit it to the full. One must act with *speed*, which is a function not only of the celerity that the forces are able to sustain in the course of a prolonged strategic action but also a function of the *activity* that one employs in the operations and of the care that one exercises to avoid unjustified and useless halts. Activity is particularly necessary in the exploitation of the favorable situation, created at great effort, from which it is important immediately to draw the possible benefit—this concern is all the more commanding in our day than formerly because the duration of the favorable situation is much briefer now.

The forces placed in front of secondary objectives or in secondary theaters play a very important role that varies according to the enemy dispositions facing them. For example, the enemy forces in a secondary theater can either intervene to reinforce the principal theater against our principal force so as to disrupt and to compromise the favorable situation created by our *manoeuvre*, or they can attack our interests in the secondary theater. It is necessary to oppose both of these types of enemy undertakings so as to assure the *security* of the *manoeuvre*.[11] Security, one will see, can be divided into two components. To oppose enemy initiatives of the first type involves the *security of the principal body;* to check those of the second type is to achieve the *security of the plan* itself. And this double security is indispensable; without it our combination will fail.

Security is consequently the soul of *manoeuvre*. Only

11. The French is *sûreté*.

when security is obtained can one pretend to possess *freedom of action*. This is a fundamental principle. Security is one of the essential bases, one of the necessary conditions of freedom of action.

Because the principal mission of the secondary forces is to assure security, the coefficient of economy of force, defined earlier as the ratio between the forces assigned to the principal objective and to the secondary objectives, has sometimes been presented as being the ratio between force and security.

To prevent enemy reinforcement from the secondary theaters, our secondary forces struggle to immobilize the opposing forces for the duration of the action. This mission demands a clearly aggressive posture marked by secondary attacks. Constant threats against the enemy's interests, especially his coasts and communications, will force him to defend them and prevent him from going to the secondary theater to mix in what does not concern him, and draw him back if he has gone. In short, our secondary forces provide *diversions* whose value is measured by the number of the enemy that they draw to them.

To prevent the enemy from upsetting our overall plan by gaining victories in the secondary theaters, our secondary forces must operate defensively, especially in protecting coasts and communications. They defend in naval style: that is to say, without relying, as on land, on the exploitation of terrain features as obstacles. At sea, terrain is tactically nonexistent. Strategically, however, our secondary forces can profit from possibilities offered by the bases or positions upon which they support themselves. Thus, their defense will be essentially defensive-offensive, acting, seeking always to attain and conserve the initiative of operations through "minor counter-attacks."

In both cases, therefore, our secondary forces will usually be in an offensive posture, though of the special type appropriate to their means. Their posture will depend on the many factors alluded to in mentioning the problem of "dosage." Their role will be very difficult because the very economies achieved for the purpose of *manoeuvre* condemn them to a serious inferiority in resources. Their task is so difficult and, at the same time, so important that the commander himself sometimes retains direct control of the task in spite of its painful and unrewarding character. De Ruyter, Suffren, and Nelson acted thus more than once in the tactical realm.

The importance of the security function of the secondary forces means that *there is a limit to the economy of forces.* The title "secondary" cannot be interpreted too narrowly or in too disparaging a sense. The numbers dedicated to secondary tasks cannot fall below a certain level, particularly because of the need to defend coasts and communications. Intolerable gaps in indirect coverage will force a return to direct protection and reduce one's freedom of action. If one's economy of forces exceeds this prudent limit, security disappears—freedom of action also—everything fails, and, a curious detail, the operations of the main body will prove to have been compromised by having been too much favored in the allocation of forces. Thus, reduction of the secondary forces to the minimum *possible* must nonetheless ensure them the means necessary to accomplish their mission. The distribution of forces requires artistry, surety of touch, and discernment, not simplistic brutality; herein the talent of the great commanders manifests itself. In all of the examples that they have left us, one is struck by the prudence with which they have resolved the problem, restraining themselves from the exaggeration to which their passionate desire for *manoeuvre* could have hurled them.

Security is only one of a multitude of necessary conditions for *freedom of action*. To have freedom of action, the principal force must not be hampered by demands foreign to its own actions and to the operation in progress—for example, by obligations relating to communications, coasts, geographical position, or useless bases, all duties that ought to be left to other forces. Ships must be available and have adequate range of action, endurance, and quality of material and personnel, training, and morale. All these modest qualities have more importance for freedom of action than do other flashier ones. There are *manoeuvres* that one cannot attempt except with certain tools and that will fail if these elementary factors are lacking.

Freedom of action also demands that forces be provided at the proper moment with indispensable supplies of every sort, from fuel and munitions to provisions. Even the health situation demands attention. Many belligerents have been brought to a standstill by such mundane matters. Since *manoeuvre* does not live in the blue of abstraction, these technical and material factors have a singular importance.

Freedom of action requires relieving our surface units from excessive fear of submarines and aircraft, which must be countered by forces of the same nature, by organizing passive defense, by reducing the tonnage of surface ships, and by other measures. Movement demands a relatively clear field, not too much encumbered by mines and diverse obstructions. It is necessary to have one's forces united, as we have said before, in a flexible disposition permitting easy response to the unforeseen. . . .

By virtue of the difficulties that it imposes on the enemy, taking the initiative in operations automatically ensures a certain degree of security. Finally, though one lacks the necessary forces to immobilize the enemy, one must at least be able to predict when they will move. Thus, security demands *intelligence.*

Surprise confers considerable advantages; it is *manoeuvre*'s trump card. Surprise demands conserving the *secrecy* of one's own plans and dispositions. Among the various procedures and methods that contribute to the achievement of secrecy is the shapeless character of the initial disposition of forces, which ought to reveal nothing of the chosen plan and keep the enemy in a state of uncertainty and ignorance. Diversions are indicated, as are false news reports, especially when they are accompanied by false movements that appear to confirm them. In the realm of ruse, as old as the world, the possibilities increase with the geographical dispersal of the enemy's interests. Speed and movement are also excellent elements of surprise. Rapid and unexpected concentrations, the shifting of unexpected forces, can achieve, at least for a certain period of time, the surprise *manoeuvre* that can produce a great event.

Finally, it is particularly desirable to benefit from the *liaison of arms* by making all forces participate in the decisive operations undertaken by the principal body. For submarines and aircraft, these operations impose conditions of time and place that are not always convenient. Geography intervenes significantly here.

One may ask whether it is possible to predict the value of a *manoeuvre* or even to compare two antagonistic *manoeuvres* and to rate them in advance according to their chances of success.[12] Though *a priori* comparison is very delicate, it seems, however, that one can usefully employ for this purpose two elements of analysis.

The first is the *value* of *the principal objective* targeted by each of the two *manoeuvres*. The second is the probable *time* that each requires to achieve its objective. The absolute value of the two lengths of time is of very secondary importance and, also, impossible to calculate in advance. What matters is their difference or the relative length. It is a mat-

12. This section and the remainder of the chapter are new in the second edition.

ter of judgment, of predicting which of the two *manoeuvres* will attain its objective quickest, *before* that of the enemy.

When the two elements above favor one of the two *manoeuvres,* there are strong probabilities that it "crowns" the other, that it has what has sometimes been called "superiority of orientation." One example is the German *manoeuvre* in the land campaign of August 1914 as compared to that of the French.[13] Another is any naval *manoeuvre* aimed against enemy forces able to escape easily and against inaccessible enemy coasts, while the same enemy simultaneously has the capability to threaten essential maritime communications— which is obviously the case of France and Germany today. If, after considering everything that it is possible to foresee, circumstances give the advantage in *manoeuvre* to the enemy, it may be that we are compelled to renounce our own *manoeuvre* and that we have no better move than simply to assume a parade rest, for the time being at least, and await better conditions for another *manoeuvre.* This course is perhaps less elegant, less brilliant, less ingenious, but it is infinitely safer.

When the two *manoeuvres,* friendly and enemy, are aimed in different directions, each commander runs up against the security provided by the other and in effect asks his own security to give him the necessary time to achieve a decision in the theater that he deems to be principal. The "time" factor, the second of the two elements considered, reduces itself in this case to a balance between the two securities. Whichever of the two belligerents has better and more durable security has a stronger possibility of reaching his ends before his enemy. If each player attempts to attack with his head while holding his tail out of reach, the winner will be the one who manages to bite the other's tail before his own is bitten. The judgments of the two above elements, value of

13. Schlieffen's plan versus the French Plan XVII.

the objective and time, also help us to rank various projects of *manoeuvre,* from which we have to choose and thus to guide our decision.

The logical result of *manoeuvre* can only be to affirm superiority at the chosen point. When the *manoeuvre* is oriented from the outset against the enemy fleet, the goal is nothing other than battle, which is the summit of the edifice. When the *manoeuvre* is designed to satisfy a mandatory requirement foreign to naval strategy, it is still battle that one must, if not immediately, seek out, at least anticipate, and it is with battle in mind that one must arrange the compromise to which one yields under the pressures of contradictory needs. In sum, there is no *manoeuvre* without battle at the end, immediate or deferred. Every *manoeuvre* that fails to respect this obligation is empty and without value. War is not an excuse to perform what is nothing but empty show. It demands the act of force. These observations may appear odd and unnecessary, but past experience demonstrates that they are neither. Many past *manoeuvres,* however well-conceived and executed in other respects, turned out to be mere caravans on a grand scale, utterly devoid of impact.

So far, we have envisioned a *manoeuvre* of offensive character. But all of the considerations addressed on this subject apply also when inferiority of means condemns one to the defensive. The defender relies even more heavily than the attacker on *manoeuvre* as the only antidote to the disadvantages he suffers and as the best possible use of his limited forces.[14] Lest diffusion of effort result in a serious check,

14. Though he mentions that the sea's lack of terrain features eliminates the tactical advantages that commonly accrue to the defender on land, Castex never explains his consistent assumption that the defender will always be at a strategic disadvantage nor does he consider that policy might demand defensive strategy.

the defensive situation also demands the choice of a decisive direction and of a principal objective or a principal theater and that one cultivate them at the expense of secondary objectives, achieve the corresponding economy of force, establish a system of forces, ensure security, etc. It is necessary to organize active diversions against enemy interests in secondary theaters by means of "minor counterattacks" in order to clear forces from the principal theater and to create a situation there less disadvantageous than at the beginning and favoring the desired defensive success.

Similarly, the principles established for strategic *manoeuvre* are easily transposed to other realms. First, they apply to tactics. Without dwelling at length on this subject, which does not really fall within the framework of this study, it is easy to see by consulting history that the splendid naval victories, or splendid battles that should have been victories, have been characterized by *manoeuvre* and that this *manoeuvre* was usually conceived, prepared, and organized in advance. One always discerns in the commander's mind the necessary ingredients of *manoeuvre:* a principal objective chosen in preference to the secondary objectives, the establishment of a force charged with the destruction of the principal objective, an economical distribution of the forces to secondary objectives, security, etc. This entire classic ensemble shows up clearly in documents from the past, whether they be the celebrated instructions of Suffren to Tromelin or Nelson's memoranda before Trafalgar.[15] The question is simply a bit more complicated in our day, given the new

15. The memorandum of 9 October 1805 informed his captains of the plan to divide the fleet and break the enemy's line in two places. Acknowledging the possibility of confusion during the battle, it concludes with the famous injunction "in case signals can neither be seen or perfectly understood no captain can do very wrong if he places his ship alongside that of an enemy," quoted in Corbett, *The Campaign of Trafalgar* (London, 1910): 448.

weapons, torpedo boats and aircraft, which are likely to figure on both sides and in both the principal field of operation and in the operations of security. Historical examples, however, remain valid. Independent of its physical means, the idea of *manoeuvre* persists, reincarnated under successive and changing material conditions by a kind of metempsychosis.[16]

Some of the governing principles of *manoeuvre* operate in the more limited field of matériel and technology, in the establishment of the characteristics of the combat ship itself. Give a set displacement, one also *manoeuvres*—this time with tonnage. One obviously seeks the greatest offensive power, armament, and speed, which, the first above all, constitute the principal objective. Other things, protection especially, generally play the role of secondary objectives.

One always tries to emphasize the primary at the expense of the secondary, and one practices economy of force in limiting the weight of ships. But one cannot go too far on this road. It is necessary to provide every ship with appropriate protection, even and especially the offensive vessels because they cannot deliver blows unless they can first absorb them. Protection represents security, always the foundation of freedom of action, which is itself understood in this case as the possibility of practicing the offensive. Protection cannot fall below a certain level, but the argument concerning range of action is equally powerful. In every aspect of shipbuilding, economy of force has its limit, and secondary elements cannot be entirely forgone.[17]

One can also apply the general rules of strategic *manoeu-*

16. In language evocative of Buddhism, Castex replaces his usual pseudo-scientific formulation of the historical method with a peculiarly spiritual one.

17. A battleship design submitted by Castex while a student at the *Ecole de Guerre Navale* demonstrates the *reductio ad absurdum* of the principle of economy of force, Coutau-Bégarie, *Castex*, 64–65.

vre to air *manoeuvre,* which also enjoys capabilities foreign to *manoeuvre* on land or sea. Air power always has the necessary space because it finds it in the third dimension. It can easily use the freedom imparted by speed to operate on interior lines.

Strategic *manoeuvre* includes some particular cases deserving of attention. For example, we have supposed above that at the outbreak of hostilities the two parties will disperse their forces in order to cover their various and scattered interests and to attack those of the enemy. The imagined *manoeuvre* consists consequently of a struggle to create from this dispersed disposition a situation superior to the enemy's at the point (the principal objective) where one seeks the decision. It is the division of forces that makes *manoeuvre* possible.

Matters can be entirely different when the conditions of the war impose upon the belligerents a preliminary concentration and one finds two blocks opposing one another in a single region. Such was, for example, the situation in which the Germans and the English found themselves in the North Sea during the 1914–1918 war. In this case, the determination of the principal objective and the principal theater is much simplified, since only one objective and one theater qualify. But if the formulation of the problem is elementary, its solution is singularly formidable. How can one obtain the advantage over the enemy forces at which every *manoeuvre* aims, especially if our force is inferior to the enemy's? How does one practice strategic art under such adverse circumstances? There is no solution other than to recreate dispersion, working to substitute it for the initial concentration. . . . By means of diversions one makes the enemy detach from his principal body forces larger than those that one has oneself devoted to these operations so as to improve one's relative position in the struggle between the two main forces and to attack with chance of success.[18] One will also have to focus the decisive effort not against the main force itself but against contingents that one manages to detach from it. In this way one will put out of action either the whole or a part of the enemy's principal force, depending on the circumstances. This was how the Germans attempted to operate, admittedly without great success, and it appears to be the only *manoeuvre* solution to this difficult case.

These observations demonstrate the importance to *manoeuvre* of premeditated and intentional dispersion. To *manoeuvre* it is necessary to know how to disperse, but to disperse less than the enemy. In other words, one must create and maintain an enemy dispersion greater than one's own. Dispersion ought to be exploited for maximum return and so as to avoid excessive risk.

It is a dispersion of this type, based on the intention of *manoeuvre,* that one finds in the second plan of the Count de Broglie, in Napoleon's naval plan of 1805, or even in von Spee's[19] decision to detach the *Emden* rather than join that vessel to his van. On the contrary, dispersions like those of the eighteenth century, like those of the Russians in 1904, like those of the Allies in the Pacific in 1914, entirely lack this character and were highly culpable.

Another approach is to employ space and distance to achieve a sufficient security without the dispatch of a secondary force. Moving rapidly and consolidating suddenly in the chosen principal theater, one takes advantage of the delay before the enemy has recovered from his surprise and

18. One can also, to the same end, attempt to weaken the enemy's principal force by the action of submarines or aircraft (author's note).

19. Admiral Maximilian von Spee (1861–1914) commanded the German Cruiser Squadron in the Far East in 1914.

succeeded in effecting a parallel displacement of forces. If distance assists, one can obtain a favorable situation in this theater for a sufficiently long time, delaying the moment when the adversary arrives to upset matters or turn them to his advantage. Towards the same end, as a sole means or as an accompaniment to the preceding system, one can spread false information, misleading noises that instill in the enemy imaginary fears and lead him to dispatch large forces on wild-goose chases that divert him from the action at the vital moment.

Many *manoeuvres*, willingly or not, have been built upon this single base. Examples are the movements of d'Estaing towards the United States and towards the West Indies in 1778, and Bruix's progress to the Mediterranean in 1799, while thanks to the false information disseminated by the Directory, Bridport[20] tarried for a month uselessly on the coast of Ireland. Another example is Napoleon's plan in 1805. But these are events from the distant past. The methods used then are much more difficult to employ in our own time because of the potential for rapid movement on both sides and the intensive development of communications that make possible the very rapid transmission of intelligence and information. The adversary will quickly tear the veil and will not be long taken in by deception. In making use of the system for the operation envisaged, one must be content with a favorable situation that can only be transitory. . . .

Here are some other specific considerations. It can happen that the principal objective, the enemy fleet that is the target of the *manoeuvre* escapes the effort directed against it. The

---

20. Admiral Alexander Hood (1726–1814), victor at the battle of Groix, was created Viscount Bridport in 1801.

fleet can conceal itself, or remain dispersed, or take refuge in its bases, etc., so that the *manoeuvre* falls on empty space.[21] It fails for the moment if its purpose was to put out of action the principal enemy force or the force situated in the principal theater. On the other hand, it can be considered a success if it only intended to satisfy a non-naval requirement (protection of a convoy, combined operation, transport of an army, etc., . . .), for the relevant waterway thus becomes empty of enemy surface ships. One cannot rest, however, since nothing has been achieved towards the essential object of the war, the destruction of the enemy fleet.

In this situation, one can attempt to revive the *manoeuvre* by pressure on the enemy's interests, coasts, or communications to compel him to sortie to their defense. For this method to bring a return, the interests in question must be of great importance to the adversary, who will otherwise remain unmoved by the action.

Thus, for example, de Ruyter was forced by the threat of an Anglo-French landing in Holland to abandon his bases and to give battle at Texel,[22] the fear of an action by Howe[23] against the American convoy obliged Jean Bon Saint-André and Villaret-Joyeuse[24] to sortie from Brest and to engage in the battle of Prairial,[25] the attack at Lissa by

---

21. An example from land warfare would be the German withdrawal to the Hindenburg Line in February 1917, which caused the Nivelle Offensive to waste its momentum on vacant trenches.

22. Second battle of Texel, 11 August 1673.

23. Admiral of the Fleet Richard, Earl Howe (1726–1799).

24. Louis-Thomas, Comte de Villaret de Joyeuse (1748–1812) commanded the Brest fleet from 1793 to 1796 under the more republican name Villaret-Joyeuse.

25. "The Glorious First of June."

Persano led Tegethoff to appear from Pola,[26] and Mr. Churchill and Admiral Fisher, in 1914, conceived of assaulting the island of Borkum so as to force the German fleet to come out and fight.

To destroy or at least gravely injure an enemy fleet that has taken refuge in a port, there are obviously other means including blockade and the siege and capture of the base from the land (Santiago and Port Arthur) and, in our day, aerial attack. But we will limit ourselves here to *manoeuvre* in the strict sense.

In other cases, it is possible that the enemy force, initially barricaded in its own port, will escape from its blockader and, by an initiative symmetrical with the preceding, undertake operations against the interests, coasts, or communications of its antagonist. Moving to the vicinity of these interests in order to defend them, the erstwhile blockader will have the greatest chance of attacking—and wholly or partially destroying—the enemy forces that had escaped it. The fleet thereby achieves two goals at one time—the principal one of dealing with the enemy fleet and the secondary one of protecting its own assets.

The English acted no differently with regard to our privateers, operating independently or in divisions during the War of the Spanish Succession, the Seven Years War, and those of the Revolution and the Empire. In this way they destroyed de Brueys's squadron at Aboukir, Leissègues's division at Santo Domingo, Bompard's division on the coast

26. After studiously avoiding contact with Admiral Baron Wilhelm von Tegethoff's Austrian fleet, Admiral Carlo Pellione di Persano finally shelled Lissa in July 1866 in obedience to instructions from the Italian government. Tegethoff accepted the challenge and sank two Italian ironclads while losing none of his own, Lawrence Sondhaus, *The Hapsburg Empire and the Sea: Austrian Naval Policy 1797–1866* (West Lafayette, IN, 1989): 253–56.

of Ireland,[27] and many other ships or groups of ships involved in similar enterprises. The Federals similarly put an end to the Confederate raiders who had passed through the net of the blockade that enveloped their coasts. The English, again, thus destroyed the German cruisers in 1914, even managing to eliminate their largest group at a single blow in the Battle of the Falklands. If the German High Seas Fleet had escaped, all together or in pieces, to support and strengthen attempts like those of the *Moewe* or the *Wolf,* the principal English force would have matched the move in the necessary numbers, and one would have seen several repetitions of the Falklands battle. If Admiral Scheer[28] had, with the same High Seas Fleet, renewed his attempts against the Norwegian convoys, the Grand Fleet would very probably have given battle at the northern end of the Orkney Islands, and one would perhaps have seen a second Battle of Jutland fought over lines of communication. In the next war, if the German navy operates with major forces against our Atlantic communications, it is undoubtedly there that the major clash will take place and not, as one could believe, in the North Sea, considered from the beginning to be the principal theater.

In such circumstances, whether created by one's own *manoeuvre* or in consequence of an enemy counter-initiative, there is a kind of shifting, at least for the moment, of the objectives and of the theaters. The principal objective superimposes itself temporarily on a secondary objective. The principal theater comes to be confounded briefly with a secondary theater.

27. Jean-Baptiste-François Bompard (born 1757) was captured attempting to invade Ireland in 1796.

28. Admiral Reinhard Scheer (1863–1928) commanded the High Seas Fleet from January 1916 until his elevation to Chief of the Naval Staff in 1918.

Such are some of the theoretical considerations that one can offer on the subject of strategic *manoeuvre*. But all this abstraction is actually disagreeable and obscure. We can express ourselves more clearly and better by examining some real, concrete examples.[29]

29. The ensuing chapters discuss such historical cases as Tourville's operations in 1693, Bruix's voyage of 1799, and Admiral Von Spee's operations in the Pacific in 1914.

CHAPTER 7

GERMAN OPERATIONS IN THE NORTH SEA (1914–1916)[1]

THE THEATER OF OPERATIONS

GEOGRAPHICAL AND technical conditions in the North Sea from 1914 to 1916 closely parallel those likely to be encountered in most of the regions where future maritime conflicts will be fought.[2] The North Sea is an insignificant basin, barely 480 nautical miles from north to south and 360 nautical miles from east to west at its widest point, the latitude of Rosyth. The space therefore offers meager possibilities for movement and, in consequence, *manoeuvre*. Since belligerent fleets at sea at the same time will never be very far from one another, especially given the speed of modern ships, favorable opportunities will be more ephemeral unless the enemy is fixed in place.

1. Raoul Castex, *Théories stratégiques,* 2nd ed., vol. 2 (Paris: Société d'Editions Géographiques, Maritimes et Coloniales, 1939): 206–41. (Author's note: For this period one can fruitfully consult the excellent analytical works by professors and students at the *Ecole de Guerre Navale* and the *Centre des Hautes Etudes Navale.* I will especially cite those of Captains Richard, Laborde, and Gensoul, Frigate Captains Platon and Landriau, Corvette Captain Aubin, and Lieutenants Coignet, Michaud, Tracou, Mesnager, and Bard. These works were very useful to me as a historical base for my synthesis, and I here express my profound gratitude to the authors.)

2. Unlike the Pacific Ocean, the subject of his previous chapter.

127

The small size of the basin will facilitate the intervention of forces with a limited range of action, aircraft for example. Submarines, which require reasonable odds of encountering the enemy, will bring much increased returns. Both will give operations an entirely new shape.

Geography confers to Britain the indisputable advantage in blockading Germany, but this geographical superiority will bring little benefit unless supported by a superior British Fleet. Geography only truly contributes to the decision when it serves the action of the fleet. Otherwise, as in the past, it is relevant mostly to maritime communications and of little importance for maneuvering fleets.

The British fleet will have several bases after the necessary arrangements have been completed: Scapa Flow (Orkney Islands), Cromarty (Scotland), Rosyth (near Leith), the Humber Estuary, Harwich, and Sheerness (Thames). In fact, the problems of defending the anchorages and of supplying the fleets at these bases are only gradually being resolved. Moreover, some of the bases (Harwich) are accessible only to small vessels and, of the others, only Scapa Flow can hold the entire British fleet. Scapa Flow, which has great virtues, is unhappily too far from the important operational area of the southern part of the North Sea. However imperfect, this situation nevertheless offers remarkable possibilities for *manoeuver* because the British forces there have several possible directions of attack and retreat.[3]

The German fleet is less happily placed. With the Danish Straits closed, it must rely only on the limited system of bases at the estuaries of the Elbe, the Jade, and the Ems,

---

3. For the argument that the imperfections of British bases in 1914 were more striking than their geographical advantages, see Arthur J. Marder, *From the Dreadnought to Scapa Flow*, vol. 1 (Oxford, 1961), 421–22.

which are difficult to navigate at certain tides. From these bases, the High Seas Fleet can *maneuver* only in a single direction. As Admiral Scheer complained, "every sortie of ours against the English coast exposes us to attacks on the flank while the British approach our coast worrying about no threat but that in front of them."[4]

The North Sea presents an expanse of uninterrupted water almost devoid of islands. Numerous banks, through which one cannot navigate without buoys, impede navigation in its southern part. The coasts of this region, particularly those of the Helgoland Bight, are difficult to access.

The shallow depth of the North Sea is useful for submarines, which are able in many places to rest on the bottom, but more important still in permitting the intensive use of mines. Spread in large numbers by both sides, fields of mines will soon extend from Tershelling to Horn's Reef. A protective shield, the mines will also serve the Germans offensively as cover for forces steaming from the three major channels that they keep open at all times, those of Horn's Reef, the northwest, and the coast of Frisia.

The minefields will quickly reach the high seas as the two belligerents sow them liberally throughout the theater of operations. The British will establish two huge fields, at the eastern exit of the Pas de Calais and at the mouth of the Thames, while the Germans will sow theirs off the Thames, the Humber, the Tyne, the Forth, Cromarty, etc. At sea, the Germans will mine Dogger Bank as well as the center of the North Sea up to the 56th parallel. Every minefield will naturally be as constraining for friends as for enemies. Thus,

---

4. Marder is less critical of the German bases, whose defenses he describes as "simply terrific." Admittedly difficult of egress, they were correspondingly difficult for the British fleet to approach, Marder, vol. 1, 426–27.

mines and submarines will transform the southern part of the North Sea into a vast trap into which the British fleet will be loath to venture.

In sum, submarines and mines will seriously restrict the freedom of action of both adversaries and consequently hinder their *manoeuvres*. The new restriction on freedom of movement imposed by modern conditions offsets our liberation from hindrances formerly caused by calms or contrary winds. What is gained on the one hand is lost on the other. It should be noted that German *manoeuvre* is also restricted by the slight range of action, only forty-eight hours, of their torpedo boats.

At the higher latitudes of the North Sea, the season greatly influences operations, both because of weather conditions and because of the very disparate lengths of days and nights depending on the time of year. That the days are extremely long in summer and extremely short in winter will confer advantages on one side or another according to the season and the nature of the enterprise. Ice, of which the North Sea is free, is not a factor.

Visibility is generally poor in the North Sea. Statistics show that on three hundred days of the year the range of visibility does not exceed eight or ten nautical miles, the maximum range of heavy artillery. Fog is frequent, especially in the summer and early autumn, and horizons are frequently veiled by rain or snow. These meteorological factors make strategic and tactical surprise common while rendering precautionary scouting and reconnaissance completely ineffective. *Manoeuvre* must therefore always expect to meet sudden and unforeseen situations.[5]

Even in 1914, radio easily covered the whole of the North Sea, which is well endowed with coastal stations. This new

5. Written in a world without radar.

method of communications intervened at all times and in every place to facilitate the commander's task in a way not true of the Pacific Ocean at the same time, while new methods of radio interception, decryption, and radio direction finding played their part in intelligence gathering and contributed, in consequence, to security and to liberty of action.

Far from ignorant of the importance of geographical and technical conditions, the two adversaries had very conscientiously studied the future battlefield. An article in the German *Marine Rundschau* of 1911 examined the peculiarities of the North Sea and, curiously enough, mentioned Rosyth's value as a central point and that of Scapa Flow for blocking the northern egresses from the North Sea. On the English side, Admiral Fisher, already First Sea Lord, claimed to have made the same discoveries "while playing with a compass," as he put it, when studying the theater of operations of a possible Anglo-German conflict.[6] Such observations led the British to begin the work at Rosyth in 1903 and to decide to adopt Scapa Flow and Cromarty as fleet bases. Their 1910 and 1911 maneuvers illuminated the matter and led to their war orders of 1912, which foresaw a *distant blockade* of the German fleet while maintaining the British fleet in those harbors. The first fleet or *Grand Fleet* was to retain its main force at Scapa Flow; the second or *Channel Fleet* was to remain in the Pas de Calais and on the southern coasts of Britain. The third fleet would provide a reserve and local defense. Patrol flotillas were charged with coastal surveillance. At irregular intervals the Grand Fleet was to ensure the blockade and to make itself felt by means of limited sorties as far south as 57 degrees. Its light forces could sail as far south as Helgoland (54 degrees). Below this paral-

6. Marder calls Fisher's claim "fanciful," vol. 1, 424–25.

lel, surveillance was the responsibility of the Harwich force.[7]

Such was the disposition against which the Germans were going to pit themselves, and we will study the vicissitudes of their wartime *manoeuvre* plan solely from their point of view.

THE INITIAL SITUATION

If one ignores the British Second and Third fleets and all of their secondary vessels and the German Fourth, Fifth, and Sixth squadrons of old battleships of little military value, the balance of forces as of 1 August 1914 was as follows. The British forces consisted of twenty-eight battleships (twenty dreadnoughts[8]), four battle cruisers, and eight armored cruisers, eleven light cruisers, and forty-one destroyers of the Grand Fleet and the Harwich Force with its three light cruisers, thirty-six destroyers, and seventeen submarines. The German High Seas Fleet contained twenty-three battleships (fifteen dreadnoughts), three battle cruisers, one armed cruiser, fourteen light cruisers, eighty-eight destroyers, and twenty-eight submarines.[9]

7. Castex conflates the orders issued by Admiral of the Fleet Sir George Astley Callaghan on 25 November 1912 replacing close blockade with observational blockade with those of 3 July 1914 establishing a distant blockade. Only with the second did Scapa Flow become the base of choice, see Marder, vol. 1, 371–72.

8. Fast, armed solely with big (12–inch) guns, and driven by a turbine engine, HMS *Dreadnought,* launched 10 February 1906, rendered all previous battleships obsolete and multiplied the cost of Anglo-German naval competition.

9. Slightly different numbers of capital ships: twenty-one dreadnought and eight pre-dreadnought battleships for the British and thirteen dreadnoughts, sixteen pre-dreadnought battleships, and five battle cruisers for the Germans appear in Richard Hough, *The Great War at Sea 1914–1918* (Oxford, 1984).

Looking at numbers alone, the Germans had a marked, but not insupportable, inferiority in capital ships and a slight superiority in destroyers and submarines. . . .

Though the disparity in force should not have been paralyzing, the Germans were from the beginning convinced of their impotence against the British navy. From the Agadir affair[10] of 1911 to August 1914, naval leaders repeatedly expressed a pessimism that was reinforced at the war's beginning when Germany saw the British fleet strengthened by the addition of French and Russian naval forces. Denying that German naval forces were ready for war, Tirpitz wrote in a letter of 22 August 1914 that "we, the navy, can do very little, and that makes our situation very painful." The army general staff understood that Britain would entirely dominate the sea.

At the same time, there arose among some Germans the singular idea, more political than military, that it would be possible to avoid active war against Britain, that the navy's role was not to fight the Royal Navy but to "manage" her. On 19 August 1914, while German armies surged across Belgium in an irresistible tidal wave threatening the imminent erasure of France, Admirals von Pohl and Tirpitz explained their cleverness to Chancellor Bethmann-Hollweg. At the end of the war, Germany's territorial acquisitions in France and Russia would largely balance Britain's naval power and the loss of German colonies. With Germany the master of a good part of the French Channel coast and the

10. The Second Moroccan Crisis began on 1 July 1911 when the German gunboat *Panther* appeared off the Moroccan harbor of Agadir to insist on German colonial compensation for French occupation of Fez, the Moroccan capital. Britain rallied to the support of France, and Germany suffered a second diplomatic humiliation over Morocco, but some British leaders were alarmed to discover how closely their nation's military policies had become tacitly bound to those of France.

Turks threatening the Suez Canal, Britain would have to make concessions to Germany. Germany would have achieved what Germans called "the First Punic War," after which the modern Carthage could be destroyed in a second or third conflict.

Moreover, the Germans continued to live on the famous "risk theory" formulated in 1900. In this view, German naval power was intended not to defeat Britain directly but to paralyze her with the fear that her losses in a conflict with Germany would demote her to the second rank of naval powers.[11] Infantile in ignoring British capabilities for ship construction and repair, the risk theory obsessed many Germans.

Though these ideas of "bargaining" and "risk" dominated German naval circles at the outbreak of the 1914 war, what led them to virtual inactivity was their conviction of their at least temporary impotence. The navy's depressed spirit, lack of energy, which affected even the Kaiser himself, stands out clearly in the initial plan of operations of 31 July 1914. The major objective of these orders was "equalization," that is, the gradual elimination of British units by minor attacks until a parity of forces had been achieved. To this end, the navy was ordered "to *damage the British fleet*" by attacks against surveillance or blockade forces *within the Helgoland Bight* simultaneously with an energetic offensive

11. The risk theory implied that the German navy was constructed not to fight against Britain but to deter Britain from responding militarily to German provocation. "For the opponent the risk of war was to be made so costly that he would not dare to turn the cold war that had been forced upon him into a hot one and would rather abandon his position peacefully," Ludwig Dehio, quoted in Volker R. Berghahn, *Germany and the Approach of War in 1914* (London and Basingstoke, 1973): 39. The "bargaining" theory seems merely a component of the "risk" theory, since it is the risk inherent in fighting that is expected to lead Britain to the negotiating table.

with *mines* and, if possible, *submarines*. Battle was to be sought only after *equalization of force* had been achieved. Supplementary orders stressed the Kaiser's intention that *"the High Seas Fleet ought not to be engaged"* and the political importance of conserving the High Seas Fleet as a lever to be employed at the peace negotiations. In the meantime, *commerce destroying* was to be carried out within the constraints imposed by the laws of war.[12]

The plan of operations is defensive, appropriate to a party that believes itself to be much inferior to its adversary, but the defensive is only temporary. Battle is only deferred. One envisions it for the future or at least pays lip service to an offensive idea belied in actual operation orders. One would naturally strive to undertake the battle under favorable circumstances of time, place, and, above all, forces.

How will one obtain these? By an operation in some sense material, mathematical, mechanical; by the simple effect of "equalization"; by the sum of the losses inflicted on the enemy; by the procedures described above. One will thus pit "all one's forces" against British forces diminished to a total approximately equal to that of the High Seas Fleet. Before this situation has been achieved, one limits oneself to seizing an "opportunity" should it present itself, that is to say, one relies on chance to produce a happy combination of circumstances.

Thus, arithmetic or chance, but not *manoeuvre*. The plan's essential characteristic is the almost total absence of the *manoeuvre* idea, of which one finds only the merest glimpses. The reference to blows against British blockaders in the Helgoland Bight appears to correspond to the intention to attack a portion of the enemy fleet with a superiority of means while there is also a provision for war against enemy commerce, which could be a *manoeuvre* plan. The for-

12. A condensation.

mer is not a true *manoeuvre,* however, because the Germans intended merely to wait until the enemy himself created an appropriate circumstance by moving vulnerable forces into the Helgoland Bight. The advantageous situation would result from British miscalculation, not German manipulation. The German plan also made reference to *guerre de course,* a classic component of *manoeuvre* when used to force an advantageous redistribution of enemy forces, but the connection between commerce war and the fleet action received not the slightest acknowledgment.

The German plan to equalize forces not only lacked the element of *manoeuvre* but was doomed to failure from the very beginning of the war. It did not take into account the energetic British program of naval construction that promised to offset their battle losses. Predicated on the assumption that the Royal Navy would maintain a close blockade of the Helgoland Bight, the plan offered little return because the British confined themselves to the system of distant blockade foreseen in 1912 and only entered the North Sea in rapid sorties carried out at moments of their own choosing. . . . [13]

FIRST OPERATIONS (AUGUST–SEPTEMBER 1914)— BIRTH OF A *MANOEUVRE* IDEA

Equalization operations commenced at the beginning of the war. On 5 August the unsupported auxiliary minelayer *Königin-Luise* laid mines at the mouth of the Thames and was sunk by a British destroyer flotilla. At almost the same time, the Germans, believing that the bulk of the British forces was stationed towards the center of the North Sea in

13. Distant blockade was the 1914 plan, while the 1912 plan mandated an observational blockade, but Castex is correct in the sense that neither called for British capital ships to enter the Helgoland Bight.

support of a close blockade, dispatched ten submarines to sweep the North Sea from north to south from 6 to 11 August. Meeting the Grand Fleet on its return, the screen proved unable either to attack or to report any information about it. Two submarines were destroyed, one of them rammed by a British light cruiser. Three submarines reconnoitered the Firth of Moray, the Firth of Forth, and the Humber from 14 to 21 August, discovering defensive installations but no British forces.

The transport of British troops to France began on 9 August. Warned on 7 August of the imminence of this movement, the German General Staff did not think it dangerous and advised that the navy need not concern itself. However, on 8 August, the Kaiser ordered the navy to attack the British transports, though without employing the High Seas Fleet. The German command entrusted the operation to four submarines, which acted independently and had the additional mission of attacking the warships covering the transports in order to contribute to the desired equalization. These submarines left Helgoland on 6 August. Two returned without having reached the presumed position of the British covering forces. The third found nothing, and the fourth, spotting only a cruiser and some British destroyers, was unable to attack any of them.

Meanwhile, the Grand Fleet was at sea and its cruisers approached within one hundred miles of Helgoland without finding anything or being attacked even though they had put themselves into the situation desired by the Germans. . . .

The German command attributed their lack of submarine success to the British surface fleet's staying stubbornly out of reach. To entice the capital ships to come out and be torpedoed seemed to require raids by surface ships, cruisers, and destroyers against the British coast. Herein lay a rudimentary *manoeuvre* idea but only at the minor level of equalization operations. The objective of genuine *manoeu-*

vre would have been to create a favorable relationship between the main British and German fleets. Though *manoeuvre* on a very low level, it did contain a seed that would develop later.

With the idea of drawing British ships from harbor, the cruisers *Stralsund* and *Strasburg* were sent on 17 August, alone and rather imprudently, to attack the British transports. The *Stralsund* encountered light elements from Harwich but broke off the contact. The two cruisers retired without being pursued and without managing to draw the enemy to the east. The only effect of the raid was to lead the British to station several cruisers, including two battle cruisers, in the Humber. The move is of some importance as the beginning of British dispersion, a theme to which we will have occasion to return.

On 31 August, a group composed of the light cruisers *Rostock* and *Strasburg* and a flotilla of destroyers, supported from behind by the cruisers *Mainz* and *Hamburg* and three submarines, raided Dogger Bank and sunk several trawlers. On the night of 25–26 August, the minelayers *Albatross* and *Nautilus,* each escorted by a light cruiser and half a flotilla of destroyers, sowed mines in the mouths of the Tyne and the Humber. The latter minefield was discovered in time, and the two battle cruisers based in the Humber were shifted northwards to the Firth of Forth. All of these operations failed to create the desired equalization and would be interrupted by a disagreeable enemy blow.

On 28 August 1914, at 0600, Admiral Beatty's[14] Battle Cruiser Squadron, the eight cruisers of Commodore

14. David, First Earl Beatty (1871–1936) commanded the Battle Cruiser Squadron of the Grand Fleet from 1913 to 1916 and the Grand Fleet from 1916 to 1919. He was First Sea Lord from 1919 to 1927.

Goodenough's First Light Squadron, and the two light cruisers, thirty-three destroyers, and eight submarines of the Harwich Force[15] made a surprise entry into the Helgoland Bight and destroyed three light cruisers, the *Köln, Mainz,* and *Ariadne,* and the destroyer *V-187* before disappearing as quickly as they had come. The British had approached the Helgoland Bight but not in the manner the Germans had intended. Far from offering themselves as a target, they had remained mobile, active, agile, and slippery in the face of fixed German dispositions. It was the British whose actions had constituted a *manoeuvre,* who had created a favorable situation and surprised the foe. . . .

The fight at Helgoland naturally made a deep impression on the Germans, one which translated into both immediate measures and reflections with long-term implications. . . . Since the defeat appeared to have stemmed above all from the lack of support for the light vessels by the forces of the line, it was decided to bring the High Seas Fleet into the action in the future.

High Seas Fleet commander Admiral von Ingenohl made himself the spokesman at headquarters for spirits imbued with these ideas and proposed modifying the war plan so as to increase the initiative of the fleet. The suggestion appeared inopportune to higher echelons; the Kaiser treated the Helgoland battle as further proof of the impotence of the German navy compared to that of the British. He also focused on the political and military effect of the mere existence of the High Seas Fleet—of its influence on the neutrality of Scandinavian powers and on the mastery of the Baltic. Finally, he had held firmly since the beginning to preserving the fleet intact to play a role at the peace negotiations that

15. Commanded by Commodore Sir Reginald Tyrwhitt (1870–1951), later Admiral of the Fleet.

the rapid victories on land made appear imminent. . . . Supported by Bethmann-Hollweg and von Falkenhayn, he instructed the fleet to continue to exercise restraint. The original plan remain entirely unchanged. . . .

Within the High Seas Fleet, however, disputes continued between proponents of the status quo and advocates of a more active strategy. Those German officers who favored an offensive posture for the fleet used the engagement of 28 August to argue that the Helgoland Bight was unlikely to provide favorable conditions for battle but was, on the contrary, the one locale where the High Seas Fleet would never have the initiative in operations and would encounter the enemy only when he was alert and his forces concentrated. Opportunities for surprise would occur only if Germany took the initiative with sorties to the open sea.

Pushed by these officers, Admiral von Ingenohl proposed to the Kaiser a battle cruiser raid near the Skagerrak to take place on 20 September and, some days later, suggested expanding the operation by adding the support of the entire High Seas Fleet. Admiral Hugo von Pohl unilaterally rejected the latter proposal, and the whole project was soon abandoned at the news that the Grand Fleet had weighed anchor. On 25 September, Admiral von Ingenohl repeated his case in a more complete and better-prepared memorandum that stressed the impossibility of achieving the desired conditions for battle with any plan depending on British willingness to sail of its own volition into the Helgoland Bight. Nor could equality be achieved by a mine and submarine campaign. It would be perfectly possible, however, by taking the initiative oneself and sortieing *with united forces,* to obtain success *against parts of the British fleet,* even outside of the Bight, by operating, for example, near the Skagerrak.

In this memorandum was born the idea of *manoeuvre.* Previous plans had aimed only at equalization through minor operations in the Helgoland Bight, but von Ingenohl envisioned using *manoeuvre* to achieve a favorable ratio between the main forces of the German and British fleets. Still shapeless, sketchy, and lacking a program for implementation, the new concept nevertheless constituted an immense improvement over the preceding strategic vacuum. It did not, however, enthuse the highest leadership, and on 2 October the Kaiser renewed his order that the fleet eschew battle.

Directives issued on 6 October in accordance with "the imperial will" actually constituted a true plan of operations and revealed the intentions of the high command. The order repeated the fundamental importance of the fleet's mere existence for the defense of Germany's coasts, the mastery of the Baltic, and maintaining communications with Scandinavia. It observed that losses suffered in even a victorious battle would destroy these advantages and end the fleet's impact on neutral powers. Thus, the fleet was ordered "*to stay in reserve* and avoid actions that could lead to large losses," though it should take advantage of favorable opportunities to inflict *damage* on the enemy. Even within the Helgoland Bight, an encounter with the Grand Fleet was to be avoided until the Kaiser had determined the moment to be appropriate. The order of 6 October emphasized the vigorous pursuit of the war by submarines, destroyers, and mines and the possibility of *battle cruiser* raids.[16]

Thus, the Kaiser and his counselors von Pohl and von Müller[17] (head of the naval cabinet) had hardly modified their initial concept. The bulk of the High Seas Fleet would remain at its base and abstain more firmly than ever from all major action. They gripped tightly to the mirage of

16. Compressed.
17. Vice Admiral Georg Alexander von Müller (1854–1940).

equalization through submarine war. In spite of everything, the instruction did retain something of von Ingenohl's suggestions. It no longer treated a battle in the Helgoland Bight as desirable; eyes had been opened by the engagement off Helgoland. That it allowed for a battle cruiser sortie was also progress.

But the Kaiser, von Pohl, and von Müller had not understood the basis of von Ingenohl's *manoeuvre* idea. They remained unreceptive to the creative intention manifested by the chief of the naval staff, to which they would agree only later in what appeared to be encouraging circumstances.

FIRST ATTEMPTS AT *MANOEUVRE* (NOVEMBER 1914–JANUARY 1915)

In September and October, several events occurred of a nature to instill confidence in the proponents of equalization by means of the little war.[18] On 22 September, three British armored cruisers, the *Aboukir, Hogue,* and *Cressy,* steaming slowly and without precaution along the Dutch coast, were torpedoed by submarine *U-9.* On 15 October, it was the turn of the armored cruiser *Hawke* to go down in the southern part of the North Sea. Scapa Flow not yet being defensible, the Grand Fleet took shelter at Lough Swilly on the northern coast of Ireland. On 22 October, moreover, the auxiliary minelayer *Berlin* sowed her mines in well-trafficked waters off Ireland. One of her mines sank HMS *Audacious,* one of Britain's most modern battleships, on 27 October.

Other German minelaying operations were less successful. On 17 October, British light forces drove the minelayer *Nautilus* and the cruiser *Kolberg* away from the mouth of the Forth. On the same day, the German 7th half-flotilla of

18. *"La petite guerre."*

142

four destroyers was entirely destroyed in the region of the Thames by a British cruiser and four destroyers.

The chief of the High Seas Fleet concluded that further minelaying on the British coast would require support from heavy forces. On 29 October, he telegraphed supreme headquarters to ask permission to lay mines near Yarmouth. In direct support of the minelayers would be battle cruisers, a squadron of light cruisers, and a flotilla of destroyers, while the bulk of the High Seas Fleet would hold itself ready forty miles to the north of Terschelling. His *manoeuvre* idea having been rejected by the high command, von Ingenohl sought to resurrect it in the form of mine warfare.

Surprisingly, in view of the restrictive instruction of 6 October, the Kaiser immediately approved von Ingenohl's plan with the sole reservation that the High Seas Fleet go no farther than 120 miles from Helgoland and fervent advice to maintain a major reconnaissance effort, including aircraft, to the north.

Von Ingenohl's plan proved the first cog in a wheel that would turn inexorably towards a genuine German offensive. The coming transformation should come as no surprise. When one commits forces to action, one must either leave them to their fate or support them with other forces. Moreover, the concept was logical, even solely from the point of view of equalization. Experience had shown and reason suggested that to lead British vessels to expose themselves to mines and to submarines it would be necessary to offer German surface ships as bait, a line of analysis that led naturally to a sortie by the High Seas Fleet.

This is not to say, however, that Admiral von Ingenohl's sortie involved *manoeuvre* on a large scale—unless Admiral von Ingenohl, fearing a rebuff, voluntarily concealed grander ideas behind what appeared to be only an ordinary minelaying operation. His proposals contained no hint of attempting to attack an isolated part of the British fleet.

143

Whatever von Ingenohl's intentions, no moment in the war would be more favorable for the Germans either to pit themselves against the united British forces or to seek to encounter them dispersed and to defeat them in detail. At the end of October, the Grand Fleet's capital ship situation was unusually poor. Of the battleships, the *Audacious* had been sunk, the *Iron Duke* and *Ajax* had damaged condensers, the *Orion*'s turbines were undergoing repair at Greenock, and the *Erin* and *Agincourt,* newly joined to the fleet, were not yet battle ready. The battle cruiser *New Zealand* was being repaired at Cromarty. The Grand Fleet could count on only seventeen dreadnoughts, five battle cruisers, and forty-two destroyers, while the German numbers were fifteen, four, and eighty, respectively. (It was at this time that serious consideration was given to moving four French dreadnoughts from the Mediterranean to the North Sea.) Moreover, at the beginning of November, their defeat at Coronel would lead the British to dispatch from the Grand Fleet the battle cruisers *Invincible, Inflexible,* and *Princess-Royal* to the Falklands and the Caribbean. The arrival of HMS *Tiger* would only partially compensate for these detachments.

Also, on 12 November, the British instituted a very questionable redeployment. In October, the British government and high command were haunted, as so often in their history, by fear of invasion. Under the circumstances, this fear is easily demonstrated to have been unreasonable and unjustified, even absurd. Nevertheless, concerned that the Grand Fleet at Scapa Flow was too distant to repel a German landing, the British determined to distribute forces along the coast so as to better oppose such an enterprise. The Third Battle Squadron (eight *King Edward*-class cruisers) and the Third Cruiser Squadron (eight *Antrim*-class armored cruisers) were removed from Scapa Flow to Rosyth on 20 November, and the Fifth Battle Squadron (old battleships of the *Formidable* class) was stationed at Sheerness, in the area also containing the Harwich and Nore flotillas. Refusing even to consider that the Harwich Force was an essential component of the Grand Fleet, the Admiralty kept it under its own control.

In sum, the British were in the process of creating a dangerous dispersal of ships between Scapa Flow, Cromarty, Rosyth, Harwich, and Sheerness, which, especially given the weakness level of the Grand Fleet at the time, offered up the necessary conditions for a German *manoeuvre*.

Von Ingenohl's raid against Yarmouth by battle cruisers and some light cruisers took place on 3 November. The minelaying was accomplished without incident but in the wrong place, while a bombardment of the coast achieved insignificant results. Meanwhile, the High Seas Fleet held itself ready in the Terschelling area and sighted only light British elements. The Germans retreated finally without anything interesting happening, while the British sailed from Cromarty too late to meet the enemy. Though only moderate in scope, the operation had gone well, and everyone on the German side was of a mind to continue.

On 16 November, Admiral von Ingenohl sent to headquarters a plan for the bombardment of Hartlepool and Scarborough by forces supported by the High Seas Fleet, which would advance this time up to 130 miles out to sea. He received permission for the operation on 19 November. Von Pohl, von Müller, Tirpitz, and the Kaiser himself now hoped that the High Seas Fleet would achieve some successes against detached elements of the Grand Fleet; they were now less resistant to von Ingenohl's *manoeuvre* proposals, admittedly more modest than those before the sortie of 3 November. They also knew that the British were weakened by the absence of the ships sent against von Spee. Only the naval staff in Berlin limited its ambition to minelaying.

The operation, delayed from day to day for various reasons, finally took place on 16 December 1914 and unrolled in a succession of extraordinary chance encounters. The *first act* in the drama and first chance occurrence saw British and German forces clashing unintentionally and unaware of the situation.[19] About midnight, Hipper, who led the advance guard of battle cruisers, passed several miles in front of Beatty's Battle Cruiser Squadron and Warrender's[20] Second Battle Squadron.[21] About 0500, these two squadrons found themselves sandwiched, alone and unsupported, between Hipper and von Ingenohl, who followed with the German van. Here was von Ingenohl's chance to achieve the goal of his *manoeuvre* by attacking with superior forces an isolated part of the Grand Fleet—a magnificent opportunity for the Germans.

Second act—From 0515 to 0600 von Ingenohl's light forces (torpedo boat *V-155*, then cruiser *Hamburg*) met Warrender's destroyers. A firefight ensued, and von Ingenohl, alarmed by a sudden conviction that he had engaged the whole Grand Fleet, reversed course and headed back for the Helgoland Bight. Thus, unknowingly, he lost the sought-after opportunity that would never reappear during the war. Moreover, since he neglected to inform Hipper of his countermarch until 1045, the battle cruiser force was left in the air and found itself confronted by the united forces of Beatty and Warrender. A splendid situation for the Germans had suddenly turned tragic.[22]

19. Not entirely true for the British, who had been brought to sea by radio intercepts.

20. Sir George John Scott Warrender, 7th Baronet (1860–1917).

21. Beatty had four battle cruisers, Warrender six dreadnoughts and a destroyer flotilla. Also at sea were the four vessels of Pakenham's Third Armoured Cruiser Squadron, Goodenough's First Light Cruiser Squadron, and eight submarines under Keyes.

22. But Hipper, off bombarding Scarsborough, Hartlepool, and Whitby, was too distant from the High Seas Fleet to spring the trap.

Third act—In sailing west, however, Beatty and War-render had opened an eighteen-mile gap between their forces through which Hipper's destroyers and three light cruisers passed miraculously between 1130 and 1215. Aided by poor visibility, by a misunderstanding among the British light cruisers, and also by the sending of false recognition signals, they managed to escape.[23] Hipper's battle cruisers stole away northwards in a move that would not have saved them had not Beatty's change of course averted a certain intercep-tion. Thus, chance intervened a third time and saved Hipper from a desperate situation.

The British Admiralty did everything on this occasion to disperse its ships in a manner favorable to the planned Ger-man *manoeuvre*. It would be difficult to find a better illus-tration of dispositions preventing forces from giving another mutual support. . . . In spite of these exceptionally good conditions, the German *manoeuvre* failed even though it was directed by its principal instigator and, so to speak, godfather.

Admiral von Ingenohl offered excuses of varying degrees of merit, including insufficient intelligence and orders from the high command, for missing the excellent opportunity of-fered him on 16 December. . . . The truth is that such a *manoeuvre* is highly susceptible to chance, especially in a theater of operations like the North Sea, where the forces are close together and can move very rapidly from place to place, and, finally, where poor visibility increases the risk of being surprised.

Something looms up. What is it? Is it an isolated detach-ment? Is it the enemy's main force? Has one achieved the desired situation or steamed into one full of danger? And if

23. An ambiguous signal by Beatty caused the light cruisers that were the only British forces in contact with Hipper to break off the action, Hough, 126–27.

this is an enemy detachment, where is his main force? Near? Far? So many terrifying questions assail the commander and plunge his soul into doubt and anxiety, especially when his forces are smaller overall. Even if, at the beginning, he has faith in his *manoeuvre,* he now feels less sure of himself, he sees the perils that had not appeared to him when far from the action, and if the horizon is not absolutely clear he retreats . . . if he can. All of this is quite understandable.[24]

Success in such an affair requires special conditions of execution. Perfect *security* is especially necessary. *Manoeuvre* is, above all, a question of security. Intelligence, which the Germans so sorely lacked, is indispensable. Their espionage service in Britain having been disorganized by arrests at the beginning of the war, they had only vague reports about the strength of the Grand Fleet, the locations of its various components, and the type of blockade that it practiced. The British were far better served by their efficient secret service. Seizure of a German codebook from the wreck of the *Magdeburg* made the decryption of enemy radio messages easy after November 1914, and a net of radio tracking stations did the rest.[25]

When German headquarters learned, however, that the High Seas Fleet on 16 December had tangled with only a part of the Grand Fleet and that it had missed an opportunity for the desired *manoeuvre,* all of the new converts to the idea of *manoeuvre*—the Kaiser, von Pohl, von Müller, Tirpitz—were, ironically, furious with von Ingenohl, who was its father. These men, who had not experienced his apprehensions in the theater of action, now surpassed him in

24. Thus, for Clausewitz, the most important elements of friction are the commander's fear and uncertainty, *On War,* book 1, chapters 4–6 (Howard, 113–21).

25. See Patrick Beesly, *Room 40: British Naval Intelligence 1914–1918* (London, 1982).

their offensive thinking. On 23 December, the commander of the High Seas Fleet received a note denying the earlier defensive posture: "His majesty has expressed that efforts to preserve the fleet, or certain parts of the fleet, *ought not under any circumstance to go so far as to impede the exploitation of promising opportunities* for success, under the pretext that this exploitation will bring the possibility of losses." What the note did not say was how a commander was to identify a truly favorable situation, but, in any case, von Ingenohl's replacement as head of the High Seas Fleet was soon decided.

Like those of 6 October 1914, the new imperial instructions of 9 January 1915 constituted a genuine plan of operations. . . . They addressed the role of the submarines and dirigibles and stressed the High Seas Fleet's *manoeuvre* role. Greater freedom of action accrued to the fleet commander, who was authorized "to undertake *more often* and according to his own judgment *offensive* actions in the North Sea, in order to *cut off advanced enemy forces and to attack them with superior forces*. . . . " These instructions constituted an incontestable advance over those of 6 October 1914. The idea of *manoeuvre* is now allowed and clearly expressed. It has conquered the high command, certainly still influenced by the missed opportunity of 16 December.

Though Admiral von Ingenohl pronounced himself very satisfied with these instructions, whose emphasis on *manoeuvre* marked an incontestable advance over those of 6 October 1914, in practice, however, he was less daring than before. Seemingly assailed by doubt, he reassessed the affair of 16 December and decided that Beatty's apparently isolated forces had probably been supported by others not far distant. He became ever more doubtful of the feasibility of bringing a mere part of the Grand Fleet into an engagement. . . . Diminishing ardor did not afflict von Ingenohl alone but would occur in other German leaders confronted with similar conditions.

Shortly thereafter, a battle cruiser engagement occurred at Dogger Bank on 24 January 1915, in which Hipper was repulsed sharply by Beatty and lost the armored cruiser *Blucher* in his retreat. The Germans brought this upon themselves. Overanxious to engage, they acted before they had the use of all of their forces. The Third Line Squadron, their most modern, was exercising in the Baltic with some destroyers. The rest of the High Seas Fleet was at anchor, and some important vessels were undergoing repair. Thus, Hipper was sent off alone and unsupported. . . .[26] Although telegraph messages reported contact with a sizable enemy force and allowed the command to follow the alarming evolution of the situation, von Ingenohl was very late in ordering to sea what remained of the High Seas Fleet. . . . It was 16 December again—but not produced by chance. '

Thus, the Germans voluntarily placed themselves in the situation in which they had hoped to see the British. It was inconceivable. It was the opposite of *manoeuvre*, and it was done by von Ingenohl, pioneer of the *manoeuvre* idea!

Ironically, von Ingenohl's mistake happened exactly as the enemy was in the process, once again, of offering the Germans an excellent opportunity to achieve the situation that they claimed to seek. Though the Admiralty, warned since 14 January of a German fleet movement, had decrypted communications on the morning of 23 January revealing the timing and composition of that evening's sortie, it repeated its usual glaringly dangerous dispersal of effort. As of 0747 on 24 January, Beatty's battle cruisers and the destroyers of Harwich Force were at Dogger Bank, the Third Line Squadron and Third Cruiser Squadron were thirty miles north,

26. With *Seydlitz* (flag), *Derfflinger, Moltke,* and *Blücher.*

and the remainder of the Grand Fleet was halfway between Aberdeen and Jutland. Imagine that, as on 16 December, not Hipper alone but the entire German High Seas Fleet had steamed to Dogger Bank on 24 January. What would have happened? Did the British dispositions not depend too blindly on intelligence reports?[27]

But it is results that count, and Dogger Bank led to the replacement of Admiral von Ingenohl and his chief of staff Admiral Eckermann. Admiral von Pohl, chief of the naval staff at general headquarters, took command of the High Seas Fleet on 4 February 1915. On the same day, the submarine blockade of the coasts of Britain, the prelude to true submarine warfare, was declared.

A YEAR OF WAITING (1915)

Admiral Bachmann, maritime prefect of Kiel, replaced Admiral von Pohl at the head of the navy staff at general headquarters. . . .[28] Bachmann's operational ideas added nothing new to the existing *manoeuvre* idea. He favored sorties of the entire German fleet in an attempt to surprise isolated contingents of the Grand Fleet, and he thought that a submarine commerce blockade just as British vessels were dispatched to the Dardanelles would afford the desired opportunities. Bachmann was no innovator.

Though von Pohl himself had begun to advocate these ideas when he was at general headquarters, surprisingly, they seemed less attractive to him now that he was responsible for their execution. A victim of the same mental process that afflicted von Ingenohl after 16 December 1914, he expressed his uncertainties in a memorandum to the Kaiser on

---

27. In fact, Jellicoe was only 140 miles north of Beatty at the height of the battle-cruiser action, Hough, 139.

28. A discussion of naval politics is omitted.

23 March 1915: "I do not know the position of the enemy naval forces. My reconnaissance forces are so weak that I do not know when I encounter weak enemy forces whether or not the main body is in the neighborhood. I can, therefore, find myself unwillingly engaged in a naval battle that I ought to avoid. Thus, our two desired goals contradict one another. . . . In the present military situation, I think that offensive thrusts ought to be *very short* and to limit themselves to showing our dominance of the Helgoland Bight."

The neophyte advocate of *manoeuvre,* who had so much reproached von Ingenohl for failing to win on 16 December, had developed cold feet. The Kaiser approved his views and, on 30 March 1915, sent him an order, which while leaving him complete freedom of action, offered a counsel of prudence that would not be rejected.

Thus, during of all 1915 the High Seas Fleet abstained from active operations, even cruiser raids. The Germans returned to the chimera of achieving equality by means of the little war—submarine action and minelaying. . . .

For Germany, 1915 was a year of waiting but also one of preparation characterized by increased naval resources. The High Seas Fleet was reinforced by the four new battleships (*König, Grosser-Kurfürst, Markgraf,* and *Kronprinz*), two battle cruisers (*Derfflinger* and *Lützow*), and three light cruisers. In spite of losses, the number of submarines grew over the course of the year from forty-one to fifty-five. The Germans worked actively throughout the entire year at improving their matériel, especially their naval artillery. They lengthened the range of their guns, achieved new fire control arrangements, replaced the 100-mm. guns of the light cruisers with 152-mm. guns, and increased the armor of their magazines and munitions hoists.

The High Seas Fleet improved its training through a dogged and intensive effort. Long-range gunnery and torpedo practice, once requiring that the ships be dispatched to the Baltic, could now take place under the protection of mine-fields around Helgoland. . . . Aerial reconnaissance was supplied by the end of 1915 by a dozen well-trained dirigibles. In sum, all of these improvements, of which Admiral Scheer was the beneficiary, gave the Germans very superior resources for *manoeuvre* in 1916 than those they had had in 1914. . . .

Unhappily, the British did not remain inactive in the face of these improvements in the High Seas Fleet. Reinforced in 1915 by the new dreadnoughts *Queen Elizabeth, Barham, Canada,* and *Warspite,* the battle cruisers *Australia, Inflexible,* and *Indefatigable,* eight light cruisers, and twenty-two destroyers, the Grand Fleet's superiority over the German fleet increased considerably during the year, although it was lessened in practice by the fact that the Germans could choose the timing of the encounter so as to act when their own forces were consolidated.[29]

The British strongly pressed their own training. After establishing themselves properly at Scapa Flow, they practiced short-range gunnery, night gunnery, and torpedo launching. Long-range gunnery training took place on the crags of the west coast of Scotland, then at targets towed to the opening of the Bay of Cromarty behind the barrier of the mine fields. Finally, British morale was maintained at a high level by the frequent sorties at sea to which the British forces, contrary to certain folklore, committed themselves. German morale, on the other hand, fell sharply as a consequence of interminable periods at anchor. While the High Sea Fleet's technical competence remained high, the same could not be said of

---

29. The initiative of operations devolving upon the belligerent who practices an defensive-offensive is one of the characteristics of naval war (author's note).

their psychological condition because the maintenance of morale demands regular activity and experience at sea.[30]

The British retained and increased their advantage in intelligence. Though the Germans improved the security of their radio transmissions, the British established a highly effective network of forty radio triangulation stations between the Orkneys and Dover directly connected to the Admiralty. Henceforth, as soon as the High Seas Fleet stood to sea, it could easily be located and followed by the enemy. Such were the factors, favorable and not, that would affect German *manoeuvre* in 1916.

30. A suggestive difference between the two navies is that, while British sailors lived in their ships, Germans remained in barracks until the ships sortied.

CHAPTER 8

GERMAN OPERATIONS IN THE NORTH SEA (1914–1916) (CONTINUED)[1]

RESUMED ATTEMPTS AT *MANOEUVRE*

FOR VARIOUS reasons, the year 1916 had to see the resumption of active naval operations in the North Sea. The war as a whole was not going as the leaders of the Central Powers desired. The offensive against Verdun appeared to have been checked. Russia, cruelly tested in 1915 but not out of the war, would counterattack vigorously in June 1916. The Serbian army had reentered the fray and stabilized the Balkan front for the Allies, while the value of the Austro-Hungarian army was diminishing. Finally, as the Germans themselves admitted after the war, economic conditions in Germany were becoming disquieting and giving rise to widespread pessimism. Doubtful that any understanding with Britain could be reached, German leaders saw the need for a vigorous offensive.[2]

The very ill Admiral von Pohl had to give up command of the High Seas Fleet on 9 January 1916, and the command

---

1. Raoul Castex, *Théories stratégiques,* 2nd ed., vol. 2 (Paris: Société d'Editions Géographiques, Maritimes et Coloniales, 1939): 242–76.

2. But Wilhelm II approved Scheer's concepts on 23 February 1916, two days after the Verdun battle had begun and long before the German leadership had reason to be depressed.

fell to Vice Admiral Scheer on 24 January.[3] Scheer was an extremely energetic man who did not shrink from responsibility. The advocate of vigorous action against Britain, he had been much distressed by the inactivity of the High Seas Fleet in 1915. His intention to inaugurate a completely new system was aided by a strength of character that allowed him to impose his own ideas on headquarters. Accepting neither directives nor control, he alone governed operations in the North Sea and even, in many ways, in the whole naval war.[4]

Determined to seize and retain the initiative in operations, he argued that: "The present disparity of forces forbids us from seeking out decisive battle against the united British forces. Our conduct of operations ought therefore to ensure that a decisive battle not be imposed upon us by the enemy. . . . The many ways we have of attacking the enemy give us the advantage, even given our inferior forces, *of always being the aggressors*." Taking the initiative in operations is indeed especially necessary for the weaker party.

To execute his intention, Scheer advocated "a constant and methodical pressure on the enemy" so as to force him to "send against us forces that we can attack." This pressure would be achieved by the submarine war against commerce, mine warfare, attacks on commerce in the North Sea, air war, and, finally, active sorties by the High Seas Fleet.

Admiral Scheer insisted, moreover, that these various operations be tightly linked to one other. "The mine war, the

3. Von Pohl died in Berlin on 23 February 1916 (author's note). Admiral Reinhard Scheer (1863–1928) commanded the Third Squadron from 26 December 1914 until taking command of the High Seas Fleet.

4. And he would lead it even better after being named to the post of chief of the general staff in August 1918, the date that, to be sure, marked the beginning of the end of the German war at sea (author's note). For a less positive appraisal of Scheer, see Holger H. Herwig and Neil M. Heyman, *Biographical Dictionary of World War One* (Westport, CT, 1982).

commerce war, and the sorties of the High Seas Fleet are *closely interrelated*. The more they are combined within the framework of a program of operations, the greater their chances of success."

To this end, the admiral laid out a comprehensive set of coordinated operations. Thus, the aerial attacks were henceforth to be supported by light units or even by the entire High Seas Fleet. Bombardments of the English coast would bring about engagements with responding British detachments, while dirigible reconnaissance would prevent the disagreeable surprises of previous occasions.

The official history of the German navy credits Scheer with a new system of coordinated operations designed to ensure that "from now on," encounters would be with only a fraction of the enemy forces. Though the appraisal is interesting, "from now on" is an exaggeration. The *manoeuvre* idea remained unchanged from that of 1914. . . . Scheer's only improvement, other than pursuing *manoeuvre* with new energy and intelligence, was his coordination of submarines and aircraft with the surface fleet. . . .[5]

On a visit to the High Seas Fleet on 23 February 1916, the Kaiser approved Scheer's plan and gave him full freedom to carry it out.

Scheer began by reorganizing the security arrangements of the Helgoland Bight.[6] New air and surface patrols were established, and minesweeping units cleared the channels. Destroyers were placed as pickets, while a conveniently located force consisting of about half of the High Seas Fleet

5. Castex is unfairly dismissive of Scheer. Submarines and aircraft added significantly to the *manoeuvre* idea, which Castex himself hardly saw as fully developed in 1914.

6. "Security" is Castex's *"securité,"* which, sometimes confusingly, combines the search for information about enemy movements with screening one's own.

stood ready to weigh anchor within three-quarters of an hour.

Finally, the sowing of new and larger minefields contiguous with those laid by the enemy opened to the High Seas Fleet for deployment and exercises a hitherto forbidden zone extending from Helgoland to the Terschelling–Horn's Reef line. The High Seas Fleet now had a vast training area from which it could exit by the three channels already mentioned.[7]

The undersea war, which we have examined elsewhere, continued at the prevailing relatively moderate pace with a reduced number of submarines and with political limitations still observed. Mining, done mainly by submarines, achieved no significant results. The *guerre de course* underwent a brief renaissance with the efforts of the *Moewe* and the *Greif*.[8] The first of these vessels left Germany in the last days of 1915, sowed mines north of Scotland that sank the battleship *King Edward VII*, cruised the Atlantic for some time, and returned to Germany on 5 March 1916. Thanks to surprise, she had achieved noticeable results against enemy shipping. The *Greif* was sunk by the British Tenth Cruiser Squadron in the North Sea. In sum, this revival of the *guerre de course* was too brief and too minor to change the conditions for the *manoeuvre* of organized forces.

The air war was very active during the first months of 1916, and it occasionally drew British counterattacks against centers of German air activity. On 18 January, a bombing operation by the Harwich Force against the hangars at Emden was stopped by fog. On 23 January, German

7. Below, 129.

8. The mysterious *Moewe* and *Greif* caused considerable grief both to enemy navies and to the editors of naval reference works attempting to pin down their exact specifications; see *Brassey's Naval Annual* (London, 1916): 175.

airplanes bombed the harbor of the Dunes, and on 29 January, a second British attempt against Emden was not vigorously pressed. On 31 January, nine dirigibles raided Birmingham, Derby, Nottingham, and Liverpool. Returning, the dirigible *L-19* sank in the sea off Grimsby. On 4 March, three dirigibles bombarded Hull in an expedition coinciding with a sortie of the High Seas Fleet.

On 25 March, the British made an air attack against the hangars of Tondern. The operation was executed by a seaplane carrier escorted by the Harwich Force, which advanced almost to Horn's Reef. The attack failed; three seaplanes out of five were captured by the Germans. A collision sank the destroyer *Medusa* and badly damaged the light cruiser *Undaunted*. On their side, the Germans lost two destroyers and two trawlers.

Beatty's battle cruisers covered the Harwich Force and retired northwards with it during the night, returning at daybreak on 26 March towards Horn's Reef. At the same moment, Admiral Scheer, warned by his aircraft, ordered the High Seas Fleet to weigh anchor and steam towards the enemy. But at 0630, faced with very bad weather, he turned his fleet around. Thus, unknowingly, he lost a magnificent opportunity to engage in detail an enemy that had presented itself to him. The British were, as usual, badly scattered, with the Grand Fleet far off to the north.

Six successive Zeppelin raids took place on the first six days of April. A number of important British centers were hit, notably London, Sunderland, Leith, Edinburgh, Yarmouth, and Whitby. The *L-15* was destroyed by antiaircraft artillery. Two other German attacks took place in early May. In the course of the second, the *L-20* was forced to land in Norway, where she was interned.

In truth, one cannot perceive between these aerial operations and Admiral Scheer's *manoeuvre* the link claimed in his plan of operations. The connection would have been genuine and useful only if the dirigibles had been employed to attack British naval or air forces at their bases or to reconnoiter for the German fleet, in either case contributing to the fleet's *manoeuvre*. It is hard to understand certain expressions used by the Germans in their operations orders or in their official history when referring to the relationship of surface forces with Zeppelins. What does it mean for the former to "support the action" or to "protect the return" of the latter? One cannot see how ships are to intervene in air action. . . . Only after the middle of April, when poor results and shortening nights led the Germans to renounce Zeppelin raids almost completely, were airships employed principally for High Seas Fleet reconnaissance, that is, in aid of security and, consequently, *manoeuvre*.[9]

FIRST MAJOR OPERATIONS

Admiral Scheer promptly sought to execute his *manoeuvre* plan. His first project envisioned a sort of triangular sweep, covered by dirigibles, of the North Sea up to Fisher Bank and Dogger Bank in the hope of an encounter with isolated enemies. Conceived for 8 April, when the new moon would provide good conditions for night torpedo attacks, the plan had to be abandoned because of bad weather. A second idea, using the full moon for a sortie by the High Seas Fleet to the Skagerrak on 13 April, was given up in the face of reports of a British incursion into the Helgoland Bight. . . . When the anticipated British movement failed to occur, Admiral Scheer decided upon an operation in the Lowestoft region in conjunction with the Irish revolt planned for Easter Sunday. . . .

9. Further detail on Zeppelins are omitted.

The inspiration for the enterprise undertaken on 25 April 1916 was still that conceived by Admiral Scheer in February. The battle cruisers would exert pressure on the enemy by bombarding the towns of Lowestoft and Yarmouth while the High Seas Fleet waited off Texel to intervene against the British units that would sortie from their separate harbors and present themselves for attack in isolated contingents. . . .

Both submarines and airships had important parts in Scheer's scheme. The Flanders submarine force sent seven U-Cs to lay mines on the British coast, four U-Bs as a barrage in front of Southwold, and two U-Bs to serve as markers for the cruisers handling the bombardment. The role of the dirigibles was even more significant. Six of them, *L-11*, *L-13*, *L-16*, *L-17*, *L-20*, and *L-23*, were to bomb Britain during the night of 24–25 April and, on their return trip, perform reconnaissance for the fleet. Three other Zeppelins, *L-6*, *L-7*, and *L-9*, were assigned wholly to fleet reconnaissance. Thus, for the first time, the security of the *manoeuvre* was assured by a large-scale use of aircraft. . . .

There is no need to recount here the details of the Lowestoft affair, which one can find in the histories published on the subject. German operations proceeded as planned without any incident other than the temporary loss of the battle cruiser *Seydlitz* to a mine.[10] On 25 April, the German battle cruisers bombarded Lowestoft and Yarmouth before engaging the three light cruisers and eighteen destroyers of Commodore Tyrwhitt's[11] Harwich Force. At 0455 the German cruiser retired, shadowed by a battered Harwich Force, towards Scheer's main body.[12]

10. The *Seydlitz* was barely repaired in time for Jutland.

11. Commodore Sir Reginald Tyrwhitt (1870–1951), later Admiral of the Fleet.

12. Due to Hipper's illness, the German scouting force was commanded by Rear Admiral Friedrich Boedicker, whose four battle cruisers,

Admiral Scheer's order at 0930 for the High Seas Fleet to retire reflected two considerations. First, he had received information suggesting that British forces had been instructed to abandon the Belgian coast and would therefore not give battle that day. On the other, Scheer had already sent home his three reconnaissance dirigibles (*L-6, L-7,* and *L-9*) and three others that had arrived at dawn as reinforcements. Without aerial reconnaissance, he lacked complete information. Since *manoeuvre* in the North Sea rests essentially on security, Admiral Scheer naturally gave up *manoeuvre* after his security was seriously compromised. Nonetheless, his decision cost him yet another excellent opportunity to close with a badly dispersed British fleet.

By 24 April, intelligence had alerted the British to the German sortie, and at 1200 on 25 April the British forces were at sea in five groups. . . . The bulk of the Grand Fleet was 100 miles from the Firth of Forth. Thirty-five miles ahead and to the southeast were the Third Battle Squadron and Third Cruiser Squadron. The Fifth Battle Squadron was a further thirty-five miles ahead. The battle cruisers and their light cruisers were 110 miles farther out, while the Harwich Force was south, parallel with Yarmouth. Had the Germans not turned around at 0930, they would have encountered a completely dispersed British fleet. The British battle cruisers were particularly isolated and far from immediate help. At noon, in spite of the German turn, they were only forty-five miles from the German battle cruisers bringing up the rear of the procession towards the Helgoland Bight, and Admiral Scheer unknowingly missed exploiting

---

four light cruisers, two flotillas of destroyers, and submarines had an immense superiority of force over the Harwich Force but retired in the belief that Beatty's battle cruiser squadron lay in support of Tyrwhitt, Holger H. Herwig, *"Luxury" Fleet: The Imperial German Navy 1888–1918* (London, 1980): 174.

the very situation that his *manoeuvre* had been designed to achieve.

Moreover, examination of the routes shows that if the aerial reconnaissance had remained in place, *L-6*, whose post was to the southwest of Dogger Bank, would shortly after 1000 have detected the British battle cruisers heading towards the German main force and determined that no other British force followed them even at a distance. It would have signaled these facts to Scheer, who would have exploited the happy circumstance. The *manoeuvre*'s failure can be attributed to the lack of security stemming from the disappearance of the aerial reconnaissance.

The dispersion of the British forces, a result in part of the distribution of forces along the British coast, was a strategic weakness in all of the major operations that took place in the North Sea. . . . In April 1916, the Admiralty proposed as a remedy placing the Grand Fleet farther south at Rosyth or even in the Humber, and suggested as a provisional solution the detachment of the new Fifth Battle Squadron to the Firth of Forth and the incorporation of the battle cruisers into the fleet. Admiral Jellicoe,[13] who wished to preserve the new fast battleships of the Fifth Battle Squadron as his own *"masse de manoeuvre,"* turned a deaf ear, and the transfer of forces was put off until later.

In the meantime, the Germans bombarded Lowestoft, and public opinion demanded a regrouping of British forces to prevent further such incidents. At the Admiralty's insistence, Admiral Jellicoe agreed to send the Third Battle Squadron and the Third Cruiser Squadron from Rosyth to Sheerness, where they arrived on 2 May. . . . On the eve of the Battle

---

13. Admiral of the Fleet John Rushworth, First Earl Jellicoe (1859–1935), commanded the Grand Fleet 1914–1916 and was First Sea Lord 1916–1917.

of Jutland (31 May–1 June 1916), the principal British forces were distributed as follows: The bulk of the Grand Fleet (minus the Fifth Battle Squadron) and the Third Battle Cruiser Squadron were at Scapa Flow. The Second Battle Squadron was at Cromarty. The battle cruisers (minus the Third Squadron) and the Fifth Battle Squadron were at Rosyth. The Harwich flotillas were at home, and the Third Battle Squadron and Third Cruiser Squadron were at Sheerness. Thus, the earlier dispersion had been aggravated by further detachments to the south, and, on the day of the Battle of Jutland, the Admiralty would formally order the retention on the south coast of the Harwich and Sheerness forces. This scattering of resources could only facilitate the German plan.

The effect of coastal bombardments on enemy deployments is clear. While such operations produce only mediocre material results, their effect on morale can contribute to diversion, fixation, and, consequently, *manoeuvre,* to say nothing of the opportunities they offer for combat.

. . . The High Seas Fleet was also aided in its *manoeuvre* plans by the availability of a new weapon—the submarine. On the very day he returned from the Lowestoft raid, Admiral Scheer received from headquarters the information that the submarine war against commerce, resumed the previous month, would henceforth have to be conducted in conformity with the provisions of international law. That is, ships would not be sunk without warning, and personnel would have to be rescued. These restrictions resulted from protests by the United States following the sinking of the *Sussex* on 24 March 1916. In response to the new orders, which in his view vitiated the submarine war, Admiral Scheer informed headquarters that he would terminate the submarine campaign and summon home all of the submarines at sea. Henceforth, the submarine would collaborate with the High

Seas Fleet in the North Sea, aiding in both security and battle, and its contribution to *manoeuvre* would be a genuine innovation.

JUTLAND

In May Admiral Scheer returned to his customary *manoeuvre* idea, and to achieve it, he devised the following plan. Supposing, accurately enough, that the British fleet would be divided among the Scottish ports, the Humber, and the Channel bases, he contemplated having his battle cruisers and fastest destroyers bombard Sunderland at daybreak so as to draw out the enemy forces. During this time, the bulk of the High Seas Fleet would remain in support between Dogger Bank and Flamborough Head, ready to attack any isolated enemy contingent. Although he wanted to leave the old vessels of the Second Squadron in port, its commander's entreaties led him to include the squadron in the operation. The dirigibles would reconnoiter in the directions whence the British could be expected to come, that is, towards the Forth, the Humber, the Thames, and the Skagerrak.

The role planned for the submarines is particularly noteworthy.[14] At the suggestion of the submarine force commander, on 15 May nine submarines steamed to occupy a square about 150 miles on a side in the southern part of the North Sea. There they would wait from 17 to 23 May, watching for enemy forces and signaling their presence if necessary. After 23 May, they were to station themselves off the British coast for ten days, two submarines in front of Scapa Flow and the other seven at the Forth, before returning to base. One submarine was sent into the Firth of Forth itself on 20 May with instructions to return after four-

---

14. Castex gives more complete details in *Théories*, vol. 1, part 3, chapter 6.

teen days, and another was to remain on watch off the coast of Sunderland during the night of 21 to 22 May and then in the Peterhead region until 2 June. Three submarines were to lay mines in the Forth, off Cromarty, and in the western Orkneys. Two submarines steamed on 21 May to watch the Humber and were to remain off the estuary for ten days beginning 23 May, and two others were posted near Terschelling on 22 May. All of these submarine cruises had strict time limits. That they would have to break off their operations by 2 or 3 June would have great consequences.

The submarines' limited periods of action magnified the consequences of certain misfortunes that delayed the beginning of Scheer's operation and forced the Germans to acknowledge a grave impediment to the essential condition of *manoeuvre*—freedom of action. Planned for 17 May, the operation had first to be pushed back to 23 May because of damaged condensers in certain vessels of the Third Squadron. Then badly done repairs to the battle cruiser *Seydlitz* forced a further postponement to the 29th. That the submarines had already been sent out, however, meant that the starting date could be no later than 31 May. Bad weather predicted for 30 May prevented the necessary dirigible reconnaissance.

Faced with a cruel choice between waiting for good weather in order to use the dirigibles, and thereby renouncing the use of the submarines, or steaming at once while the submarines were on station but without aerial reconnaissance, Admiral Scheer determined on 28 May to act without air support and revised his *manoeuvre* plan in consequence. Abandoning the operation against Sunderland, he decided instead to act in the direction of the Skagerrak. Lacking aerial reconnaissance, he would rely on distance from the enemy and the proximity of the Danish coast. This was a *manoeuvre* of the second order, infinitely less brilliant than the original, of which it was a crude copy. To do better, however, was impossible except by abandoning the entire project.

Admiral Hipper, with the First and Second Scouting Groups (battle cruisers and light cruisers) and three destroyer flotillas, was to weigh anchor at the first hour of 31 May and appear before nightfall on the Norwegian coast. If on that day or the next he were to meet the British forces that were frequently reported in the vicinity, he was to try to destroy them or, should they prove to be superior to him, to draw them to the bulk of the High Seas Fleet that followed behind and would be about forty-five miles south of Cape Lindesnes at 0400 on 1 June.

But, by a singular coincidence, the British had at the same moment conceived of a similar plan. They, who until this time had done virtually nothing but await events, were going to take the initiative, to force the German fleet to battle, and, moreover, to do so with a *manoeuvre* approach. Two squadrons of light cruisers were to find themselves at daybreak on 2 June off Cape Skagen and steam southwards down the Kattegat in order to induce the Germans to send major forces to the north. The line and battle-cruiser squadrons would attempt to intercept the German main body from a position near Horn's Reef. A minefield and a line of submarines would also be in place in the German channel that ends near this point.[15] The British set aside their own plan, however, when they received on the morning of 30 May news of the imminent departure of the German High Seas Fleet. Learning at 1100 that the enemy would very probably sail on the morning of the 31st, they were further

15. Castex, who praises Scheer for his innovative incorporation of submarines in his *manoeuvre*, glosses over the parallel element in Jellicoe's plan and ignores the reconnaissance role assigned to the British seaplane carrier *Engadine*.

informed at 1700 of a major enemy operation planned for that very day. At 1740 the Admiralty ordered Admirals Jellicoe and Beatty to steam and to concentrate their forces in the usual manner. At 2230 the movement was executed, several hours ahead of the German movement.

Incontestably, though fortuitously, the Germans had the initiative in this affair. Their *manoeuvre* had trumped the other, forcing the enemy to abandon his prepared plan, but the excellent British intelligence that allowed them to be ready before the Germans largely compensated for their initial disadvantage.[16] While the Germans believed the Grand Fleet to be still in port and condemned to react in its usual fashion, tardily and in some disarray, the British were already at sea. On the other hand, however, the British found themselves irreparably divided, according to their usual faulty conception, into two groups separated by seventy miles and threatened by serious difficulties because Admiral Scheer had decided this time to keep his main force immediately behind Hipper's cruisers.

For his part, Admiral Scheer courted great risks due to inadequate security. Since weather conditions precluded reconnaissance by dirigible, everything depended on reports from submarines. The *U-32*, standing off the Forth, saw at 0410 and reported at 0537 two large warships, two cruisers, and several destroyers sixty miles east of the Forth *heading south* (these were Beatty's battle cruisers). The *U-66*, an hour later, signaled that at 0500 she had seen eight capital ships, light cruisers, and destroyers sixty miles east of Peterhead *heading northeast* (this was the Second Battle Squadron coming from Cromarty). The other submarines saw nothing.

The composition of the enemy groups, the divergence of

---

16. Castex's rigid score keeping gives the British no credit for having achieved the objective of bringing the High Seas Fleet to battle.

their courses, and their occurrence in advance of German movements led Scheer to deny any connection between British actions and his own operation. Rather than alarming him, a further report from the cryptographic station at Neumunster of a sortie from Scapa Flow temped Scheer to exploit the enemy's penchant for dispersal.

Thus, without any other intelligence about the enemy, Scheer moved to meet the British in the North Sea and experienced the very disagreeable surprise of finding himself unexpectedly nose to nose with the entire Grand Fleet. The complete breakdown of security on the German side placed them in the greatest possible peril.

The Battle of Jutland is too well-known to require recapitulation here, especially in a work that does not deal with tactical questions. From the point of view of strategic *manoeuvre*, a subject that is, however, central to this work, Jutland presents a curious tangle of entirely opposite, radically dissimilar situations linked not by coherent evolution but by the vicissitudes of chance. For a little more than twelve hours each adversary was unknowingly bounced by a sort of blind fate between a magnificent and a disastrous position, between two extreme poles of wonderful luck and black misfortune.

First Act—Shortly before making contact with the enemy on 31 May 1916, Beatty, alone and about seventy miles south of Jellicoe, was, due to British miscalculations, steaming almost due east. Had he continued in that direction, he would have inserted himself into the gap between Hipper and Scheer about forty miles from the former and twenty from the latter, that is, right into the pincers formed by the German battle cruisers on the one hand and battleships on the other. Scheer would finally have fulfilled his dream of crushing an isolated British detachment with superior forces. Fortune would have rewarded the Germans.

Second Act—Turnabout! At 1415 Admiral Beatty headed north, not because he had discerned the trap into which he had at first been going to stick his head, but simply because it was time to join Jellicoe. Pure luck. At a blow, the Germans' beautiful situation had vanished. It was Hipper now who, blindfolded, hurled himself towards Jellicoe even as Beatty was moving to join him. It was Hipper who would find himself alone in a clinch with the united British forces. The German position, magnificent as it had been, threatened rapidly to become disastrous.

Third Act—The disaster did not happen because, at 1420, the scouting forces of Beatty and Hipper met with the *Galatea* and *Phaeton* on the one side and the *Elbing* and two torpedo boats on the other.[17] Pure chance again. Beatty and Hipper engaged in combat and, turning to the south, headed towards Scheer and the High Seas Fleet. Each passing minute worsened Beatty's position. Thus, by this simple change of course, we return instantly to situation number one. Soon the British would find themselves taken into the trap that the German *manoeuvre* had prepared for months. It was Beatty's turn to march towards catastrophe.

Fourth Act—The catastrophe was averted because Beatty, perceiving the German van at 1640, steered back to the north away from the united forces of Hipper and Scheer and towards Jellicoe. Though Hipper no longer faced the prospect of a single combat with the entire British fleet, the German position was far from brilliant as the Grand and High Seas Fleets steamed towards a battle that Scheer did not want and that his entire plan was designed to avoid.

Fifth Act—The encounter so feared by the Germans took place; the High Seas Fleet was gripped in a mortal embrace—only to be saved by fortune from certain destruction.

---

17. Light forces of both sides had stopped to investigate the same Danish merchant vessel.

Admiral Jellicoe's hesitations, his formation's slowness to maneuver, his "turn away," Scheer's desperate improvisation, the lateness of the hour, in a word, the proverbial combination of fate and friction[18] allowed the German fleet finally to disengage.

Sixth Act—But the escape could only be temporary. The Germans, whose sole direction of retreat was no secret to the enemy, could not expect to elude pursuit during the hours of a too-short summer night. It was certain that the two forces would meet again at dawn and that the fate of the High Seas Fleet was indelibly written. No! And no again! For chance, if one really wishes to use that name for the errors committed by Admiral Jellicoe in interpreting the information he received, caused the British to head towards the northwest channel of the Helgoland Bight, while the Germans steered for the Horn's Reef channel.[19] At daybreak on 1 June, the Germans had no British ships in view. Though Scheer's *manoeuvre* had failed, he was allowed to escape a total catastrophe.

In sum, Jutland appears to us as a strategic drama in six acts, which for the German actor gives the impression of being a sort of "Scotch shower."[20]

Admiral Scheer's *manoeuvre* idea was certainly seductive. Since it should have succeeded on more than one occasion when all that was required was the creation of a favorable situation for a few hours, its lack of success cannot justify its summary condemnation. The facts do, however, reveal the hazards that *manoeuvre* presents. . . . Jutland reaffirmed the lesson of 16 December 1914, that *manoeuvre* de-

18. *"Fatalités et frottements."*

19. Jellicoe's guess that Scheer would take the Ems Channel, the longest and most southerly route, proved wrong but need not have been, Marder, vol. 3, 135–38, 150–52.

20. That is, one alternately hot and cold.

mands security. One must have, if not absolute security, at least sufficient intelligence concerning all enemy units. But how can the side forced to *manoeuvre* in consequence of numerical inferiority safely carry out the necessary reconnaissance to prepare and secure that *manoeuvre*? The problem is almost irresolvable and well explains why in these conditions there arose among the Germans[21] the very interesting idea of using other weapons, such as submarines and aircraft, to provide security. These units run only insignificant risks compared to those awaiting surface reconnaissance units and are always more or less free to escape. . . .

But submarines are slow and have little range, especially if circumstances compel frequent dives, while aircraft have limited range and duration of action. Security can only be achieved by these means if they are in place at the desired moment, that is, if one has the initiative and can impose a perceived plan upon the enemy. This observation is of special relevance to the present *manoeuvre*.

19 AUGUST 1916

When they began to prepare for the next operation, the Germans knew perfectly well, exaggerated claims notwithstanding, that Jutland had been an extraordinarily lucky escape. It is regrettable that Admiral Scheer, who has just title to our high esteem and even our admiration, compromised the excellent opinion that one ought to have of him by his later tasteless boasts about the spirit reigning in the German fleet on the morning of 1 June after it had returned precipitously to port in order to escape the British fleet.[22] Lieutenant

21. Whose means of surface reconnaissance were notably inferior to those of the British (author's note).

22. "Just as dawn was about to break on this historic day, June 1st, everyone expected to see the rising sun reveal the British line of battle

Commander von Hase's report more honestly expresses the indescribable relief with which the Germans surveyed the empty seas on 1 June. This sentiment and the fall in morale that resulted from it are what really made Jutland a German defeat—incomplete, certainly, but a defeat nonetheless—whatever the results of the material calculations done after the battle.

That the dominant note on the German side was apprehension and pessimism about such future undertakings is revealed in the admiral's new enthusiasm for submarine warfare against commerce. During the Kaiser's visit to the fleet on 5 June 1916, Scheer told him that "the atmosphere is favorable for the renewal of rigorous economic warfare." Scheer's *Memoirs* put great emphasis on the prospects for commercial war during June 1916, and he wrote to the general staff that "the essence of naval war is to annihilate enemy commerce." On 20 June, he again advocated unrestricted submarine warfare, arguing that if the fleet's submarines were not used for this purpose, he would withdraw them from all other military use. On 30 June, he praised the submarine war to the chancellor, who had come to visit the fleet.[23]

But Admiral Scheer must have known that to divert the submarines to the war against commerce would prevent

---

deployed ready to renew the combat. This hope (?) was not to be fulfilled" (author's note).

23. In his report to the Kaiser of 4 July 1916, Scheer proclaimed that "there is no doubt but that even the greatest success in battle will not force Britain to make peace. The fleet cannot neutralize the military disadvantages of our geographic situation compared to that of the island empire and the enemy's enormous material advantages even if they were devoted entirely to military objectives. One can only achieve a victorious end to the war within a reasonable period of time through the ruin of the British economy, a result that can be achieved only by devoting the submarine arm to the struggle against British commerce" (author's note).

their use in combination with the High Seas Fleet. It meant depriving *manoeuvre* of a trump card or even renouncing *manoeuvre* altogether. Thus, his sudden and misplaced enthusiasm for the submarine war as a single panacea reflected lost faith in *manoeuvre*. Scalded as von Ingenohl had been on 19 December 1914, but more severely, Admiral Scheer, too, had seen his illusions undermined. His new uncertainties explain the tentativeness of the last German *manoeuvre* effort, that of 19 August 1916. . . .

Though prepared without great conviction, the sortie of 19 August demonstrated, nonetheless, great technical progress in the employment and combinations of different weapons for *manoeuvre*. At Jutland, submarines had been deployed in static ambushes off the British bases, a major investment of force that had brought only slight return at high risk. Immovably fixed in advance, these submarine had not been available for *manoeuvre*. This time, the Germans would arrange their submarines in a series of lines, one capable of moving in conjunction with the High Seas Fleet. Assigned primarily to destroy enemy warships, they contributed to security by sending reports of what they saw.

Admiral Scheer wanted more than ever to entrust his security to aircraft, to dirigibles. Overly impressed perhaps by the raids against Britain, which had no relevance to the problems of reconnaissance at sea, he exaggerated the visual range of the isolated dirigible. Moreover, when he proposed to begin his next *manoeuvre* with another bombardment of Sutherland, he supposed that the Grand Fleet would not move until alerted by the bombardment and would therefore still be at Scapa Flow that morning. Granted these conditions, sufficient warning of the fleet's approach could be assured by placing a line of dirigibles at the latitude of Peterhead during the morning, but events would demonstrate the precariousness of this gratuitous assumption.

A change from the usual practice was that the bombardment of Sunderland was scheduled to begin not at dawn but at the end of the day on 19 August 1916 so as to allow the German fleet to sail from the Helgoland Bight on the previous night, with consequently little chance of being seen, and to benefit from the reconnaissance by submarines and dirigibles during the day preceding his arrival on the English coast. Complete secrecy was to be ensured. Radio would be used as sparingly as possible, and at the moment of sailing, both the transmission frequency and the cipher key would be changed.

The advance guard, weakened because two battle cruisers were under repair[24] and another had been sunk at Jutland,[25] would be reinforced by three fast battleships. In addition, the distance to the main body would be reduced to a mere twenty miles to avoid the risks clearly demonstrated by the events at Jutland. Finally, this time the old Second Squadron would stay in port.

The *manoeuvre* of 19 August 1916 was provided with a protective skeleton of unprecedented scale that perfectly utilized the aptitudes of the submarine and air arms for the tasks required of them. At the latitude of Peterhead (Scotland), Scheer placed an east-west barrage of three dirigibles, the *L-30*, *L-32*, and *L-22*, covering the northern egress of the North Sea. Other dirigibles took station along the length of the British coast: the *L-31* at the Forth, the *L-11* at the Tyne, the *L-21* at the Humber, and the *L-13* in the southern part of the North Sea. There were four lines of submarines, two of them perpendicular to the British coast, almost at the height of the Tyne and Flamborough Head, and two

24. *Derfflinger* and *Seydlitz*.
25. *Lützow*.

others on both sides of the minefield northwest of Terschelling.[26]

Behind this screen, Admiral Scheer expected to be able, in complete security, to achieve his perennial desire of mauling one part of the British fleet while being guaranteed, thanks to timely forewarning, against intervention by their main force. He intended to enjoy the maximum degree of protection, exactly what he had lacked at Jutland. Security, which appeared so complete, would collapse, however, at the moment of need!

Admiral Scheer assumed that the Grand Fleet would not steam from Scapa Flow until sometime during the day of 19 August, when his own movements would have been revealed to it, and that the northern Zeppelin line would need only be in position that morning to provide warning. Thus, the Zeppelins were entirely in place only at 1000. At that hour, however, the Grand Fleet, which had been warned by certain indications and had steamed from Scapa Flow at 1800 on 18 August, was already south of the pickets, which, ignorant of the fleet's movement, remained there unaware of their uselessness.[27] Confident in his northern picket line and the excellent visibility, Admiral Scheer enjoyed during this time the most dangerous tranquility.

The reconnaissance reports he received were not of a sort to trouble him. A little after 0600 on 19 August, the *L-13,* in the south, signaled the presence of destroyer flotillas and

26. In the course of the action these lines, in particular the last two, moved considerably in response to the demands of the fleet (author's note). Twenty-four submarines were assigned to the operation, Marder, vol. 3, 236.

27. Warned by radio interceptions of the German fleet's departure time, the Grand Fleet steamed at 1600 on 18 August 1916, the Battle Cruiser Fleet at 1820, and the High Seas Fleet last of all at 2100, Marder, vol. 3, 237.

light cruisers steaming southwest and then northeast. At 0800, the radio intercept facility post at Neumunster reported that the British forces seemed to be at sea but did not give their location. At 1000, the *L-31* reported that at 0900 she had seen "large forces" off the Forth but gave neither course nor speed. Shortly thereafter, the *L-31* indicated a sighting at 0950 of the "principal forces" of the enemy in a position much different from the first report and wrong, incidentally, by more than sixty miles. Also at 1000, Neumunster reported that the Grand Fleet was at sea but, again, did not report its position.

Then the submarines entered the scene. At 1010, the *U-53* announced that she had seen "three capital ships and four light cruisers *heading north*" at 0810 in a position close to that of the *L-31*'s first report. At 1140, the *U-52* indicated that at 0700 she had encountered four light cruisers *heading north* and had sunk one (the *Nottingham*). Though the *L-11* spotted the British forces at 1100, she did not report anything.

In sum, by noon all of this information gave Admiral Scheer a completely inaccurate picture of the situation. He believed that there were two light squadrons in the south, which was not far from the truth, and that in the north there were numerous separated forces whose divergent, but generally northward, courses indicated ordinary patrolling activities and ignorance of his own arrival.[28] The northern forces had, however, been heading towards him since 0900, and by holding his course, the unsuspecting Admiral Scheer impaled himself ever more deeply on the enemy blade.

At midday, many British radio messages were heard. Admiral Scheer, who thought that the submarine that had tor-

---

28. The effect was the same produced by submarine reports on the morning of Jutland (author's note).

pedoed the *Westfalen*[29] in the morning had reported the German sortie and that the British reaction was only commencing at that moment, was terribly far behind actual events.

Thus had the magnificent security system so carefully prepared in advance failed to warn Scheer of the precipice towards which he rushed and of the complete ruin of his *manoeuvre*. On the point of being destroyed by false intelligence reports, Scheer was going to be saved by another, also false, report!

At 1222, he received from the *L-13* to the south a message reporting "large naval forces, approximately thirty ships, steaming north." Shortly thereafter, a second message announced with greater precision "thirty ships, comprising sixteen destroyers, heavy and light cruisers, and *battleships* sailing towards you between 1130 and 1200 in the area of Swarte Bank." This, however, was only the Harwich Force, which was heading north at the time and which never included battleships. Upon receiving the first of these two telegrams, at 1223, Admiral Scheer made a half-turn. At 1245, he changed course to the west to recover his advance guard and, having met it, turned east-southeast at 1315 and, at 1400, southeast.

This rapid about-face has given rise to discussion that continues to the present day. Some have interpreted it as a simple retreat stimulated by Scheer's awareness of the difficulty of his position and unwillingness to repeat the experience of Jutland. I would be inclined to accept this hypothesis, which the rapidity of Scheer's reflex renders very credible. On the other hand, the admiral claims in his *Memoirs* that he had concluded from the reports of the *L-13* that

---

29. The *E-23* torpedoed SMS *Westfalen*, the last ship in Scheer's line, at 0505 on 19 December 1916, 60 miles north of Terschelling, Marder, vol. 3, 241.

a fairly major but inferior enemy force lay to the south and that he had gone southeast in the hope of intercepting it, even sending a flotilla of destroyers to reconnoiter in that direction. By this account, he was obeying his *manoeuvre* idea, except that he steamed towards a phantom target produced by a failure of aerial reconnaissance.

Whatever the case, while hastening southeast, Admiral Scheer received a new report. At 1415, the *U-53* signaled that at 1315 the Grand Fleet had been seventy-five miles east of Hartlepool, heading south, a position wrong by twenty-three miles. A little later, the same submarine indicated that the enemy's main body comprised only ten battleships, which was also inaccurate. At 1420, the *L-20* reported that at 1415 she had seen isolated enemy forces heading south in the same area.

Admiral Scheer now had every reason to think that the Grand Fleet, which he had believed to be dispersed, was steaming towards him threateningly from the north. At 1515, not having succeeded in catching the group that he fancied himself to be pursuing, he changed course to east-northeast and definitely headed home to the Helgoland Bight while the Harwich Force retained very distant contact.[30]

We now know that Scheer was saved by two unexpected events. First, the *L-13*'s erroneous news led him to make a lucky half-turn. Second, the Grand Fleet, which would have moved inexorably to contact had it continued on the course taken early on 19 August, had detoured north-northeast at

30. Marder's reconstruction puts the *L-13*'s first message at 1203, the second at 1222, and a third at 1250. The first led Scheer to turn south towards what he believed to be significant enemy forces. Unable to catch his prey, which would have proved to be the Harwich Force, he headed home at 1435 in response to a message from the *U-53* establishing the Grand Fleet's position sixty-five miles to the north, Marder, vol. 3, 242–43.

0700 in response to the torpedoing of the *Nottingham* and had only reverted to a southward course at 0900. This pernicious detour created a delay that the Grand Fleet could not make up. Furthermore, the first confirmation of the High Seas Fleet's sortie, the *E-23*'s report after torpedoing the *Westfalen,* was received only at 1010 and incorrectly placed Scheer far behind his actual position. The Grand Fleet concluded from this information that there was no need to hurry, and Admiral Jellicoe's keenness to encounter the Germans began to decline from this moment.

Thus, the German *manoeuvre* had again misfired. Catastrophe had again been averted, in spite of the failure of security and—a curious note—even because of it (the case of the *L-13*). Security had proved deficient, moreover, even though Admiral Scheer had understood its preeminent importance. In spite of his efforts, the northern picket line of Zeppelins was put out of the picture at the first blow. The reconnaissance craft sent incomplete or false intelligence. Position reports erred by as much as twenty-three miles for the submarines and forty-five and sixty miles for the dirigibles. In other cases, the scouts signaled incorrect enemy courses or failed to indicate course and speed at all (*U-31*). Sometimes they forgot to fix the position of the perceived elements (*U-52*). Other vessels failed to recognize what they saw (*L-11*). The *L-13*, finally, proved to be possessed of an overflowing imagination. Thanks to these errors, Scheer remained until noon, in spite of his precautions, in a state of mind dangerously removed from reality.

Taken as a whole, even this well-prepared *manoeuvre* turned out to be fragile and problematic. Progress had been made since Jutland, but much remained to be done. The Germans did profit in their *manoeuvre* from taking the initiative of operations. The initiative permitted the calculated placement of a submarine and aerial screen that, ineffective though it proved in its security function, would have done better in combat. That the two light cruisers *Nottingham* and *Falmouth* were torpedoed by submarines made a profound impression on the mind of Admiral Jellicoe, who expressed after 19 August 1916 the firm intention to renounce future engagements of the Grand Fleet south of Dogger Bank. To him the southern region appeared entirely contaminated. The Germans were there, however, though in much less force than Jellicoe imagined, only because they took the initiative and because they had deployed their submarines for their *manoeuvre* plan. The British could have entered the same zone four days later without meeting a single submarine. The area was not, therefore, completely barred to the British. Moreover, can we not attribute the lack of success by the British submarines on 19 August to their lack of initiative, to the need to respond to the enemy *manoeuvre*?

A comparison of the operations of 19 August 1916, 28 August 1914 (the Battle of Helgoland), and 4 May 1916 (British raid against Tondern) suggests the extent to which the German action gained from the exercise of the initiative in operations and lost from its absence.

Happily for the British, however, 19 August 1916 marked the final twilight of German *manoeuvre*. With the decision in mid-October to begin the submarine war against commerce again, the High Seas Fleet saw itself deprived, with Scheer's full consent, of all of its submarines. Without this essential arm of *manoeuvre,* the High Seas Fleet would henceforth effect only the tiny sortie of 19 October 1916. . . .

The material results of the German efforts at *manoeuvre* in the North Sea from 1914 to 1916 were virtually zero.

181

The German fleet inflicted some losses on the British fleet, but it did not free itself from its bonds nor, still less, did it seize control of maritime communications from the enemy or even partially reestablish them for Germany. To do this, it would have been necessary to put the Grand Fleet out of action by battle. The Germans tried to eliminate the Grand Fleet indirectly, by means of *manoeuvres* designed to destroy it one part at a time, but nothing came of their effort. All the activity that we have witnessed cannot conceal their essential lack of success. . . .

If German *manoeuvre* always failed, let us hurry to add that it was always attempted under conditions rendered strongly unfavorable by the special geographical and atmospheric features of the North Sea, the speed of the two adversaries, the ephemeral nature and rapid evolution of the situations, the difficulty of ensuring security, and the superiority of the British intelligence service.

Moreover, these attempts at *manoeuvre,* in spite of their lack of success, are interesting to study and contain lessons. First, their setting resembles that which is encountered today in a number of theaters of operations and especially in European waters where *manoeuvre* will no longer find the favorable conditions of the past. The events that occurred in the North Sea in the course of the last war can usefully serve as a base for prudent and rational extrapolation.

Finally, Admiral Scheer has shown us—one cannot forget it—how a belligerent who is inferior on the surface and reduced to the defensive can manipulate new weapons to attempt to *manoeuvre* in spite of the obstacles that oppose him everywhere. He shows us not to give up, not to be deterred from every enterprise by adverse conditions. Above all, he has taught us how one can give to the defensive an active and relatively offensive character, how one can avoid depressing inaction and absolute stagnation and, disadvantaged as one may be, conserve to the end the initiative in operations, and, thereby, the morale factors that are the supreme reserve for the future. These are more than enough reasons for us to pay homage to this persistently tenacious practitioner of *manoeuvre*.

CHAPTER 9

STRATEGIC
MANOEUVRE
IN OUR DAY[1]

E VEN THE most recent of the preceding historical analyses[2] will have only a Platonic value unless rounded out
by a brief look at the nature of *manoeuvre* in the present
and the immediate future. . . . *Manoeuvre* has been transformed both externally, that is, in its geographical framework, and internally, in the tools that it employs. . . .

Geographically, the battle theaters should be fairly limited
in scale, smaller at least than the immense areas allowed to
or imposed upon belligerents of other days. The most likely
future maritime conflicts will occur in circumscribed regions. . . . Even where the adversaries are separated by
large expanses of ocean, the theater of operations will tend
to be on one coast or the other for reasons having to do
with the need for bases and the range of action of surface
vessels and airplanes. The validity of this conclusion is made
clear from studying hypothetical wars between, for example,
Britain and the United States or the United States and Japan.

1. Raoul Castex, *Théories stratégiques*, 2nd ed., vol. 2 (Paris: Société
d'Editions Géographiques, Maritimes et Coloniales, 1939): 291–313.
2. This chapter follows the chapters analyzing *manoeuvres* by Bruix
in 1799, Villeneuve in 1805, von Spee in 1914, and Germany in World
War I.

. . . Fighting in smaller arenas deprives *manoeuvre* of the benefits that are provided by large distances. A force too weak to immobilize the enemy cannot hope to compensate by exploiting space. . . .

The impact of smaller theaters of operations on *manoeuvre* is exacerbated by the increased speed of surface ships. Distance as conceived in terms of duration of travel is effectively shrunk by speed. Thus, the framework of the struggle has been twice contracted, first in linear distance and then in time. . . . The high speed of surface vessels, very high speed of aerial elements, and infinite speed, as it were, of communications, all combine to shorten the duration and increase the rapidity of events. *Manoeuvre* finds itself thrown into the maelstrom that has transformed everything in our day. It is a film projected at high speed compared to the slow motion of the past, and we find ourselves struggling with difficulties unknown to our predecessors.

One of the direct consequences of these changes is the diminished duration of the favorable situation. That is *manoeuvre*'s aim. Now the enemy is likely to arrive and turn the situation, which has become transitory, around. Decisions must be rapid and exploitation of the situation aggressive.

The impact of the internal factors—the submarine, the airplane, mines, and communications—on strategic *manoeuvre* can be assessed adequately by examining how each side will use them in both the principal and secondary theaters and in terms of both combat and security. . . .

In the principal theater, or in regard to the principal objective, the submarine contributes to *manoeuvre* as a combatant. The employment of the submarine in *manoeuvre* here is profitable and conforms to the principles of combined arms[3] and concentration of force. . . .[4] As the arrangements made by Admiral Scheer for the *manoeuvre* of 19 August 1916 demonstrate, the submarine functions particularly well in indirect liaison with surface vessels and when serving as one component of a deployment in depth. In the principal theater, submarines should not be immobilized in static positions outside of harbors or in picket lines but stationed ready to participate in *manoeuvre*. Their effectiveness will obviously be intensified if some kind of bait, a threat against a point on the enemy coast or the appearance of a friendly convoy, for example, draws the enemy out and forces him to take a predictable course.[5] One can see the extent to which having the initiative enhances the action of submarines.

As an instrument of security, the submarine is of secondary importance in the principal theater. Security itself, although always of appreciable value, is not of capital importance here, and it is primarily achieved by the advantage we gain by taking the initiative.[6]

Enemy submarines naturally constitute a danger, especially in the principal theater, but less so than people believe. They certainly call for taking constant precautions, but no defense against the submarine works better than speed, activity, and initiative, the very qualities required by *manoeuvre* itself, and one's own *manoeuvre* therefore provides a certain automatic guarantee. The enemy submarines

3. The importance of combined arms is the theme of Castex's *La liaison des armes sur mer,* Coutau-Bégarie, ed. (Paris, 1991).

4. *"Masse"* to Castex.

5. . . . the use of such bait to bring about battle does not by itself constitute a favorable *manoeuvre* as long as the enemy can appear at the chosen point with excessive force (author's note).

6. In analyzing Sheer's *manoeuvre,* however, Castex stresses the primary importance of security, which he elsewhere calls "the soul of *manoeuvre,"* above, 111.

will perhaps prove more troublesome in their role as agents of security.[7] Even if unable to attack the oncoming fleet, they can ruin the *manoeuvre* by locating it and depriving it of the essential advantage of surprise.

In the secondary theaters or for secondary objectives, submarines can be very useful combatants because they are difficult to get rid of, do not themselves run great risks, and serve to immobilize the enemy's light surface and air units. . . . Also, their diversions against enemy coasts or communications can contribute greatly to a planned *manoeuvre*. Because submarines are so useful in secondary theaters, their deployment there implies an economy of force greater than that achieved by deploying surface vessels and that ought to be taken into account in distributing resources between the primary and secondary theaters.

The submarine has an equally great value in secondary theaters as an element of security and is entirely suited to guard against events in unexpected directions. Although too slow to function as scouts or reconnaissance vessels, submarines can as least cooperate in surveillance. Placed in warning posts along the probable routes of enemy units, they can ward off disagreeable events.

On the other hand, the submarine is less useful to the enemy in secondary theaters, because he will be challenged there only by limited forces whose actions will not be seriously hindered by submarines acting in either a combat or a security role. Offering little target to the former, they are virtually indifferent to being reported by the latter.

In sum, if the appearance of the submarine has noticeably changed the execution of *manoeuvre,* it has not disturbed its general conduct. The submarine's relatively minor impact, especially in contrast to revolutionary expectations once held for it, can possibly be explained by its lack of speed.

7. That is, in their reconnaissance and screening roles.

The submarine has not shared in that general evolution towards speed that we noted above.[8] If the mine is immobile, the submarine suffers from a semi-immobility relative to the other instruments of modern war. It is like an ox cart in the face of the automobile. . . . Its star pales a bit from the special point of view of *manoeuvre* in spite of the contribution that it brings to it. This conclusion, however necessary, implies no denigration of the submarine's other important qualities and its usefulness for missions appropriate to its capabilities.

The participation of aviation in our *manoeuvre* in the principal theater or towards the principal objective is completely consistent with the principles of combined arms and concentration of forces. The great mobility of the air arm promises rapid and massive concentrations of force under certain conditions of distance, that is, geography. The speed of aviation is considerable, while its range increases daily but remains limited. Finally, since the period during which an airplane can remain aloft remains brief in the context of a major operation, aviation can contribute only when the action is compressed into fairly tight time limits. To make its intervention effective at the chosen point requires taking the initiative in the action. One must not forget, moreover, that aircraft carriers can supply only a limited number of planes, and that successful aerial attacks will always require the cooperation of land-based aircraft. By being able to pursue and attack the enemy from the air, airplanes can also prevent his surface forces from confounding our *manoeuvre* altogether by taking refuge in port.

8. The submarine's surface speed has increased in recent years with growing displacements but remains much inferior to that of the new surface vessels and, more important, submerged speed has improved only insignificantly (author's note).

The use of aviation as an instrument of security concerns us less in the principal theater because, as we argued above in reference to the submarine, security is not fundamental there. Conversely, in the same theater, the enemy's combat air power poses a serious threat to surface vessels of which we have already spoken at length elsewhere.[9] Though enemy air action may inflict losses, it cannot itself block *manoeuvre* or render it impotent. Incontestably, however, aviation introduces a new factor because it makes possible a defensive reaction so rapid compared to the speed of surface ships that the latter lose much of the advantage that they once drew from taking the initiative. But, as a corrective, one must add that there are defenses against aviation, the best of them being the achievement of air superiority at the relevant point. Air superiority requires that one has the initiative of operations, which retains its value once again.

If scouting by aircraft is of only minor importance to the attacker in the principal theater, it greatly assists the defender in warding off attack. Permitting the enemy to see clearly into our hand, to be warned of our approach and of the blow that we wish to strike, a single airplane's prying look may suffice totally to ruin our *manoeuvre* combination.

In the secondary theaters, the situation is identical but the players are reversed. The attacker's combat aircraft will have a secondary role and cannot be relied upon to stop the enemy forces, though, because security in these regions is absolutely essential, his aerial reconnaissance will be of capital importance. That the enemy's combat airplanes may efficaciously oppose our operations in the secondary theaters need not be disquieting since these operations are intended precisely to keep away from the main arena of operations the largest possible enemy force, especially his airplanes. As

9. Castex, *Théories*, vol. 1, part 3, chapter 7 (author's note).

for the security that they can furnish our adversary, it will not be a great boon to him because our principal attack is not oriented in this direction.

For each of the cases envisaged above, some important reservations must be made about the airplane's contribution to missions of intelligence. Theoretically, aviation excels in this function, supplying both combatants with a clear view of things. Clarifying the most tangled situation, it promises to render impossible the risks, the surprise blows, that we saw at Jutland or even on 16 December 1914. In practice, however, as the example of 19 August 1916 demonstrates, aviation's claims must be moderated. Bad weather can paralyze airplanes, which cannot pierce rain, snow, fog, or the shadows of night. An airplane can inaccurately report the forces it sees. It may wrongly calculate their position through uncertainty about its own. Sometimes, as we have seen, it fails to send any report at all. Finally, its technical difficulties may render communication impossible. Thus, it would be imprudent to rely entirely on aviation to assure security. In particular, it is a good idea not to accept negative aerial reports with blind faith but to act upon them only after considering other sources of information.

On the other hand, one is not entirely at the mercy of enemy aerial surveys. Even if their reconnaissance is not hindered by unfavorable circumstances, the speed of modern surface ships permits night voyages of 250 to 300 miles and allows appreciable opportunities for surprise in spite of the security efforts of aircraft. Moreover, there are cases where the enemy's air reconnaissance, though effective, is irrelevant because he is too weak to attack even with complete and up to date intelligence.

From this rapid overview of the influence of two new weapons arise several general conclusions about contemporary *manoeuvre*. Generally, the side intending to *manoeuvre* will find that the submarine and the airplane contribute combat power in the principal theater or against the principal objective and security in the secondary theaters and against secondary objectives. It is the reverse for the side that is the target of *manoeuvre.*

As the events of 19 August 1916 demonstrate, exploitation of the *manoeuvre* potential of the airplane and the submarine absolutely requires the initiative of operations, which is the foundation of *manoeuvre.* Initiative gains in importance for the weaker party, the one with the greater problems to overcome in order to create a favorable situation.

The conditions of *manoeuvre* in a modern theater of operations make the notion of security even more important than in the past, and, if the submarine and the airplane are powerful additions to security, two shadows darken the balance between the increased demand for security and the improved means of achieving it. In the first place, the new agents reinforce not only our security but that of our enemy. No one, obviously, monopolizes an improvement of technique or of armament, but we do well to remind ourselves that the security improvements work against us also. In the second place, however good the new tools, absolute security never exists and we must never forget its probable deficiencies.

Rapid communications—telephone, telegraph, and, especially, radio—allow high commands to coordinate elements far removed from direct control. They provide the possibility of very quickly sending information or intelligence provided by diverse sources—even if the accuracy of the information can no more be guaranteed than in the past.

In *manoeuvre,* rapid communications generally favor the defender because he wants to use the forces of the secondary theaters to reinforce the primary theater.[10] On the other hand, they work to the disadvantage of the attacker's principal attack and diversions.

The role of neutral ships in the propagation of news is naturally multiplied by technological innovation. As if telegraphs were not enough, it is now possible to send information immediately by radio. Even without radio, a cargo ship that happens upon a naval fleet can report at its next port of call the fleet's composition, position, and route. One can acquire very important information by this means or, alternatively, find one's principal attack severely compromised.

What remains now of the old method of hampering the enemy by using false intelligence to lure him in the wrong direction? Not much, certainly, at least in most cases. The effect of such fraud will now be brief and limited. Information from many sources, quickly transmitted, will promptly correct the enemy's errors.

The benefit that the radio brings in the diffusion of intelligence and enhancement of security contains its own antithesis as well. Having no discretion as to who receives its messages, radio furnishes intelligence to the enemy, who exploits it by means of interception, decryption, and radio direction finding. Secrecy and surprise disappear because one can rarely abstain altogether from radio transmission in the course of an operation. *Manoeuvre* must defend against enemy curiosity, particularly so as not to reveal the principal attack prematurely. . . .

In our day, strategic *manoeuvre* suffers from some new and grave restraints on its freedom of action. We have already noted the vulnerability of surface vessels to subma-

---

10. Castex at his most obscure: *"quand on cherche à déjouer des réactions des théâtres secondaires sur le théâtre principal c'est à dire dans la partie négative de l'affaire."*

rines, aircraft, and mines and will pass over the subject except to note that the effect of mines depends on the theater of operations. In some regions, the North Sea for example, mines are very much to be feared because the shallow water allows them to be sown everywhere. In the Mediterranean, however, minefields will be in limited and well-known areas and will offer only a slight impediment to movement. Improvements allowing mines to be laid at greater depths are to be expected, as are more sophisticated types that are more difficult to sweep or neutralize.

A still more important restriction on freedom of action is the limited range of oil-burning ships. This is a permanent constraint, which exists in every time and every place. . . . It is a good thing that the conditions of present and future wars tend to restrict the field of battle, but one cannot be too hasty, however, in reckoning up gains here. If the distances of travel have diminished, security now requires travel at such great speed as to negate the gain.

Also, since security demands protection by torpedo boats or small vessels, the whole force finds its range of action limited by that of the flotilla, which, though much improved recently, remains below that of capital ships. . . . The need to refuel after two or three days at sea will continue to pose a heavy constraint on *manoeuvre*.

In sum, our era has created for strategic *manoeuvre* difficulties that increase its risks and diminish its chances of success. Very happily, however, on the other hand, various new resources permit us to struggle to defend ourselves. *Manoeuvre* remains the object, promising to achieve major results in itself, to maintain the initiative, and to avoid yielding it to the enemy. The duration of favorable opportunities has obviously much diminished, but it remains sufficient since, with modern weapons, a short space of time suffices to eliminate a naval force. By the same token, a short span of time suffices for an important convoy to pass safely through or to undertake operations against the enemy coast. If this condition of rapid decision is satisfied, one can content oneself with a brief window of opportunity, and *manoeuvre* is to be recommended. But *manoeuvre* must not aim too high in expecting a favorable situation to last longer than today's circumstances allow.

A means exists for visualizing the subtle evolution of military methods over time. It consists of choosing a representative case from the past and examining how the actors of that day would behave if they were to return to earth today and face a similar situation with modern tools. Though well known, the procedure is, unfortunately, little practiced, despite the important educational and professional benefits it offers soldiers. Let us apply the method to strategic *manoeuvre* and ask, for example, how Bruix's campaign in the Mediterranean would have unrolled had it taken place in 1930 with today's machines replacing those of 1799.[11]

Let us first note the initial positions of the two adversaries. In April 1930, Bridport blockades Bruix at Brest, but in the modern fashion with his main force stationed at Plymouth and the close blockade entrusted to light surface vessels and to submarines placed at the exits of the Four, the Iroise, and the Raz-de-Sein.[12] British and French minefields seal off the area but with channels for the defender. British aviation, based on the other side of the Channel, periodically examines Brest harbor and the ships anchored there. The airplanes drop bombs from time to time, and French planes

---

11. Castex analyzes the 1799 campaign in *Théories*, vol. 2, chapter 3.

12. Close blockade became obsolete with the steam ship, which gave blockaders a limited endurance on station and allowed the blockaded to act independently of the wind. Also, the invention of mines and torpedo boats barred capital ships from inshore activities.

respond in kind. Keith[13] uses similar methods to blockade Mazzaredo in Cadiz from Gibraltar.[14] In 1799, Admiral Duckworth[15] and Nelson are at Minorca and Palermo, respectively. The numbers are the same as in 1799, except that the ships of the line are replaced by contemporary cruisers of 10,000 tons.[16]

On 26 April 1930, Bruix steams from Brest, taking advantage as he did before of bad weather and very poor visibility.[17] His scouts chase to open sea a patrolling British light vessel (the *Nymph* of today), which loses contact.[18] Meanwhile, the bulk of the fleet takes the mine-swept channel out to sea. Bruix steers southwest, preceded by his mine-sweepers, which he sends home as soon as he thinks himself outside of the mined area. The sole British submarine scouting south of Raz-du-Sein is harassed by surface patrols that have been particularly active since morning and has to re-

13. At the time of Bruix's breakout from Brest, Admiral Lord Keith was in the process of relieving the ailing St. Vincent as commander in chief in the Mediterranean.

14. Assuming, which is pure fiction, that Gibraltar would be usable as a base in the case of an Anglo-Spanish war (author's note).

15. Admiral John Duckworth (1748–1817).

16. Mazzaredo's Spanish fleet at Cadiz comprised eighteen ships of the line and eight or nine others lacking crews. Melgarejo had five or six at Ferrol. The French had no significant naval force in the Mediterranean after the battle of the Nile, but Bruix had twenty-five ships of the line, six frigates, and seven corvettes at Brest. Keith had sixteen ships of the line in the Mediterranean, Duckworth four at Minorca, Nelson nine, and Rear Admiral Sir Alexander Ball blockading Malta and Captain Sir Sidney Smith of the Levant Squadron three each. Admiral Bridport's Channel Fleet nominally contained fifty-one, A.B. Rodger, *The War of the Second Coalition* 1798–1801 (Oxford, 1964): 94–97.

17. Bruix's ill-defined mission included joining Mazzaredo's squadron, driving the British from the Mediterranean, and, eventually, relieving Corfu, Malta, and Alexandria, Rodger, 98–99.

18. Rodger refers to errors by the frigate *Nymph*'s captain but not to her being chased from her station, Rodger, 102.

main submerged. Poor visibility prevents it from spotting the enemy sortie.

Let us note that Bruix's forcing of the blockade, though an extraordinary event in 1799, is much less so given the distant blockades of 1930. On the other hand, that his sortie was not reported and contact with him was not retained is just as astonishing today as it was in the past and constituted an exceptional piece of luck for Bruix. But visibility was bad, and human eyes cannot penetrate fog any better today than in the past. Because of the weather, the usual British aerial reconnaissance did not take place on 26 April. When flights were resumed on the morning of the 27th, they established that Brest's harbor was empty.

The news produced a predictable impression on Bridport. He weighed from Plymouth at noon on 27 April and headed for Ireland, as in 1799, at an average speed, after deductions are made for zigzagging, of twenty knots. In the afternoon of 27 April, British reconnaissance aircraft from Cornwall and Ireland explored the sea without finding any trace of Bruix, who was already far away and steaming southwest at an average speed of twenty knots. The enemy was completely fooled but would very soon be able to restore control over the situation.

First, the Danish merchantman that encountered Bruix in 1799 is now a cargo vessel of twelve knots, which, arriving at Southampton at 2000 on 27 April, reports that she has met the French navy at 2000 on the 26th ninety miles southwest of Raz-du-Sein on a southwest course. The information goes immediately to London. Next, the frigate *Success* is now a British cruiser, which happens upon Bruix on 27 April at 1900, slightly south of the parallel of Oporto. Darkness allows her to elude the French pursuit, and she is soon able to advise Keith and Jervis by wireless of the enemy's position and route. Jervis immediately repeats the message to London, Duckworth, Nelson, and Sydney

Smith.[19] London has the information by midnight on 28 April. Moreover, at 2000 on the 27th, Bruix has used his own wireless to warn Mazzaredo of his arrival and to plan a rendezvous for the next day. This pernicious transmission is tracked, and the British locate Bruix near the Berlengas Islands off the Portuguese coast. The information is confirmed by a report from a Portuguese cargo ship. Thus, shortly after midnight on 28 April, the Admiralty is in possession of a sheaf of critical intelligence reports that permit a clear appraisal of the situation and prevent it from falling for false French reports implying that the fleet's goal is Ireland.

Absolutely certain that Bruix is heading for the Mediterranean, the Admiralty warns Bridport and orders him to detach Cotton[20] and a dozen ships at once to the Mediterranean. Bridport, on the west coast of Ireland, receives the order at 0400 on 28 April and executes it without delay. The British, held for more than a month off the Irish coast in 1799, are released within twenty-four hours in 1930. Thus has the correction of faulty decisions been accelerated by improvement in communications. Since Cotton is at worst forty-eight hours behind Bruix, the duration of the favorable situation in the Mediterranean acquired by the French admiral's *manoeuvre,* thirty-three days in 1799, is now only *two days!*[21] Security today is frail indeed if based on space and on false intelligence.

In any case, Bruix, who by 0600 on 28 April had reached a point ninety miles west of Cape Saint Vincent, steers southeast. Mazzaredo, alerted by Bruix at 2000 on the pre-

19. Sir William Sydney Smith, born 1764, promoted to full admiral 1821.

20. Admiral Sir C. Cotton eventually succeeded Collingwood as commander in chief in the Mediterranean.

21. Author's emphasis.

vious day, steams from Cadiz at midnight and joins Bruix at noon on the 28th about forty miles to the south of Cape Saint Vincent and with much greater ease than in the age of sail.[22]

Mazzaredo had left Cadiz as easily as Bruix left Brest, more easily even, for the movement happened at night. A British submarine on the surface did see something, however, and warned Keith. Aerial reconnaissance dispatched at daylight on the 28th confirms the sailing. Juxtaposing this departure with information about Bruix received the previous day, Keith deduces that the French and the Spanish have already managed to join forces. Since together they have forty-two ships (twenty-four and eighteen) against Keith's sixteen, Keith cannot take the offensive and shuts himself up at Gibraltar so to deprive Bruix's *manoeuvre* of its preliminary objective—the British fleet. Keith does, however, mobilize his submarines and aircraft to attack the Franco-Spanish fleet when it broaches the Straits of Gibraltar.

Bruix and Mazzaredo, after having reached the Moroccan coast at the latitude of Larache[23] at 2000 on 28 April, pass through the straits at night at twenty-five knots. They are at the latitude of Gibraltar at midnight and at the Cape du Gate at 0600 on 29 April.

Now one must reflect upon supplies. Bruix has steamed at an average of twenty knots since leaving Brest, and his tanks are three-quarters empty. In 1799 this constraint did not exist, but, in 1930, Bruix and Mazzaredo head for Cartagena to refuel and arrive there at 1000 on 29 April. Cotton, with his twelve ships also averaging twenty knots, joins Keith at Gibraltar at 1200 on 30 April. He, too, is forced

---

22. In 1799 Mazzaredo left Cadiz very hesitantly, suffered severe storm damage, and holed up in Cartagena while Bruix himself was safely in Toulon, Rodger, 105.

23. El Araish in Spanish Morocco.

to lose time refueling since his ships have steamed for three days. . . .

Supposing the two forces are able to refuel quickly enough at Cartagena and Gibraltar,[24] Bruix and Mazzaredo leave first, at 0000 on 1 May, while Cotton and Keith, reunited under the command of Jervis, follow on 2 May at 1200. The Franco-Spanish forces still retain the two-day advantage achieved by their *manoeuvre*, but it remains to be seen what use they will make of it.

Having escaped Keith at Gibraltar, they now head at fifteen knots towards the Balearic Islands in order to attack Duckworth, whose four ships would prove merely a mouthful. But the aerial reconnaissance of Minorca provided by aircraft carriers[25] from the Island of Formentera reports that Duckworth, completely forewarned, has found safe haven at Port Mahon. From the neighborhood of Minorca, where they were at 2000 on 1 May, Bruix and Mazzaredo head for the island of San Pietro southwest of Sardinia. There, at 0600 on 2 May, they join the large convoy dispatched to resupply Malta and Egypt, which had left Marseille at 0000 on 1 May. Escorting this convoy to its destination had been, one remembers, the principal reason for sending Bruix to the Mediterranean.[26] Steam engines confer on the convoy a rapidity and surety of movement previously unknown and make possible a prompt and precise rendezvous with the protecting force. Once reunited, the group travels towards Cape Bon at twelve knots to enter the Sicilian Channel.

Thanks to Duckworth's aerial reconnaissance, the British

24. And also that these ports are capable of containing forty-two and twenty-eight 10,000-ton cruisers, respectively. Here we are fully in the realm of fiction, but it is perfectly admissible for the type of study that we have in mind (author's note).

25. Later described as two French and one Spanish.

26. Castex gives a misleading simplicity to Bruix's convoluted orders.

know Bruix and Mazzaredo's location and heading as of 2000 on 1 May, but they are less certain about enemy intentions. Nelson, warned by wireless, has no intention of installing himself at Marittimo with his mere nine ships as he would have done in 1799. Thinking it prudent to barricade himself instead in his favorite base, Palermo, he nevertheless sends, for his conscience' sake, reconnaissance aircraft westward, and they discover on 2 May at 1600 the enemy forces north of Bizerte. That Malta is the enemy object becomes clear, and Nelson so informs Captain Ball and orders him to give up his blockade there and fall back to Messina. He also attempts to deploy submarines to attack the enemy in the Sicilian Canal, but the operation is too late.

On his side, Bruix wants information about the chances of encountering Nelson, which he very much desires in view of his overwhelming superiority of means. At 1200 on 2 May, while south of Sardinia, he sends a scout plane to Sicily that two hours later reports Nelson's presence at Palermo. Not wanting to allow Nelson to escape as Keith and Duckworth had done, Bruix dispatches the three aircraft carriers (two French and one Spanish) escorted by light forces to Marittimo and launches two bomber squadrons towards Palermo. They attack Nelson's squadron at the end of the afternoon and very seriously damage two of his ships.

Meanwhile, Jervis, grouping under his command Keith's and Cotton's twenty-eight ships, has left Gibraltar, as we have seen, at 1200 on 2 May and steered a course towards Sicily along the Algerian coast. Alongside Algiers, Jervis is joined by Duckworth's four ships from Minorca. He continues his course at twenty knots and at 1200 on 4 May reaches Palermo where he joins with Admiral Nelson and his seven serviceable ships. There he decides to remain for twenty-four hours to allow the ships from Gibraltar to refuel.

The last act has for its theater the Eastern Mediterranean. The Franco-Spanish force had safely managed to traverse the Sicilian Channel. Arriving south of Malta at 1000 on 3 May, it releases the blockade by its mere presence. The members of the convoy destined for Malta enter the port while the remainder continue their route to Egypt. Bruix's force has maintained its two-day lead over the British even after joining with the convoy, which steamed at only twelve knots, because Jervis's stop at Palermo reestablished the balance. Such was its lead, that the combined fleet would travel the 810 miles from Malta to Alexandria and arrive without difficulty at the latter port on 6 May at 1500 with reinforcements and provisions for the army of Egypt. . . .

But afterwards? The Franco-Spanish fleet must first resupply, which is only possible if the convoy has been joined by enough colliers and oilers to take care of its needs. The allies do not have a base in the eastern Mediterranean since besieged Corfu cannot be used. The British, on the other hand, can make use of Sicily. Except in the unlikely event of southern Italy and Taranto being conquered by land, the allied situation in the eastern Mediterranean will remain precarious. It is clear that the situation, which appeared serious enough to Bruix in 1799, is much more so in our day because of the fuel problem. The questions of bases, and consequently the geographical considerations upon which they partially rest, is much more important today than in the past.

As for the balance of forces, it is, after these diverse movements, very close to even. Jervis, having reunited at Palermo the thirty-nine ships commanded by Cotton, Keith, Duckworth, and Nelson, can now meet Bruix and Mazzaredo, who have forty-two ships between them. The allied period of numerical advantage has ended.

What results have they obtained by their *manoeuvre*? Not

much from the point of view of dealing with the enemy fleet. Keith, Duckworth, and Sydney Smith all eluded their attack. This is a common phenomenon in naval war and more frequent today because of warning by radio. They hurt Nelson somewhat with an aerial attack, a method that somewhat reduces the enemy's ability to avoid action, but the consequences were minor. On the other hand, the objectives foreign to naval war, the resupply of Malta and of the army of Egypt, were fully achieved. The duration of the favorable situation, two days, was short, but it sufficed for the planned operation, which, thanks to contemporary means, could be conducted with a speed and synchronization of movement hitherto unknown. An essential condition of *manoeuvre* in our day thus finds itself achieved.

One sees how we can use this example from 1799 to evaluate the change of strategic *manoeuvre* over more than a century. Though a simple outline, limited to major themes and passing over many details, the exercise illuminates the transformation of the methods of execution and the repercussions that this transformation ought to have on the conception and possibilities of modern *manoeuvre*.

PART III

EXTERNAL FACTORS

CHAPTER 10

THE ACTION OF POLICY ON STRATEGY[1]

RELATIONS OF POLICY WITH STRATEGY

STRATEGY AND policy, two distinct but equally important servants and executors of the national will, are necessarily intimately linked. Our earlier metaphor from physics compared strategy to the visible part of the solar spectrum and policy to the infrared with the two separated only by a blurred zone into which both penetrate.

The undisputed links between strategy and policy are repeated in an abundance of common circulated aphorisms like "war is a violent form of policy" or "war is nothing other than policy continued in arms" (it is, I believe, Clausewitz, who said this or something similar).[2] Another German scholar, Bernhardi, said that "war is the extension of policy by other means and is at the same time the most efficacious, if most dangerous, instrument of policy."[3] Our reflections on the relationship between policy and operations will not reiterate these truisms but show instead that the facts suggest a slightly altered situation.

1. Raoul Castex, *Théories stratégiques,* vol. 3 (Paris: Société d'Editions Géographiques, Maritimes et Coloniales, 1931): 3–53.
2. This offhand reference to Clausewitz's celebrated dictum from *On War,* book 1, chapter 1, para. 2 (Howard, 87) and book 8, chapter 6B (Howard, 605–7) sums up Castex's treatment of the German theorist.
3. Bernhardi, *Notre avenir* 59 (author's note).

The conventional approach implies that the link between strategy and policy is a serial one, that the two never function at the same time. Policy and its extension, strategy, operate successively, one yielding to the other at the appropriate time. The two activities are compartmentalized. On Bernhardi's argument, for example, policy defines the objective of the war, the importance and the nature of the interests involved, the choice of the opening moment, the desired success, etc. He adds, "War remains a means of attaining an objective completely outside of its competence. It cannot chose the goal itself."[4] Thus, the strategist receives his mission at the beginning of a war from the policy maker, who steps back to watch his acolyte perform. Only after the strategist has fulfilled his task, well or badly, successfully or otherwise, does the policy maker return to the scene. In peacetime, the policy maker acts alone, and the strategist rests. In war, it is the reverse. But is this really how things work, or is the reality of human conflicts not infinitely more complex?[5]

We can find the answer by searching the historical experiences of our ancestors for examples from the past. We will thereby be on firm ground and in the practical world. In this concrete realm we see that, far from effacing themselves in the course of a war while only the strategists operate, policy makers continue to act in wartime. The two zones of activity are neighbors that mix and become entangled with one another.[6]

4. *La guerre aujourd'hui*, vol. 2 (author's note).

5. Castex is unjust to Clausewitz, whose description of war as a trinity of violence, policy, and chance, though notoriously vague about practical mechanisms, demands that all three elements function in wartime, *On War*, book 1, chapter 1, para. 28 (Howard, 89).

6. We will discover the link between policy and strategy exemplified in the relationship between the government and the high command, which we will examine with attention (author's note).

In particular, policy undertakes to aid strategy. With more or less success, policy strives to lighten strategy's task by negotiating with other nations for support or, at least, benevolent neutrality. Sometimes, in spite of its good intentions, policy blunders and adds to the problems with which strategy must cope. These are indirect influences of policy on strategy.

More directly, policy intervenes to orient strategy in specific directions. Such interventions can be positive, that is, prescribing actions, or negative, forbidding specific enterprises. Obviously, political demands are not always the most judicious; their inspiration can be good or bad; they may be lacking in foresight. Frequently policy comes to trespass on the domain of strategy and interferes excessively in the conduct of operations and in other matters that do not concern it. Nonetheless, the demands made by policy cannot be neglected or distrustfully dismissed; they have a preponderant weight. Consequently, strategy cannot abstract itself from policy and work in isolation.

OLD MEMORIES

Direct negative action by policy on strategy can be seen at the end of the First Anglo-Dutch War, when British military leaders led by Monk[7] dreamed of exploiting Britain's maritime victories with a final campaign to crush Holland. Thanks to the exceptional skill gained by the British army during the Civil War, Monk's ambitions extended to the conquest of the Low Countries. Cromwell, however, stopped him in the name of policy. The Protector required not total victory but merely Dutch acknowledgment of the

---

7. George Monk (1608–1679), First Duke of Albemarle, defeated Tromp's fleet at Scheveningen, the last battle of the First Anglo-Dutch War, on 31 July 1653.

Navigation Act.[8] Further attacks would have undermined higher policies based on the two countries' joint interest in opposing a marriage[9] that, by uniting the Houses of Orange and the Stuarts, threatened both Britain and Holland with monarchy. Also, Cromwell hoped to attack Spain after taking on Elizabeth's role as protector of the Protestants. Because the annihilation of Protestant Holland went against Britain's larger aims, Monk had to renounce his larger offensive aspirations.

Similarly, during the War of the League of Augsburg, Herbert,[10] who commanded the British fleet, had conceived a defensive plan of withdrawing from a confrontation with Tourville[11] and holing up in the Thames where he would both avoid destruction and be ready to react to events.[12] He counted, rightly or wrongly, on the real advantages of the "fleet in being," but politics intervened.[13] Queen Mary, regent of England, alarmed that continuous retreat would demoralize the country and stimulate Jacobite activities, ordered Herbert to fight. The military result was the defeat at Beachy Head.[14]

8. Navigation Act of 1651.

9. Between Charles I's daughter Mary and William II of Orange.

10. Arthur Herbert (1647–1716), created Earl of Torrington in 1689.

11. Louis XIV's most distinguished sailor, Admiral Anne-Hilarion de Cotentin, Comte de Tourville (1642–1701).

12. His Anglo-Dutch force was outnumbered seventy to fifty-five because King William had part of the British fleet with him off Ireland, Michael Lewis, *A Social History of the Navy 1793–1915* (London, 1960): 467.

13. Castex discusses the "fleet in being" in chapter 16.

14. France could not exploit her greatest naval victory, that at Béveziers (Beachy Head to the British) on 10 July 1690, because of bad weather, wretched conditions on Tourville's overcrowded ships, and poor coordination of land and naval forces. See Etienne Taillemite and Pierre Guillaume, *Tourville et Béveziers* (Paris, 1991); Symcox, *The Crisis of*

Two years later, it was the turn of Torrington's foe to experience the pernicious effect of excessive political interference in military operations. Before engaging in the great battle designed to allow the troops of James II to cross the Channel, Tourville wanted to unite his forces and, especially, to join with those arriving from Rochefort and the Mediterranean. The impatient Louis XIV, anxious for the much desired invasion of England, insisted on immediate action. If the resulting battle of the Hogue,[15] fought at odds of two against one, was the most admirable of its day, it ended indecisively, and losses in the ensuing retreat paralyzed France for an entire year and blocked progress towards attaining the political objective. . . . [16]

MODERN EXAMPLES

Such are the memories of the past, but more recent events present the same observations. Let us take, for example, the American Civil War. On the Northern side, during the campaign on the James River, political considerations led Lincoln to prevent McDowell's corps from reinforcing McClellan in spite of the imminence of a clash that could have given victory to Richmond. On 27 May 1862 Lincoln recalled McDowells's corps to defend Washington.[17] Simi-

French Seapower, 99–100; and J.R. Jones, _Britain and Europe in the Seventeenth Century_ (London, 1966): 88, 91. For Torrington's controversial decisions, for which a court martial exonerated him, see Corbett, _Principles_, 214–19, and Mahan, _Influence_, 162.

15. Tourville was defeated by Admiral Sir George Rooke (1650–1709) at the Battle of Barfleur-The Hogue on 23 May 1692, Peter Kemp, ed., _History of the Royal Navy_ (London, 1969).

16. Other eighteenth-century examples are omitted.

17. Castex's terse narrative does no justice to the complex series of orders and counter-orders given to McDowell's corps in April and May 1862.

larly, political concerns were at least partly responsible for the great Federal offensive in the Mississippi Valley. If it was partially a matter of cutting the Confederacy in two and preventing provisions from moving from the Trans-Mississippi region, the Union also wanted to reopen the mouth of the river to its western states like Missouri and Ohio, which were inclining towards compromise with the South. It was for this reason that Lincoln chose to make a great effort to take Vicksburg and Port Hudson.

On the Confederate side, Jefferson Davis conceived the idea of invading Maryland for political reasons and imposed it on an unwilling Lee. The Southern President hoped thereby to satisfy Virginian desires for vengeance and to win over Maryland to the pro-slavery cause, to which he believed public opinion was favorable. In reality, his political hopes were disappointed; Maryland remained unmoved, and the venture ended at Antietam.[18]

Jefferson Davis tried again the following year; he ordered the second invasion of Maryland for similar reasons and again against the advice of Lee, who preferred to relieve Vicksburg.[19] Counting on the machinations of the "peace democrats" of the "copperhead" party, that is, on Northern

18. Castex is no historian of the American Civil War. If many of the reasons to invade Maryland in the summer of 1862 were indeed political, foremost among them the hope that another victory following upon the Second Battle of Bull Run and Jackson's Shenandoah campaigns would finally bring about European recognition of the Confederacy, it was General Robert E. Lee who sought battlefield victory in the North while President Jefferson Davis preferred a defensive strategy, Russell Weigley, *The American Way of War* (New York, 1973): 114, and Frank E. Vandiver, *Their Tattered Flags: The Epic of the Confederacy* (New York, 1970): 151.

19. Castex again reverses the roles of Davis and Lee. Lee hoped that by invading the North he could draw the war out of Virginia and distract Union efforts from Vicksburg, Edwin B. Coddington, *The Gettysburg Campaign: A Study in Command* (New York, 1984): 5–7.

proponents of a peaceful entente with the South, Davis wanted to penetrate into Maryland in order to encourage them and to support the uprisings that he predicted in Washington and Baltimore. Hence, Lee's operations, which were more political than military, looked more to the occupation of the country and the requisition of foodstuffs than to seeking the organized forces of the enemy. Gettysburg, however, soon put an end to this enterprise.

Policy's impact on strategy is not representative of any one particular kind of government. France's shift during the 1870 War from an imperial regime to a government of National Defense did not change the tendency of government to intervene in strategy. . . .

That policy does not always have perfect perception is clear from the Second Balkan War. After their victory over the Bulgarians at Bregalnitza,[20] the Serbians could have exploited their success to put their enemy out of action. At the end of July 1913, however, Marshal Radomir Putnik, the Serbian generalissimo, received orders to stop his pursuit from a government that insisted on tying the army's actions to those of the Rumanians, who had the initiative from the political point of view. The subordination of strategy to policy was of disputable value here, for it retarded the military action and the final victory. Fortunately, the enemy was—at the same time—even less well served by his policy makers.

POSITIVE AND NEGATIVE POLITICAL ACTIONS

Policy is not always so badly directed. It achieved an exemplary intervention in the French "ten kilometer withdrawal" of 30 July 1914. By ordering her troops to move back from the frontier, France convinced a still-wavering Britain of her

20. 2 July 1913.

peaceful intentions. . . . Adopting a similar policy towards Italy, on whose neutrality she counted, France delayed dispatching to Bizerte the battleships intended to bring the force there to wartime strength. . . .[21] Later events showed the political leadership to have been very happily inspired in both cases.

Alongside this type of intervention, negative in the sense that it prohibited certain operations, the 1914 war also produced examples of positive interventions or political insistence on certain actions. At the end of 1914, the British and French governments decided to undertake operations in the Orient over the objections of the army commanders on the Western Front. Similarly, in April and September 1915, the French government required the general in chief to dispatch four additional divisions to the east in order to extend the Dardanelles offensive to the edge of Asia. A month later, the government conceived of the Salonika landing and imposed it upon the military commander, pushed in this direction not only by the necessity of aiding Serbia but also by the hope of achieving political benefits in the form of changed attitudes on the parts of Greece and Bulgaria.[22]

ECONOMIC POLICY AND STRATEGY

One part of naval strategy includes the operations for economic and military exploitation of mastery of the sea (as we understand the concept) after mastery has been obtained by

21. Bizerte, now Banzert, was France's naval base in Tunisia.

22. Castex ignores another kind of political motivation behind the dispatch of the French Eastern Army, the Left's insistence on establishing an adequately important command for republican General Maurice Sarrail, whom General Joffre had relieved from command of Third Corps, Jan Karl Tannenbaum, *General Maurice Sarrail 1856–1929: The French Army and Left-wing Politics* (Chapel Hill, 1974): 57–62.

eliminating the enemy fleet. This exploitation has both military and economic components, and the latter, blockade, naturally impinges upon the neutrals and brings politics into play. From the beginning of the 1914 war, the Allies attempted to cut off German supplies through increasingly restrictive interpretations of the London Declaration regarding contraband.[23] In suppressing contraband, however, they were obliged to heed the concerns of the United States, not only to avoid acquiring a new enemy but because of their own dependence on the Americans for significant quantities of supplies. It was necessary to find a compromise, as Sir Edward Grey[24] says, "to maintain the tightest blockade possible without breaking with the United States." There was, as in mechanics, a sort of state of equilibrium between pressure and resistance.

Difficulties appeared when the Allies manifested the desire to include in the absolute contraband list rubber, copper, and cotton, products formerly considered to be conditional contraband. Certain of American protest against the inclusion of cotton, the Allies dealt at first only with rubber and copper, commodities whose shipment to Germany they were able to bar. They had less luck with objects destined for neutral European ports because the United States refused to acknowledge the absolute contraband label in these cases. Britain was forced to undertake long and painful negotiations on the matter. . . . Occasionally, as in the *Dacia* case, relations between Britain and the United States were pro-

23. See *Théories* vol. 1, part 2, chapter 1 and vol. 3, part 3, chapter 6 (author's note).

24. Sir Edward Grey, Viscount of Fallodon (1863–1933), whose memoirs Castex cites, was a liberal imperialist and Asquith supporter. Secretary of State for Foreign Affairs in the Campbell-Bannerman cabinet in December 1905, he retained the office until David Lloyd George assumed the premiership in December 1916, Herwig and Heyman, 169.

tected by having a French cruiser stop the American ship, a subterfuge suggested in this case by the American ambassador to Great Britain.[25]

Cotton always remained merely conditional contraband because the Allies could not block this indispensable American export, especially given the degree to which the war itself had gravely hampered the cotton trade. United States merchant ships traveled in armed convoys, which the Allies could stop only at risk of war against the United States. Tolerance of American cotton shipments was a painful concession to policy by strategy, which saw the material used by the enemy in producing munitions.

All of these complications obviously disappeared after the United States entered the war . . . but given the extent of the difficulties in a case relatively favorable for the belligerents, one can imagine the problems in a future war in which the neutrals are numerous and powerful. Economic strategy will be paralyzed to a much greater extent by political considerations.

POLICY AS AN AUXILIARY TO STRATEGY

Coalition politics also acted during the 1914 war to enhance strategic opportunities, principally by securing foreign aid and benevolent neutrality. From the beginning Sir Edward Grey divided the neutrals into four classes: (1) genuine neutrals (Spain, Denmark, Norway, Holland, the states of Central and South America); (2) neutrals with pro-German tendencies (Turkey, Bulgaria, Sweden); (3) neutrals with pro-Allied tendencies (Italy, Rumania, Greece); and (4) the United States. Political actions towards the nations of the first category had to be, at least at the beginning of the war,

25. See Grey, *Memoirs*, 407 (author's note).

limited to seeking good relations and benevolent neutrality. Here, the Allies were generally successful in spite of occasional tensions with the northern powers over the issue of contraband of war and Allied insistence that benevolent neutrality extend to the abolition of trade with their German neighbor.

The Allied political effort in regard to Turkey focused entirely on persuading that nation to remain neutral despite the influence of a very powerful pro-German party. Turkey's stance was of particular concern to Britain in view of its proximity to the Suez Canal and because an anti-Turkish policy could anger Britain's Muslim subjects. Thus, the Allies showered manifestations of their good intentions upon Constantinople. Denying any threat to the territorial integrity of the Ottoman Empire, they dangled before the eyes of the Turkish government suggestions of economic advantage and the suppression of the Capitulations,[26] all, of course, on condition that Turkey remain neutral and repatriate the crews of the *Goeben* and the *Breslau*.[27] Turkey, however, disregarded Allied concerns by incorporating the German ships at least notionally into her own fleet, an action that the Allies bore without protest. Allied forbearance on this matter managed to slow Turkey's inevitable adhesion to the German cause, which occurred only on 28 October 1914, on the occasion of the Turkish fleet's hostile demonstration

26. The "Capitulations" were a series of increasingly unfavorable trade agreements between a declining Ottoman Empire and various European powers.

27. In August 1914, the *Goeben*, a new German battle cruiser armed with 11-inch guns and capable of doing twenty-seven knots, and the light cruiser *Breslau* eluded British Mediterranean forces and made their way to neutral Constantinople, where their appearance aided the pro-German lobby and contributed to the Turkish decision in October 1914 to enter the conflict alongside the Central Powers, Hough, 70, 82.

off the Russian Black Sea ports.[28] Allied policy had won two and a half months to transport Indian and Australian troops to Egypt and to reinforce positions in the Mediterranean. Moreover, the coalition avoided assuming in Moslem eyes the appearance of aggression against Turkey. These were substantial advantages. British policy intelligently avoided the grave error of following Turkey's entry into the war with the annexation of Egypt. By contenting herself with a protectorate, she mollified both Allied suspicions and Moslem sensitivities.

Similar considerations led the British to decline Greece's offer of 18 August 1914 to join the Allied camp. Though the offer was a seductive one, acceptance would have provoked immediate Turkish and Bulgarian entry into the war, and Russia had made clear her anxiety to avoid Turkish hostilities as long as her efforts against Germany and Austria left the Caucasus stripped of forces. Since a vigorous Russian military action on the German eastern front was absolutely essential to the Allied cause in August and September 1914, objections from St. Petersburg militated decisively against an inopportune Greek offensive against still neutral Turkey. In declining the advances of Mr. Venizelos,[29] the policy makers wisely abstained from complicating the strategists' task at a particularly critical moment. . . . In general, Allied policy suffered only one defeat in forming the coalition—continued Bulgarian hostility. Never before, except in the wars of the Revolution and the Empire, had politics acted so energetically to the benefit of military strategy. . . .

---

28. Turkish naval forces, including the *Goeben* and *Breslau*, initiated hostilities on 29 October 1914 by shelling Odessa, Sevastopol, and Novorossiisk, Alan Morehead, *Gallipoli* (New York, 1956): 18.

29. Eleutherios Venizelos (1864–1936), six times premier of Greece, headed a pro-Allied faction in opposition to King Constantine I.

INTERNAL POLICY

In coalition warfare, policy also has a vital internal role. A coalition is not an idyll, a cloudless marriage of devoted partners, but a transitory assembly of nations brought together by temporarily shared interests on some points but still disagreeing on others. Conflicts spring up within coalitions, causing anything from minor dislocation to complete disintegration, the latter a catastrophe that destroys strategy as well.

Policy alone can guard against these dangers, avoid them, minimize discord, level differences, and maintain cohesion. In coalitions, policy sees open before it an internal field—inter-allied policy—in addition to the external arena. Both kinds of policy aid and support strategy.

Staying with the war of 1914, we have seen already that Russia raised difficulties in the negotiations concerning the entry into the war of Greece, Italy, and Rumania that could be ended only by firm and open pressure exercised by Britain and France in the name of the common cause. In the month of January 1915, the Turks, very demoralized by their defeat at Sarikamish[30] in the Caucasus and by the Russian squadron's raid in the North Sea, showed signs of weakness. The Turkish liberal faction hoped to make a separate peace with the Allies, retaining as its only condition respect for the territorial integrity of Turkey. The commandant of the 1st Army Corps at Constantinople, Mechemed-Pasha, suggested to Mr. Venizelos that he launch a coup in order to free Greece of its German alliance. Russia, aware of these intrigues, was disturbed and irritated because guar-

30. Russian General Vorontsov stopped Enver Pasha's offensive on 29 December 1914, and his counterattack of 3 January 1915 destroyed the Turkish army.

217

antees of Turkish integrity directly challenged her own ambitions toward Constantinople. On 27 January 1915, Sir George Buchanan, ambassador to Petrograd, was charged to remind Russia in the names of France and Britain that the inter-Allied convention of 5 September 1914 barred any separate peace.

The Dardanelles attack soon provoked another grave crisis in the alliance. In November 1914, the Russians had received from Britain a vague assurance that Russian interests would be taken into consideration in any postwar settlement of the fate of Constantinople and the Straits, and matters remained there until the first naval attacks against the outer forts of the Dardanelles of 19 February to 2 March 1915. In Russia, this operation provoked considerable ill-feeling, skillfully exacerbated by the maneuvers of the pro-German Count Witte. It was said that while Russia did her duty for the common cause on the German front, Britain and France would take advantage of the opportunity to seize the Straits. Some ambiguous phrases pronounced by Sir Edward Grey in the House of Commons heightened the tension. The Russian legislative assembly (Duma) and public opinion at large became excited and angry. On 1 March, Russian minister of foreign affairs Sazonov,[31] demanded of the French and British ambassadors a clear statement yielding Constantinople to Russia at the conclusion of the war. On 3 March, Sazonov further extended Russian ambitions to include the Sea of Marmara, southern Thrace, the Dardanelles, Imbros, and Tenedos.

Policy found its work cut out to appease an explosion of Russian discontent that could have put an end to the coalition. The moment was critical, and on 8 March 1915, Del-

---

31. Sergyei Dmitrievich Sazonov (1866–1927) was Russian foreign minister four times.

cassé[32] authorized a declaration to Sazonov that Russian aspirations would meet with the goodwill of the French government. But the Russian required a formal official declaration, and for Britain, such a declaration was completely inconsistent with her long-term policy on the Straits that had led to the Crimean War and dictated her position during the Turko-Russian War of 1878. So serious was the matter that the liberal government called the leaders of the opposition to join in the deliberations. On 12 March, the Cabinet, bowing before the hard necessity of maintaining the coalition at any cost, yielded to Russian demands and transmitted on the following day the necessary reassurances to the Russian government.[33] The crisis of the alliance was averted, but, in the meantime, the western Allies had been forced by Russian veto to renounce Greece's offer to collaborate in the Dardanelles attack. Thus, policy managed to avoid the nightmare of a separate peace, but the threat had been a near one. . . .[34]

POLICY AND ITS CONVERSATIONS

But policy deals with more than neutrals and holding alliances together. So far is it from lethargy during a military conflict that it confronts the enemy through direct conversations in which the two parties probe one another, test their respective appetites, and sketch the contours of the future negotiations through which they will eventually lay down their arms. Communication with the enemy never absolutely ceases in the course of a war. Conversations continue, some-

32. Théophile Delcassé (1852–1923), French foreign minister 3–4 August 1914 and 27 August 1914 to 12 October 1915.
33. These "reassurances" included a secret treaty promising Russia Constantinople, the Bosporus, the Sea of Marmara, and the Dardanelles.
34. Pages 25–26 are omitted.

times directly and sometimes through third-party intermediates. These do not always act disinterestedly but, like the Bismarckian "honest courtier" draw from their mediatory role commissions in the form of material or morale advantages. Even the most destructive wars cannot escape this rule because they are almost always the longest, and long wars are likely to have moments in which weariness overtakes the belligerents and pushes them to preliminary negotiations likely to lead, if not to a stable and definitive peace, at least to a truce.

Such was the case of Britain in 1796. Three years of war against France had produced no result suggestive of eventual victory—far from it. France had overcome the external dangers pressing her on the Continent, and the Basel treaties of 1795 had marked a significant victory.[35] Next had come Bonaparte's brilliant campaign in Italy which, joined with Corsica's change of heart and the Franco-Spanish alliance of August 1796, forced the British to evacuate the Mediterranean. Britain's situation was far from brilliant. After the imminent Austrian peace,[36] she would be alone against France. Her successes at sea in the battles of Prairial, Groix, Noli, etc., had all been indecisive. The invasion of French political exiles at Quiberon, supported by Britain, had proved abortive. Finally, Britain was suffering a grave internal crisis. New industrial machines created overproduction which, because of the interruption of continental trade, led to lower prices and diminished wages. At the same time, the cost of living had increased (the price of wheat having almost doubled from 1792 to 1796), and discontentment became general. Confidence plummeted, public funds were low, and the

35. The Treaty of Basel of 5 April 1795 took Prussia out of the War of the First Coalition.
36. Campo Formio.

government found itself unable to borrow. The entire British nation prayed for the return of peace.

In such circumstances, it is not surprising that the British showed themselves interested in conversations with their enemy. From October 1796, Lord Malmesbury began privately sounding the waters in Paris, and official negotiations opened in Lille in July 1797. The British envoys were very conciliatory, recognizing the French territorial gains in Europe and asking only foreign compensation. The French delegates, however, intransigently ignored popular desires for peace until the *coup d'état* of 18 *fructidor* (the last month of the French Revolutionary calendar) ousted the pro-peace faction from the Directory and the Councils.[37] The French plenipotentiaries increased their demands, and the conversations broke off on 18 September 1797. At the beginning of the Consulate,[38] Bonaparte sent new peace initiatives to the King of England[39] and the Emperor of Austria,[40] but the Peace of Amiens was concluded only on 25 March 1802.[41]

37. The pro-peace faction described by Castex was made up of the royalists, who had made substantial gains in the 1797 council elections but were ousted in September 1797 in a coup by the directors Reubell, La Reveillière, and Barras supported by the generals, Alfred Cobban, *A History of Modern France. V.1: 1715–1799* (1963): 253, Gordon Wright, *France in Modern Times*, 2nd ed. (Chicago, 1974): 63–65.

38. The consulate was established by *coup d'état* on 9 November 1799. Intended by the conspirators to be a triumvirate, it fell immediately under the domination of the first consul, Napoleon Bonaparte.

39. George III (1738–1820).

40. Francis II (1768–1835), Holy Roman emperor from 1792 until 1806 and thereafter emperor of Austria.

41. The Peace of Amiens allowed France to retain her conquests up to the Rhine and in northern Italy and required Britain to give up all of her overseas conquests except Trinidad and Ceylon. That the British public so warmly welcomed a peace thoroughly incommensurate with their military successes supports Castex's claims of British economic hardship. Hostilities between Britain and France resumed in March 1803.

Inconclusive talks occurred again in 1806 after Trafalgar had been followed by Austerlitz[42] and the French seizure of Dalmatia and the kingdom of Naples, which directly threatened the British situation in the Mediterranean. When the despondent Pitt died on 23 January 1806, his successor, Grenville,[43] resigned himself to seeking conversations with Napoleon, who welcomed his overtures. Initially productive, the talks soon stalled over the kingdom of Naples and Napoleon's intransigence over the Dutch colonies. Negotiations broke off at the end of September, and Britain reasserted herself by launching the Fourth Coalition against Napoleon. Thus, the conversations of 1806 ended as unhappily as those of 1796. Only one more such attempt, a vague one in 1809, would occur before the end of the wars of the empire.

Such were the most important attempts at Franco-British rapprochement between 1793 and 1815, and there were others too trivial to recall here. What is important is that France and Britain never ceased, throughout this whole period, to remain in political contact directly or indirectly.

The most striking of the peace initiatives during the 1914 war was the German offer of December 1916.[44] It was rejected, but was the rejection inevitable? Some individuals in the Allied camp felt considerable uncertainty about the value of continuing the war. Sir Edward Grey's memoirs recount his own fear at the beginning of 1916 that the war had become unwinnable by either side.[45] Hoping for United

---

42. 2 December 1805.

43. William Wyndham Grenville, Baron Grenville (1759–1834) was foreign secretary from 1791 to 1801.

44. Details in Gerhard Ritter, *The Sword and the Scepter: The Problem of Militarism in Germany*, vol. 3: *The Tragedy of Statesmanship—Bethmann Hollweg as War Chancellor (1914–1917)*, trans. Heinz Norden (Miami, 1972), chapter 8.

45. Grey, *Memoirs*, 420ff. (author's note).

States' mediation to put an end to hostilities, he communicated with Colonel House,[46] *éminence grise* of President Wilson, who had already himself conceived of such an intervention. The two men drafted a memorandum in February 1916 defining a course of action for the President of the United States. The challenge was to contrive an arrangement judged by Colonel House to be acceptable to both sides and that would include the restoration of Belgium, the return of Alsace-Lorraine to France, Russian acquisition of access to the sea, and compensations for Germany outside of Europe. The Grey-House memorandum was communicated to the British War Committee, which decided not to act on the matter at that time, and was transmitted to the French government purely as a matter of information.

Certain favorable events of 1916, such as the failure of the German attack on Verdun, the battle of the Somme, the success of the Brusilov offensive, and Rumania's entry into the war, somewhat increased Sir Edward Grey's confidence.[47] That autumn, however, Rumania was knocked out of the war, and Grey's returning pessimism led him to present to his colleagues once again the memorandum composed by himself and Colonel House. His hopes were raised by the knowledge that Colonel House, in addition to his visits to London and Paris, had gone to Berlin and made inquiries implying American willingness to mediate between the two adversaries. . . .

It is no secret now that many individuals among the Allies, discouraged by the persistent and apparently permanent military stalemate, shared Grey's discouragement. Though such feelings were stigmatized in the light of the later vic-

46. Edward Mandell "Colonel" House (1858–1938) was Wilson's closest adviser.
47. Positive appraisal of the outcome of Verdun or the Somme was probably more difficult at the time.

tory, they were perfectly explicable and natural at the time.[48]

At the same time, moreover, similar doubt and perplexity attacked the enemy. To Chancellor Bethmann-Hollweg,[49] especially, the military situation did not appear much brighter than it did to the Allies. Seeing Colonel House in Berlin in early 1916, Bethmann-Hollweg spoke to him of "the universal merit which the President could earn as the founder of the peace."[50] In the course of the summer, he told Ambassador Gérard, who was leaving for the United States, that Germany would welcome with favor United States' action to this purpose. Behind his pessimism were the same considerations that induced a moment of despair in the Allies in 1916. Even the victory over the Rumanians seemed to the chancellor a bargaining chip at best since total victory appeared improbable.

Except for the parties of the Right, all of the various political factions held the same view. All believed peace absolutely necessary, especially in view of the economic hardship caused by the blockade.[51] Victory seemed impossible. As Deputy Conrad Haussemann wrote to the chancellor on 25 October 1916, a favorable moment for peace negotiations had arrived, and diplomatic inertia threatened delay and lost

48. Moreover, as we shall see later, *Théories*, vol. 3, part 2, chapter 2, the Allied financial situation was extremely grim at the end of 1916 (author's note).

49. Theobald Bethmann-Hollweg (1856–1921) was chancellor of Germany from 1909 to 1917, when the German army forced his resignation. At the Crown Council at Pless on 9 January 1917, he yielded against his better judgment to the navy's call for unrestricted submarine warfare, see Herwig and Heyman, 87.

50. Bethmann-Hollweg, *Considerations sur la guerre mondiale*, 261ff. (author's note).

51. Hardships denied by Castex elsewhere to have existed as early as 1916.

opportunity.[52] Others, like von Jagow, were not loath to describe the continuation of the war as folly. Kaiser Wilhelm II spoke in favor of peace, and he pressed Bethmann-Hollweg to that effect in a letter of 31 October. . . .[53]

Given that the two adversaries shared virtually identical attitudes towards peace and that the terrain had been well prepared on both sides by active and adroit third parties, one might expect that direct conversations would have had good chances of success. At that moment, however, the Allies were bracing themselves for a supreme effort to carry on hostilities. In Britain, on 8 December 1916, Lloyd George[54] replaced Asquith as prime minister. Affirming his resolution to carry the struggle to the end, he created a new, smaller War Cabinet. The same tendency was evident in France. After secret debates in the Chamber of Deputies from 20 November to 7 December, the Cabinet was reorganized on a narrower basis and a War Committee established. In Russia, after Sturmer's[55] disgrace on 24 November, one saw a violent reaction against the Germanophile party.

It was under these unfavorable conditions that the Germans made their peace offer. On 12 December 1916, the chancellor, not wanting to await a United States' initiative, delivered to the neutral representatives in Berlin a proposal for negotiations whose terms implied a complete end to the war. On 19 December, President Wilson entered the scene with a demand that the belligerents announce their war

52. Conrad Haussemann, *Journal d'un député au Reichstag* (Paris, 1928): 97 (author's note).

53. Bethmann-Hollweg, 266 (author's note).

54. David Lloyd George (1863–1945) served as Liberal prime minister of a coalition government from 7 December 1916 until 22 October 1922.

55. Boris Vladimirovich Sturmer (1849–1917) was a prime minister, minister of interior, and minister of foreign affairs of such striking incompetence that he was alleged to be a German agent, Herwig and Heyman, 330–31.

aims. On 27 December, Germany and Austria responded with a short note offering no illumination of their views. On 30 December, the Allies rejected the German offer and responded to President Wilson's interrogative by stipulating peace conditions implying the definitive defeat of Germany. Thus, prospects for peace were checked. . . .

Throughout these and other wartime attempts to negotiate, policy continued to work to the benefit of strategy. Having attempted at the war's beginning to launch strategy in the best possible conditions and during the conflict to facilitate its tasks, policy acted when strategy appeared deadlocked to seek an honorable exit by means of exchanging views preliminary to an acceptable settlement. Such is the teaching of experience. . . .

This is not to say, however, that one ought to welcome all conversations, whether public or secret, whether initiated by oneself or by the enemy. Why make war at all only to seize every possible opportunity for negotiation? Neither desirable at all times nor a perversion always to be rejected, communication with the enemy must be treated as a natural phenomenon, sometimes appropriate and not to be rejected out of hand. Everything depends on the specific case.

Peace negotiations constitute a severe challenge for a people at war, testing not only their will to struggle and their moral solidarity, but also the political and military judgment of their leaders. Whether or not to continue the battle is an agonizing dilemma whose resolution demands as much energy and clairvoyance as did the original entry into the war itself and which assumes both certainty of information and firmness in its exploitation.

The test is even stiffer for a coalition than for a single nation because the prospect of peace and postwar settlement reveals fissures within the alliance that prevent the adoption of a single, unanimous line of conduct. Here one ought to acknowledge that the fact of having weathered such crises without damage, having continued without deviation to the point of victory, was certainly the most glorious success of the anti-German coalition of 1914–1918.

The many services that it renders or tries to render to strategy give policy the right to be heeded by its associates. Although political counsel cannot be followed blindly and can, even if inspired by the very best of intentions, lead to military disaster, it cannot be disregarded. Soldiers, both past and present, often misunderstand this relationship. Failure to acknowledge that policy must direct strategy explains the refusal of some of them during the 1914 war to see beyond their fixation on the Western Front. Citing Clausewitz, of whom they were novice acolytes, they deemed an eastern approach "a fatal example of mixing policy and strategy" and considered the idea of breaking Austria "nothing but pure politics. . . ."

Prime Minister Lloyd George ran up against the single-mindedness of military strategy when he decided after Caporetto[56] to send British reinforcements to the Italian front over the objections of General Robertson,[57] the Chief of the Imperial General Staff, and Sir Douglas Haig.[58] The latter, engaged at the time in his Passchendale offensive,[59] refused to yield a single division for the Italian front. Annoyed by this resistance, Lloyd George answered, "It's perfect. You soldiers take a village in Flanders and Serbia collapses. You

56. Its army's collapse on 24 October 1917 in the face of an Austro-German offensive northwest of Trieste almost knocked Italy out of the war.

57. The only British field marshal to begin his career as a private soldier, Sir William Robertson (1860–1933), was chief of the Imperial General Staff from December 1915 to February 1918.

58. Field Marshal Sir Douglas Haig (1861–1928) was commander in chief of British forces on the western front from 1917–1919.

59. The Third Ypres offensive of October–November 1918.

take another, and it is Rumania which falls. Possibly you will take Passchendale next week, and it will be Italy's turn for annihilation."[60] The prime minister overrode military objections for reasons of overall policy. What he criticized in this sally was less military hostility to his ideas, for strategy was not required to bow without discussion before the suggestions of policy, than its rejection of arguments foreign to pure military necessity.

POLICY AND STRATEGY IN TIME OF PEACE

These examples show that policy and strategy are not juxtaposed end to end with one succeeding the other when one passes from a state of peace to a state of war. Policy does not hibernate in wartime but works in liaison with strategy. Does this condition of "operation in parallel" cease with the end of the abnormal situation that is war? Does peace see policy completely eclipse strategy?

Not at all, for there exists, as we have remarked earlier,[61] a true "peacetime strategy" that encompasses all of the measures, ranging from new-construction programs and provisioning to training of personnel and drafting plans of operations that one can take to increase the power of an army or a fleet. As Admiral Sir Cyprian Bridge said, "The work of strategy never ends" and its field of action remains immense in peacetime. Strategy's incursions into a peacetime arena seemingly reserved to policy mirror the actions of policy in entering into strategy's wartime realm. We find the two together again, always side by side.

One ought then to expect to find between policy and strategy in time of peace the same tight links that unite them

60. Wickham Steed, *Mes souvenirs,* vol. 2 (Paris: Plon): 111 (author's note).
61. See *Théories,* vol. 1, part 1, chapter 1 (author's note).

in time of war. Are the two not both servants of the same cause?

Nothing of the sort. It is easy to grasp why their peacetime bonds are generally much looser and sometimes altogether absent. The intimate collaboration evident in wartime reflects tragic, imperious, and implacable necessity. Problems of a political-military nature constantly arise and demand immediate solution at any cost. Since cooperation must be daily and constant, the links that develop naturally assume a semi-permanent character.

In peacetime, however, things are entirely different. The threats are eventual, hypothetical, distant. Demands can be deferred, at least for a time. Events are awaited at leisure. Nothing presses. Circumstances do not demand the collaboration of policy and strategy for immediate ends, and the two often disassociate themselves from one another.

The nations that present exceptions to this generality are those animated even in peacetime by the will to struggle. Expanding and conquering peoples manifest in all of their actions an offensive drive conducive to long-term projects. In other nations, one usually finds in peacetime only a vague defensive and conservative instinct, lacking an established direction and stirred up by every possibility without attaching itself to any one of them. Policy is inchoate, uncertain, changing; strategy lacks orientation or precise objective. Ignorant of the path to follow and of the nature of future hostilities, it can only offer static measures for organization and mobilization. Active dispositions such as plans of operations cannot develop because they require determination of the enemy to be fought and of the objective to attain. If neither policy nor strategy properly exists, then there can logically be no rapport between them.

This pernicious state of affairs does not improve until the nation becomes the object of a direct threat and the desire for self-defense fosters the creation of both policy and strategy, which can then cooperate with one another. The situation is now similar to one of war, to which it is generally a prelude.

The rise of Prussia in the second half of the nineteenth century exemplifies the liaison between policy and strategy in a nation motivated by unchecked ambition. A clear and vigorous will for struggle presided over Bismarck's Machiavellian plan to destroy the old German edifice of 1815. Each of the successful stages of Prussia's growth marked the unceasing collaboration of policy and strategy. She drove Denmark out of the Duchies and used this event to catalyze the desired break with Austria, who was left isolated diplomatically by Prussian agreements with Italy and by French inertia.[62] Bismarck's Prussia led the resisting German states to the Austrian war and unification in spite of anti-Prussian sentiment.

Incarnating Prussia's will to expand, Bismarck directed the whole program and inspired what might be called Prussia's "war plan." Though foreign minister in title, Bismarck also managed internal politics and thereby conducted both the whole of the war and one of its component parts.[63] But he could have achieved nothing without the support of a powerful strategy and without a collaborator both adept at the preparation and conduct of military operations and cognizant of their political implications.

Chance filled Bismarck's need in the form of Moltke, Chief of the General Staff, that is, of the organ that became the principal lever of the chosen policy. Bismarck allied with

62. In the Danish War of 1864 Austria and Prussia allied to wrest the duchies of Schleswig and Holstein from the King of Denmark. A three-month alliance between Prussia and Italy was signed on 8 April 1866.

63. Otto von Bismarck (1815–1898) was minister president, not foreign minister, of Prussia from 1862 and chancellor of the new German Empire from 1871 to 1890.

Moltke; their shared hopes united them. Before Sadowa,[64] Moltke took an active part in the alliance with Italy. He inspired the draft of the Usedom note to General La Marmora of 17 June 1866, which outlined the military requirements for cooperation with the Florentine cabinet. The solidarity of the Bismarck-Moltke team reinforced itself on the field of Sadowa during the four agonizing hours they spent together awaiting the arrival of the army of the crown prince.

After this campaign, in August 1866, Bismarck sought Moltke's advice on measures to take against France, and Moltke then contributed to writing the secret treaties with the southern states.[65] In the spring of 1867, Bismarck again asked for Moltke's written opinion about disquieting French military preparations, and Moltke responded with two memoranda on the very same day.[66] In June 1867, Bismarck and Moltke visited France together, taking advantage of that year's exposition for purposes one can easily divine.[67] The famous falsification of the Ems telegram marks the culminating point of this collaboration between Bismarck and Moltke.[68] Before Bismarck's *démarche,* the partners feared

64. Sadowa, or Königgrätz, was the Prussian victory over Austria in Bohemia on 3 July 1866 that determined the result of the Austro-Prussian War.

65. *Correspondance militaire du maréchal de Moltke* (author's note).

66. *Ibid.,* no. 10 and 11 (author's note). What Castex does not say is that Moltke advocated war against France in 1867, a policy Bismarck entirely opposed.

67. Though widely believed in France after 1870, the insinuation that the true purpose of the visit was to reconnoiter the defenses of Paris has no basis in fact, A. J. P. Taylor, *Bismarck: The Man and the Statesman* (New York, 1967): 108.

68. The Ems telegram of 13 July 1870 reported to Bismarck King William I's acquiescence to Leopold of Hohenzollern-Sigmaringen's withdrawal from candidacy for the vacant throne of Spain and the resulting moderation of tensions between Prussia and France, but Bismarck, set on

the possibility of a peaceful settlement of the Hohenzollern incident, in the foreign minister's words, that "the affair be lost in the sands." Rarely does one see such tight intercourse between policy and strategy in peacetime preparations for war. At the decisive moment, they supported one another with a clear and stimulating vision of the profits to come.[69]

Modern Italy gives another possible picture of the intimate peacetime union of policy and strategy in a nation aspiring to expansion or hegemony. Here, policy is primary; it finds its milieu. It is ordinarily farsighted, informed, capable, flexible, resourceful. It helps strategy, which is less assured, to achieve, at the least cost, the advantages that strategy cannot win on its own, always careful that strategy not be left unsupported except against the weakest adversaries. Politically, the Italian method consists of approaching objectives serially; militarily, it is to insinuate themselves into the conflicts of others or to assure from the beginning the assistance of reliable allies and to act only in entirely favorable circumstances. . . .

Nations that live in a state of political and military expectancy, nations that have no positive program for the growth

war, offered the press a version implying that Franco-Prussian relations were on the verge of collapse, Halo Holborn, *A History of Modern Germany: 1840–1945* (New York, 1969): 213–14.

69. Castex is unusual in praising the Bismarck-Moltke partnership, usually treated as a model of civil-military relations gone wrong. The two disagreed on such important matters as Moltke's preference for aiding Austria against France in 1859, the desirability of war against France in 1867 and 1875, the provisions of the peace with France in 1871, and Bismarck's plan for a Russian alliance. Their arguments during the Franco-Prussian War, especially Moltke's complaints about civilian interference in military matters, were notorious, Fritz Stern, *Gold and Iron, Bismarck, Bleichröder, and the Building of the German Empire* (New York, 1979): 121, 130, 137, 144–46, and A. J. P. Taylor, *Bismarck,* 105, 133, 210. Castex himself echoes the conventional view below, 255.

of their power, are generally afflicted with a mutual semi-indifference of policy and strategy. The two cooperate with one another only when a direct threat forces them to contrive the necessary defense. In France between 1870 and 1914, the German menace was obvious to everyone, the people and the government alike. It dominated the national consciousness, which never lost sight of it in spite of temptations posed by other European or colonial objectives. Because the need to face Germany was accepted with unanimity, conditions were eminently favorable for a collaboration of policy and strategy, conditions which were not, however, always exploited as they should have been. . . .

NEO-POLITICS

But our discussion of policy, strategy, and their mutual rapport may appear outmoded and obsolete since the event in 1928 that claimed to eliminate war from world affairs. I speak of the Kellogg Pact, whose central idea was the repudiation of war *as an instrument of national policy*. The fifteen states that signed the Kellogg Pact on 27 August 1928 agreed to settle all disputes by peaceful means, thus establishing a new kind of politics to which strategy is irrelevant. . . .[70]

The lessons of forty centuries, however, support Bern-

---

70. French foreign minister Aristide Briand first proposed a bilateral renunciation of war by France and the United States as a means of achieving a *de facto* alliance with the latter. Hostile to any special relationship with France and contemptuous of peace advocates, United States Secretary of State Frank B. Kellogg subverted Briand's plan by proposing instead a multilateral agreement abjuring the use of force as an instrument of national policy. The irrelevance of the resulting Kellogg-Briand Pact to events of the 1930s is hardly surprising, given that neither of its sponsors had any interest in the abolition of war, Arthur Ferrill, *Peace in Their Time* (New Haven, 1952).

hardi's conclusions that "war is the most efficacious instrument of policy" or, more exactly, that life is a struggle, whether for gain or for self-preservation. There is no reason to believe that things will be different in the future, that politics will have no recourse to force nor need for concourse with strategy. Experience has proved such ideas artificial and unrealizable. . . .[71]

71. Omitted are a further five pages of Castexian denunciation of the chimera of a politics that disavows war.

CHAPTER 11

THE REACTION OF
STRATEGY ON POLICY[1]

THE FORMS OF THIS ACTION

STRATEGY RETURNS to policy, with interest, the pressures exerted upon it from that direction. When well-conducted and crowned with military success, strategy contributes to the achievement of policy's objectives. Its impact stems from the impressiveness of the use of force, from a sense of awe that the "neo-politics" described in the previous chapter pretends to have abolished. On the other hand, military failure can raise insoluble problems for policy.

These indirect influences of strategy on policy are accompanied by direct influence in the form of demands by strategy for specific policy acts. Such demands are natural and perfectly acceptable; strategy has requirements that cannot be ignored because they affect the outcome of the war in progress or to come. In some cases, however, and they are less rare than one might think, strategy restrains policy by acting independently and contrary to the requirements of policy. In ignoring policy, strategy can create catastrophes that the former must impotently watch and for which the latter ultimately pays the price.

1. Raoul Castex, *Théories stratégiques*, vol. 3 (Paris: Société d'Editions Géographiques, Maritimes et Coloniales, 1931): 59–114.

235

INDIRECT AND DIRECT INFLUENCE OF STRATEGY

A brief glance at the 1914 war reveals some typical examples of the repercussions of strategy on policy. . . . The sad history of Allied efforts before September 1915 to draw Bulgaria into their camp shows the futility of any policy insensitive to the military situation. The moment was certainly ill-chosen. The year 1915 had seen the Russian disaster on the eastern front, and the Dardanelles expedition[2] had achieved nothing at all. It was asking too much of policy to attract the Bulgarians to a cause that must have appeared militarily hopeless. . . . Thus, the failure in the Dardanelles proved less serious from a strategic point of view than in its political consequences. . . . Such an operation should only have been undertaken with sufficient means to achieve total success or, given the political repercussions of failure, not at all. . . .

The influence of strategic requirements on policy can also be seen in the Anglo-French military accords that formed the foundation of the alliance between the two countries before 1914. In 1905, when relations between France and Germany were tense as a consequence of Moroccan affairs,[3] negotiations began between the military and naval general staffs of France and Britain. Taking place without the participation of civilian diplomats, the conversations were independent of policy, though Sir Edward Grey and French Am-

---

2. The attempt to knock Turkey out of the war lasted from 25 April 1915 to 10 January 1916, employed half a million Allied troops, and cost about 250,000 casualties.

3. Long at odds over colonial issues, Britain and France resolved their outstanding differences on 12 April 1904. Hoping to undermine the new *Entente Cordiale* before it could become a military alliance, Kaiser Wilhelm II's Germany challenged French expansion in Morocco only to find herself in a position of humiliating diplomatic isolation at the conference in Algeciras, Spain, which settled the so-called First Moroccan Crisis.

bassador Cambon asserted that the military discussions were opportune and should continue as long as the governments, that is, policy, were not committed to anything.[4]

From 1906 to 1911 the military technicians continued their intermittent talks. Foreign Minister Sir Edward Grey reports that during this period he did not even know whether military negotiations were being pursued.[5] In any case, the British cabinet was not informed officially, and many British leaders were shocked when the Agadir crisis of 1911 displayed the potential dangers of such conversations. Minister Asquith warned against allowing the French to rely on British cooperation, and those ministers not party to the negotiations raised the matter in the full cabinet. They asked that Britain obtain from France a declaration that exchanges of military views would not compromise the government's freedom of action and that joint plans established by the general staffs would be put into effect only should the governments decide to act in common. A notable demand was that French and British naval dispositions would not be based on a promise of wartime cooperation. Speaking for France, Ambassador Cambon immediately offered the assurance demanded by the British cabinet, while, at the same time, the Anglo-French military conventions were committed to writing. . . .

When the war came, the British, though holding firmly to

4. On Anglo-French military conversations see Michael Howard, *The Continental Commitment* (Harmondsworth, Middlesex, 1974), chapters 1–2, and Samuel R. Williamson, Jr., *The Politics of Grand Strategy: Britain and France Prepare for War, 1904–1914* (Cambridge, MA, 1969).

5. Only Prime Minister Campbell-Bannerman, Lord Ripon, Secretary of State for War Haldane, and Chancellor of the Exchequer Asquith knew of the proceedings before they were explained to the full cabinet on 23 August 1911, John Terraine, *Douglas Haig: The Educated Soldier* (London, 1963): 59, and Zara Steiner, *Britain and the Origins of the First World War* (London, 1977): 76.

the principle of liberty of action, were committed to preventing the German fleet from erupting into the Channel to shell the French coast. The Anglo-French naval conventions calling for concentration of the French fleet in the Mediterranean and the British fleet in her home waters created a compelling sense of moral obligation that did the British the greatest honor. As Sir Edward Grey put it, by agreeing to keep her fleet in the Mediterranean, France exposed her coasts unless Britain intervened to protect them. *Was Britain not bound by obligations independent of any formal agreements?*

Thus, in conformity with sentiment and in spite of the reservations enunciated in 1911, on the afternoon of 2 August 1914, Ambassador Cambon received assurance from Sir Edward Grey that the British fleet would intervene if the German fleet acted against France in the Channel. The equivalent of a declaration of war, Grey's act was an excellent example of the pressure placed on policy by strategic dispositions.[6]

. . . The very successes of strategy can have an unhappy effect on policy. To take a hypothetical example, had the Dardanelles campaign achieved the expectations of its advocates, the ultimate political results might have nullified any military success. By forcing the Straits and seizing Constantinople, the Allies would have put themselves in an awkward diplomatic position. Compelled to cede their conquest to a clamoring Russia, they would have faced demands for compensation from the Balkan powers and Italy that could not have been met without stirring up further discontent. The pernicious implications of such a victory have become clear only after the event, and the only consolation for our

6. For a denial that the cabinet's decision resulted automatically from the naval agreements, see Steiner, 230.

military failure is having been spared an almost insoluble political quandary.

The enemy would have faced a similar situation in November and December 1915 had he tried fully to exploit his great Serbian success by pushing on to Salonika. Taking Salonika would have brought into the open Austrian and Bulgarian appetites for that city, which belonged to Greece, that is to say, to Wilhelm II's brother-in-law,[7] and created major fissures within the Central Powers. Thus, very wisely, the Germans rejected Austrian General Conrad's[8] demands to press their offensive and demonstrated their awareness of the potential for military victory to undermine policy. Of course, the enemy's halt at the Greek frontier granted the Allied army an unexpected respite to reorganize within the Salonika camp and await better days.

Similarly, Chancellor Bethmann-Hollweg reveals that there was some hesitation in German political circles at the war's beginning about the propitiousness of declaring war on Russia.[9] General von Falkenhayn,[10] the minister of war, opposed the declaration for fear of the repercussions on world opinion. General von Moltke,[11] chief of the General Staff, on the other hand, favored war against Russia because it would bring France into the game and allow the application of the pre-established plan for a war on two fronts.

---

7. King Constantine I (1868–1923), whose pro-German sympathies led to his abdication in 1917, though he returned to the throne in 1920.

8. Field Marshal Franz Count Conrad von Hötzendorf (1852–1925) was chief of staff of the Austrian army from 1912 until July 1918.

9. *Considerations sur la guerre mondiale,* 118 (author's note).

10. General Erich von Falkenhayn (1861–1922) was minister of war from July 1913 until he became chief of the German General Staff from September 1914. Author of the Verdun bloodbath, he was removed in August 1916.

11. General Helmuth von Moltke (1848–1916) was chief of staff from 1806 until September 1914.

Moltke won his point when the chancellor admitted the impossibility of contesting "the absolutely plausible military arguments of the general responsible for the operations."

It was equally under the compulsion of pressing military needs that the Allies concluded on 26 April 1915 the Treaty of London, which brought Italy into the war at the price of political concessions completely incompatible with the Entente's fundamental principles. In particular, promises to Italy of territorial aggrandizement violated the principle of nationality with regard to Germans in the Tyrol, Croatians east of Trieste, and Yugoslavs in Dalmatia. The highly impolitic treaty threatened to provoke violent discontent among the Serbs and the Croatians and even to stimulate a singular revival of South Slav affection for the Hapsburgs, but military necessity demanded Italian adherence to the Allied cause. As Delcassé said to Wickham Steed,[12] a million Italian and six hundred thousand Rumanian bayonets were worth even a sacrifice of principle. Here strategy imperiously commanded policy, making up for having been under other circumstances its subordinate.

EXAGGERATION OF STRATEGY'S INFLUENCE

Just as policy sometimes exceeds its sphere and invades the zone legitimately reserved for strategy, strategy takes its revenge through frequent incursions into the domain of policy. Condemnable in theory, these excesses are explicable and unsurprising in practice. Tools of human beings, policy and strategy are imperfect and subject to passions. . . . Hence, it happens that in the yoked team of policy and strategy the one with more character, more personality, more audacity, and fewer scruples dominates. . . . Strat-

12. Journalist and later editor of the London *Times* Henry Wickham Steed (1871–1956).

egy's influence on the affairs of state becomes exaggerated by customs, institutions, or circumstances that give the military a disproportionate weight in the decision-making process.

The actions of Napoleon Bonaparte during 1796 exemplify the soldier's increasing usurpation of the policy maker's role. At the beginning, the relations between policy—that is to say, the government—and strategy, the military leader, were normal. Bonaparte obeyed the instructions of the Directory and fully shared their views. For example, writing to the Directory from Cherasco on 27 April 1796 to explain the benefits of the armistice with Piedmont, he announced that he would be greatly distressed to discover that his action had been in any way contrary to the Directory's wishes.[13] Until September 1796, Bonaparte had corresponded with the Directory in the measured tones of confident collaboration between policy and strategy. The commander in chief remained perfectly in his place and handled only those matters within his competence.

A clear change manifested itself from October 1796, after his great success against Würmser.[14] Feeling greater assurance about the military situation, Bonaparte began to take the initiative in the political domain. Thus, he reported to the Directory on 2 October his assessment of the Italian sit-

13. At Cherasco, Napoleon negotiated an armistice to end a brief campaign against Austria's ally, Piedmont. Taken by Castex at face value, Bonaparte's letter was disingenuous. Behind superficial deference to the Convention lay the truth that the entire campaign had contravened instructions to avoid unnecessary conflict with Piedmont in the hopes of wooing a potentially republican state to a French alliance, David Chandler, *The Campaigns of Napoleon* (New York, 1966): 61, 75.

14. Count Würmser commanded Austrian forces that raised Napoleon's first siege of Mantua before being defeated at Castiglione on 3 August 1796. A second attempt to save Mantua in September 1796 led to Würmser's army being pinned up within the city.

uation and offered a plan to "revolutionize" Modena. On 8 October, he wrote of the need to temporize with the Italian states, especially with Rome. His intervention he attributed to selfless motives:

> *Whenever your general in Italy is not at the center of everything, you will run great risks.* Do not attribute this language to ambition; I have too many honors.

The first storm cloud arrived over Bonaparte's project to import revolution to Modena and a second, in December 1796, when he declared his opposition to negotiations with Austria before the fall of Mantua. Here the military leader was in his proper role because the armistice was an essentially strategic matter.

On the other hand, on 28 December 1796 and 1 February 1797, Bonaparte proposed his own Italian settlements including, among other things, turning Modena, Ferraro, and Romagna into republics, giving Rome to Spain, and restoring Parma to the emperor. At Macerata, on 15 February, he indicated his conditions for a peace with Rome. At Leoben, raised to the rank of plenipotentiary, Bonaparte decided policy matters.[15] He had won his own total independence, even dictating decisions that involved other theaters of operations. . . .

Thereafter, Napoleon's political activity could only increase. . . . Throughout the summer of 1797 he governed Italy from the palace of Mombello outside Milan without concern for the ideas of the Directory. In signing the treaty of Campo Formio with Austria in October, he disobeyed the

---

15. Imposed by Napoleon upon both the Directory and the Hapsburg emperor, the agreement of 18 April 1797 obliged Austria to cede Belgium, the right bank of the Rhine, and Milan and formed the foundation of the Peace of Campo Formio.

instructions of his government by allowing Austria to keep Venice and other territory east of the Adige.[16]

Circumstances had aided the soldier's entry into the zone of policy. The commander in chief was far from Paris, and with the rudimentary means of communications of the day two weeks were required to obtain the central government's responses to his requests or suggestions. He had with him no government representative responsible for presenting the political point of view. Given that the circumstances often demanded urgent action, the strategist was led to resolve policy issues. Finally, war as fought by the French in those days had a clear component of political propaganda.[17] The power of our arms was in large measure put in the service of propagating a particular political and social concept with which the military leaders were imbued. Themselves a product thereof, they could not but put it in the forefront of their thoughts.

Napoleon represents an anomaly in civil-military relations. His expansive, authoritarian, and centralizing tendency, combined with a personal education as much political as military, led him to dominate his political masters. Given a different commander placed in the same conditions, relations between the military leadership and the government could have been very different.

During the 1914 war, Ludendorff[18] set out to emulate Napoleon. After having relegated the conventional and col-

16. In exchange, Austria ceded control over Belgium, the Rhine's left bank, and Venice's Ionian Islands to France and recognized the Cisalpine Republic and Venetia.

17. As would a war fought in our own time by the Soviets, for example (author's note).

18. Erich Ludendorff (1865–1937) was Hindenburg's chief of staff in the eastern theater of the war and became first quartermaster general after Hindenburg succeeded Falkenhayn as chief of staff in August 1916. Be-

orless Hindenburg to second place at German headquarters, he used the pretext of military necessity to infiltrate the political domain. His claims to instill unity in the war effort covered dreams of dominating everything, diplomacy and domestic policy as well as strategy. His success was incomplete. For one thing, Germany was by that time almost a constitutional state whose legal institutions could not be entirely disregarded. The vicious struggles initiated by the former quartermaster-general led the country into serious disorder. Finally, the military situation withheld from Ludendorff his best instrument—victory on the battlefield. Strategy had not achieved such success that it could supersede policy.

. . . After the war, Ludendorff attempted in his *Conduit de la guerre et politique* to explain his failure as war leader on the grounds that he had been denied the full powers over the nation necessary to the strategist.[19] Exonerating the military command, he attributed Germany's defeat to her people's poor guidance by their clergy and teachers and to paralyzing judicial rulings.[20] The Jews were also to blame for supporting the *Entente* and undermining the state's resistance. The high command had done its duty in spite of obstructions from a government that, failing to comprehend

---

hind the figurehead provided by the ineffectual Hindenburg, Ludendorff functioned as a virtual "silent dictator" of Germany until he was ousted by Prince Max von Baden in October 1918, Herwig and Heyman, 233–34.

19. See also Hans Delbrück, *Ludendorff peint par lui-même* (author's note). Ludendorff's *Kriegsführung und Politik* was published in German and French versions in 1922 and *Der Totale Krieg* appeared in 1935.

20. One finds in books written in Germany since the last war a constant and pernicious alteration of the truth in the service of personal or national interests. When his own or his country's interests are at stake, the German naturally behaves this way (author's note).

the total character of the war, did not offer the command the necessary support and, in particular, refused it complete political mastery. . . .

Ludendorff had an excellent remedy for these evils in the establishment of a dictatorship by the high command. He regretted that headquarters, that is, Ludendorff himself, had not taken the direction of the state into its own hand, *"the only solution that would have led policy to have the same conceptions as the high command."* This remarkably original solution elegantly cut through the conundrum of civil-military relations. In eliminating the contradictor, it eliminated the contradiction. Pride had unhinged an otherwise remarkable mind.

Ludendorff was not an aberration but, rather, the product, if an extreme case, of a specifically German mentality and milieu that believed that, especially in time of war, the military ought to take command of the state and absorb its other agencies. Others reasoned similarly, and Ludendorff simply personified their thought. . . .[21] Even civilian politicians deferred to the military. Having noted that political and military considerations were often contradictory, Bethmann-Hollweg admits ungrudgingly that "the overall direction, the single line to follow, ought to be determined only from a military point of view." So self-effacing is he as to denigrate politics from the second rank to the third and to the fourth. . . .[22]

21. Castex's description of Ludendorff as a *"réduction homothétique,"* in mathematics a conformal transformation of the type called a dilation, is even more technical than is his wont.

22. See Bethmann-Hollweg, *Considerations sur la guerre mondiale,* 162–68, 184–88, 192, 223–26, 267, 277, 312, 319, 325 (author's note). Four pages of examples of the German general staff's impositions upon policy are omitted.

In Germany during the 1914 war the normal relations between policy and strategy were completely transformed. Strategy's influence was excessive and unbalanced. With the omnipotence of an unchallenged military, the greatest and most baneful stupidities took root and flourished. Two particular events will be cited until the end of time: Germany's violation of the Belgian neutrality and her adoption of a policy of unrestricted submarine war.[23]

These two colossal blunders by strategy are intimately connected. By invading Belgium, Germany provoked Britain and condemned herself to irremediable inferiority at sea. To escape the consequences, Germany had to use, and finally to abuse, her submarine force, which led inexorably to America's entry into the war.[24] Everything was inevitable from the moment German troops entered Liège. In such cases, the future is all the more predictable the more strongly the state is intoxicated with power and the more completely the appetites of an omnipotent strategy overcome its political reason. The aggressor is essentially maladroit, and his mistakes contribute to his defeat and to the salvation of his opponents and to the liberty of the world.[25]

Juxtaposing on the one hand the violation of Belgian neutrality and the unrestricted submarine campaign, and on the

23. Castex devotes thirty-two pages, omitted here, to these episodes, arguing that, had German political leaders not abdicated their responsibilities, they would have impressed upon the soldiers the foolishness of an attack on neutral Belgium certain to bring Britain into the war. In disagreeing with Bethmann-Hollweg's suggestion that Britain would have supported France even in the absence of a threat to Belgium, Castex ignores his own earlier argument that the Anglo-French naval arrangements led Britain into World War I.

24. Castex means abuse in a political sense; that he had no doubts as to the legitimacy of the use of submarines against unarmed merchant ships is clear from his arguments in chapters 2 and 16.

25. Castex's liberal ideology has no place for a rational and skillful aggressor.

other, France's ten-kilometer withdrawal and British policies regarding American cotton reveals one of the principal causes of the outcome of the 1914 war. The comparison demonstrates that strategy usually has no reason to rue yielding to the well-founded demands of policy.[26]

26. The caveat "well-founded" hints that the soldier's duty may lead him to defy a poorly conceived policy.

CHAPTER 12

THE LEAST BAD COMPROMISE[1]

Policy and strategy act independently and without co-ordination. As in classical mechanics they achieve an equilibrium that is simply a compromise between their contradictory requirements and desires.[2] The position of the compromise, whether it is closer to the demands of policy or of strategy, depends upon the forces in play. Moreover, no solution ever wholly satisfies anyone. Always an imperfect outcome, compromise offers inconveniences as well as advantages.

The diverse compromises imaginable can be evaluated; some are more or less good, others more or less bad, and among all there is one that is, if not the best, at least the least bad. That human weakness and errors conspire to ensure that this least bad compromise will very rarely be achieved in practice does not permit us to avoid the necessary and constructive effort of seeking to identify it by examining the lessons of the past.

Let us first identify the parties. On one plane we find the twin sisters, policy and strategy. The first is directed by the

1. Raoul Castex, *Théories stratégiques*, vol. 3 (Paris: Société d'Editions Géographiques, Maritimes et Coloniales, 1931): 115–33.
2. A pointless metaphor because Castex offers no mechanism to explain the alleged equilibrium.

organ of the state devoted to foreign affairs, the second by the military or naval high command. Above both policy and strategy is their common ancestor, the nation's will to fight. The national will is represented by a plan of action or, in time of war, by a war plan. The plan lies in the exclusive domain of the government.

The problem is to establish contact and liaison between the plan of action or war plan, between policy and strategy.[3] As we have already observed, one cannot conceive of relations between persons or entities unless they exist. But do the government's war plans or plans of action, the diplomats' policy, and the strategy of the generals always exist?

The answer depends on whether or not the nation is at war. In wartime, one can answer the question affirmatively. Nations at war are driven by inexorable and sometimes tragic necessity to struggle in every domain. In peacetime, however, things are often very different. While nations that are expanding and conquering or are threatened by serious perils manifest a peacetime collaboration of policy and strategy almost as active as that in time of war, otherwise joint planning falls into a deep sleep.

Strategy is the favored sister and can more or less escape the fate of disappearing altogether in peace.[4] Peacetime

3. The argument is confusing. Having just asserted the existence of only one plan at any given time, a war plan if the nation is at war or a plan of action if not, Castex then introduces the need to coordinate the two. Surely the problem is rather to coordinate the elements of strategy and policy within whichever plan exists at the moment, an interpretation consistent with the paragraph's later introduction of a tripartite scheme of government plans, policy, and strategy. The superimposition of a national will over the "twin sisters" undermines, moreover, the assumption of conflict between the two and reveals that Castex's real concern is not in the theoretical realm (who will make plans?) but in the practical (how to get the French government to do so?).

4. Castex returns here to a simple opposition between government policy and military strategy.

strategy can be uninspired, incomplete, ill-conceived, but it will not disappear altogether because military forces continue to exist and strategy controls their maintenance, future, and training. Strategy must concern itself with possible future employment and can never be completely extinguished. That the military always retains a certain level of activity explains why the nation's will to struggle and awareness of that struggle's requisites ordinarily find refuge in the military during periods when the people as a whole no longer feel the need to protect their existence. Moreover, the military bears a heavy weight of responsibility in times of trouble.[5]

But strategy, though it continues to exist in uncertain and vacillating form in peacetime, will not always find in the government's plan of action the support, nourishment, and inspiration that it has the right to expect. The phrase "government war plan" often appears in the treatises of specialists, but rarely corresponds to anything real. Like the great sea serpent, many people speak of the government war plan, but no one has ever seen it, and one is not very confidant of its existence.[6]

It is not that the government renounces all peacetime control over the military command and over strategy. Ministers often return from cabinet meetings to announce to the army or navy chief of staff: "My dear general (or my dear admiral), the government has instituted this or that policy—operate accordingly." But these interventions usually concern urgent problems. Government action rarely begins with

5. It is for these reasons that, during international negotiations, the politicians of certain countries tend to diminish the participation of technicians of all sorts and soldiers in particular, whose concern for the interests of the nation renders them inconvenient (author's note).

6. One of Castex's favorite lines, repeated elsewhere and cited in Jean Baptiste Duroselle, *La Décadence, 1932–1939* (Paris, 1979): 267.

premeditated, methodically analyzed, long-term prognostications developed through a process of leisured thought and implemented with consistency and perseverance. Government influence will rather be discontinuous, hesitant, sporadic, and empirical. Acting in fits and starts and living from day to day, it has little to do with planning.

One ought not to be surprised by this state of things. Politicians do not generally operate in conditions permitting the development of large-scale plans of action or war plans. Most of them lack the necessary special training, both technical and moral. Even if they had such an education that reasoned argument could replace rhetoric, ministerial instability would deprive them of the time necessary to undertake any useful large-scale work. However good their intentions, politicians find their ephemeral periods in office dominated by current affairs, by political struggles, by agitations in the parliamentary assemblies, etc. Such an atmosphere is not conducive to devising a major political and military plan. . . .[7]

To avoid the serious inconveniences that result from the lack of peacetime government policy, countries have sometimes thought to reinforce their government with an instition capable of furnishing the elements it lacks: competence, stability, and permanence. Examples are the *Conseil Su-*

7. Unstable government was particularly characteristic of the French Third Republic, which saw 107 cabinets overthrown between 1875 and 1940 or an average of more than one a year, William L. Shirer, *The Collapse of the Third Republic: An Inquiry into the Fall of France in 1940* (New York, 1969): 38. One can go too far, however, in decrying French political instability. Cabinets came and went, but their personnel went largely unchanged. It is useful to remember that throughout this discussion Castex uses the word "government" where an American would say "administration." Omitted is a discussion of Britain's exceptional ability for peacetime planning.

périeur de la Défense Nationale (C.S.D.N.) in France and Britain's Committee of Imperial Defence.[8] We will discuss these in greater detail later in this chapter. These institutions not only provide policy stability, at least in theory, but reinforce the executive and coordinate the ministerial departments in addressing specific tasks.

For such an organ to achieve the desired results, it must exercise the full measure of the attributions that logically belong to it. On one level, the national defense council must ensure the cooperation of the diverse ministries to achieve the purposes of the war. It must manage the wartime functioning of the wheels of government and administration, economic mobilization, industrial mobilization, transport, communication, etc. All of this is important, but a national defense council cannot, however, limit itself to the sphere of organization, supply, and administration. Using the language of the general staff, these are matters for the "first bureau." The council must take up the challenge of reasoning, to stay with staff jargon, at the "third bureau" level and concern itself with operations, as operations are to be understood at the high echelons of "government" and "nation." It is with this operational focus that I would like to see our C.S.D.N. pose and resolve questions like the following:

What are France's interests?

What is the best direction in which to focus French effort?

How should we pursue our historic development and the work of our predecessors?

Where should we struggle for profit, to improve the present situation?

8. See, respectively, Kiesling, 30–39, and Franklyn Arthur Johnson, *Defence by Committee: The British Committee of Imperial Defence 1885–1959* (London, 1960).

Where, on the other hand, should we resist to conserve what we have?

Whence are the mostly dangerous threats likely to come?

To what attacks are we particularly exposed?

What should we do to meet our needs, be they positive or negative, expansionist or conservative?

What specific plans stem from these needs?

What are the appropriate political, military, maritime, colonial, economic, moral, etc., plans for the situation?

Perhaps our council poses and answers these questions. Not being party to the secrets of the gods, I do not know. I only hope that this is how they act, because such an approach is necessary to produce a war plan or a plan of action worthy of the name. Only after having established such a permanent and lasting plan of operations can the council create the necessary organizational and administrative dispositions.

Such a process is the only one through which strategy can receive a plan of action upon which to rely, a plan to take the place of the one vainly sought from the government itself.[9] Similarly, diplomacy acquires from the national defense committee the foreign policy program that it had demanded from the government with similar lack of success.

Of course, such resolutions will not always prove satisfactory. The military will do well always to assume either a complete dearth of responsible planning organs or regrettable errors in the plans themselves and must be ready to act and to act judiciously in either case. This observation will be useful later on.[10]

9. Note both the reification of "strategy" and "foreign policy" and their independence from the government.

10. See below, 262–64.

Let us suppose that our first condition, that is, existence, is fulfilled, that the government war plan, policy, and strategy are alive and flourishing side by side.[11] If policy and strategy are to enjoy good relations, they must not mix in one another's business nor attempt to control one another.[12]

This requirement is easier proclaimed than met. All of history shows us the frequency of trespasses over the policy-strategy frontier. Well-intentioned minds have thought to solve the problem of transgressions by policy into strategy, at least, by distinguishing positive from negative interventions. Policy would forswear any but negative interventions into strategy, stepping in only to block operations likely to produce unhappy diplomatic consequences and abstaining from positive interventions, those meant to direct operations along roads it deemed to be favorable. But this distinction between positive and negative interventions is a false panacea. Experience indicates that the actions of policy on strategy are always as much positive as negative and cannot be one or the other depending on the case. Moreover, positive actions are perfectly admissible as long as they do not exceed reasonable limits and do not mix in details of execution. In sum, the danger does not stem from the nature of the intervention but its degree. Excess alone constitutes a problem. However difficult the task, we must seek a better dividing line between the actions of policy and strategy.

While remaining in their respective places, policy and strategy must retain a tight liaison, each facilitating the

11. Throughout the chapter, Castex moves carelessly between the strategy-policy duo and the triad of strategy, policy, and government war plan.

12. Logic suggests an arrangement not of three independent elements "side by side" but with strategy and policy subordinate to the government war plan, but Castex is skeptical of the government's ability to formulate a war plan.

other's task or at least not further complicating it.[13] This union is a beautiful thing, as beautiful as its manifestations are rare. Ludendorff cites as a model the cooperation of Bismarck and Moltke, but although steady and constant in time of peace, their relationship experienced some clouds during the 1870 war.[14] Moreover, the constant success that crowned all of the Prussian efforts greatly facilitated the collaboration. Acrimony is much more difficult to avoid in hard times for, as the proverb says, "When there is no more hay in the manger, the asses fight."

As we have seen, for bad times, Ludendorff offers the radical remedy of giving strategy control over diplomacy and over the direction of the state—"the only solution," he says, "that causes policy to have the same conceptions as the high command." In offering this analysis, he cites, interpreted in his own fashion, High Priest Clausewitz:

> To bring a whole war to a brilliant result, it is necessary to possess a deep knowledge of the higher affairs of state. The conduct of war and of policy are intermingled, and the military leader becomes a statesman. . . . But he must not cease to be a leader. He must, on one hand, embrace all matters of state and, on the other, have exact knowledge of what he can do with the means at his disposal.[15]

Ludendorff is not the sole proponent of unifying policy and strategy under the same hat.[16] Gustaf II Adolf,[17]

13. "War, like peace, is not a double thing but a *unity*. It does not consist of military and civil compartments. The two are tightly united," Marshal Foch, quoted in M. Recouly, *Le Memorial de Foch,* 45 (author's note).

14. Castex himself exaggerates the intimacy of the Bismarck-Moltke partnership for his own purposes, below, 230–31.

15. *On War,* book 1, chapter 3 (Howard, 112).

16. Castex conflates a theoretical stance on Ludendorff's part with the actual behavior of the soldier-monarchs.

17. King Gustaf II Adolf of Sweden (1594–1632) was the most successful Protestant soldier of the Thirty Years War.

Charles XII,[18] Frederick II,[19] Napoleon, and others are only the most brilliant examples. Such monocephalism can manifest itself in ministers as well as in sovereigns. During the Seven Years War, for example, the Elder Pitt, as "Minister of Foreign Affairs of the South," controlled British policy and corresponded directly with the military commanders.[20] Under his authority, the Secretaries for War and the Admiralty, Barrington[21] and Anson,[22] were mere technicians and executive agents. Corbett and Mahan praised the system, to which they attributed Britain's success in this period.[23] In seventeenth-century France, Colbert also found himself to have control over policy and strategy from a triple point of view—naval, economic, and colonial.[24]

The coin has another side, however, and civil-military consolidation has not been without failures. Charles XII's martial adventures in Russia produced political catastrophe,

---

18. Charles XII of Sweden (1682–1718) led his country during the eighteen-year Great Northern War, during which Swedish aspirations against Russia were crushed at the battle of Poltava (1709).

19. Frederick II (1712–1786) assumed the crown of Prussia in 1740 and immediately, by invading Silesia, initiated the War of the Austrian Succession (1740–1744).

20. William Pitt, 1st Earl of Chatham (1708–1778), was called to office as "Principal Secretary of State" under Prime Minister Newcastle late in 1756 where his effectiveness was undermined by George II's dislike for "the Great Commoner," Sir Sidney Low, ed., *The Dictionary of English History* (London, 1928): 849.

21. Vice Admiral Samuel Barrington was no mere administrator but won high praise from Mahan for his energy and diligence as British commander in chief in the West Indies in 1778, Mahan, *Influence*, 322–23.

22. George, 1st Baron Anson (1697–1762) was First Lord 1751–1756 and 1757–1762.

23. Sir Julian Corbett, *England in the Seven Years' War* (author's note).

24. Jean-Baptiste Colbert (1619–1683) served Louis XIV simultaneously as controller general of finance and secretary of state for the navy.

while Napoleon's enormous political blunders towards Russia and Spain led to disastrous military consequences. When policy and strategy are in different hands, they tend to neutralize one another and, as in dynamics, reach an equilibrium. Because each side works as a brake upon the other, the equilibrium offers the possibility of harmony, wisdom, and prudence. When, on the contrary, policy and strategy inhabit the same skull, their contest must take place within it without possibility of compromise. One dominates the other, and the internal struggle produces not compromise but a single force, not equilibrium but an accelerated movement that is by its very nature immoral and illogical. In the absence of a counterpoise or a brake, things roll towards the abyss. The unity of policy and military direction in an all-powerful individual is not to be desired; better that they be separated but living side by side in a tight liaison and a confidant union.

To achieve such a situation, policy and strategy must understand one another, appreciate one another's importance and particular requirements, and know how to communicate their own. There is no other way of achieving this basic object except through a long process of education for those charged with the two forms of combative activity.

It is first necessary to ensure that politicians, statesmen, and diplomats receive a basic initiation into military and naval questions and understand the organization and employment of the armed forces. Many thinkers, especially those writing after their nations have undergone major crises, have adumbrated this necessity. "The political leadership of a state must not lack knowledge of military matters," Clausewitz observed.[25] Mahan spoke "of the need of states-

25. *On War*, book 8, chapter 6 (Howard, 608).

men and people to know something about the ABCs of Naval Strategy."[26] Such knowledge allows policy to know at least whether its advice or requests are reasonable and to avoid unreasonable or pernicious demands.

The British have demonstrated a notably clear awareness of this fundamental prerequisite for the proper functioning of the politico-strategic machine. Especially since the South African War,[27] they have given a major place in their universities and establishments of higher education to the study of naval and military questions. Courses on this subject, whether historical or contemporary case studies, have had a great success in the universities, and the students have profited greatly from them in the high posts which they later assumed in the various branches of the state administration.[28] For example, in 1903, Corbett, the Ford lecturer, held the chair of maritime history at Oxford and devoted his teaching to the history of British activities in the Mediterranean. In 1905, Oxford created a lectureship in military history, which became a chair in 1909 and was held first by Spencer Wilkinson[29] and then by Charles Oman,[30] author of *The History of the Art of War in the Middle Ages* and *The History of the Peninsula Wars.*[31] The same trend existed at Cambridge where a chair of naval history was cre-

26. Mahan, *Naval Strategy* (Greenwood Press, 1975): 6.

27. Boer War of 1899–1902.

28. That the courses existed is indisputable, but Castex offers no evidence for their efficacy.

29. Spencer Wilkinson (1853–1937) was a journalist for *The Manchester Guardian* and *The Morning Post* and military writer.

30. Sir Charles William Chadwick Oman (1860–1946).

31. Castex has confused the Chichele Chair of Modern History, held by Oman, with Wilkinson's Chichele Chair of the History of War. See John Hattendorf, "The Study of War History at Oxford, 1861–1990," in Hattendorf and Malcolm H. Murfett, eds., *The Limitations of Military Power: Essays Presented to Professor Norman Gibbs on his 80th Birthday* (London and New York, 1990): chapter 1.

ated under the auspices of Lord Northcliffe in 1920.[32] Its first holder was Holland Rose,[33] whose primary thesis was that military history and the history of the nation were so inextricably bound together that they could not be presented separately. The famous maritime historian Laughton[34] taught at King's College, while at University College was to be found General Sir G. Aston[35] of the Royal Marines, one of the creators of the navy's intelligence service and the author of several valuable writings on strategy.

More recently still, in 1925–1926, a series of military lectures was given at the University of London. Vice Admiral Richmond[36] treated naval war, Major General Sir Edmund Ironside[37] land war, Vice Marshal Brooke Popham[38] air war, and Brigadier General Hartely chemical war. The collected lectures were published by Aston in a volume bearing the significant title: *The Study of War for Use by Statesmen*

32. The Vere Harmsworth Chair of Imperial and Naval History was established by Northcliffe's brother Harold Sidney Harmsworth. "Imperial" was added to the title in 1932, and Sir Herbert Richmond succeeded J. Holland Rose in 1934.

33. John Holland Rose (1855–1942) was Vere Harmsworth Professor of Naval History 1919–1933.

34. John Knox Laughton (1830–1915) was a professor at King's College of the University of London 1885–1914.

35. Major General George Grey Aston (1861–1938) of the Royal Marine Artillery.

36. For the parallels between the careers of Castex and Sir Herbert Richmond, see above, xxxvi.

37. Field Marshal William Edmund First Baron Ironside (1880–1959) was commandant of the Staff College at Camberley and later served as chief of the British Imperial General Staff from September 1939 to July 1940.

38. Air Chief Marshal Sir Henry Robert Moore Brooke Popham (1878–1953) was the first commandant of the R.A.F. Staff College from 1921 to 1926. Though he retired from the air force in 1937, he returned to serve as Commander in Chief Far East from October 1940 to 27 December 1941.

and Citizens (Longmans, 1927). The British effort has been a most admirable one and offers a valuable model.[39]

Conversely, it is no less indispensable that soldiers have that sufficient knowledge of political questions without which they cannot establish plans in peacetime nor execute and revise them during the course of hostilities. Moreover, one can only work effectively in the military realm if one understands the *raison d'être* of one's effort, if one can clearly perceive the political goal behind the military one. Let us hasten to add, however, that the soldier must not play at politics, a profession that is not his and for which others are better qualified. He need receive a minimal initiation into policy questions but has no business piloting the ship of state. When things follow their normal course, he is not to seek to impose his personal conceptions in a sphere in which he is, at least apparently, hardly competent. He ought, in the beginning, to leave matters to those responsible and only to intervene in certain particular cases.[40] Mahan has written several felicitous lines on the subject.

> To better prepare for war and to establish a plan of campaign, the generals and admirals ought to be perfectly in-

39. Castex would later become aware of the best example of British civil-military education, the Imperial Defence College (now the Royal College of Defence Studies), established in 1926 under Richmond's directorship. The college, designed to introduce officers from the armed forces of Britain and the Commonwealth and a few civil servants to "the broadest aspects of Imperial strategy," served as a model for the *Collège des Hautes Etudes de Défence Nationale* of which Castex was the first director, Kiesling, 87–91. It is striking that Castex did not add a reference to the Imperial Defence College, let alone to the French college, to the second edition of *Théories*.

40. Castex's argument slides from "the soldier is and should be incompetent to exercise political influence" to "the soldier is, apparently, not really competent" to "the soldier may have to intervene whenever his competence appears to exceed that of the civilians." There are other hints in the text of Castex's tacit belief, one common in the French armed

formed about the international situation . . . Every naval officer ought to study current events, in foreign countries as well as his own, for he may be able one day to advise his government or at least sometimes to influence events favorably by means of his understanding of the world situation. . . . The sphere in which the navy operates is uniquely international, that is, intimately linked to the realm of the statesman. The naval officer must therefore try to be as much statesman as sailor, and the most glorious names in our profession have been both.[41]

The British, who are again the advance guard, put this idea in practice by having some eighty naval officers study at Cambridge as a counterpart to the measures taken to introduce future civilian leaders to military matters.

The study of contemporary politics does not offer any serious difficulty. Contrary to what some would have one believe, foreign policy is not the private preserve of so-called specialists. One need not understand all of the intricacies of diplomacy to have a sane opinion. The man on the street who reads his newspaper carefully each morning and who has a solid educational foundation in geography and military history can easily arrive at clear views on the problems of the day. Merely by applying his faculties and common sense to the objective analysis of the specific case, he can reason as well as a diplomat. Military officers are even better off than civilians because they have at their disposal not only serious publications dealing with these subjects but also the material furnished by their own reconnaissance services. The repercussions that policy has on their own work provide them with greater justification than common mortals for concerning themselves with political matters. Strategy is

---

forces of his day, that officers had a truer understanding of the nation's needs than did the politicians of the Third Republic.

41. Mahan, *Naval Strategy*, 20–21 (author's note).

the beginning and the end of all policy speculations. The military factor dominates policy. The balance of force underlines everything. Someone has said that "the history of nations is that of their armies."[42]

For the military to understand the political situation is especially valuable when strategy finds itself trying to pursue its peacetime preparations in the absence of a governmental plan of action. To avoid the grave consequences of such situations, the military will have to call upon their own political understanding, which serves as an emergency reserve and is not employed in normal times but saved for such eventualities. An example of this sort of thing, which is more frequent than one would think, can be seen in the Anglo-French military conversations and the arrangements of 1906 to 1914. Because of the hesitations and reluctance of the British government, France and Britain were unable to achieve the political dispositions that the situation required. The military leaders, alert to the coming storm, understood that they could not afford to wait for diplomacy to act, and they did well to make their own arrangements.

I know well that there are people in our profession who invoke the absence of government directives as a pretext to avoid taking necessary and urgent military action. This kind of reasoning, of which there are many sensational examples,[43] has the incontestable advantage of favoring laziness,

42. The last four sentences rest uneasily with the overall argument of balance between strategy and policy.

43. In Britain in 1912 an official article in the *Army Review* responded in these terms to a demand for the augmentation of the army made by the National Service League: "Until the government tells us that the expeditionary force is too weak to support a good national policy, we ought to assume that it is sufficient, and we ought *to count on the government* to foresee the appropriate moment to increase our forces" (Marshal Robertson, *Conduite générale de la guerre*, 50). It is with that same blind

inertia, and abdication of responsibility. But does one believe the sophism of Pontius Pilate and that this bizarre respect for constitutional form will be well received by the public should it result in a future catastrophe? The military must remember that their intelligence services provide them with an even better ability than others to predict what is going to happen. One cannot understand how they can remain inert when the situation demands action nor accept the pathetic excuse of lack of orders from the government or Foreign Ministry. Public opinion will rightly demand the heads of those military people who try to abdicate their responsibility.

Moreover, even if a government plan exists, there will be times when it contains inappropriate dispositions or even dangerous mistakes. In this case, the military must advise the government in accordance with their view of the situation. Strategy is not bound blindly to assent to all political claims. If, for example, as I have seen happen, an ambassador posted abroad errs badly in his appraisal of that nation's sentiments towards us and this more or less fantastic intelligence contrasts with that available from other sources, should the military remain quiet and fail by their protests to draw the anomaly to the attention of the political leadership? Should they not insist on a revision of the assumptions behind the political plan?[44]

The Admiralty, which enjoys an unusually privileged position, frequently expresses its views on British foreign policy

---

faith in others, even concerning their own profession, that the heads of the British army marched towards the events of 1914 (author's note).

44. Witness the behavior of Marshal Foch towards the French and Allied governments during the drafting of the Treaty of Versailles (French Council of Ministers 25 April 1919 and Peace Conference meetings of 31 March and 6 May 1919) (author's note). Foch objected that the terms of the treaty did not satisfy France's defensive requirements but was checked sharply by Prime Minister Clemenceau.

and is listened to with attention. Governments pass, the Admiralty remains. Sometimes it has found itself in marked opposition to the Foreign Office and won its case only after lively struggle. During the last war, the Admiralty reacted strongly against the American conception of freedom of the seas that had invaded Sir Edward Grey's Foreign Office. At the time of the Armistice, a strong sentiment manifested itself among the British against imposing overly rigorous conditions upon the Germans. Field Marshal Haig shared these views, and Lloyd George was not in favor of demanding that the Germans hand over their fleet, but the Admiralty was adamant on the matter, and no one cared to oppose its formal demand.[45] Finally, for too many long years after the war, the Foreign Office policy had a secret, if not open, anti-French orientation. By a singular aberration at odds with all the facts, it imagined that our country, like Germany before, had suddenly become the *perturbateur* of the European equilibrium, and the ramblings of Lloyd George on this subject hearkened to the period before Fashoda.[46] British diplomats, businessmen, and colonialists took a jaundiced view of things and added their tiny contributions of vinegar to Anglo-French relations. This crisis of distorted vision lasted until December 1926, when the Admiralty intervened. Thanks to its excellent intelligence service, it had attentively observed the changes in the political situation over the past several years. It nosed out and revealed the true *perturbateurs* of the future, noting Germany's state of mind, its desire for revenge, and the resurrection of German commerce, industry, merchant marine, and aviation. It followed the de-

45. Lloyd George only later changed his mind. Foch opposed overly harsh naval clauses in the treaty, and wrote a note to the government on the subject on 29 October 1918 (*Mémoires du Maréchal Foch*) (author's note).

46. French and British forces confronted one another at Fashoda in the Sudan on 18 September 1898.

velopment of Moscow's grand hegemonial plan in Asia and identified Germany's failures, especially in China. Thus the Admiralty, conscious of new perils brewing and of the need for a solid partnership between Britain and France to preserve the status quo, pulled the alarm bell and forced the Foreign Office to open its eyes and to acknowledge that France was not the enemy of the future but an indispensable ally. Admiralty policy was successful, and 1927 saw a sudden improvement in British policy towards France, Poland, and Russia and a happy and fruitful reaffirmation of the *Entente Cordiale.* Unhappily, the Labour victory has come to darken the picture.[47]

These are characteristic examples of military intervention in the policy domain. Though sometimes imperative, it should occur only under exceptionally unavoidable circumstances. It is preferable that things happen in a regular manner according to the natural functions of each agency, the military being restrained to the less brilliant role inherent in their own proper sphere of activity.

Moreover, nothing can replace duty and devotion to the higher interests of the country, which give the strategist and the policy maker the strength to perform their respective tasks, allow them to work together, and make them willing to remain in their respective places. Through duty, each can eschew all pretense to domination over the other, discovering, in a word, the necessary degree of self-denial.

---

47. The Admiralty also returned to the scene in December 1929, in the preparatory phase of the London Conference, but, apparently, with less force than heretofore. Serious evidence of Britain's current weakness, this is disquieting for us (author's note).

CHAPTER 13

THE INFLUENCE OF GEOGRAPHY IN NAVAL WARFARE[1]

GEOGRAPHY IS an essential factor in strategy and, along with history, an indispensable subject of study for statesmen, soldiers, and sailors. It is par excellence the science of government and command or, as Strabo puts it, "the science of princes and military leaders." Geography has long been a favored study of maritime belligerents. During the age of sail, the difficulties of navigation made it of prime importance, sometimes to such an exaggerated degree as to constitute a pernicious influence on the conduct of operations. With the discovery of steam, the importance of geography was rather hastily forgotten, but the wars of the second half of the nineteenth century, with their almost uniquely coastal emphasis, restored attention to it. The new interest in geography was limited, however, to the contours and hydrographic[2] characteristics of coastlines and their implications for inshore forces. There was little concern for the repercussions of geography on fleet operations, which had more or less disappeared from the scene.[3] Then, around

1. Raoul Castex, *Théories stratégiques,* vol. 3 (Paris: Société d'Editions Géographiques, Maritimes et Coloniales, 1931): 137–81.
2. Castex uses the word "hydrographic" in the strict sense of charting water depth.
3. But Castex notes below that Mahan's *Influence* was a seminal discussion of geography as a fundamental element of sea power.

1900, in the French navy especially, there arose a movement aimed at restoring the preeminence of the fleet,[4] which momentarily eclipsed the study of geography. This brings us to the 1914 war, during which this physical element gained a deserved revenge. To make use of geography in the future, it is appropriate to seek a balance by putting that science in its proper place.

SOME HISTORICAL EXAMPLES

The Anglo-Dutch wars of the seventeenth century provide oft-cited evidence of the influence of geography on naval operations. The geography entirely favored Britain, whose coasts virtually blockaded those of Holland. To assure the passage of their convoys across the Channel, the Dutch had to consolidate their high seas fleet as an escort force, depriving it of the opportunity to conduct operations against the enemy fleet. Freeing up the fleet for battle during the military phases of the struggle meant almost complete interruption of commercial traffic, even of herring fishing in the North Sea, and consequent economic hardship. The more fortunate British escaped this constraint. Their foreign commerce traveled in safety, and the Royal Navy remained unshackled.

To remedy this disadvantageous situation, the Dutch would have needed sufficient numerical superiority to allow simultaneous fleet operations and commerce protection. Thus, their unfavorable geographical position translated in the final reckoning into an entirely detrimental balance of forces. . . .

The geographic factor evolves with politics and with the course of operations. It also modifies itself through the ac-

4. The French School.

tions of the belligerents. We will return to this point in treating the subjects of bases and positions.

Discussions of the Crimean War often stress the unfavorable geographical conditions in which the Allies had to operate; in reality, however, the conditions were only partly disadvantageous and the balance differed according to the theater of operations. Though operating far from home, the Allied forces in the Black Sea were able to support themselves on the Turkish and Asian coasts, right at the scene of the action. Though the local coasts contained only limited resources, supplies could be shipped from Britain and France, and everything reduced itself to a not unsolvable problem of transport. Moreover, the Russian fleet remained completely inactive and made no effort to exploit the advantage of being in its home waters. It was only in the Baltic and Kamchatka that geography placed the Allies in a truly disadvantageous situation.

During the war of 1870, the physical layout undeniably hampered the French fleet from desired actions against the Prussian coast. Against her were distance, lack of bases for rest and resupply, and bad weather. Moreover, the hydographical peculiarities of the German North Sea and Baltic coasts reinforced the strength of the defense and prevented our vessels from approaching close enough to achieve any material success. Unable to win, France did not press the offensive.

The Spanish-American War is a case in which, on all the evidence, geography was singularly partial. It would have been a major achievement for the Spanish, already distinctly inferior at sea, to carry on a successful war on the other side of the Atlantic given that their adversaries were conveniently placed to exercise their power.[5] If, however, the Spanish had

5. One can make an analogous observation with regard to a war between the United States and Japan in Asian waters. A glance at the

succeeded in properly preparing Cuba and Puerto Rico with naval supplies and land defenses, the war would have been infinitely more taxing for the Americans. Their lack of a land army and the very unpleasant climatic and health conditions in Cuba would undoubtedly have long delayed the decision and, with a little bit of activity, better prepared Spanish ships could have posed a considerable problem. This example shows that one must not attribute everything to geography alone. The attitude of the combatants can tilt the balance by reinforcing or diminishing the undeniably important geographic factor.

The role of geography in the Russo-Japanese War, important though it was, seems to have been exaggerated by commentators. Generally, it worked against the Russians, who had to sustain separate naval forces in the Baltic, the Black Sea, and the Far East. The Black Sea fleet was far from the action, and the union of the Baltic and Yellow Sea fleets delayed by the great distances involved. Geography does not, however, fully explain the events. It was the exigencies of European politics that prevented Russia from shifting forces from the Baltic to the Far East in time of peace, and things would have been altogether different had the Russian fleet been adequately trained and appropriately commanded. In these conditions, Rodjestvensky's expedition would have begun much earlier and been carried out more efficiently. Rather than arriving at Tsushima in May 1905 with a random conglomeration of ships, he could have brought a fleet to the Sea of Japan in May or June 1904 while the Russian First Pacific Squadron remained virtually untouched and could blockade Japan with considerable effect. While the final result cannot be predicted, Russia's geographical disadvantages would have been largely rectified.

---

map reveals the difficulties to be encountered by the Americans (author's note).

Unhappily, there was no remedy to the problems that lo-cal conditions also imposed upon the Russians. The war zone was cut by Korea and the Japanese islands into two distinct theaters. To move from one to another, the Russian naval forces were obliged to used the Straits of Korea, Tsu-garu, or La Pérouse (Soya), all of which were in Japanese hands. Their interior lines placed the Japanese particularly well to oppose any Russian attempt to shift theaters. This was the major obstacle to the union of the Port Arthur and Vladivostok groups after the sortie of 10 August. The Vladi-vostok division was surprised and defeated by Kamimura in the Korean Straits on 14 August. The *Novik,* having escaped from the battle and seeking to reach Vladivostok, was de-stroyed on 20 August in the Straits of La Pérouse. . . . The Russians would have been able to overcome these grave lo-cal obstacles only by a real superiority of forces and by un-dertaking energetic offensive operations.

In the North Sea in 1914, Britain benefited from the same geographical advantage against Germany that she had en-joyed in the Anglo-Dutch wars. Roughly equal in terms of fleet action, the situation gave Germany a serious disadvan-tage in the struggle over communications.[6] The British Isles could not have been better placed to paralyze German ocean traffic and to block German ports while British communica-tions were virtually immune to German surface action.

One knows how the Germans broke out of their North Sea prison by the use of the submarine. Modern technology thus undermined the geographical obstacles that it had ini-

6. Wegener would object to the distinction. Because the High Seas Fleet could not bring the Grand Fleet to battle by threatening British ship-ping, "the Helgoland Bight was, is, and remains a dead angle in a dead sea," VAdm. Wolfgang Wegener, *The Naval Strategy of the World War.* Translated with an introduction by Holger Werwig (Annapolis, 1989): 22.

tially served to aggravate. But technology solved only one part of the problem. If it provided the means with which to attack enemy communications, it was impotent to safeguard Germany's own, which were largely paralyzed by geography.

I say "largely" only because some participants and commentators have overstated the case. It would not be correct to represent the excellent situation that Britain enjoyed during the war as uniquely a gift of geography and to ignore the contribution of the Royal Navy. The exaggeration becomes clear if one imagines what would have happened had the balance of naval forces been reversed and Germany had had naval superiority to match her superiority on land. In this case, the Germans would obviously have struggled to break free of their stifling geographical position. They would very probably have seized islands like the Orkneys or the Shetlands or even points on the British coast and achieved at least the defensive objective of assuring an open route north of Scotland to the high seas. Though unable entirely to stop British traffic, which would have continued to take advantage of the favorable situation in the west, they would have considerably hampered the cross-Channel communications of the British armies in France. And, under these circumstances, would the British forces have gone to France? Would they not have remained at home to defend against possible invasion? . . . One can see how often a shift in the balance of the fleets profoundly alters the situation in spite of the immutability of the geographic framework. However important, geography is clearly not everything.

ATLANTIC AND MEDITERRANEAN

There is certainly no better example of the influence of geography on naval operations than the demands placed on

France by the separation of her two coasts by the enormous mass of the Spanish Peninsula. This state of things, though very favorable from the economic point of view, has often led us to divide our squadrons between the Atlantic and the Levant, a division with the gravest consequences for our strategy.

Whenever Britain was our enemy and Spain either neutral or hostile, only good fortune allowed the reunion of our widely separated forces. Sometimes, the attempt ended in a serious disaster. The movements necessary to join our forces in the face of a superior British fleet concentrated at Ushant and Gibraltar against our Mediterranean group were always perilous. In 1689, Tourville, coming from Toulon, only managed to reach Brest through masterly exploitation of a fortuitous southwest wind. In 1690, Châteaurenault,[7] who led the Mediterranean contingent before the Beachy Head campaign, reached his destination only because he had the good fortune to shake off the pursuit of Killigrew,[8] who had been placed at Gibraltar to intercept him. On other occasions, France has not been so lucky, and the arrival of the Mediterranean vessels was so delayed by distance and contrary winds that it was necessary to commence operations in the Channel without them. During the Second Anglo-Dutch War, the Dutch had to fight the Four Days Battle[9] without waiting for the arrival of the Duc du Beaufort. Simi-

7. François Louis Rousselet, Marquis de Châteaurenault (1637–1716).

8. Admiral Henry Killigrew (died 1712).

9. The Four Days Battle of 1–4 June 1666 ranged from the Dutch coast to the mouth of the Thames. Admiral Monk, now the Duke of Albemarle, divided his forces, sending Rupert's squadron down the Channel to prevent the French from joining their Dutch allies. The Dutch and, eventually, the French had the better of this extremely hard-fought battle.

larly, Tourville gave battle at the Hogue without d'Estrées,[10] who did not reach Brest until the very day of the battle.[11] In 1759, the attempt to pass from the Mediterranean to the Atlantic Ocean ultimately led to de la Clue's complete defeat at Lagos. . . .[12]

In these conditions, a forward concentration, the unification of troops near the enemy, has proved a singularly dangerous idea, and it would have been much simpler to concentrate at the rear by sending the Atlantic detachment to meet that of the Mediterranean. The process, though full of disadvantages on land, is admissible in naval war. Unlike on land, where it involves giving up territory to the enemy, concentration at the rear merely, and only momentarily, cedes water and the brief interruption of certain communications. The meeting of Tourville and d'Estrées occurred in the Mediterranean without any trouble in 1693. Similarly, during the War of American Independence, the concentration of French and Spanish forces took place on the Spanish coast, either off Ferrol or Cadiz, in 1779, 1781, and 1782 before the combined fleets cruised the Channel. Political factors undoubtedly contributed to these decisions, but they proved very successful from a strategic point of view.

The geographical situation during the last war differed from these earlier cases because an essential factor had altered in our favor. Spain had become our ally, and the Iberian Peninsula offered ports and bases to facilitate the move-

10. Marshal Jean d'Estrées commanded Tourville's rearguard at Beachy Head but was prevented by weather from joining his superior in time for Barfleur-Le Hogue, Etienne Taillemite, *Dictionnaire des marins français* (Paris, 1982): 114.

11. It is fair to add that Tourville also failed to wait for Villette and La Porte before sailing for the central Channel. Villette joined him three days before the battle, and La Porte never went beyond Brest (author's note).

12. By Admiral Boscawen on 18–19 August 1759.

ment of our forces around its periphery and to address the needs of our ships. The difference is vital, as we learned during the wars of the Revolution and Empire. The Spanish alliance allowed Bruix safely to conduct his campaign of 1799 between Brest and the Mediterranean, and every Napoleonic combination of 1805 was based on the possibilities of movement around the Spanish littoral.[13]

These Spanish geographical and political factors have hardly diminished in importance over time and continue to be almost as important to naval strategy as in the past. The peninsula is always in the same place and remains almost as great a barrier as ever. It is easy to imagine how grave our situation would be if, while we were engaged in a European war against an enemy to the east, we had Spain for an enemy as well. Not only would the movements and concentrations of our fleets be rendered extremely difficult, but our communications, Mediterranean as well as Atlantic, would be threatened from the Spanish coast itself, from the Canaries, and, especially, from the Balearics, which nature has so disagreeably placed on the routes that link Marseille with Algiers and Oran. The conflict would be singularly difficult, if not hopeless from the start.

One sees how much interest we would have, in such a conflict, in ensuring that Spain was with us or, at least, not against us. Her neutrality alone would be a great prize for France. On the other hand, our enemy, whoever he be, cannot but strongly desire to draw Spain into his camp or, failing that, at least to obtain the use of her well-situated ports as bases for his forces. These obviously were the secret motives that inspired the treaty between Italy and Spain of 7 August 1926. . . . If its contents and results were less com-

---

13. That these naturally disappeared in 1808 reveals the serious mistake committed by Napoleon in provoking war with Spain (author's note).

plete than Rome would have liked, it was a step towards greater aspirations. Here, policy was led by geography and put itself at her service. It was because of geography that everything that happened in Madrid had such great importance for both sides. If there is a sector in which one can not afford to err, it is this one.

Our diplomacy must maintain good relations with Spain so as to prevent our enemies from plotting against us there. An easy task! Nothing divides France and Spain; rather, their collaboration in the Riff in 1925 showed how solid their mutual interests are. Only the Tangiers question remains to be settled. While it is not clear what France had to gain from opposing Spanish wishes on this subject, from a maritime point of view, the great dangers we would run and still run by making an enemy of this power are obvious. . . .

The Tangiers affair offered France a profitable opportunity at a very low price. It is too bad that we failed to understand that the integrity of our maritime communications in wartime was worth the insignificant sacrifice involved in this advantageous transaction.[14] I apologize for this political parenthesis, to which geography led me naturally and imperiously.[15]

A MEDITERRANEAN CASE

The importance of geography is equally clear from examining the conditions of a Franco-Italian war. Not that anyone in France favors such a war, which would come about only

14. "When a frontier separates two countries whose interests are not opposed, the government should at least seek the neighbor's benevolent neutrality by supporting its interests," Colonel Culmann, *Stratégie*, 416 (author's note).

15. Castex rarely writes so prescriptively.

if we were attacked, if Fascist imperialism were to pass from threats to acts, but this altogether speculative and theoretical case is very interesting in the study of the influence of geographical factors.[16]

The theater of operations, the Mediterranean's western basin, is a very limited area in which the belligerents possess numerous bases. Their cruises can be very short; the region is particularly suited to quick raids and to operations by fast ships of moderate size. The proximity of the opposing positions lends itself to amphibious operations. As an extended peninsula with long coastlines, Italy is very vulnerable to naval action, but France is no better off since her combined coastal perimeter in Languedoc, Provence, Corsica, and North Africa equals that of the Italian shores of the Western Mediterranean.

Italy has, moreover, the advantage that the Tyrrhenian Sea, set off by the Corsica-Sardinia-Sicily barrier, constitutes a relatively closed sea. Two of the three passages connecting it to the west, the strait between Corsica and Elba and the Strait of Bonifacio,[17] are difficult, and only the third, between Sicily and Sardinia, can be traversed easily. It will always, therefore, be very risky for enemy forces to penetrate deeply into the Tyrrhenian Sea except for operations of short duration. Moreover, this relatively protected water provides Italy with a coastal passageway extending from the Gulf of Taranto to the Gulf of Genoa. Unlike the Tyrrhenian Sea, however, the Gulf of Genoa is largely open to enemy action from the west.

Corsica is an island position of capital importance. It sur-

---

16. Admiral Bernotti treated part of this question in his important work *Il potere marittimo nella grande guerra* (Livorno, 1920): 535–45. See also Captain Bertonnelli, *Il nostro mare* (Florence, 1929) (author's note).

17. Between Corsica and Sardinia.

veys the three nearby passages and permits a timely warning of movements by Italian forces using them. Its western coast provides useful bases for enemy forces. Its salient position gives Corsica an offensive value of the first order against a significant part of the Italian coast but exposes it, on the other hand, to converging attacks.

Sardinia provides similar advantages for Italy. Protecting the Tyrrhenian Sea, it offers excellent bases of departure for Italian naval and air forces against French north-south communications. . . .

The northern part of Tunisia is particularly well placed for naval and air surveillance of the nearest coasts of Sardinia and Sicily, of the entrance to the Tyrrhenian Sea, and of the Malta Channel but is, therefore, an obvious target for enemy attack. For a raid against French communications with North Africa, the Italian forces have three lines of approach and retreat based on Spezia (to the north of Corsica), La Maddalena (through the Strait of Bonifacio), and Cagliari (to the south of Sardinia). This multiplicity of directions for maneuver gives the Italians great flexibility.

The geographical conditions of the western Mediterranean are eminently favorable for the use of air power. The basin can be entirely covered by reconnaissance aircraft, while the Italian littoral from Vintimille to Civita Vecchia, as well as La Maddalena (northern Sardinia), is within range of bombers from Nice or Corsica. Inversely, Corsica and all of the Provençal ports east of the Rhone are within the field of action of Italian airplanes leaving from fields near the frontier. Northern Tunisia can be reached by aircraft from Sicily or Sardinia. Bone and Philippeville (both in Algeria) are within range of airplanes based at Cagliari. The Italians have the important advantage of having bases at Naples, Messina, Augusta (Sicily), and Taranto that are beyond the range of French land-based aircraft, while Toulon and Bizerte (Tunisia) are within the Italian sphere of action.

Much of the Italian coast from Cape Passaro to Cape Santa Maria di Leuca looks to the Ionian Sea. Relatively far from the principal theater of operations, it is difficult to reach for French forces leaving from their closest point of access, Tunisia. The Italians, on the other hand, have so many well-appointed bases at Augusta, Messina, Taranto, Tripoli, and Cyrenaica and important observation points at Pantellaria and Lampedusa that it would be difficult for an enemy to undertake a sustained action in the basin, which is a zone of obvious Italian predominance. The Italian monopoly is even more evident in the Adriatic.

The communications routes of the respective nations are particularly striking. Those of France that begin at the North Sea, the Channel, and the Adriatic are protected by nature herself.[18] Our relations with northern Europe, Britain, Spain, the two Americas, Morocco, West Africa, etc., would hardly be affected by the outbreak of war. For once, geography benefits us, paying reparation owed for difficulties suffered over the long span of our history.

The Mediterranean will be a different matter. French communications with Algeria and Tunisia, very threatened by enemy flank attacks, will have to be moved, perhaps shifted west of the Balearics, so that their terminal points will not be east of Marseille and Algiers. Our communications with the eastern Mediterranean will be more precarious because of Italy's predominance in the central Mediterranean and her possession of positions in Tripoli, Cyrenaica, and the Dodecanese that flank our routes. Only with difficulty will we ensure our relations with the Levant, in particular with that damned[19] Syria, the dead weight of our strategy in that region. Since our traffic through Suez to the Far

18. The Adriatic is out of place here.
19. Castex explains the adjective below, 299–301.

East and the Indian Ocean will have not only to run the Mediterranean gauntlet but meet additional threats in the Red Sea from Italian positions in Eritrea, indispensable commerce will probably have to be routed around the Cape.

Italy's communications situation is somewhat symmetrical to ours. Her communications with northern Europe, the two Americas, with West Africa through the Straits of Gibraltar will without doubt completely disappear. This will be a very serious hindrance to Italy, for four-fifths of her imports come by way of Gibraltar. On the other hand, most of her coastal and Adriatic trade will survive, since both follow routes protected by geography. Finally and most important, Italy will retain easy communications with the eastern Mediterranean, the Black Sea,[20] and the seas beyond Suez, whither travel a third of the ships departing from her ports.[21]

In sum, as is natural, the communications of the two countries will be blocked on the front facing the enemy but unimpeded on the protected side (the Atlantic for France and the eastern Mediterranean for Italy).

Such, in theory, will be the shape of the conflict from the physical point of view. It goes without saying that we pray sincerely that this study will remain an exercise for mental recreation and a geographical pastime and that France and Italy remain united in the common defense of western civilization, a future challenge overriding all of the problems of the present day.[22]

20. Hence fascism's current policy towards the Soviets, which can seem illogical from other points of view (author's note).

21. In this passage it is not only a matter of Italian or French shipping but of neutrals, with whom it will be much more difficult to deal (author's note).

22. Castex refers not to Hitler's Germany but either Russia or, in the longer term, Asia.

GEOGRAPHY AND THE DEFENSIVE

The situation that we have just studied is only a verification of the general principle that a war involving the attack and defense of communications is conditioned to the utmost degree by geography. Geography furnishes or withholds positions from which commerce raiders can base their action. It can give a means of establishing a blockade. It can permit special procedures such as the rerouting of suspicious vessels and their examination in friendly ports. The 1914 war demonstrates all of these possibilities, most of them to the advantage of the Allies. Conversely, it also shows how certain communications, such as those of Germany in the Baltic, are protected by geography from enemy action.

Geography explains the mindless and incomprehensible hostility that many Britons have evidenced towards France since the last war. If some of them consider France, one does not know why, to be Germany's heir as the disruptive continental power, for others France has simply resumed her ancient role as the nation whose geographical situation makes her a special threat to British communications, a threat now exacerbated by the existence of aircraft and submarines. It is a matter not of our intentions but of geography. . . .

The geography of the littoral, that is to say, its hydrographic character, can serve the defender by protecting his coastal communications and hiding them from the actions of the attacker. Outer islands belonging to the defender constitute positions of defense behind which coastal traffic can circulate in more secure conditions. It is the same when the belligerent possesses internal channels or navigable canals. Reefs and shallow water can render the same service. . . . These advantages can be achieved elsewhere by: (1) rationally managing the terrain; (2) establishing minefields and various obstructions; and (3) placing artillery at important points. . . .

The influence of geography on the general situation of communications has repercussions for the fleets because the number of forces that they have to detach to attack enemy communications and to defend their own will increase to the extent that geography places them at a disadvantage.

GEOGRAPHY AND TECHNICAL PROGRESS

The influence of geography on operations is not a constant but evolves with technical change. In the era of sail, ships could go anywhere, their range of action limited only by supplies of food, munitions, and water. But the steam engine that freed them from the wind reduced the range of action by introducing dependence on the resupply of fuel. Combat vessels now had a leash, even a veritable chain. Naval vessels had to make their presence felt in the brief period before having to break off to coal. Certain regions were now too far away unless one had well-placed local bases. Technical change allowed geography to reassert itself more imperiously than ever. . . .

Ships are not the only elements affected by this; aviation faces similar restrictions. Since one can never transport more than a limited number of airplanes on an aircraft carrier, the greatest part of the air power acting in a given theater will be land-based and constrained by distances from airfields to targets. . . .

In former days, underwater topography was of importance only for navigation. If greater than about ten meters, water depth was of no interest for operations, except, possibly, when evaluating opportunities to anchor against a contrary current (as in the Channel). Now everything is changed. Water depth affects strategy because of its consequences in employing submarines, mines, and underwater obstacles. Alongside the "horizontal geography" of the position and contours of land masses, one has seen the birth of

281

a very important "vertical geography." During the last war, Germany supplied her submarines in the Channel with minute details about the precise nature of the sea bottom in different places, the currents at different depths, the places where vessels could safely rest on the bottom, etc. The Allied blockade was facilitated by the shallow water that allowed the Allies to place mines in the Pas de Calais and sow the huge Anglo-American minefield from the Shetlands to Norway.

Another technical factor has noticeably altered certain aspects of geography—the great speed of modern surface ships and aircraft. Unchanged when measured in linear kilometers, the physical arena has shrunk considerably in terms of duration of travel. Formerly, distances dilated or contracted by chance according to the effect of contrary or favorable winds. A voyage over the same stretch of water could be shortened for a ship traveling in one direction but simultaneously lengthened for one going in the other. The new temporal calculation is homothetic, however, since all of the dimensions vary in the same way.[23] Under these conditions, certain geographical accidents have a different value than they would have had formerly, and the problems that they raise are perhaps easier to solve. The Iberian Peninsula still impedes our naval travel between the Atlantic and the Mediterranean, but we have at our disposal more effective remedies than those of our fathers. Today, the voyage from Brest to Toulon, which in 1799 took Bruix seventeen days in one direction and forty-one in the other, would require only four days at the not extraordinary speed of twenty knots. The convergence of forces leaving from Toulon and Brest, formerly impeded by difficulties and delays, can now occur in forty-eight hours in the Gibraltar–St. Vincent region.

23. This second use of the notion of homothetic reduction makes more sense than that of chapter 11.

Improvements in wireless communication facilitate such operations by permitting the participants to remain in radio contact and to coordinate their movements. Forces are no longer isolated from one another; their thoughts, if not their bodies, have overcome geography.

ACTION OF THE LAND ON THE SEA

The influence of geography in naval war makes itself felt throughout the entire domain of maritime communications. It affects the struggles of fleets both indirectly by its action against communications and directly through its impact on bases and positions, movement, and possibilities for uniting forces.[24]

Geography's impact changes with time and technical progress, but equally for everyone. Its effect can be exacerbated or mitigated by the condition of the belligerent's mobile forces and by his ability to make more or less good use of them. Fundamentally, the influence of geography is nothing other than the *action of the land on the sea.*

From the strategic point of view, the land exercises power over the sea as if the continents overflowed the oceans as oil spreads over water. Awareness of the resources that the land can give to certain belligerents leads one to speak of a "command" of the sea imposed by the geography of specific regions.[25] To characterize this situation, people have used expressions like "zone of control," "zone of influence," or "zone of preponderance," formulas that more or less hap-

24. Geography affects not only military but social and political actions. A state of affairs like that in Russia [the Soviet union] has survived only because it has been protected by distance, that is, by geography, against moral, economic, and military reaction from outside. In other regions of Europe, "this human cancer" would probably soon have been eliminated. Witness Bela Kun's adventure in Hungary (author's note).

25. See above, chapter 5 (author's note).

pily describe the influence of the land on the sea. The mind, however, insists on the preeminence of the fleet and begrudges the admission that geography might undermine its domination. If my force is superior to that of the enemy, I can go into the zone in question and force the enemy to retreat into port and remain there. How, then, can one speak of his "preponderance" in that zone when it is I who reigns there as master? Indeed, this will be the state of affairs for some period of time. Eventually, however, I shall have to return to my bases to revictual, effect repairs, and clean the hullls of my ships. If these bases are badly placed and too far from the zone in question, that is, if geography is unfavorable to me, I shall be absent for a considerable period of time. As soon as I have turned on my heels, the enemy, who is at home and supported by facilities I lack, will reenter the theater of action and dominate it during my absence. Even in my presence, he may be able to accomplish some operation that would have been impossible without some collusion between the earth, the coast, the depths, etc. He will have opportunities forbidden to me. It is in this sense that one must understand the terms "control" and "preponderance."

The influence of the land on the sea is not, then, an empty one. It has been increased, moreover, by technical developments. In the days of sail, the superior fleet could maintain its preeminent situation, even on the coasts of a belligerent having a geographical advantage, much longer than at present. Because his range of action was limited, his mastery had a more permanent character. One need only think of the British fleet during the Revolution and Empire.

Certain new inventions, like the torpedo boat and the submarine, increase the influence of the land because they are most effective in the neighborhood of their coastal bases. Since fleets will avoid them as if they emanated a special repulsive force, they reduce the ability of the superior surface fleet to approach enemy shores.[26] Aviation also increases geography's role. Because aircraft carriers do not allow an equal response, whoever holds the land has the advantage in the air. Mines are similar because they are used in shallow waters, which tend to be found near land.

Consequently, the preeminent fleet, once the master of the sea, enjoys a much less favorable situation than in the past. Wherever geography favors the enemy, it is handicapped by concerns of resupply and by the enemy's torpedoes, submarines, air power, and mines.[27] Future fleets will emulate the British during the last war, who, acting as if the German coasts had advanced into the middle of the North Sea, refrained from applying their special formula of "moving their frontiers to the enemy coast." With ships of the line, at least, one will have to proceed by means of rapid and intermittent raids, and only the ships of light or moderate tonnage will inherit the favored situation of the past. If not totally paralyzed, one will nonetheless be considerably hampered and limited to special kinds of operations.

Finally, bizarre as it may seem, the land plays a greater role than before in operations, especially in the area of communications. The great transmission stations, upon which one constantly calls to ensure communications with the vessels, exist on land, and only there can one operate the special stations for interception, direction finding, and transmissions to submarines. Intelligence services also must do the bulk of their work on land.

Thus, looking at new elements of naval war including fuel

26. Thus, with the advent of the torpedo, the French *Jeune Ecole* somewhat hastily invented a coastal war destined in theory to replace war on the high seas forever; the sudden increase in the shore's power has somewhat unhinged people (author's note).

27. Consider, for example, the difficulties that a French fleet would encounter in cooperating in the defense of the east coast of Corsica (author's note).

resupply, torpedoes, submarines, mines, aviation, and wireless communication, one concludes that the influence of the land on the sea *has significantly increased with technical progress.* This is one of the principal reasons why one cannot transpose unaltered into our epoch certain methods or processes of the past. . . . [28]

GEOGRAPHIC STUDY OF A
THEATER OF OPERATIONS

Clearly one cannot elaborate on any plan of operations without profound study of the relevant theater. . . . Admiral Mahan excelled at geographical analyses of this kind but presented them in a particularly indigestible form. In fact, his emphasis on such study is, after the notion of the importance of the fleet, the most remarkable feature of his work. This special side of naval strategy appeared to him early with clarity. He succeeded in giving the fleet and the terrain their appropriate respective weights, although the two factors are ordinarily treated as contradictory.

In a series of articles appearing from 1893 to 1904 and united in a work called *The Interest of America in Sea Power,* Mahan outlines several case studies of primary importance for American naval policy.[29] He first examines the Pacific from the point of view of American interests. Ex-

28. The influence of the land will become preponderant if the strange and novel American theory of freedom of the seas should be adopted because that theory would have the effect of limiting hostilities to the territorial waters of belligerents (author's note). Discussions of narrow seas and meteorology (pages 165–75) are omitted.

29. Translated by M. Izoulet, professor at the *Collège de France,* under the rather imprecise title *Le salut de la race blanche et l'empire des mers* (author's note). "Imprecise" to say the least.

haustive evaluation of routes and distances leads him to stress the great military value of the Hawaiian Islands, which, in any case, leaps to the eyes after a single glance at the map.

Mahan then occupies himself with the Caribbean, an American Mediterranean none of whose islands belong to a serious continental power. . . . He traces the major Caribbean routes linking Europe and the Atlantic coast of the United States and identifies the points that permit command of these routes. The Mississippi Delta, Pensacola, Key West, Santa Lucia, Martinique, Cuba, Jamaica, and the Isthmus of Panama draw particular attention. Of these, the Mississippi, Cuba, and Panama seem by far the most important. Under the control of a foreign power, Cuba and Jamaica threaten to interfere with American communications, but the United States could free herself from Jamaica's geographic influence and even dominate the British possession *if she were master of Cuba or if Cuba were independent and solidly allied with the United States.*

One sees how Mahan's geographic studies, a reflection of the preoccupations of his country and his time, directly inspired the contemporary naval policy of the United States and oriented American expansion in these regions. The coincidence of dates is revealing. The study of the northern Pacific was in 1890 and the occupation of the Hawaiian Islands, which the United States did not want in 1881, occurred in 1898. The study of the Caribbean Sea was in 1897 and the Spanish-American War, more or less provoked by the Americans who were still far in their thought from the Kellogg Pact, in 1898. Spain was chased from Cuba and Puerto Rico, doubtless on the basis of the principle, dear to Mahan, of "the expropriation of incompetent races." Next America took control over the isthmus and canal of Panama, and the Hay-Pauncefote Treaty of 1900 gave her free access to the former British coast.[30] The purchase of the French company's rights rendered the Americans financial masters of the canal, and the 1904 constitution of the Republic of Panama gave them political supremacy. Finally, in 1914, they reduced Haiti to vassalage. At present, the United States looks towards Central America and a future Nicaraguan Canal.[31]

Some contemporary Americans do not find this sufficient. The *Army and Navy Journal* of 25 November 1922 argues America's need to possess not only the canal itself but its advanced posts, the islands now held by European powers. Amiable financial agreements have already been negotiated for the Danish West Indies, but it remains to persuade Britain, Holland, and France to cede their possessions. The American journal offers an ingenious argument. If these nations are at peace with the United States, the islands are of no value to them. In war, the islands pose a grave threat to the Americans but could not, in American hands, threaten the metropolitan territories of Britain, Holland, or France. The Bermudas, Trinidad, and Jamaica seem especially irritating to Uncle Sam, more so because the British fleet has no serious European enemy and its activities in the Caribbean impinge on American's self-proclaimed sphere of interest. . . .

30. Actually dated 1901, the treaty allowed the United States to build an isthmian canal.

31. They have even proposed establishing a protectorate over the republics in this region, launching a financial appeal to this end in 1927. In the course of a grand tour of Central America, the Secretary of State for War visited all of the points in Honduras, Guatemala, Costa Rica, and Nicaragua suitable for naval bases. For this purpose, Cuba has already ceded Guantánamo, Panama Colón, and Nicaragua Fonseca Bay and the Corn Islands. See J. Crockaert, *La Méditerranée américaine*, French translation (Paris, 1929), and Léon Rollin, *Sous le signe de Monroe*, 1930 (author's note).

In our day, other authors have also treated the geographic elements of different possible conflicts. Before the 1914 war both the British and the Germans studied the North Sea theater. Admiral Bernotti's *Guerra Marittima* analyzed once again the situation of the Germans and the British in the North Sea during the last war.[32] Previously, in his work *Il potere marittimo nella grande guerra,* he had, as we have seen, considered in detail the situation of the eastern Mediterranean in a war involving Italy, and our example reminds us of the importance of such a geographical study in developing any plan of action in that theater.

32. Castex, *Théories,* vol. 1, 50–59 (author's note).

CHAPTER 14

COLONIAL EXPANSION AND NAVAL STRATEGY[1]

PERHAPS A better title would be simply "Colonial Expansion and Strategy" since colonial expansion is part of general strategy and has not only land, sea, and air components but policy elements as well. Because maritime communications are its principal element, however, naval strategy is primary and the title appropriate. Naturally, we will treat the subject as it concerns our own country and ask how France could improve her colonial position.[2]

Opening an atlas, what do we see? An enormous mass draws our eyes—our African empire. It strikes us not only by its extent, but by other characteristics. First, it is a single territory and capable of being more solidly unified than it is today. From the shores of the Mediterranean to the Sudan and the Congo, one never leaves French territory—an extraordinary, magic notion that the mind finds difficult to grasp. From the military and political point of view, the unity of our African possessions means that the various parts are easier to maintain and defend, that they support one another now and will do so even more in the future. There will be a day when inland roads will render them mu-

1. Raoul Castex, *Théories stratégiques*, vol. 3 (Paris: Société d'Editions Géographiques, Maritimes et Coloniales, 1931): 269–334.

2. Narrative history of French colonization (pages 269–86) are omitted.

tually supportive and when, though completely independent of maritime communications, they will be able to exploit the sea offensively. Moreover, the northern part of our empire lies so close to metropolitan France that Tunisia, Algeria, and Morocco form virtually an integral part of it, and one can ask whether France's center of gravity is north or south of the Mediterranean.[3] North Africa is the only French possession within our immediate range that we can rapidly support and that can easily contribute to the defense of France herself. Our strategic position in Africa, already good, will become even more solid in the future. . . .

In the meantime, however, the picture has some darker spots. First, this territorial continuity is compromised by inconvenient foreign enclaves. Since the last war, German Togo and the Cameroons have passed under our aegis, theoretically as mandated territories but, given the condition of the local populations, actually as protectorates. Moreover, there remain within French Africa British Gambia, Portuguese Guinea, Sierra Leone, the Republic of Liberia under its bizarre American moral tutelage, the British Gold Coast, and, above all, the large and disagreeable chunk of British Nigeria, which bars us from particularly rich and profitable lands.

Moreover, land communications remain rudimentary. In North Africa much railway building must be done. In West Africa, the railway from Dakar [Senegal] and Konarky [Guinea] barely reaches the Upper Niger River but has not yet joined the lines from the Ivory Coast and Dahomey. In Equatorial Africa, it will be a long time before the line from Duala and Yaoundé [the Cameroons] reaches Bangui [C.A.R.] and Chari [Chad]. Finally, the Sahara continues to

3. In *Mélanges,* Castex uses this notion of France's Mediterranean center of gravity to argue that in 1940 France should have transferred its capital to Marrakech in order to continue the fight against the Germans.

separate the north and south to a scarcely diminished degree. The automobile and the airplane have triumphed over the sand, but only for picturesque tourist expeditions into the grand desert whose practical return is insignificant.

The situation is infinitely less bright in Indochina. Unlike Africa, Indochina is terribly far from France. Marseille is only 400 nautical miles from Algiers but 7,300 from Saigon. There is no reason to believe that we will have the strength to achieve or even to dispute command over this interminable expanse of sea. In most wartime scenarios we risk being unable to sustain our colony and seeing it succumb since it will not be able to defend itself.

Additionally, Indochina is exposed to its own particular dangers. Not only will it be threatened more or less seriously if we should find ourselves engaged in a European war . . . but it also faces local dangers that have singularly grown in the last quarter of a century. Onésime Reclus describes our colonies as surrounded by five wolves, the "three red wolves"—Britain, America, and Germany—and the "two yellow wolves"—Japan and China.[4] If at the moment some of these seem less fearsome, others continue to be disquieting. There is also a young wolf whose teeth have considerably grown—Siam.[5]

The Japanese danger that so much preoccupied us after the Russo-Japanese War in 1905 seems to have evaporated since the Franco-Japanese accord of 1907 and especially now, but one is never sure about the diplomatic future, and

4. Onésime Reclus, *Lâchons l'Asie, prenons l'Afrique* (Paris, 1904); 40 (author's note). Reclus's thesis was sufficiently popular to warrant denunciation by the French colonial ministry, C. M. Andrew and A. S. Kanya-Forstner, "The French 'Colonial Party': Its Composition, Aims and Influence, 1885–1914," *Historical Journal* 14 (1971): 99—128.

5. Now Thailand.

it is important not to forget the conclusions reached by studies made of the defense of Indochina in the days when we feared the Japanese. In military terms, the dangers have increased. In 1906, we thought that Japan could attack Indochina with 125,000–150,000 men on the twenty-fifth or thirtieth day of the war with reinforcement to follow. . . . Rightly abandoning our once vaunted but entirely unrealizable plan for defending Indochina itself, we limited our ambitions to defending for our fleet's base of operations the port of Saigon, which would have to hold out for a month until our forces from Europe could cut the enemy's maritime communications and unhinge his attack. Even to attain this limited objective, however, would require installing powerful defenses in Saigon and Indochina. The occupation force would have to reach 50,000 men in peacetime and be further increased by major reinforcements in time of war. Even in 1908, this program would have required an initial outlay of 340 million francs and an annual expense of 24 million.[6] One recoils before such numbers, which, moreover, are no longer adequate today. The balance of naval forces has considerably shifted in Japan's favor, and she has the capability to launch against Saigon and Indochina an attack as powerful as that which made her master of Tsing-Tao at the beginning of the 1914 war.[7] Defense of Indochina against the Japanese is an illusion.

From the Chinese side, risks once vague have recently taken tangible form. Where along the 500 kilometers of the Tonkin frontiers we used to worry only about the Black Flags or poor-quality regular troops, we now face large Chi-

6. Captain Sorb, *Armée, Marine, Colonies* (1908): 91–102. See also the budget report for the colonies, 1906 and 1907 (author's note).

7. Tsingtao (Ch'ing-tao, Qingdao) was a port in the German enclave of Kiaochow seized by the Japanese in the autumn of 1914.

nese armies with modern equipment and good commanders that, solidly based on land, are relatively immune to our naval mastery. Considerable reinforcement will have to come from France—if public opinion will accept the weakening of metropolitan France to safeguard a distant and less-than-vital part of our colonial domain. Events of 1926–1927, when we hastily reinforced Tonkin, led us to understand then that the future defense of Indochina against China was perhaps as illusory as was that against Japan.

Siam has made immense military progress in the last twenty years, consistently devoting 20 to 25 percent of her annual budget to military expenses. . . . Her various weaknesses notwithstanding, the possibility of attack along the Cambodian frontier by 120,000 combatants makes Siam an enemy to be reckoned with by Indochina. It is probable that Siam would choose to act only in conjunction with China or Japan during a period of internal troubles in Indochina, or when a European war distracted France from naval action in the Pacific. None of these scenarios is a happy one, and none was imagined by Rigault de Genouilly when he first set foot in Saigon.[8] In the most favorable of them, where we have mastery of the sea, we can respond to a Chinese or Siamese or Sino-Siamese attack by using our naval power to hold positions in the two deltas of Tonkin and Cochinchina.[9]

Our policies in the Far East have accentuated the insufficiency of our inherently inadequate resources. For reasons

8. Charles Rigault de Genouilly (1827–1873) commanded the French expedition that invaded Cochinchina in 1858 and took Saigon the following year.

9. Respectively, northern and southern Vietnam. Between the two lay Annam.

of religious propaganda, the July government and the Second Empire undertook the responsibility of protecting Catholic missions of every nationality in China.[10] This policy, whose undeniable benefits in prestige are exaggerated in the passionate cliches[11] to which the subject lends itself, greatly strains our resources. Moreover, the same policy gained us "concessions" here and there in China, territorial enclaves that we had to defend in troubled times.[12] Trouble, however, was the normal state of affairs in the Celestial Empire, and local conditions generally rendered defense difficult. In modern China, the concessions and French protection of the Catholics are archaic and undoubtedly destined soon to disappear.[13] Meanwhile, however, these policies divert excessive land and sea forces that lack credibility in the face of modern Chinese military might. . . .

Let us look now at America, where we rediscover in the Antilles the same problem that we tried vainly to solve for Indochina. The Antilles also face, in addition to the general and normal risks associated with a European war, a local and entirely grave peril that could not have been foreseen in that distant time when we planted our flag on the Windward Islands. Already the radiation emanating from their enormous neighbor touches the islands and warms them more than pure reason would suggest. We have already

10. The July government (1830–1848) was the Orleanist monarchy of King Louis Philippe, the Second Empire (1852–1870) was the regime of Napoleon III.

11. *"Clichés conventionnels et dithyrambiques."*

12. Every European power had concessions, that is, areas of exclusive trading rights, in China.

13. Britain gave up the concessions of Han-Këou and Kiu-Kiang in 1927, Chin Kiang in 1929. It negotiated the retrocession of Wei-Haï-Weï in 1929 while France persists in clinging to Quang-Tchéou-Wan, which is even less defensible than Indochina (author's note).

noted American views on the sea that they consider their Mediterranean[14] and seen the looks of brutal avarice that they cast upon European offshore possessions, which they treat as "outposts of the Panama Canal." We have seen how, consistent with their own logic, they have constantly pursued their southward expansion, marked by the war against Spain, the seizure of Cuba, Puerto Rico, and Panama, and the acquisition of the Danish Antilles. Everything has been consistent, from the Monroe Doctrine of 1823, to President Grant's 1870 declaration opposing the transfer of any American territory to a nation on the old continent, to President Cleveland's intervention in 1895 between Venezuela and British Guyana.[15] President Coolidge reiterated the theme on 26 April 1927 by announcing the United States' claims to the tutelage of all nations situated between the United States and the Panama Canal, that is to say, all of Central America. In the beginning of 1928, the American journal *North American Review* proposed openly that European war debts to the United States be forgiven in exchange for cession of their Caribbean possessions. An idea acceptable as a whole, but one can foresee the outcome of what the American periodical called "the *progressive* Monroe Doctrine."[16]

How does one resist such an inexorable expansion? The proposal made by the British in 1929 of neutralizing the Caribbean and demolishing its fortifications would give only an ostrich's illusion of security. . . . On the other hand, France is absolutely incapable of defending the Antilles

14. Cf. below, 286–88.

15. An ancient quarrel to which Britain had refused arbitration as early as 1841. Cleveland's assertion of the United States' rights to settle such questions greatly extended the Monroe Doctrine.

16. One of the prayers preached by American Christian Science missionaries contains the exquisite phrase "I believe in the Monroe Doctrine and the American Constitution" (author's note).

when the day comes that it pleases the Americans to attack them. Even were they covered with batteries and mines and saturated with submarines, these island positions would succumb before an assailant possessed of a crushing superiority of naval force and a geographical proximity so favorable to his enterprises. Thus, on this side, irremediable weakness and the prospect of great humiliation.

Furthermore, geographical proximity renders practically invincible the fatal phenomenon of attraction that tends to unite tiny morsels of territory to the neighborhood colossus. The attractive force is, as in physics, proportional to the mass of the larger power and the reciprocal of the square of the distance.[17] The small bodies lack their own inertia to resist the movement to which they are pulled. Thus went Cuba and all of the other lands we have mentioned. The exception that proves the rule was the tragicomic incident in 1929 in which the proximity of Curaçao to Venezuela saved it from Holland.

Must one deplore this inexorable march of destiny that will lead us to see the Antilles one day separated from us? They are merely a memory of the past, and they hold only a tiny place in our economic and political existence. The brilliant "isles" of the eighteenth century have lost their ancient splendor. If the last war and the following years gave them a superficial suggestion of renewed prosperity, it is to be feared that these artificial conditions cannot last and that the colonies will fall once again into the commercial decay of before the war. Moreover, internal politics and electoral struggles periodically shred these societies. The opening of the Panama Canal, from which one expected marvels, seems not to have appreciably influenced their evolution.

17. This time Castex's exaggeratedly scientific claim comes from Newtonian gravitational physics. All too often he implies that such models explain rather than merely illustrate a point.

And Guyana? What is she worth and what shall we do with her? Though all are hypnotized by fabulous visions of great wealth in this equatorial strip, no one goes there but gold seekers and the condemned.

At the other end of the world, in the Pacific, our position is both weakest and most overextended. We hold in the Marquesas, the Society Islands, the Tuamotu Archipelago, the Gambier Islands, etc., a cluster of valueless atolls. Before 1914, their foreign commerce, consisting almost exclusively of mother-of-pearl and copra, did not exceed 20 million francs. Tahiti, French in name, became increasingly Americanized under the impact of maritime relations, Yankee tourism, and Protestant missions. Whatever the Americans did not absorb went to the Chinese. Only some bureaucrats remember that France still owns this island that has played no role in our history but to give rise to the artistic and literary ideas that attached themselves to Queen Pomaré, to Rarahu, and to other banalities of Pierre Loti.[18]

New Caledonia, more favored, possesses incontestable mineral wealth, but the suppression of deportation, decided in 1896 to facilitate free colonization, created a manpower crisis that greatly compromised a brilliant beginning. More fortunately, the New Hebrides developed remarkably; we are not entirely alone there, however, and Australia impatiently tolerates our presence in the archipelago.

Given their distance from France and the maritime effort required, defending these positions is obviously impossible. They are at the mercy of the United States, the Australian Commonwealth, or New Zealand as soon as one of these should decide to attack, as the last two did with New Guinea and Samoa in 1914. Moreover, would the New

18. Pseudonym of French naval captain and prolific novelist Louis-Marie-Julien Viaud (1850–1923).

Hebrides and New Caledonia not volunteer for this fate? Are they not attracted by forces we described in reference to the Antilles? . . .

Our position in the Indian Ocean is somewhat better. We cling, no one knows why, to five Indian establishments that have no value to us. These useless vestiges of the past are far from one another, forming a mosaic of tiny fragments separated from one another by British territory. They are coveted by their enormous neighbor, to whom they are united by economics and politics. They no longer matter to France, and France matters very little to them.

In the sea to the south, Madagascar, less distant than Indochina, is favored by an almost complete isolation that protects her from all local danger. Only a European war could create enemies for Madagascar, and Britain, the most genuine threat, is not a likely foe. Moreover, since Madagascar's economic value is certain and her future sure, we can accept the situation that our fathers made.

For the same military reason, one can condemn our establishment at Djibouti. It is a useful stopping point on the sea route to Madagascar only if it can be adequately defended.

Like Indochina and the Antilles, Syria is surrounded by local perils of which we have had hard experience ever since taking possession of this long-coveted land. . . . The painful balance sheet of the Syrian mirage is the following roster of French dead.

	Officers	Men
1920	65	1,176
1921	59	649
1922	9	271
1923	8	133
1924	4	93
1925 (to 1 October)	15	251

Such is the price we paid for taking up the problematic advantages offered by the League of Nations mandate. . . . [19]

Though much better today, the situation is far from simple. Threats continue to exist. The enigmatic Turk remains to the north. To the east there is the Arab danger. In the interior, finally, troubles continuously arise, instigated by Palestine, Transjordan, Egypt, and others. Highway robbery is rife. Racial and religious hatred divide populations that remain on the brink of explosion.[20] All of this requires us to maintain in Syria a large and costly military establishment. . . .

We have paid and continue to pay dearly for our presence in Syria.[21] Providence has made us a singular present that we have greedily grasped. And this calculation has been purely military, ignoring the three billion francs that the country has cost us from 1919 to 1925. All this to have the empty satisfaction of exercising a mandate without tangible

19. Britain and France agreed on postwar French jurisdiction over Syria and Lebanon in the secret Sykes-Picot Treaty of 1916 and publicly at San Remo in 1920.

20. Britain has similar difficulties in Palestine, where the Zionist dream leads to frequent skirmishes between Jews and Moslems and among the Jews themselves. Witness the troubles of 1929. Lord Balfour has left a singular heritage to his compatriots. They doubtless ought to adopt the old-fashioned Turkish method of hammering on everyone regardless of religious persuasion—if the very powerful Jews and Moslems of Britain and the United States would allow this practical and paternal procedure (author's note). The "heritage" of Arthur James Lord Balfour, first Count Balfour (1848–1930) was a letter to Lord Rothschild on 2 November 1917 expressing His Majesty's government's support for the creation of a Jewish state in Palestine.

21. An anonymous work of official flavor entitled *La Syrie et le Liban sous l'occupation et le mandat français (1919–1927)* (Paris, 1929) passes in complete silence over the military side of the question (author's note).

benefits and to suffer at the end of the year, when we make our report to Geneva, the disagreeable humiliation of seeing our actions dissected and criticized while we agonize internally over difficulties that others have thoughtfully bequeathed to us.

Some people perceive Syria to be geographically important to our navy, arguing that France cannot maintain her position in the Mediterranean without bases in Syria, Alexandretta, and Mersine.[22] We must remember, however, that Syria does not belong to France; it is not a colony, but a mandate territory. The mandate requires us to defend the country against any aggression, but it does not give us the right to use Syria as an offensive base for our navy. Even were it permitted, Syria may not be appropriate for that use. Isolated, she cannot protect herself but is threatened simultaneously by attacks from the sea, by enemies on her frontiers, and by internal disorders. Except perhaps for foodstuffs, she lacks all of the necessities for making war, which can come only by sea. We have here another example of a supporting base for the fleet which, ironically, itself depends upon the fleet for support. . . . Like so many other parts of our foreign domain, Syria is a house of cards, further evidence of the danger of believing that one always improves one's strategic situation simply by increasing the number of positions.

GENERAL CHARACTERISTICS OF THE PRESENT SITUATION

A century of colonial expansion, sometimes judicious, sometimes incoherent, has led us to a situation of incontestable

22. See the orders to the vice admiral commanding the Syrian division of May 1919 and the letter from the Ministry of Marine to the Ministry

weaknesses and serious danger whose distinctive trait is *dispersion of effort.*

We persist in being everywhere, at the decisive points and those that are not. We attribute the same importance to Tonkin as to Gabon, to Tahiti and Morocco, to Syria and Madagascar. We do not know how to choose, to establish a hierarchy of our possessions. For us, everything is of the same importance, and we want to play the same, very large, role everywhere. Our refusal to sacrifice anything costs us because it leads directly to dispersion in the domains both of policy and of strategy. It leads to a cordon, to a scattering of effort, to a linear organization. In a word, it prohibits *manoeuvre* because the essential characteristic of every *manoeuvre* is precisely to determine a principal objective or a principal theater and to concentrate there exclusively at the expense of the secondary objectives or secondary theaters.[23]

What ought to be the principal objective or the principal theater of our foreign expansion? The question seems never to have been officially posed, even though its timely resolution would have prevented us from ruinous wanderings. Never having addressed the question, never having determined the principal objective of our colonial development, we have naturally not envisioned the second half of the problem, which consists of evaluating the principal foreign objective's impact on the defense of metropolitan France. It is certainly pertinent to ask whether the chosen principal objective serves the defense of the home state or is served thereby. . . .

In our own day, when the stakes at play in the western Mediterranean include our national greatness or even our survival, when we are gravely threatened and the principal

---

of Foreign Affairs of 23 July 1919 (author's note). Alexandretta and Mersine are now Turkey's Iskenderun and Mersin.

23. See *Théories*, vol. 4, chapter 6 (author's note).

objective obviously lies at home, it is strange to see people, even members of our own profession, speaking seriously of the "Pacific problem," of the Yangtse flotilla, or the effort to be made in Tahiti.

Geographical dispersion has also diluted the effectiveness of our external propaganda. Naval cruises, propaganda's chief instrument, are acceptable and advantageous when they do not diminish the training or material condition of the ships involved. Their effect depends, however, on the places visited. In logical consequence of our colonial dispersion, we have sent our forces across the entire world and doubtless made a strong impression, but only on countries that are relatively unimportant. It is obviously agreeable to think how our cruisers have pleased the few French residents of Durban or inspired the natives of the Marquesas. During this same time, however, our Italian rivals have concentrated more productively on showing their flag in Spain, Portugal, Greece, Turkey, the eastern Atlantic, and northern Europe. Our lack of concentration reflects our failure to establish a hierarchy among alleged interests scattered to the four corners of the globe.

One can make the same observation about our religious missions. These costly and inconvenient establishments can be a remarkable instrument of national propaganda and foreign influence if focused in the regions most significant to us or where a hearts-and-minds campaign will bring us the greatest benefit. In a word, they must be aimed at the principal objective. If, however, we plot the distribution of our religious missions on a map, we are astonished to find them scattered across the globe without regard for political principles. Their principal centers are not to be found in the countries where it is of absolute importance to ensure our moral preponderance. Our missionary centers have their maximum density in four regions: China, the near-East (Asia Minor,

303

Syria, and Palestine), British Nigeria (!), and South Africa. The density is moderate in Madagascar. Finally, a shocking detail, it is extremely thin in our own French Africa where there could never be too many devout apostles to open souls to the rays of French civilization, to teach the French language and the love of France. . . . [24]

In 1922, in Constantinople, at the moment of the Turkish offensive, the head of one of our most important instructional establishments in Asia Minor told me of the risk that his institution ran. "Father," I replied, "you should have founded your school in Marrakech (Morocco)!" My disconcerted interlocutor did not understand, but I had compressed into this single comment the whole of my thesis about disaccord between our religious effort and our principal political objective. . . .

Mahan warned of the strategic repercussions of this sort of colonial dispersion, observing that scattered colonial holdings undermine the concentration and the tight lines of communications that are important in war. Every distant colony *weakens and disperses the efforts of the state.* . . . Scattered possessions constrain a nation to fight a defensive naval war. . . . [25]

A PLAN OF ACTION

To save the situation will require a line of conduct that will strike more than one Frenchman as the ravings of a revolutionary or an anarchist but which, with the natural omnipo-

24. This nationalistic concern does not exactly match the Vatican's view of proselytizing work and offers an excellent subject for negotiation with the Holy See (author's note).

25. Mahan, *Stratégie navale,* 175–76 (author's note).

tence of all just ideas, will come to be entirely acceptable. The necessary solution will be very difficult to put into practice. Paradoxically, it is infinitely simpler to install oneself in a country than to withdraw from it after years have passed and woven between it and the present state a web of material and moral interests. One clutches the country in question as if holding a lobster by the pincers. This is the tragic side of our situation.

With energy and will, however, we can put an end to the problem. To do so, we must chose a *principal objective* and elevate it above all others. Which? Naturally that which is closest to metropolitian France, our closest neighbor, our African domain. Africa has the advantage of being connected to France by short, and therefore relatively secure, maritime communications. A vast territorial expanse, it can sustain itself in the event of foreign naval domination. The defenses of this part of the world can contribute to those of the homeland. . . . What would Ferry's[26] old adversaries, whose principal argument was colonization's threat to France's eastern defenses, have said had they witnessed the part played by Africa in the 1914 war?[27]

Concentration of effort on our African empire implies considerable work. As promising as that domain is, there is much to be done to improve its strategic value. First, to the extent that international arrangements allow . . . it is important to unify our holdings by eliminating foreign enclaves like the British possessions of Gambia, Sierra Leone,

26. Premier 1880–1881 and 1883–1885 and president of the Senate in 1893, Jules Ferry (1832–1893) was one of France's chief advocates of colonial expansion.

27. The author's note enumerates the 216 colonial battalions in France in 1918, eighty-six percent of whose 545,000 soldiers were African. The colonies also contributed 220,000 laborers, 180,000 of them African.

the Ivory Coast, and Nigeria; Portuguese Guinea; and the Liberian republic over which the United States extends a vague protectorate likely to prove annoying to us. . . . [28]

It is also strategically necessary to unite the various parts of our African empire by rail. Much remains to be done in both the northern and southern regions, while the two must be connected across the Sahara. . . . Strange as it may seem, *the Transsaharian railway appears to be an essential component of naval strategy.* Its most ardent champions ought to be sailors. One could even logically suggest that the Ministry of Marine ought to defray part of the cost of construction. . . .

The effort to improve African communications[29] ought to be accompanied by an intellectual and morale campaign intended to weld the European and indigenous races living there into a single powerful block. This is a project of public education. As M. Roumne formerly said, "Railways and more railways!" our motto must be "Schools and more schools!" . . . If only we could transport to French Africa, as if with a magic wand, all of the railways, roads, and educational establishments already built in places like Syria!

In the meantime, we must minimize investments in the secondary areas while waiting to be relieved of them advantageously.[30] Who will relieve us of Indochina? The best solution appears to exchange it for British Nigeria, a wealthy region interposed between our eastern and equatorial possessions in Africa. The Antilles cannot be defended from the fate of Cuba and Puerto Rico, and it would be folly to at-

28. Pages 319–21 are omitted from *Théories*, vol. 4.

29. Which ought to extend to aerial communications. What profits it to be able to fly from Paris to Tokyo? A regular Marseille-Algiers-Sudan air-mail service would interest me much more. When will we have it? (author's note).

30. The remainder of the chapter condenses *Théories*, vol. 4, 325–34.

tempt to hold on to them. It has been suggested for some years that we deliver the Antilles to America in exchange for forgiveness of debts accumulated during the 1914 war, but it would be better to exchange them for recognition of a French protectorate over the Republic of Liberia, meanwhile selling Guyana to Brazil.

The rest follows. We can cede our Pacific holdings to Australia and New Zealand in the expectation of compensation from Great Britain in the form of West Africa territory. I would personally choose Sierra Leone. We can also give Britain our Indian stations, asking perhaps for Gambia in return.

It remains to disengage ourselves from our Syrian mandate by transferring it to another power. It would be very shrewd policy to cede Syria to Italy, thus simultaneously disembarrassing ourselves of Syria and providing Italy with needed space for her surplus population. This repository for the overflow of Italians would also satisfy Fascism's expansionism and bellicosity since the proximity of the Turks and the Arabs would furnish ample opportunity to exercise that "spirit of conquest" that Mussolini hopes to instill in the youth through "warrior education." Meanwhile, we will have peace in the western Mediterranean and be paid for giving up our mandate by Italian renunciation of her pretensions towards Tunisia and our African territories.

Such are the decisions necessary to redress a colonial situation whose strategic vices leap to the eyes. As painful as they are, let us be firm. Free from the paralysis of the past, let us take care for the future. Let us accept these amputations, these necessary surgical interventions. If we do not, they will happen later in any case, in an infinitely more brutal fashion without anesthesia or compensation.

Have courage. Let us go to the operating table.

Strategy demands it.

PART IV

INTERNAL FACTORS

CHAPTER 15

THE OFFENSIVE[1]

CHARACTERISTICS OF OFFENSE AND DEFENSE

OFTEN DESCRIBED by military writers and by the regulations of every army, the characteristics and properties of the offensive and the defensive require only brief review. Offense represents action and movement. Its virtues are dynamic. When successful, it physically changes the positions of the two antagonists. It transforms power relations and modifies situations, changing one state of affairs into another of its own devising. The offensive is a creative act par excellence.

On the other hand, the pretensions of defense, at least of the pure defensive, can only be static. Defense can only maintain the present situation, can only stop the course of events by blocking the adversary's creative actions. The defender tends towards consolidation and stabilization of the present situation. Defense is an act of sterilization aimed at the germs of change.

Attack has a positive character, defense a negative one. The latter ought not to be denigrated, however, because simple consolidation may in some situations constitute an immense result. Generally, however, as Clausewitz says,

1. Raoul Castex, *Théories stratégiques,* vol. 4 (Paris: Société d'Editions Géographiques, Maritimes et Coloniales, 1933): 102–36.

311

"The different objectives that one can propose to attain through war are positive ones, and, therefore, only the offensive can achieve them." This is principally true of the most important positive goal that one can set oneself, that is, the reversal of the enemy's will to struggle and his submission to one's own.[2]

Only the offensive can definitively break the equilibrium to produce a decision. Defense, because it works to maintain the equilibrium, is impotent to create a decision. Only when accompanied by an offensive executed elsewhere can the defensive lead to a decision and end the status quo.

But the superiority of offense over defense does not limit itself to this generic trait and to this difference of possibilities. He who operates offensively knows what he wants. He is relatively master of his movements, free to choose where to direct his main effort and when to launch it. His action can be managed, or at least begun, in a precise manner. His task is greatly facilitated by having a clearly determined, preconceived goal and by having the initiative.

Thus, one generally sees the offensive achieve a better result than the defensive. Even failure is moderated by the advantage that priority of action gives. In our maritime past, we have been defeated both when attacking and when defending, but the defeat was always less serious in the first case than in the second.

While the offensive imposes, the defensive submits. He who only defends himself can only act for the better or the less bad. He does not what he wants but, and only with difficulty, what he can.[3] His absence of initiative deprives

---

2. Compare "War is thus an act of force to compel our enemy to do our will," Clausewitz, *On War*, book 1, chapter 1 (Howard, 75).

3. Echoes Thucydides, book 5, chapter 89, "The strong do what they can and the weak suffer what they must."

him of all influence over the circumstances, of which he is slave and not master. All of the threats he perceives appear equally important and, ignorant of the place and time of the attack, he must defend in every direction. He cannot achieve an efficient disposition of his forces and is often led to disperse them. Above all, an atmosphere of anxiety, uncertainty, and irresolution often leads the defender to hasty, impulsive, ill-considered, and fatal decisions.

There are certainly cases where the defense has reconquered the advantage and become, according to the classical formula, "a form of war stronger than the offensive."[4] These include those where the defender was able to force the enemy to come and fight him on known ground where he had prepared positions more solid than those of his moving adversary. Here, all uncertainty disappears. The advantage of surprise, in the form of counterattacks, is on the side of the defense. One can even imagine that, in such circumstances, the defenders would need fewer resources than the attacker. But all this is an exceptional case. In general, the respective situations of the offensive and the defensive are those we have recalled above.

This picture applies with certain easily understood modifications to naval warfare. The principal difference concerns the defensive. On land, the defensive can aspire to the complete result, at least in the negative sense, of halting the enemy entirely and creating an unbreakable obstacle to his invasion. Preservation of the national territory is in itself a great prize. The naval defensive does not operate in the same conditions. First, it cannot risk acting on the high seas

4. Castex rejects Clausewitz's assertion that the defense is the stronger form of war, *On War*, book 1, chapter 1 (Howard, 358), without directly addressing his arguments.

against superior forces because it is denied that use of terrain that can compensate for numerical inferiority on land.[5] Fighting at a marked disadvantage quickly leads to naval disaster.[6]

The first reinforcement that the naval defensive can find from terrain is a friendly coast whither it can retreat and establish itself in order to check the adversary. Having thus more or less abandoned the sea to the enemy, the defensive can expect only minor positive results. It can attack only sporadically and never against the coasts or territory of the enemy. The losses it will be able to inflict will be tolerable to the enemy and will bring about no decision.

The negative results will not be any more brilliant. Having taken refuge on its own coast and abdicated the opportunity to undertake major operations at sea, the defender is completely impotent to prevent the enemy from cutting his lines of communication. His fleet cannot even guarantee the coasts, which will have to be protected by other means—coastal batteries, mines, obstructions, and land armies—while pure naval action will be of little importance. Defense protects the fleet itself, perhaps, but in no way safeguards the interests entrusted to it. As a result, the enemy benefits, at the smallest cost, from a situation that could have been created in other circumstances only by a series of victorious battles.

The naval defensive is therefore a more disadvantageous form of war than the terrestrial defensive, and this inferiority is paradoxically strongest in the negative, the defensive domain. Deliberate adoption of the defensive has only disadvantages. One might be forced to it by lack of resources

5. Smoke screens create a sort of artificial terrain, but one should not base excessive hopes on such factors (author's note).

6. For the importance of superior force in naval tactics, see Wayne P. Hughes, *Fleet Tactics* (Annapolis, 1986).

but would never adopt it by choice. Within the limit of one's possibilities, one will always seek an offensive path, the only one that at least disputes the control of the sea.

But the chief superiority of the offensive over the defensive concerns morale. The simple difference of attitude has incalculable psychological consequences. As Montesquieu said, "The nature of defensive war is discouraging. It gives the enemy the advantage of courage and energy in the attack. It is better to undertake a risky offensive than to depress spirits by holding them back." The waiting, expectation, anxiety, and uncertainty inherent in a pure defensive tend to depress courage. Discouragement is common among blockaded forces, which rapidly lose their self-confidence while developing exaggerated fears of the enemy. Low morale, combined with the disappearance of all training, often renders blockaded forces incapable of fighting effectively. . . .[7]

DEFINITION OF THE NAVAL OFFENSIVE

For land war, it is unnecessary to define the offensive because everyone knows what it is. The question is much more complicated for naval war because of the great diversity of possible objectives and of the means that can be used to achieve them. The different combinations of objectives and means create different genres of offensive.

To understand and classify these offensives requires keeping in mind our claim that the principal merit of the offensive, that which justifies it and which raises it above the defensive, is its potential to achieve a positive result, and particularly the positive result that really counts, the decision of the war. Its decisive character is the virtue of the

7. Historical examples are omitted.

genuine offensive, and only offensives capable of bringing about a decision are worthy of the name. . . .

There are cases of attacks against enemy communications intended to bring about a decision by themselves alone. The two Ponchartrains[8] and even great minds like Vauban[9] believed that the offensive exclusively directed against enemy commerce would end the war without the considerable expense involved in combats between major fleets. By an energetic offensive of this type the Convention hoped to reduce Britain to "a shameful bankruptcy." The First Empire also practiced commercial warfare, augmenting it with the system of cruises by divisions. The Confederates calculated that pressure on Federal economic interests would force them to make peace. In our own day we have seen the Germans adopt the same approach.

This method of operation, however offensive in inspiration, has clearly proved completely unsuccessful.[10] The *guerre de course* has never achieved significant results unless preceded or accompanied by a fleet offensive, as, for example, in the War of American Independence. To achieve a decision, the *guerre de course* requires support by the "*guerre militaire*." Since an offensive directed uniquely against communications and commerce cannot be decisive, it cannot properly be called an offensive at all.

The same observation applies to attacks on coasts and territories. These nominal offensives succeed only when sup-

8. Louis de Phélypeaux, Comte de Pontchartrain (1643–1727) and his son were successive ministers of the navy: the father under Louis XIV and the son under Louis XV.

9. The Marquis Sébastien Le Prestre de Vauban (1633–1707), the preeminent military engineer of the seventeenth century, wrote a pamphlet, *Mémoire de la course* (also called *Mémoire sur la caprerie*), advocating reliance on the *guerre de course*, Symcox, 4 and J. R. Jones, *Britain and Europe in the Seventeenth Century* (London, 1966): 91.

10. See Castex, *Théories*, vol. 1, part 3, chapter 1 (author's note).

ported by fleet operations. For example, the landing of James II in Ireland at the beginning of the War of the League of Augsburg would have failed had Châteaurenault not managed to dominate Herbert's fleet at Bantry. On the other hand, when we revived the idea of an offensive against British soil in 1759, the fleet only had to be defeated at the Cardinals to wreck the plan. . . .

During the War of American Independence, the decisive offensive at Yorktown was crowned with success by virtue of the superiority of de Grasse's fleet over that of the British, but the offensive against Gibraltar accomplished nothing because we could not subdue the British squadrons and prevent the resupply of the fortress. During the Revolution and the Empire, the expeditions of Hoche[11] and Humbert[12] to Ireland and the expedition to Egypt were offensive in concept but reduced to nothing by naval defeats.

The vast scheme of 1805 was a broad offensive envisioning a complete decision through an invasion of the British Isles. But Napoleon had to subordinate success in that venture to achieving a pronounced superiority over the British fleet, and Trafalgar determined the fate of the whole enterprise. Similarly, British naval mastery assured the success of the offensive in Spain.

The destinies of territorial offensives in the Crimea, at Lissa, of the Chileans against Peru, of the Americans against Cuba, of the Japanese during the wars of 1894 and 1904 were settled by the preeminence of the attacker's fleet over that of the defender.

These obvious examples demonstrate the preponderant

11. General Lazare Hoche (1768–1797) failed to reach Ireland in December 1796 after being blown out into the Atlantic.

12. General Joseph Amable Humbert (1767–1823) arrived on 22 August 1797 to support Irish rebels only to surrender to British forces a month later.

influence of organized naval force in any offensive against territory. The fleet is the most efficacious instrument for operations of this sort. Hence, every offensive against a territory that neglects the enemy fleet is badly oriented. To obtain a decision, the offensive must aim at, or at least not ignore, the enemy fleet.

Where communications or territories are concerned, the only real offensive, the only one that can attain complete results, is that which strives to put the enemy fleet out of action. Only events like Bantry, Beachy Head, the Hogue, Minorca, the Cardinals, Aboukir, Trafalgar, Lissa, Santiago, the Yalu, Tsushima, and even Jutland, only the blockade of the weak by the strong, can determine the outcome of wars and constitute a naval offensive worthy of the title.

But these observations concern only surface warfare, which is already a thing of the past. Modern technology has complicated the problem of the naval offensive by multiplying the means available to pursue it. Could one, for example, obtain a decision by means of an offensive against communications, as in the past, but entrusted to the submarine?

The only case to study is that of the German submarine war of 1914–1918. That was certainly a powerful offensive and intended to be decisive. But the independent submarine offensive, though undertaken in exceptionally favorable conditions, proved unable to achieve mastery of the sea. Not only was it incapable of gaining German control over essential surface communications, but it could not even wrest sea control from the enemy, who continued to enjoy it until the end of the war.

The campaign could not be decisive because the submarines lacked support from a surface fleet, which alone could have swept the seas of the enemy's antisubmarine forces. To be successful, the submarine offensive requires a parallel surface offensive, which Germany did not dare to undertake. Left to themselves, the submarines were expected to do the impossible. The lesson remains valuable for the future. The master of the surface will always dominate the essential surface communications, and an undersea offensive alone will not dislodge him.

In their submarine war, the Germans made errors both of objective and of means. The first was their exclusive focus on commerce and communications rather than against the enemy fleet. But this error of objective was trivial compared to the larger error of relying solely on the submarine, a new kind of error because the opportunity to make it was obviously as novel as the instrument itself. The purely submarine offensive is not an offensive at all because it does not lead to a decision.

Will an offensive undertaken entirely in the air, sometimes proclaimed as the method of the future, prove any more successful? Will it have decisive effects from the naval point of view? The subject is extremely important, and we have addressed it previously,[13] but it is necessary to reconsider it from the special perspective of the offensive.

Against party A, equipped with normal surface, submarine, and air armaments employed in conventional ways, let us place party B, which employs only an air offensive. Can air power alone bring about B's goals of protecting his own surface communications and paralyzing those of the enemy? Let us examine B's situation offensively and defensively.

Offensively, his air force can attack A's surface force. But A will react, first with his own means (artillery, smoke, etc.) and then by coopting aviation to the defense. Given this reaction, the attack will achieve results considerably less impressive than against an inert target. But A's most effective and radical response is dispersion, against which B has no

13. Castex, *Théories*, vol. 1, part 1, chapter 7 (author's note).

remedy. A's surface force, or at least the part that is dispersed, will retain a mastery that B's aviation will be unable to overcome. The persistence of A's surface fleet is a capital element of the question.[14]

Against A's communications, B's air force can hope to achieve fairly serious results, but these must not be exaggerated. Against isolated commercial vessels, the return will be mediocre because the aircraft will run up against the delicate problem of reconnaissance and because it will have trouble distinguishing enemy vessels from neutrals.[15] Against convoys, the effects will be much greater, because all uncertainty will be removed. But by grouping his ships in very large convoys, A is assured of the initiative and can organize a strong defensive air contingent. The game will then be two-sided; while A can expect to lose some ships, he will not suffer the great slaughter that some have predicted.

B's air force will naturally drop bombs on the military and commercial ports along A's coasts. Though the bombardment will create considerable problems for A, its effects will be somewhat mitigated by his defensive arrangements. Moreover, B's air force will obviously be powerless to invade and occupy A's homeland. It is not by air but by sea that one transports large and well-equipped armies.

Defensively, B's situation is still worse. He will be incapable of protecting his vital surface communications against that part of A's fleet that has victoriously resisted the air offensive. Nor will B be able effectively to protect his coasts from the enemy's superior fleet. In addition, the enemy will exploit his initiative and coordinate his own air units with

14. But dispersion also vitiates the offensive potential of A's fleet while thinning its antiaircraft defenses.

15. Not a problem for B if he adopts for aircraft Castex's own thesis for the treatment of neutrals by submarines.

the fleet's attacks so that B will have to meet an aerial enemy as well.

In sum, one does not see that an air offensive *alone* can, from the naval point of view, bring its employer victory or even a decisive superiority. Its weakness lies in the evident incapacity of aviation to *occupy* the surface of the sea and the ground or even to hold the air permanently. Like the submarine, the airplane is a limited weapon. To obtain decisive results, an air offensive must be supported on the surface. The participation of the fleet does not constitute a sufficient condition for victory, for it must obviously be supported by submarine and air forces, but it is an absolutely necessary condition. Unsupported submarine offensives and unsupported aerial offensives are only second-order offensives, but they can be extremely important in situations where, for lack of a surface fleet, one has no other option. Hardly surprising, this conclusion merely extends the general principle of liaison of arms.

The restoration of the surface forces to the offensive avoids an error of method and returns us to old-style surface warfare. Now we must escape the error of objective often characteristic of the wars of the past. The surface fleet must take as its objective the enemy fleet without allowing itself to wander towards other targets. If certain constraints prevent it from taking this path at once, at least the fleet ought not to lose sight of its antagonist and ought to return to it as soon as possible.

We can summarize our thoughts with the proposition that *the offensive occurs only on the surface,* while admitting, however, that this brief formula requires interpretation in the light of everything we have said.[16]

---

16. Omits a long refutation of arguments denying the existence of a clear distinction between offense and defense in naval war.

THE CONDITIONS OF THE OFFENSIVE

However great the virtues of the offensive and whatever value it generally has in practice, it would be illogical, contrary to good sense, and clearly dangerous to derive from it an absolute system. One must mistrust the mystique of the offensive, the sentiment that would lead one to adopt it regardless of circumstances without considering its appropriateness to the situation or its consistency with a rational plan of *manoeuvre*. It it necessary to avoid the "passive offense" spoken of by General Colin, the pointless movement forward, the tendency to advance simply for lack of a better idea.[17]

The offensive has preconditions that force one to limit one's ambitions in accordance with one's circumstances. First, offensive action requires resources sufficient in both quantity and quality. The once-popular maxim, "the weaker one is, the more one attacks," describes the mentality of the pre-1914 era, but we have become more cautious. Certainly when taken literally, it is nothing but a glaring absurdity. Why should one accept the notion of aiming as high as one is poorly equipped to succeed? Clearly the maxim requires a critical interpretation. If it intends to say that the only means of remedying a numerical inferiority is to *manoeuvre* so as to retain the initiative in operations to the greatest extent possible, than the maxim can be accepted and its exaggerations forgiven as intended to make a point. Otherwise, interpretation depends on the type of operation. On land, such an attitude may be practicable in the realm of tactics, where the inferior forces may be able to achieve the illusion of strength briefly by employing terrain and modern armaments reinforced by activity and aggressiveness. On the

17. Jean Colin, *Les transformations de la guerre*, 289 (author's note).

theater level of war, in the strategic domain, one is unlikely, however, to fool the enemy for long with an offensive lacking an adequate base of support.

At sea, the situation is simpler still. The weaker surface force can do nothing on the tactical level. Not only is the offensive forbidden but it risks ending in catastrophe. The fleet can find no help in terrain, and every fighting retreat soon becomes a disaster. On the strategic side, the perspectives are no more encouraging. Thus, the offensive possibilities of a numerically inferior fleet are almost nil. Such was the case at the beginning of the 1914 war when the French Second Light Squadron in the Channel was sent down the Pas de Calais to attack Germany's crushingly superior High Seas Fleet. Perhaps a *beau geste,* but the consequences would have been serious had not Britain's entry into the war promptly restored the naval balance. Our naval force was doubtless inspired by "the weaker one is, the more one attacks," but its conduct appears upon reflection to have been nothing but a heroic and dangerous folly.

The quality of the attacker's resources is as important as their quantity. How many past offensives failed due to the defects in the units called upon to undertake them? History is full of examples of enterprises marred by poor tools, of overly ambitious spirits who failed to take into account the poverty of their instruments. The offensives conducted against Britain during the *ancien régime* and the Revolution are striking in this regard. The campaign of 1805 is singularly suggestive; the entire Napoleonic combination was undermined, ruined at its very beginnings, by the wholly precarious state of the forces launched in that adventure. On the other hand, the superior training of the German navy during the 1914 war allowed them to escape a worse fate than they suffered. Furthermore, study of the infantry combats of that war demonstrates the clear and serious inferiority of the tactical training of the French troops in comparison to that of the Germans. One wonders how, given their numerical inferiority as well, our command could have adopted its chosen offensive plan.

Ship quality is obviously fundamental to the offensive, but appropriate personnel are equally necessary and much more difficult to acquire. It is necessary, first, that the crews be complete. Our maritime annals show how we have sometimes found ourselves paralyzed by deficiencies in manpower. Tourville had to give battle at the Hogue without filling the gaps in his ships' complements; Morard de Galles's squadron before the expedition to Ireland,[18] Martin,[19] and Villaret-Joyeuse in 1795 were in equally pitiable situations. The last was obliged to fill his ships with men from his own frigates and to transfer his ships from Lorient to Brest in three installments, returning the crews by land after each one. Undermanning hurt de Brueys at the beginning of the Egyptian expedition, Bruix at Brest, Ganteaume[20] in 1801, and Villeneuve[21] in 1805, when the Boulogne Flotilla absorbed much of the best manpower.

Peacetime fleets obviously cannot maintain their full wartime complements, but a reasonable level must be retained for training and so that each ship can make an honorable showing at mobilization when joined by a relatively small number of additional men. Personnel should be stable, with

18. Morard de Galles was naval commander of Hoche's expedition of 1796.

19. Rear Admiral Martin's Mediterranean campaign came to grief at Noli on 13 March 1795.

20. Honoré-Joseph-Antoine, Comte de Ganteaume (1755–1818) commanded the Brest fleet from 1800 to 1802 and in 1804.

21. Pierre-Charles-Jean-Baptiste-Sylvestre de Villeneuve (1763–1806) commanded the French forces in the campaign that ended at Trafalgar.

as little unnecessary shifting of crews as possible, but our own policy has been a veritable defiance of this necessity. Only ships on campaign have been spared in this regard, and it is for this reason that their cohesion is certainly very superior to that of the ships based at home.

The value of ships also stems from an impeccable internal organization, that is to say that the tasks of combat, lookout, and security are intelligently and logically organized. The chore of arranging the watch bills is enormously important. Care for organization brought glory to Jervis and provided the basis of Nelson's success. Only when its internal organization is unshakable can a vessel act as a true unit of combat, but the matter is ignored by many officers and neglected by many commanders because they concern themselves only with the exterior facades of peacetime. Lack of mental discipline has led many of them to forget the distinction between the "troop" and the "herd" and to believe that a ship is ready for war if only the designated number of men happen to find themselves on board. This is why we have seen ships, nominally combat units, transformed into training companies, into every variety of school, into depots, and into everything else, losing their organization and readiness for battle in the process.

It is superfluous to add that ships require intensive military and naval training and, consequently, constant exercises. All of these ought to follow a rational program focused entirely on the possibility of war. Eschewing tourism and frivolity, the navy must be dominated by military concerns and give individual training the major attention it deserves.

Finally, strong morale must dominate and crown everything, which is easy when all of the preceding conditions have been met. A well-trained man on a well-armed and well-organized ship has no problem with morale.

That the quality of his ships is the indispensable base of a commander's operations and, therefore, of the offensive must be repeated time and time again because this fundamental verity has often been misunderstood or at least been ignored in practice in our navy.

Many other factors, which we can only mention in passing here, also influence the outcome of the offensive. First, there is the availability of vessels. Having constantly to worry about mechanical problems is the plague of naval operations and even of the peacetime navy, while the army can almost completely ignore this kind of problem since it is unlikely to find itself suddenly deprived of units through mechanical caprice. Navies cannot act if material fails. Thus, from 1914 to 1916, the Germans had to wait until all of their ships were available to undertake their major sorties into the North Sea. The British suffered, however, because they did not choose the moment of action and could not count on their material being ready.

The offensive requires at least a minimum of intelligence about the enemy, that one know where he is likely to be and have a general idea of his movements. Though eschewing rigid prohibitions against acting in the absence of intelligence, one needs some information. Otherwise, the naval offensive always risks striking out at an empty sea, either because of the vastness of the oceans or because the enemy has taken refuge in harbor. Good intelligence allowed the opportune execution of the British counteroffensives in the North Sea.

Furthermore, even if one knows where to find the enemy, it will not always be possible to approach him, either because he is beyond the range of one's ships or because one lacks the necessary bases. The offensive can also be contraindicated if it would have to occur in an area where the enemy has improved his position with mines and obstacles, where he has a substantial reinforcement of submarines, or where he can count on superior air forces. Such conditions increase the risks of any voluntary offensive out of proportion to the likely gain. Such was the case for the British in the Helgoland Bight and the Germans with regard to the Pas de Calais. In such a circumstance, it will prove better to try to draw the adversary out of his prepared position or even to reverse roles completely. The solution may be a geographically or pseudo-geographically based offensive with a well-chosen bait. Such projects require the cooperation of the enemy, and, though the result can be as brilliant as Tsushima, this is only a subordinate offensive. But one cannot always do what one wants.

Let us now concern ourself with the enemy. An offensive must be planned with reference to the adversary's material, training, and morale. Obviously one will not act in the same fashion against an ill-armed, badly trained, inert, and poorly commanded foe as against one solid, well-trained, and intelligently commanded. Understanding this element is very important, not only to determine what to do in specific cases, but also to achieve a correct interpretation of past events. Howe, Jervis, Nelson, Tegethoff, Ito, and Togo were certainly great sailors, but, without denigrating their achievement, one must point out that things would have gone very differently for them against opponents other than the French, Spanish, Italians, Chinese, or Russians with whom they dealt in the campaigns distinguished by the battles of Prairial, Saint Vincent, Aboukir, Trafalgar, Lissa, the Yalu, and Tsushima. At both Saint Vincent and Trafalgar, for example, one side attempted the maneuver of breaking the line. That the British succeeded where the Spanish lamentably failed can be explained by the difference in quality of the opponent each faced. Similarly, the Americans can hardly glorify their success against the inferior Spanish squadrons that they defeated at Santiago and Cavite.

A critical approach is necessary when one wants to evaluate the events correctly, to appreciate the conduct of the victors, to draw the appropriate lessons, and, especially, to use the analysis as the basis for developing strategic systems. Caution must be used in drawing lessons from historical cases because one cannot construct a serious theory of war by ignoring the particular circumstances of each case, especially the value of the adversaries. For example, Corbett falls into this error in a panegyric about former British naval methods that ignores his compatriots' usual advantages in material, training, and command. Similarly, those who extracted the theory of the *manoeuvre sur les derrières* from Napoleon's campaigns or "the weaker one is, the more one must attack" from the attitude of Avensleben[22] have fallen into the same trap. Nothing is more dangerous than generalizations based on misunderstandings of specific cases.

Certain of these elements that condition the offensive are static, but others, especially the quality and quantity of material, change constantly. Their sum, the expression of our strength, can be drawn as a curve with its high and low points, and the enemy's strength can be shown the same way. The resulting sine curve, with time the absyssa, graphs our relative situation and has maxima and minima that represent good and bad conditions for an offensive. The commander's art lies in discerning and profiting from the favorable moment.

The graph take different forms in different cases. There are belligerents for whom the curve shows a constant decrease as their power diminishes over time. These must take

22. Gustav von Avensleben (1803–1881) distinguished himself as a corps commander in the Franco-Prussian War.

the offensive at once because optimal conditions will not come later. Other powers grow stronger over time and, given a steadily rising curve, their best strategy is to temporize, to await the moment when they are strong enough.[23]

In the case, perhaps more frequent, where the conditions of power oscillate, one will practice the offensive at favorable moments and return to the defensive when the situation becomes unfavorable. Thus, we find the alternation between these two modes of conduct of operations that one often notices among the great captains and that is the hallmark of the mastery of their art. Far from considering the offensive and the defensive as exclusive of one another, they employ them in complementary fashion, mixing them up and employing them according to the circumstances. Monk fought in retreat the third day of the Four Days Battle and returned to the attack on the fourth day after he met up with Rupert. De Ruyter, beaten and pursued at North Foreland,[24] awaited better days and finished the campaign with his invasion of the Thames. Wellington operated both offensively and defensively from his base in the lines of Torres Vedras, according to the situation.[25] There are an infinite number of examples.

OTHER REFLECTIONS ON THE OFFENSIVE

Having decided that the general conditions permit application of the principle of the offensive, one enters the domain

---

23. Castex was hasty in speaking of a sine wave, since the graph can take any form. Again, Castex uses an illustration as if it had predictive value.

24. July 1666.

25. The secretly prepared fortifications behind which Wellington retired before General Masséna in 1810. Castex offers this elaborate defensive network as a model for what France should have had ready in 1940, *Mélanges*, 324.

of application, which is governed not by universals but by the technique of the day. Everything rests on means and methods, and both of these change with time.

For example, attempts during the last war to pursue the enemy submarines with gun-armed surface ships came to nothing, although to attack them obeyed an indisputable principle. When the method changed, however, when the attacks employed grenades, listening devices, mines, aviation, and submarines, the results were much more productive. Likewise, the Allies had all the material they wanted for their land offensives in 1918—powerful artillery support, tanks, gas—and the results were excellent. The permanence of the offensive principles must therefore be accompanied by the evolution of procedures.[26]

There has been a tendency in certain milieus since the previous war to compare the strategic offensive to the tactical, establishing a hierarchy of the two, or at least between the strategic and tactical result, to the advantage of the former. Such claims have exaggerated the dominance of strategy, doubtless as an overreaction. If it is obvious that tactical success has only a poor return if not exploited by an appropriate strategy, it is certain nonetheless that the tactical result is the basis of the strategic result and is its necessary, if not sufficient, condition. To underestimate tactics would be a dangerous mistake.

That this new current of thought about naval war flowed especially from Germany is worth noting because the Germans have always shown themselves to be good tacticians. Their ability in this regard has not, however, blinded them from attending to certain weaknesses in their strategy, and some of them have attempted with praiseworthy modesty

26. A clear statement of Castex's method of combining historical and material analysis. Repetitious paragraph is omitted.

and zeal to understand them. But they have gone too far in advocating very dubious solutions.

Captain von Groos, in a recent and important work, criticized what he saw as the relegation of strategy to a place behind technology in the German navy.[27] If he is right, then our enemies have blundered, but one must not overly denigrate technology, because it is one of the pillars of tactical success, itself such an important contributor to strategy.

Vice Admiral Wegener reproached the successive German admirals commanding the High Seas Fleet, including the energetic Admiral Scheer, with having practiced only a tactical offensive.[28] But tactics was the necessary prelude to the rest. Admiral Wegener wanted the German high command to adopt a more "strategic" line of conduct by opening a road to the Atlantic, enlisting the army's help in subjugating Denmark and Norway. It would have been a campaign half on land and half at sea, like Napoleon dreamed of seeing in the Mediterranean. The execution of the plan remains unclear. Possession of the Norwegian coast would have required mastery of the Skagerrak through victory over the British in the kind of tactical struggle Wegener dismisses.[29] Moreover, the plan would have thrown Norway into the Allied camp. With bases on the Norwegian coast, the British blockade would have been tightened and Germany's situation

27. *Les leçons de la guerre navale à la lumière de la guerre mondiale* (Berlin, 1929) (author's note).

28. *Stratégie navale de la guerre mondiale* (Berlin, 1930) (author's note). Wegener's treatise has recently been translated by Holger H. Herwig as *The Naval Strategy of the World War* (Annapolis, 1989). See Herwig's useful introduction for the importance of Von Groos and Wegener in German naval thought.

29. Wegener does not dismiss battle but denies the usefulness of battles fought in strategically unimportant waters. Castex might reply that fleets victorious in Wegener's "Dead Sea" could then operate elsewhere.

worsened. In sum, Wegener's analysis omits both the tactical requirements of his proposal and its dubious political and maritime consequences.

Is there in war a necessary connection between one's choice between the offensive and the defensive and one's policy, strategy, and tactics? Does practicing the offensive or the defensive in one of these domains require one to take a similar stance in each of the others, and do people actually behave this way?

One can, I believe, respond affirmatively for strategy and tactics. Whoever takes the offensive in strategy, in the overall conduct of operations, will also do so on the tactical terrain. Behind this lies the impulse of the offensive state of mind. The link between policy and strategy is more controversial. First, it is useful to distinguish between the beginning and the course of the war. When hostilities are in full swing, when spirits are heated by the ardor of battle, one cares only to bring the enemy down by the most appropriate means. Policy can intervene in two senses, to recommend or prohibit certain operations, but its influence cannot or ought not to extend to dictating an offensive or defensive strategic posture.[30] Strategy is free to make this decision.

Things are different at the beginning of the war. At this moment, in theory at least, policy and strategy are independent of one another. Policy indicates the goal of the war, positive or negative; strategy chooses the means, offensive or defensive, to attain that goal, a means that lies in its particular competence. The political factors that bring a nation to war ought not to influence military action, which knows one rule only: to reduce the enemy to impotence. The political form of the war and the military stance are absolutely distinct from one anther. The offensive and the defensive,

30. But surely this is the sort of decision most closely allied to questions of policy.

which are simply ways of making war, have nothing to do with its causes. In particular, in the case where the war's political goal is defensive, that is to say, where the government and the nation desire only to preserve the national territory, its coasts, and its maritime communications, the army and navy can and even ought to attempt—their resources permitting—to put the enemy forces out of action, which is the best means of achieving the defensive ends established by policy. One would then practice an offensive strategy just as if the objective of the war had itself been offensive.

Such is the theory, but things are different in practice.[31]

One can say as a general rule that there is at the beginning of a war a concordance between the two forms of action in the case of an offensive policy. The nation that follows an aggressive policy, that seeks a positive goal like the diminution of the adversary, the conquest of territory, etc., will necessarily adopt an offensive strategy. For her, the defensive makes no sense. Synchronized offensives of policy and strategy were common during the wars of the monarchy and of Napoleon. In 1859, Austria pursued a negative goal and Piedmont a positive one, and it was the latter that took the offensive. In 1870, Prussia was the political aggressor (although Bismarck was fairly skillful in leading France to make the declaration of war), and her armies immediately took the offensive.[32] The aggressive Germany of 1914 worked the same way.[33]

There have been exceptions. For example, at the beginning of the War of American Independence, France adopted

---

31. Very different from the tight collaboration of strategy and policy advocated in volume 3. Castex never weighs ends and means to determine whether an offensive is an efficient way of achieving the result desired by the defender.

32. Strategically, but not always tactically.

33. As did defensively minded France, Castex admits on the next page.

a positive political goal, but her unambitious naval strategy had a defensive demeanor. The Russians in 1904, politically the invaders of the Far East, were militarily defensive, even inert, towards the Japanese. But finally the rule of the concordance of the political offensive and the strategic offensive seems well established.

Concordance between the two defensives does not necessarily exist. A peaceful nation, nonaggressive, whose policy has the negative purpose of maintaining the status quo will indifferently adopt an offensive or a defensive strategy in spite of the evident advantages of the offensive. Many factors intervene: the military means, first, then the tendencies of the government, the general mentality of the nation, the military ideas and personality of the command, etc. One cannot say *a priori* on which side the balance will fall. One has seen some politically defensive states remain on the military defensive because of military weakness or for other reasons, and others adopt an offensive strategy, such as the French Revolution at its beginning, the Federals in the American Civil War, or the Japanese during the Russo-Japanese War. France in August 1914, pacific though it was, practiced the offensive even though her means were inappropriate.

In this last circumstance, policy was wise enough to give freedom of action to the high command.[34] It only imposed, for good reason, the ten-kilometer withdrawal. It is not impossible, however, given the tendencies of our country, for policy to yield to the temptation to go farther and to constrain the command to an initial defensive strategy. Given sufficient resources, for a politically defensive nation, the decision will always be the great unknown factor in strategy.

A final remark remains to be made. In discussing the mer-

34. Note that policy is "wise" to abstain from interfering even in bad strategy while Castex urges strategy to correct bad policy.

its of the offensive, we have attempted to make them more precise and to eliminate certain exaggerations. But this critical approach risks killing the spirit of the offensive, whose strength demands that it be unadulterated and even exaggerated.[35] It is the spirit for enterprises of this sort. If the search for a just equilibrium results in the reduction of the offensive spirit, the dangers will be just as great as those coming from the opposite error of adopting a doctrine relying excessively on the offensive, and this book should be thrown in the fire without reading further.

It is therefore necessary to conclude with the firm and unequivocal doctrine that one must always aim at the offensive with all of one's strength, employing all of one's means and working without respite to acquire what one needs, because only the offensive can lead to great results. But one must recognize at the same time the impossibility of taking the offensive whenever and however one wants, blindly, as a matter of absolute doctrine, at every time and place. The offensive has certain prerequisites that may or may not exist in a given situation. One must expect to meet unsuitable conditions, and the best means of not being discomfited by them is to know of their existence and to be aware that one can often do something while awaiting a better situation.

35. The exaggerated offensive-mindedness of 1914 hurt us in many instances during the last war, but it is fair to remember that it helped us in others (author's note).

CHAPTER 16

THE DEFENSIVE[1]

WHOEVER DOES not enjoy the conditions requisite for initiating an attack remains on the defensive, and the day has passed when, as before 1914, General Lanrezac[2] is said to have told his officers: "If the doors are firmly shut, then I shall discuss the defensive." Made wise by recent experience, we can now freely converse on the subject.

Defensive elements appear within even the most offensively oriented concepts. An offensive plan virtually must include defensives in certain regions because, except given a very rare superabundance of means, it is impossible to be superior at the chosen point without being weaker, and therefore on the defensive, elsewhere. Embedded in the concepts of strategic *manoeuvre* and the economy of force is the idea of a local defense even within a resolutely offensive plan.[3] Moreover, the defensive is frequently mixed with the

1. Raoul Castex, *Théories stratégiques,* vol. 4 (Paris: Société d'Editions Géographiques, Maritimes et Coloniales, 1933): 137–66.

2. No proponent of the *offense à l'outrance,* French Fifth Army commander General Charles Louis Marie Lanrezac (1852–1925) was replaced in August 1914 for his pessimistic appraisal of the situation.

3. Britain itself has frequently had to follow this line of conduct because the great number and dispersion of her maritime interests implied the existence of so many vulnerable points (author's note).

offensive in time as well as in space. The evolution of the situation can force an erstwhile attacker to the defensive even though he conducts his campaign with the intention of taking the offensive as soon as possible so as to arrive at a decision.

Indirect protection, which is offensive in nature because it rests on the threat of attacking the enemy, must not exclude direct protection, pure defense, of important objects. . . . For example, in the days of surface warfare, certain forces were always engaged in the protection of convoys. Even a naval power like Britain, though better endowed than anyone else for achieving indirect protection through its naval squadrons, protected its commercial navigation directly. Battle was sometimes sought by employing the fleet itself in the role of direct protection, thus combining the objectives of defense and *manoeuvre*.

In our day, direct protection is even more favored. Although instantaneous communications facilitate indirect protection, the great speed of modern ships and the consequently briefer duration of their operations reduces the chance of intercepting them. The new tools of war are not vulnerable to indirect protection, the submarine because it can disappear at will, the airplane because of the speed and furtiveness of its attacks. We have come, therefore, even more to rely on direct protection and to accept a great investment in light vessels and aircraft in order to defend our naval forces at sea against adversaries of the same sort.[4] One can even ask whether, given the seriousness of the threat from the air, defense should not in some cases replace the offense as aircraft's primary role. Similarly, defending ships of the line and aircraft carriers against destroyers re-

4. A parallel effort is required to provide antiaircraft defenses inland and along the coasts (author's note).

quires a large number of like vessels. These sacrifices in favor of the defensive are necessary to allow the fleet to deploy its own power offensively.

The offense-defense balance is an ancient problem addressed in the design of any combat ship. In spite of the ardent assertions of the proponents of exclusive offense, it has always been thought reasonable to trade off against armament and speed a respectable measure of protection, even—especially—for an offensive vessel. A ship intended to inflict blows must first be able to endure them. Nowadays, the question is complicated by the need for protection against torpedoes, mines, and, above all, aircraft. Antiaircraft protection—armor, guns, and ammunition—comes at an especially great cost in weight.

Direct protection, though defensive in itself, confers upon the offensive an indispensable freedom of action. It represents security, without which one cannot envision the offensive. Thus, the offensive is not exclusive of the defensive but demands its participation in every area.

Defense obviously reigns when attack is impossible. To understand defense by fleets too weak to take the offensive, we must first address the old notion of the "fleet in being."

THE FLEET IN BEING

The defensive strategy of the "fleet in being" was first introduced by Herbert Lord Torrington, Tourville's luckless enemy at the battle of Beachy Head. Torrington described his intentions both in the correspondence that he exchanged with the British government before the battle and in the defense that he presented to the court-martial that judged him afterwards.

At the beginning of the campaign of 1690, when he had not been reinforced by his Dutch allies nor by Killigrew's

Mediterranean force and was separated from Shovell's[5] forces in the Irish Sea, Torrington had considerably smaller forces than Tourville, who had united with Châteaurenault.[6] He hoped, therefore, to take a waiting position, avoiding battle and withdrawing in front of Tourville behind the sand banks in the mouth of the Thames, where he would be in a good position not only to repulse attacks but to join up with the detached ships that would make their way to him via the coastal channels.[7]

More significantly, Torrington attributed to this plan the special virtue of paralyzing French offensive operations. "As long as we observe the French," he wrote to his government, *"they can make no attack against our ships or coast without running great risks."* Rejecting this analysis, the government ordered Torrington to attack Tourville, and the defeat at Beachy Head followed. Torrington took refuge in the Thames whence he vented his anger by evoking once again his earlier plan: "Had I been left alone, I would have prevented any attack against the land and assured the security of the fleets and merchant ships." Tourville, meanwhile master of the sea, cruised a Channel empty of enemies.

The commentaries on the event make interesting reading. For Corbett, Torrington was the victor of the affair.[8] Tour-

5. Admiral Cloudesley Shovell (1659–1707).

6. Tourville had seventy ships of the line against Torrington's fifty-seven, see E. H Jenkins, *A History of the French Navy* (London, 1973): 172.

7. For sources on the Battle of Beachy Head, see chapter 10.

8. Of Torrington's initial refusal to give battle, Corbett says, "Nothing could be in closer harmony with the principles of good strategy as we understand them," Corbett, *Principles*, 215. Corbett, its best known proponent, proposed that "the doctrine of the 'fleet in being' . . . goes no further than this, that where the enemy regards the general command of the sea as necessary to his offensive purposes, you may be able to prevent his gaining such command by using your fleet defensively, refusing what

ville was not able to act against the ships in the western Channel, which had time to reach Plymouth harbor, nor to destroy the British fleet in detail. Those ships not sunk at Beachy Head were safely moored in the Thames or elsewhere.

Britain's Admiral Colomb,[9] of whom we will speak again later, was still more explicit. "A fleet in being, even defeated, even reduced and *shut up behind unmarked sand banks* was sufficiently powerful virtually *to paralyze on sea as well as land* the action of an apparently victorious fleet."

Admiral Mahan saw more clearly. "It was not the beaten and scattered Anglo-Dutch fleet which guaranteed Britain against invasion. It was the softness or inertia of Tourville and the lack of French transports."[10] Mahan is right. The victorious Tourville failed to exploit his success by pursuit of further operations, but contented himself with parading from one end of the Channel to the other and executing a minor action at Teignmouth before returning to Brest. He and the French government lacked an overall plan. Had things been different, if, as two years later, an invasion of Britain had been planned, or if there had been an attempt to intercept enemy maritime communications with Ireland, one wonders how Torrington could have responded other than by taking the offensive, that is, by abandoning a "fleet in being" attitude that protected nothing at all. One can assume that Tourville would have acted on this assumption and would have organized his forces to provide security against Torrington's likely intervention. In other words, he would have intelligently achieved the compromise that we

Nelson called a regular battle, and seizing every opportunity for a counterstroke," Corbett, 224–25.

9. Admiral Philip Howard Colomb (1831–1899) published *Naval Warfare* (London, 1891), nearly simultaneously with Mahan's *Influence*.

10. Mahan, *Naval Strategy* (1975): 267.

described earlier.[11] Furthermore, his enemy's appearance could not but have pleased him. It would have allowed him to impose a second battle upon an unwilling adversary and probably finish the work begun at Beachy Head. But at no moment would Tourville have been "paralyzed."

Born of an erroneous understanding of a situation, the theory of the fleet in being has been revived repeatedly up to our own day. We rediscover it in the eighteenth-century writings of British Admiral Kempenfelt,[12] many of whose other ideas are very good. In our day, Admiral Colomb, as we saw above, made himself Torrington's advocate and the modern exponent of the theory of the fleet in being. In the third edition of *Naval Warfare*, published in 1899, he reiterated his early thesis and affirmed dogmatically that "the sea ought to be cleared of every fleet or squadron *before advancing naval war a single step* as in the assault on territory." Inspired by Colomb, others have further expanded the thesis as far as to assert that the mere existence of a fleet, even an inferior one, even one locked in harbor, ought to block any seaborne attack and to compromise any exploitation by the adversary of his domination of communications. The exaggeration is obvious. If it is excessive temerity for the inferior party to sail out into battle and destruction, one cannot found great hopes of the method of the fleet in being against an active, enterprising adversary who is knowledgeable of his profession.

This does not prevent some from seeking in past events the confirmation of the theory of the fleet in being. . . . [13]

11. Castex, *Théories*, vol. 1, part 3, chapter 4 (author's note).
12. Rear Admiral Richard Kempenfelt (1718–1782).
13. The events recalled below have already been studied from other points of view in Castex, *Théories*, vol. 1, part 3, chapters 1, 2, and 4 (author's note). Pages 144–46 are omitted.

In 1914, our navy objected to transporting our North African soldiers across the Mediterranean until after the annihilation of the enemy fleet, citing not only the excellent thesis of the preeminence of the fleet but the rather less solid notion of the fleet in being. Under pressure from the army, which absolutely required troops from Africa, the navy had to agree to set aside these doctrines and to begin the transport at the very beginning of the war in spite of the *Goeben*'s and the *Breslau*'s role of fleet in being. The very powerful protection allotted to the operation, too powerful even in view of its wholly defensive objective, permitted its unhindered execution.

In the North Sea, another, much more redoubtable, fleet in being appeared—Germany's High Seas Fleet. Although confined to the Helgoland Bight, it merited the most serious attention. But the existence of the High Seas Fleet did not prevent such urgent Allied actions as the transport of the British army to France, which was rendered possible by the strong cover provided by the British Grand Fleet. That was the beginning. Then the situation stabilized. Behind the impenetrable rampart of the Grand Fleet, the stronger side continued, in spite of the losses inflicted by submarines, to exploit its domination of the sea to maintain external communications, transport armies, and initiate major overseas operations. All of this happened, thanks to geography's cooperation, in spite of an enemy fleet in being, whose ultimate influence on events was minimal.

Britain's strong coverage of the North Sea paralyzed the High Seas Fleet and created a singular spirit of "wait and see" among the British. What good was there in risking decisive battle, in challenging the traps of German submarines, when the German fleet was doing little harm and one already enjoyed all of the benefits that could accrue from a victorious encounter? Such ideas underlaid the passionate debates over Jellicoe's conduct at the battle of Jutland. They explain Mr. Churchill's comment in *London Magazine* in the autumn of 1918 that "the British had no need to seek this battle. . . . Even without a Trafalgar, the *entire* consequences of a Trafalgar persisted and acted." The thesis is logically false; to destroy the enemy is never irrelevant. But it is easy to see how people were led to it by the evident impotence of the fleet in being.

The error of denying the usefulness of the decisive battle is most common to those who, looking only at the western front, neglected the Baltic problem. On this matter, Churchill made belated amends in volume three of *The World Crisis*. It was important to destroy as many German ships as possible so as to prevent them from playing the role of fleet in being in the Baltic and thereby deriving the useful advantages of communication with the Swedes and support for army operations against Russia. But at the time, the matter did not receive the attention it deserved. The Baltic was treated as a secondary theater and enemy superiority there as unable to compensate for his inferiority elsewhere.

In sum, the error of the integral doctrine of the fleet in being consists of the belief that the mere existence of such a fleet suffices to produces an effect, even if said fleet is moribund, and that it will necessarily paralyze a superior enemy who is master of the sea. The concept has never impressed those who chose to act in spite of the fleet in being, who had the means and knew how to use them. Moreover, in our day, can this fleet even boast of being out of reach in its bases? Does the action of enemy aviation not undermine the very foundation of the theory, the invulnerability of the protected fleet? The doctrine must be improved if one wishes to derive an acceptable defensive method.

THE CONDUCT OF THE DEFENSIVE

The side whose inferiority on the surface condemns him to the defensive ought always, in spite of his unfavorable situation, to try to be as active and aggressive as possible. His fleet ought to remember that mere existence does not suffice to convey the title of "fleet in being" and that, to have an effect on events, it must give proof of life. Thus, it must act to impose its will to the extent that its means allow. It must take as much initiative as possible, even if nothing decisive results.

The defensive must therefore above all avoid sliding into the passive state to which abusive interpretation of the theory of the fleet in being inexorably leads. The opinions of the old masters of war are unanimous on this point, and all of them favor what one calls, for lack of a better term, the "defensive-offensive." Jomini, for example, praises "the general who waits on the defensive with the firm resolution to maneuver against his adversary in order to seize the moral advantage which the offensive gives." Clausewitz develops the same idea: "The defense frequently changes form and ought to pass during the course of the action from parry to riposte. . . . To conserve his part in directing the conduct of war, the defender must return the blows he received. . . . Defensive action therefore includes offensive actions. This form of war must not be represented as a shield but rather as an arm as quick to riposte as to parry."[14] According to Rüstow, "For the defensive to be as strong as possible, an *offensive idea* must govern all preparations."

The defender's goal, at sea as on land, will be to oppose a decision. In naval war, this means preventing the enemy from peacefully enjoying the domination of communications. It means leaving that domination in suspense, in dis-

14. Clausewitz, *On War,* book 6, chapter 12 (Howard, 357).

pute, through operations that keep the adversary from gaining definitive control of the situation. History shows this to be possible to a certain degree and that obstacles imposed upon the enemy's activities can sometimes have great value, especially if coordinated with one's own efforts to seek a decision in another domain, through land war, for example.

On land, the defensive evokes principally the idea of positional warfare and fortifications. These concepts play a role in a naval defensive through the intervention of the coast, but the principal element of the naval defensive is the activity of the inferior force. The idea of *manoeuvre* consists, in essence, of avoiding a decisive battle while unceasingly harassing the enemy by limited offensives wherever and whenever one finds a favorable opportunity. Short, rapid, intermittent tactical offensives that avoid coming to grips with superior forces are the normal method. The naval defensive ought to have a constant will to counterattack, always seeking and exploiting the minor offensive but knowing to abstain in unfavorable conditions.

Above all, this strategy demands mobility; its law is movement. Thus, although defending forces can and sometimes even must exploit coastal positions for refuge, defense, and resupply, dependence on the land must be temporary. As long as the defender utilizes these positions, he yields the sea to the enemy, leaving to his mercy what ought to be protected and failing to upset the enemy's operations. A defending fleet that finds itself on the coast should strive to leave it as soon as possible and as soon as a proper occasion for action appears on the horizon.

Counteroffensives are aimed at manageable fractions of the enemy fleet or against his communications and coasts. In principle, anything is good that in any way harms the adversary militarily, materially, economically, or psychologically. Action against communications and coasts can pay a big dividend, not only directly but also in contributing to *manoeuvre* by causing the enemy to disperse his resources in the attempt to protect himself everywhere. The disruption of the enemy dispositions, the division of his forces, and the immobilization of some of them may perhaps provide a favorable occasion for *manoeuvre* against the enemy fleet. Anything that weakens his fleet is of great importance. It remains the supreme objective, however contorted the road one must follow to seek it. Naturally, the more numerous and geographically dispersed are the enemy interests, the greater his extent of coastline, and the more lines of communications he must protect, the more successful will be the method.

The game is difficult, certainly, and easier to prescribe in theory than to put into practice. But it has been played in the past and will be again in the future because modern conditions favor it. The commander upon whom the task falls will know some unpleasant hours. He will have need of imagination, ingenuity, and vision, as well as prudence and patience. He must retain full freedom from constraints like the demands of nervous public opinion for an immediate offensive. . . .

The side that practices the defensive will naturally avail itself maximally of all of its resources. The first, passive resource, which one can use but not to any significant extent modify, is geography, that is to say, "terrain," strategic terrain because tactical terrain is virtually nonexistent in naval war. The most important geographic characteristic is obviously the location of coasts and national positions in relation to the theater of operations. It is on these positions that the defender anchors his counterattacks when he has freedom to act and his retreats when he is pressed. If their hydrographic conformation is favorable, they allow him to protect his coastal communications by dispositions on advanced islands, reefs, shallows, etc., and by arrangements of batteries, minefields, aviation, etc. These local peculiarities allow construction of defended anchorages as permanent peacetime bases. . . .

The defender will do well, if he can, to see that the theater of war is shifted to his own waters and as far as possible from those of the enemy. Here, he will be more comfortable than anywhere else—close to his own bases. Near to necessary resupply and repair, he will be able to take advantage of all of his resources, even of ships with a short range of action. He will be able to employ readily his special vessels and his aircraft. The enemy, far from his bases, a bit "in the air," will be handicapped by the lack of these facilities, especially if the two belligerents are separated by a great expanse of sea.

Thus, the position of the United States during the Spanish-American War was particularly advantageous in comparison with that of the Spanish. Similarly, considerations of this sort led the Japanese to offer their decisive battle against Rodjestvensky very close to their own coasts, though the inspiration behind Tsushima was clearly offensive, not at all defensive as some have sometimes alleged.

In our day, Japan would be well advised in the case of a war against the United States to arrange matters so that the principal operations take place only in Asian waters. Likewise, in the case of a new Franco-German war, all permanent action on our part in the North Sea will run into major difficulties, while we will be very strong in the Channel and, especially, in the Atlantic waters near the Bay of Biscay, where it will be the enemy's turn to be "out of plumb" and half-paralyzed.

But this is a rather abstract statement of an ideal that cannot always be achieved in practice. To defend territorial possessions or maritime communications in a certain region requires actions there and not elsewhere; the theater of operations is fixed. That is what happened to the Spanish in

1898; Cuba being the focus of the struggle, Spain had to fight in the Caribbean. If the United States were to fight Japan, it would probably be in the Far East and nowhere else because of America's position in the Philippines.

Finally, let us add that the defender who employs bases for protection during the intervals between his counterattacks must nowadays remember that he can no longer have the security these bases offered in the past, that he is exposed to enemy aviation. Without a powerful antiaircraft installation at his bases, this method of war will be seriously compromised.

But geography is purely passive and useless unless exploited by counterattacks that interfere with the enemy's activities. These counterattacks will be of a certain kind, obviously of limited scope, without excessive pretensions, and based on certain prerequisites that are not always fulfilled. In brief, they will reflect the relative weakness of the defensive itself. To these actions Corbett gave the apt name "minor counterattacks."[15]

Chief among the minor counterattacks is the *guerre de course* directed against the enemy's communications, which, as we explained above, is likely to pay a high return in terms of *manoeuvre*.[16] History is full of examples of this classic minor counterattack, among the most famous being those of France under the *ancien régime*, the Revolution, and the Empire, of the Confederate States of America, and of the Germans in 1914. All of these used the *guerre de course* against an enemy whose superior naval power they could not challenge in a direct struggle for mastery of the sea. But those who practiced this form of warfare generally commit-

15. Corbett, *Principles*, 227–32, directly links the notion of minor counterattacks to that of the "fleet in being."
16. See chapter 6.

ted the mistake of not integrating it into a more general system of war. Notably, they failed to use it as a part of a *manoeuvre* designed to produce favorable conditions for the clash of fleets. Scheer himself, who clearly enunciated the necessity for this liaison, was not able to achieve it after the disappearance of the surface war against commerce.

His aggressive attitude must not lead the defender to forget that he has his own communications to protect and that their defense can also create favorable opportunities for *manoeuvre*. The defender must also remember that the protection of communications is partly a matter of the geographical and political conditions that will determine the role of neutrals in supplying the belligerents. . . .

But the defensive is no longer limited to the means of the past. New machines have opened vast horizons to minor counteroffensives. The submarine relies infinitely less on the land as a refuge between counterattacks than do other units. Its sanctuary travels with it, so to speak. Because the submarine can seek the protection of the deep whenever pressed by superior forces, it has a freedom of action unknown to surface ships. The submarine is entirely suited for the kind of action behind the lines once undertaken by surface raiders. Designed to slip obstacles that stop other ships, the submarine can attack either the enemy's military force or his communications. The Germans showed us its value during the last war, though one need not imitate their excesses, their political mistakes, nor their failure to support their submarines with surface forces. The British offered us an example of the same sort in the Baltic. These two precedents have a strong link with the defensive problem because the use of the submarine in each case was the consequence of a surface inferiority that prevented a true offensive. Since this time, the launching of larger, more powerfully armed, and longer-ranged submarines capable of operating effectively against distant communications and of bombarding the enemy coastline has increased the submarine's potential usefulness. The minor counterattack of the future will therefore be largely by submarine. . . .

Aviation, another new instrument, will give to the defense another particularly useful means of activity and aggression. Certainly, the defender will have to deal with the air power possessed by the enemy, who may be superior in the air as well as on the surface. He can have two advantages at once. But the air war has the special feature that the mastery acquired by the superior side is essentially local and temporary. It is very fleeting, much more so than is mastery of the sea, and the weaker side will not be impeded by the adversary's manifestation of superiority from undertaking his own operations. Thus, whatever his relative strength, the defender can use his aircraft to execute minor counterattacks against the fleet, communications, bases, and ports of the enemy. This will be one of the strongest cards in his game. He will only be barred from the air in the case where the enemy is not only superior in forces but has the initiative of operations and is able to rule the skies uncontested.[17] Aircraft not permanently attached to the navy can naturally cooperate in these counterattacks. One can call upon reinforcement from the army or the "air force" if the country has one.[18]

The defense will use mines to a great extent to reinforce

17. Airplanes and submarines will be employed against the enemy's surface forces in order to alter the balance in the defender's favor. Let us repeat that the enemy's surface fleet remains the essential objective (author's note).

18. In the latter case, one will have two negotiations to conduct instead of one. The navy's role will be diminished and it will have to call upon the air force. Everything will be a combined operation. That is one of the beauties of this organization (author's note). Compare below, 46, note 9.

his positions and to protect his coasts as well as to inflict losses upon the enemy and to force him to devote major resources to minesweeping. Mining can be done either by surface vessels or submarines.

One can see how these modern resources allow the defense to impart to his minor counterattacks a previously unrealizable vigor and how the psychological difference between offensive and defense has tended to diminish, at least superficially.[19]

The defender ought to be especially careful to avoid an excessive division of resources, the reef that usually sinks defensive systems. A frequent vice of the defender, dispersion, further compromises an already unhappy situation. Scattering his forces deprives the defender of the means to carry out fruitful counterattacks and of the reserves to create a local superiority through *manoeuvre*.

We have seen, however, proposals to distribute flotillas of destroyers and submarines along our coasts, thereby establishing the reign of local defense. At the same time, about 1880, the Americans distributed their monitors along their coastlines in a similarly impotent cordon. Today certain foreign thinkers favor an identical arrangement for air bases, although aviation's great mobility suits it for concentration in a small number of well-positioned forts whence it can be rapidly shifted to the chosen point of *manoeuvre*.

The minor counteroffensive should not, any more than the true offensive, disperse its efforts in multiple directions if it wants to achieve results. It ought to concentrate them on a specific object or a specific region or even, if there is more than one adversary, on one of them alone—either the

19. Modern advances in communications do not violate the rule. The weaker party, though usually less well endowed with telegraph cables and bases, will make good use of radio (author's note).

most important or the most vulnerable. The division of forces and selection of objectives may be even more important on the defensive than in other situations.

Moreover, today the defender profits from a previously unknown freedom of movement. Technological improvements have rendered military or commercial blockades much more open and much less effective than in the past, except in the case where, as with the Allies in 1914–1918, the blockader benefits from particularly advantageous geography. The blockaded can escape more easily and, once out, cannot be easily caught because he has a speed and variety of routes unknown in the days of sail. He may travel safely for a long time if the need to renew his fuel supply does not put an end to his roaming. If he has several bases at his disposal, the game gains increasing complexity and uncertainly.

Furthermore, the blockaded can pick his moment. The defender is not *alone* in choosing the moment of action, but let us say more accurately that the attacker does not have a *monopoly* on the initiative of operations and that the defender can exercise his own initiative. Here we find another major distinction between naval and land warfare. Fleet action depends on the volition of the party waiting in port and happens when and only when he elects it.[20] This only complicates the blockader's task, since he must be prepared at any moment for this event that he does not control. Although he cannot put off resupply, repairs, and careening indefinitely, he always worries about being caught in a position of numerical inferiority. The blockaded, however, need not attempt any adventure until his resources are at the maximum. During the last war, such calculations sometimes

20. But experience shows that, in most cases, the blockaded, whether for lack of resources or low morale, is not very eager for adventure (author's note).

seriously disquieted the British in the North Sea and ourselves vis-à-vis the Austrians in the Adriatic.

Let us end this brief overview of the methods of defensive
strategy by noting that they apply not only at the beginning
of the war to the party that does not possess sufficient resources to adopt an offensive attitude but also to anyone
whose adverse fortune during the course of the conflict reduces him to the defensive. In this case, he must continue to
struggle with his remaining means—tenaciously, persistently, and energetically—until the moment when all resistance has become impossible and he is forced to lay down
his arms.

What benefits can one expect to achieve from defensive
operations? Materially, they will be minor. One will certainly hurt the enemy and inflict losses upon him; sometimes
one will cause serious inconvenience, but the result will usually be far from upsetting his situation of preponderance.

One will "dispute" the mastery of the sea—obviously. But
one can say more than that. There are disputes and disputes;
the concept has degrees. There is the dispute between equals
or semi-equals, when one does not reject or is unable to
reject a decisive battle. This situation belongs to the offensive and has no defensive element. It is how command of
the sea was disputed in Tourville's day, during the War of
American Independence, or, to a lesser degree, by Bruix in
1799, by Napoleon during the events leading up to Trafalgar, and by the Germans in the North Sea during the last
war. This kind of dispute leaves or can leave the command
of certain zones in suspense, giving them equally to the two
adversaries with appropriate consequences for control of
coasts and communications.

There is also the dispute between the weak and the
strong, where the former works vainly through minor counterattacks and through combinations of questionable value

to modify a position of very marked numerical inferiority. Examples are the campaigns against commerce of the War of the Spanish Succession, the Seven Years War, and the Revolution; the guerrilla war after Trafalgar; the exploits of the Confederate raiders; and the German submarine war. In all cases like these, the dispute, even if energetically and intelligently handled, failed either to achieve the necessary freedom of surface communications or, in spite of the losses inflicted upon him, to deprive the enemy of them. One managed to inconvenience the enemy, sometimes seriously, but not to shake off his yoke and transform the situation. Such is the frequent fate of the naval defensive.

More complete and decisive results can only be attained by a true offensive, which must include a surface offensive. That is to say, that it must involve a battle of surface fleets, a battle that is beyond the means of the little partial offensives, limited and conditional, that characterize the surface operations of the defensive. Therein lies all of the difference between genuine offensives and minor counterattacks. The minor counterattacks are offensives of the second or third order; they are expedients. They only appear to reduce the gulf between the defensive and the offensive, but the real difference remains unchanged. The master of the surface, whose resources will suffice for the true offensive, retains every chance of having the final word.

Though it would be imprudent to base too much hope on the material returns of even the most active naval defensive, if properly conducted it can confer considerable benefits in the psychological sphere. Every purely defensive strategy risks undermining morale and incapacitating the defender for later action. As waiting ceases to be a brief suspension of activity and becomes a definitive posture, the defensive engenders over time an increasingly severe state of psychological decay. Extended periods of passivity create a paralysis that survives even material improvements that would allow decisive operations and causes forces to remain on the defensive even after their resources have become sufficient for action. . . .

The strategy of active defense has the great virtue of safeguarding morale by preserving the offensive spirit, the will to attack, the ardor of combat, and the initiative of operations to the extent material resources allow. Thanks above all to the new machines, the defender retains the ability to *manoeuvre* and need not fall into the torpor that traps those to whom all offensive action is forbidden. . . . If the material results are minor and certainly indecisive, the morale effects will be considerable both in the short run, in salvaging and reaffirming courage, and in the long run, because the gain in prestige and respect may have great consequences for the future. . . .

For example, we French still take pride in the actions of our corsairs of the past. They prove to us that we have in us the seeds of great achievements and that it remains only to exploit our potential through organization, material, and judicious conduct of operations. The foreigner, the old enemy in particular, knows as well as we that our *guerre de course* has always been impotent by itself to redress the balance in our favor.[21] But although he weighs matters coldly and from a purely technical point of view, he cannot fail also to view with respect and sympathy the heroism that our ancestors evidenced in their struggle against destiny. He deduces from this that the Frenchman is a solid combatant, worthy of respect, and a valuable ally in time of need. Past valor, whether successful or not, enters into the political calculations of the present. Over the Anglo-French transactions

21. For a more favorable appraisal of the French *guerre de course,* see Symcox.

355

that preceded the great shock of 1914, the shadows of Jean Bart[22] and Surcouf[23] still hovered.

Similarly, the German navy will live for a long time in its own imagination and others' through the memory of events like Jutland, the cruise of the *Emden,* or the submarine war, however debatable they were from the strategic point of view.

Such is the undeniable advantage of active and aggressive defense. In spite of the material failures that history impartially records, future morale often arises from traces left in the soul by the minor counterattacks of the past. . . .[24]

22. Jean Bart (1657–1702) was the most famous French privateer of the War of the League of Augsburg.

23. The most successful French privateer of the Wars of the French Revolution and Napoleon, Robert Surcouf (1773–1827) became a national hero for his successes in the Indian Ocean from 1796 to 1799; see Patrick Crowhurst, *The French War on Trade: Privateering, 1793–1815* (Aldershot, Hants, England, 1984): 100.

24. Castex's psychological argument parallels that of Clausewitz, *On War,* book 6, chapter 26 (Howard, 483). Pages 167–76 on the defense of coasts are omitted.

CHAPTER 17

THE ATTACK AND DEFENSE OF COMMUNICATIONS[1]

GENERAL CONSIDERATIONS

THE OBJECT of maritime operations is to acquire or at least to dispute the mastery of the sea, that is, the control of the essential surface communications.[2] The goal, the *raison d'être,* the final end of naval war is communications—to reserve them for oneself and deny them to the enemy, if possible, or, at least, not to be entirely excluded by the enemy from their use.

Communications are of different kinds. Some lines of communication have a military purpose, the transport of troops, . . . while others are economic in nature. . . . The role of the latter tends naturally to diminish during modern war because of the national mobilization that is the dominant trait of modern total war.[3] So-called economic communications can also have a markedly military character because they provide supplies for the armies as well as for the nation as a whole.

The importance of economic communications varies ac-

1. Raoul Castex, *Théories stratégiques,* vol. 4 (Paris: Société d'Editions Géographiques, Maritimes et Coloniales, 1933): 282–344.
2. As defined in chapter 3.
3. But Castex is about to repeat chapter 3's argument that the modern state depends on imports more than ever before.

cording the situation of the combatants.[4] There are certain countries like the United States and Russia that possess most of the necessary resources at home and for whom external communications are of little importance. But most nations are not in that exceptional situation, and those of Europe depend greatly on foreign ties. In our day much more than before, these nations are absolutely unable to subsist on their domestic resources, and imports from abroad are more indispensable than ever. Moreover, the new threat to national production posed by enemy aviation increases dependence on foreign resources. . . .

Requirements of primary materials—coal, metals, cereals, and, especially, oil—mean that economic communications represent survival for both the army and the country. Since the continuous flow must not stop, these, unlike military communications, have a permanent importance, and their defense poses an equally *permanent* and always vital problem. Attacks against enemy communications, on the contrary, are essential in some cases but not in others, depending on his vulnerability and the significance of communications in his economy as a whole.

If the two belligerents are equally vulnerable, defense takes priority over attack. Attack is optional; defense is not. Failure to attack may result in a harmful loss of initiative; defensive failure can lead to catastrophe. To keep the enemy from breathing brings many rewards, but protecting one's own air supplies is paramount. Mutual asphyxiation solves nothing.

The problem of communications exists alongside that of mastery of the sea. Every belligerent whose resources are not hopelessly inadequate must have the latter as his constant

4. Vol. 1, part 2 (author's note). Castex discusses these matters in detail in chapters 1 and 2.

concern. Often disputed, mastery rarely comes from a single stroke; the combatants struggle ceaselessly to shift the balance in their favor. If one party achieves naval mastery, or, a rare case, has enjoyed it from the beginning, he cannot rest but must consolidate his advantage and prevent the enemy from challenging it. Hence, the action—intellectual, material, and psychological—is unceasing.

The struggle to command the sea is a military struggle between the belligerents' fleets, that is to say, between the ensemble of their combat resources, including both naval and air forces under a single chief.[5] In this continuous duel, each of the fleets has as its principal and essential objective to dominate its opposite number by destroying it or forcing it from the combat.

The struggle for mastery of the sea is strongly related to the attack on and defense of communications. The respective situations of the fleets, each party's greater or lesser degree of mastery of the sea, directly affects the war for communications. Thus the fleet (including the air force), though rarely participating directly in the communications war, provides its framework. The fleet clearly supports and sustains the elements charged with either the attack on or defense of communications. It is thanks to the fleet that they can operate without excessive hindrance by the enemy. The biggest trump card in a successful defense of communications is the defeat, destruction, or blockade of the enemy fleet by the defender's naval or air forces, although one should not rest too many hopes on blockade under current circumstances.

The problem of the attack on and defense of communications cannot then be treated separately from the military struggle between fleets for mastery of the sea. These two

5. Presumably only at the tactical or operational level, as Castex opposed a unified high command. See introduction, XL–XLI.

problems have the tightest and most permanent interconnections. They react incessantly upon one another, first in the matter of the conduct of the war, then in the chronological order of operations, and finally in the division and economy of forces.

The communications war cannot be treated as a separate operation divorced from the rest of the military effort. Certainly it cannot suppress and replace the struggle against the enemy fleets. In particular, one must not harbor the illusion that the attack on communications will by itself and without any other operation lead to a decisive victory. We know how such misconceptions have led to repeated fiascoes in the past.[6]

Of course, if the conditions of the conflict change, this conclusion will have to be modified appropriately. If the inferiority of surface and aerial resources is such that it precludes any hope of success against the enemy fleet, attacking his communications will be the only method of doing him harm, hindering his exploitation of sea mastery, and, consequently, retarding inevitable defeat. This method is particularly indicated if the enemy's communications are vulnerable. This situation is characteristic of the defensive, of which we have already spoken,[7] and the attack on communications ought therefore to be treated as one of the "minor counterattacks" by means of which, in the absence of clashes between the major fleets, the defender attempts to hold his own.

For example, if the Germans, before the last war, did not intend to pit themselves against the Grand Fleet, one does not understand why they did so little to prepare for surface warfare against British communications, given that the use

6. See chapter 15.
7. See chapter 16.

of submarines for this purpose could not have been foreseen. . . .

Finally, in this situation of such serious inferiority that one cannot pretend to mastery of the sea, one is forced to ensure the defense of certain essential communications. And this means keeping the communications in operation, not merely saving the vessels themselves. The latter could be achieved by keeping them in port, which would accomplish nothing.

Thus, there are exceptional situations in which the communications war is the only available mode of operations, but these reinforce rather than undermine the more general rule described for more balanced situations.

Just as the war of communications and the war between fleets coexist, there is also an intimate relationship, characterized by *manoeuvre,* between the elements that prosecute these two wars and between the actions of these elements. If the side that attacks communications at the same time adopts an actively offensive attitude for his fleet, the enemy will be fixed in place. Lacking the resources to parry the blow, he will only be able to devote minor naval and air resources to defend his communications, and commerce raiders will have an easier time.

Inversely, a rationally organized *guerre de course* can greatly aid the fleet, on which rests the possibility of overall and decisive success. Raids against properly chosen points can force the enemy to divert major forces to meet them, thus dispersing his resources and improving conditions for action by the main fleet. In this form, the attack on communications can usefully contribute to the strategic *manoeuvre* of the fleet.

Several simple principles govern the use of the *guerre de course* as an element of *manoeuvre.*

361

1) Threats are more important than effective destruction. The psychological impact of diversions is their greatest contribution to *manoeuvre*.

2) The effect of the diversion is much greater at the beginning of a war, while the defense is still badly organized, than later.

3) It is necessary *to exploit* the diversion by striking a blow elsewhere. Diversion without exploitation is meaningless.

4) The payoff of the diversion reflects the ratio between the enemy forces fixed and the number of one's own employed. Thus, diversions must be carried out with the minimum force possible, both in number and in the strength of individual vessels. In principle, secondary operations should not involve first-line combat ships.

The necessary liaison between the forces attacking communications and those assigned to the military struggle have not always been respected in the past. While the Barbary pirates[8] were supported by the grand Turkish fleets of the sixteenth century, the *guerre de course* of the French *ancien régime* completely misunderstood the connection. In 1904, the Russian groups from Port Arthur and Vladivostok, which ought in theory to have cooperated, acted independently. In 1914, the Germans did not attempt to link the operations of the High Seas Fleet to Spee's distant attacks on Allied communications. When the British dispatched the battle cruisers *Princess Royal, Invincible,* and *Inflexible* against Spee,[9] the High Seas Fleet, failing to take advantage of the opportunity for decisive action against the Grand Fleet, limited itself to the coastal raids of November and

8. Operating mostly from Algiers and Tunis, the Barbary pirates reached their zenith in the seventeenth century but remained a nuisance until the French occupied Algeria in 1830.

9. In response to their defeat at Coronel.

December 1914. Nor did the Germans attempt a serious offensive in the North Sea to divert British attention from Spee.

Direct intervention in the war over communications can greatly profit the fleets. For example, a fleet attack against enemy communications will probably force the enemy fleet to battle. The defense of communications can also be a useful species of *manoeuvre*. Transports can be used as mobile bait, leading the enemy to the planned point of counterattack by the defender's fleet. But the defender must operate appropriately. Scattering his communications over a broad plane favors the enemy by allowing him his choice of objectives and, hence, the initiative of operations. If one remains consolidated, one's forces are never where they need to be, but dispersion leads to weakness everywhere. In both cases, one's communications are seriously at risk. The best plan is to concentrate the transports in a single very large convoy supported, closely or at a distance, by the fleet and by air cover so that communications are protected and that one can bring about combat.

Let us recall that in both of the distinct domains in which *manoeuvre* operates—in the attack on and in the defense of communications—it is necessary to be unceasingly imaginative. One must be creative, vary one's methods, and remain mentally flexible. Routine, predictability, mental laziness, static dispositions are deadly mistakes that the enemy can exploit through *manoeuvre* and by seizing the initiative. . . .

From the clear imperative of integrating the activities of the fleet with those of the forces assigned to the war of communications, in other words, from the essential unity of the two forms of *manoeuvre*, it results that the two must be coordinated. Though separate forms of war, they must be viewed as part of a *system of operations*. Each is one component of war and is tightly linked to the others by the superior will who directs plans, prepares, and conducts the war as a whole.[10]

THE SURFACE VESSEL AND THE WAR OF COMMUNICATIONS

Most of our past experience with the war of communications has concerned surface ships. They monopolized the stage for centuries, and we have precise documentation for their actions during the last two or three hundred years. But, looking more closely, most of this experience is of a certain sort, limited to periods characterized by a complete disparity in force between the two belligerents. One so dominated the surface that the other was forced to take recourse to the attack on communications as a "minor counterattack," a kind of guerrilla war. The exclusive *guerre de course* of the past was predicated on military inferiority.

As a rule, it took the form of sporadic attacks by large numbers of individually weak raiders. Most losses were inflicted by small ships who operated near their ports, either in Europe or in the colonies, and proliferated in times of war. In spite of the evolution undergone by engines and by the laws of war, the process of attacking communications with surface ships remains much the same over time, whether practiced by Jean Bart, by Surcouf, by the *Alabama*,[11] or by the German cruisers of 1914.[12]

10. Pages 295–98 are omitted.

11. Built in England for the Confederacy in 1862, the commerce raider *Alabama,* under the command of Raphael Semmes (1809–1877), was successful against Federal shipping until sunk by the USS *Kearsarge* in June 1864.

12. Aside from *Goeben* and *Breslau,* eight German cruisers were at sea in August of 1914: Admiral von Spee's East Asia Squadron *(Scharnhorst, Gneisenau, Emden, Leipzig,* and *Nürnberg), Königsberg* off the coast of East Africa, and *Dresden* and *Karlsruhe* in the Caribbean.

First, the surface raiders always have had a choice between two distinct zones of operations. There are regions where communications are particularly dense, either around ports or in the sectors sometimes called "focal zones" where the conformation of the land and conditions of navigation force routes to converge. Elsewhere, there are vast oceanic spaces where routes diverge and where traffic is rare and scattered. The regions of the first type seem the most promising for attacking communications; unfortunately, it is also there that one must expect to encounter the most solid and alert defense. In regions of the second type, the situation is obviously reversed—smaller risks but smaller rewards. Raiders operate in each zone according to their temperament and means and with varying results.

The attack on communications obviously differs greatly according the regions where it operates. Where a preponderance of friendly forces is assured, because of the superiority of the fleet, the geography, or both reasons at once, offensive action is facilitated. On the contrary, in regions dominated by the enemy, one can proceed only through rapid and discontinuous raids and at constant risk.

It has always been necessary to increase the effectiveness of the offensive against communications by frequently changing the points of attack and by spreading them as far apart as possible so as to benefit from surprise and to complicate the defender's task.

In the attack against escorted convoys, the need to choose between attacking the transports and attacking the escorts poses a problem transcending the strictly tactical. Many raiders have hesitated when faced with a choice between these solutions. In principle, however, the attack and destruction of the escorts is certainly preferable to the destruction of the transports; the former provides an excellent preliminary to the latter, and the destruction of his warships diminishes the enemy's means and has greater consequences in the long run. This theoretical rule is subject to exceptions. There are cases where the object being transported is particularly valuable or concerns a specific operation that must be blocked at all cost. The transport of troops for a combined operation would be an example. In these cases, concerns of the moment take precedence over permanent advantage and dictate an immediate attack upon the convoyed vessels.

In our day the perennial debate over whether raiders should destroy their prizes is generally answered in the affirmative because of their lack of sea mastery. Raiders therefore have to concern themselves with the rescue of crews, often solving the problem by using a previously captured enemy merchant ship, a solution not without other inconveniences.

Finally, the attack on communications can have either a material or a psychological objective, and the nature of operations will depend on which objective is pursued. From the point of view of *manoeuvre*, the moral objective is incontestably primary. The raiders of the past did not, however, appreciate the importance of *manoeuvre*, and saw only the material effects, the tangible results of their efforts, and, most important, the financial return on their investment. Greed for loot made for poor strategy.[13] This further demonstrates the need for direction of the attack on communications by a higher will, a leader cognizant of the larger obligations invisible to those who execute his commands and strong enough to bend them to them. . . .

The defense of communications has always been practiced according to a theory that distinguishes between indirect (A) and direct (B) protection of communications and, under the

---

13. Privateers found little profit in attacking warships.

rubric of direct protection (B), between its offensive (B$_1$) and defensive (B$_2$) forms. Indirect protection (A) consists of the operations of the fleet against the enemy fleet. Offensive direct protection (B$_1$) comprises patrols, hunting down enemy raiders, and attacks on raiders' bases. Defensive direct protection (B$_2$) includes providing arms for commercial vessels, watching over lines of communications, and organizing escorted convoys.

Of course, the defender rarely has the resources necessary for all of the components of this defensive scheme. Only Britain, during her time of complete naval preponderance, that is to say, during the wars of the Empire, was able virtually to do so. Most of the time, one cannot do everything at once and must be content with doing the most important. In my opinion, A and B$_2$ ought to come first with B$_1$ added if resources permit.

A is naturally primary since no degree of protection will suffice if the enemy's organized naval and air forces are not defeated or at least held in check. But, as we have said a hundred times, indirect protection is insufficient because mastery of the sea is never complete. A must therefore be reinforced by B, especially by B$_2$. Indirect protection and direct protection, far from excluding one another, are both necessary. . . .

Patrols are one of the methods of offensive direct protection. Patrolling is, in fact, a kind of offensive, albeit a rather peculiar and problematic one. It consists of waiting in a chosen geographical area to attack the enemy—if he comes, and one can never be sure whether he will or not. Hardly an intelligent method because the patrolling side immobilizes itself. Patrols protect not vulnerable things but mere space, and aspiring to dominate space pits one against it, against the square of its linear dimensions. But space is the stronger, and one exhausts oneself in the contest, expending resources for a derisory return. . . . [14]

The system of patrolling confounds military wisdom, and, in fact, has never brought good results. It was disastrous for us in 1778, and the British tried it at great expense and to little effect during the wars of the Revolution and the Empire. In 1914, the patrol system was a complete fiasco against the *Emden* and the *Karlsruhe*; the latter, in particular, operated with impunity for three months in the patrolled zone of the central Atlantic. [15]

Hunting raiders offensively is infinitely more logical than defensive patrols. [16] Instead of waiting in a problematic ambush for an encounter with the enemy, one proceeds against him directly, taking as the objective not a geographical area of no intrinsic importance but the adversary himself. When supported by a serviceable communications network and by rapid diffusion of intelligence, pursuit of the enemy generally provides good results. So it was against the Confederate raiders, against the *Emden,* whose days were already numbered when she was destroyed in the Cocos Islands, against the *Königsberg,* [17] against von Spee's division [18] as soon as

14. Such was Castex's own experience as commander of the antisubmarine patrol boat *Altair* during World War I.

15. The *Emden* destroyed or captured twenty-three merchant ships before being sunk by the light cruiser *Sydney*. The Allies had no success against *Karlsruhe*, which blew up.

16. For the argument that not patrolling but "that very method of hunting which [Castex] praises as logical" failed against the *Emden*, see Admiral Sir Herbert Richmond's review of *Théories stratégiques*, vol. 4, *Naval Review* (1933): 62.

17. The *Königsberg* was driven to take refuge in the Rufigi River delta and was destroyed by the monitors *Severn* and *Mersey* in July 1915, Brian Farwell, *The Great War in East Africa* (New York and London, 1986).

18. Destroyed at the Battle of the Falkland Islands on 8 December 1914.

the Allies turned their attention to it, against the *Dresden*,[19] *Cape Trafalgar,* and *Kaiser Wilhelm der Grosse*,[20] etc. The system would have worked against the *Moewe*, who owed her survival to mistakes of execution.[21]

The attack, capture, or destruction of the raiders' bases constitutes a powerful means of compromising their operations. It proved the only way of finishing off the Barbary pirates. In the time of Louis XIV, the British attacked Dunkirk to deprive his raiders of their base, and the same motive led them to capture our colonies and those of our allies during the Seven Years War and the First Empire. The Federals focused on the Confederate harbors and the British on Zeebrugge and Ostende in 1918. But this method, though always profitable, is practicable only when resources are sufficient to carry out an attack and when the bases have limited defensive means. If the positions are strongly protected enclaves or, especially, parts of the enemy homeland, there will not be much opportunity there.

Among the means of direct protection of communications are arming individual merchantmen and making a careful selection of routes for commercial navigation. One may use special routes distant from the usual ones, scattered routes, neutral waters or those protected by other nations, and patrolled routes. One may choose to pass certain areas at night or frequently alter one's itinerary. The most efficacious measure for protection is generally the grouping of transports into convoys escorted by warships. This method works be-

19. Sunk by the British cruisers *Kent* and *Glasgow* on 9 March 1915.

20. *Cap Trafalgar* was destroyed at Trinidad and *Kaiser Wilhelm der Grosse* at Rio de Oro, Castex, *Théories,* vol. 5, 691.

21. During two cruises in 1914 and 1915, the *Moewe* sank thirty-four Allied merchant ships and laid the mine that sank the dreadnought *King Edward VII.*

cause it defends the objects themselves rather than space, because it reduces the chances of encountering the enemy and the risk of loss, because it allows for very rapid changes of itinerary and for instantaneous reaction to attack.

Although used throughout history, the convoy method has been out of favor since the wars of the Empire. . . . It did not seem an economical practice against raiders since steamships were no longer constrained to follow predictable routes, the multiplication of ports dispersed the flow of commerce, and the number of raiders was lower than before. Having a good chance of escaping the enemy, an isolated ship could run the risk of traveling unescorted. Moreover, modern conditions were thought to have exacerbated the inconveniences of convoys. The formation of convoys delays sailings and increases vessels' turnaround times, a disadvantage increased by the shortened voyages of our day. Because of inequalities in speed the division into fast and slow convoys was necessary. Commercial vessels were not accustomed to the risky business of steaming in formation.[22] Finally, port facilities could not be used efficiently when the normal steady stream of traffic changed to a pulsing motion. Jammed upon their arrival, ports fell into a state of complete inactivity in the intervals between convoys.[23] Influenced by prevailing opinion, the British did not organize convoys to defend their shipping against German cruisers in 1914. Only troop transports were so protected, while merchant vessels were simply advised to observe certain rules of prudence. Given the lack of sufficient escort vessels, the Brit-

22. By increasing speed, steam increased the seriousness of collisions between ships.

23. This paragraph is much compressed. Castex cites arguments against the convoy system in Ballard, *Journal of the Royal United Services Institution*, 1898, von Arnim, *Marine Rundschau*, December 1907, and Corbett, *Principles*.

ish could not have acted much differently, but the climate of ideas was certainly a determining factor in British opposition to convoys.

The war over communications involves a number of accessory concerns, which I discuss here only with reference to surface war although their importance can be generalized beyond that single sphere. First, the indispensable complement of the defense of communications is the protection of their *terminuses* in the national territory. Defense of ships at sea comes to nothing if they cannot be protected in harbor. The wise exploitation of ports and rapid unloading of cargoes are other necessary conditions for good communications and demand a constant liaison between the navy and the ministry charged with transport. Finally, every measure that reduces the volume of imports lightens the task of protecting communications and reduces the country's dependence on the outside—hence the value of severe and comprehensive rationing from the very beginning of hostilities.

In the second place, it is superfluous to reiterate the extreme importance of *political* considerations in the communications war. They intervene principally in the control that the belligerents exercise over neutral shipping, each side working to ensure that neutrals supply his adversary as little as possible. In the attack against communications, politics are a constraint, a constant brake on operations. In the defense of communications, they are an asset to the extent that they allow one to benefit from foreign trade. One cannot, however, rely exclusively on neutrals for one's supplies; both national independence and financial concerns demand maximum exploitation of the national flag.

Neutral shipping therefore plays a considerable role in the war for communications, particularly if the theater of operations is near to or crossed by major international trade routes. . . . This observation reminds us that the tyrant *geography* dominates communications by facilitating or complicating their attack and defense. . . .

Finally, *intelligence* is of capital importance in the conflict over communications. In the attack, intelligence ought to provide timely reports of movements by enemy ships and neutrals suspected of bearing contraband. Defensively, it warns of enemy plans and of the approach of enemy raiders. The rapid and secure dissemination of intelligence requires an excellent communications network. Here, as always, intelligence and communications are the arm of offensive and defensive *manoeuvre*.

Such are, rapidly summarized, the lessons concerning the attack and defense of communications by surface means that one can deduce from history or, more accurately, from historical cases involving two belligerents with greatly unequal fleets and, in consequence, the attack on communications as a minor counteroffensive by raiders numerous but individually weak.

We will see further on how these initial conclusions must be modified for the "moderate case," the case in which the two forces are closer to equality and communications can be attacked by *significant* surface units, and also how the intervention of new machines complicates both attack and defense.

THE SUBMARINE AND THE WAR OVER COMMUNICATIONS

The last war presented an experience with submarine warfare that presses upon us with such an overwhelming weight that the lessons of other wars are ignored and the systems of attack and defense derived from the particular situation of 1914 to 1918 come to be treated as definitive. Inevitably, the most recent war tends to obscure all the rest. The 1914 war certainly showed in striking fashion the submarine's extraordinary aptitude for the attack on communications, an aptitude whose exploitation promises to be very profitable. But is submarine war acceptable? Can one attack surface vessels in this manner? I answer this question with an unhesitating affirmative—there can be no doubt about the legitimacy of the method.

At the Washington conference in 1922, I was challenged on this subject by Lord Lee of Fareham, First Lord of the Admiralty, on account of a passage in an article of mine in the 1920 *Revue Maritime*,[24] in which, according to him, I advocated French use against Britain of the German concept of submarine warfare. Lord Lee was misled, however, by an error of translation. I had merely referred to the genesis of the German conception, not, it goes without saying, brandishing the submarine as a threat to Britain. The mistake having been acknowledged by the entire world press, Lord Lee found himself thoroughly confused. His only success was, as he had hoped, to make our delegates ill-advisedly sign the famous Root Resolutions,[25] about which more will be said later. For me, the incident merely provides a magnificent memory of for two months hearing my name shouted to the skies throughout the entire world and having had as my publicist, without charge, the First Lord of the British Admiralty.

But the irony is that Lord Lee was fundamentally correct on the only point that mattered, about my affirmation of the military validity of the German submarine war. Three pages below the passage about which so much noise had

24. Reprinted in Castex, *Synthèse*, 24 (author's note).

25. The Root Resolutions, proposed at the Washington Naval Limitation Talks on 22 December 1920 and finally signed by the reluctant French on 5 January 1921, required submarines to adhere to all of the humanitarian constraints applicable to surface attacks on merchant ships and thereby rendered submarine war against commerce impracticable.

been made, I actually declared that "Germany had the duty, for her cause, to put into play every means and to ask her submarine arm to do the enemy as much hurt as possible."[26] Having been proved wrong on a secondary point, the First Lord failed to convince anyone, even the compatriots who had joined him in his lively polemics, that he was correct on the main issue, and the affair ended on a truly comic note.

I firmly retain my earlier position and continue to affirm out loud what everyone secretly believes—attacking commercial shipping with submarines is perfectly licit. In so doing, I am in excellent company. In a memoir drafted in January 1914 for the May meeting of the Committee of Imperial Defence, Admiral Fisher foresaw and gave advance approval to the German submarine war: "It is to be presumed that the enemy submarine will have no regard for international law and will sink all ships destined for British ports. . . . An apparently undefended merchant ship may prove to be armed and will destroy the submarine that fails to sink her first. . . . The essence of war is violence and moderation of war is an imbecility."[27]

In the *Times* of 15 July 1914, Admiral Sir Percy Scott[28] affirmed that "in war, everything is barbarous. Is the end not to destroy the enemy? To achieve it, one ought to attack his most vulnerable point. Is our most vulnerable point not resupply in food and petroleum?" Conan Doyle[29] prophetically invoked the attack on British commercial shipping by submarines in a novel entitled *Danger* published in *Strand*

26. Castex, *Synthèse*, 27 (author's note).

27. Fisher, *Records* (author's note).

28. Percy Scott (1853–1924) was best known prior to World War I as a gunnery and fire-control reformer.

29. Though better known for the Sherlock Holmes stories, Sir Arthur Conan Doyle (1859–1930) tackled serious subjects in *Great Britain and the Next War* (London, 1914) and a six-volume history of World War I.

Magazine during the course of the summer of 1914. In an article in *Current History* (June 1923), American Admiral Sims recognized that the submarine can be advantageously employed in the war against commerce. How many others believe the same but do not dare to say it for fear of conflicting with received wisdom, of playing the role of *l'enfant terrible,* and of damaging their own interests.

If one admits the legitimacy[30] of the submarine attacks on commercial vessels, one must also see that the rules imposed until now upon surface raiders cannot, by the very nature of things, be applicable. Less for lack of offensive power than because of its weak protection, the submarine is unsuited for artillery battle. Damage that would be trivial to a surface warship can mean the death of a submarine. Nowadays, however, most merchant ships are armed, and consequently, a submarine runs a very great risk if it tries to apply the letter of the law governing surface raiders. The prescribed preliminaries to attack—calling upon the victim to halt, identifying it, questioning its captain, and sending a boarding party, would produce only a sunken submarine. . . . Even were merchant ships unarmed, radio allows them to call quickly for protection from aircraft and light forces.

Moreover, the submarine's ability to obey the regulations concerning boarding and capture are hampered by its small crew and few boats, while its small size virtually prevents it from saving the crew of a sunken vessel. For passenger ships, the problem is insolvable. . . . Whatever desire the submarine has to conduct itself in a humane fashion, it often lacks the means.

Thus, the submarine, handicapped as it is in gunnery ac-

30. Castex has addressed neither the legal nor the moral legitimacy of the submarine.

tion, must adopt as its principal method of operation against commercial vessels their simple, unannounced destruction by torpedo. Obviously it will strive, if possible, to bring all possible aid to the shipwrecked and will abstain from certain German practices of the last war.

Many people, prissy Anglo-Saxons in particular, refuse to grant the legitimacy of this method, but their objections stem from a complete misunderstanding of wartime commerce. They want to believe in the existence of normal traffic continuing peacefully during hostilities and separate from the activities of war; it is paradoxical, however, to support such a thesis given the character of modern war, "total war" to which the belligerents commit every resource at their disposal. In this sort of conflict, one must strike at the adversary's commerce, even that destined for his population, because the attack on his rear hits at his front. As the British jurist Arthur Garfield Hayes said, "There is no logical distinction between supplying food to civilians and to armies; the more the civilians have, the more will be available to the army. . . ."

In total war, the commercial vessel acquires the undeniable status of a warship. Itself a weapon, it can be torpedoed like any military vessel. The "warning" is constituted by the declaration of war itself. In consequence, *the crewmembers of a merchant ship are combatants. . . . True non-combatants (women, children, old people, citizens of neutral states, etc.) ought not to take passage on ships belonging to belligerent powers. . . .* They cannot evoke considerations of humanity to preserve themselves and, in consequence, the ship itself. . . .

The truth about the attack on communications by submarines and, more generally, by other modern instruments of war should neither surprise nor appall. Ought not the law of man, always behind the progress of armament, change with machines (the submarine) and with concepts (total war)? Is it not an illogical illusion to try to block the submarine with an obsolete law relevant to surface warfare?[31]

AVIATION AND THE WAR FOR COMMUNICATIONS

The intervention of aviation in the war over communications is the great novelty of our day. Is it also legitimate as a means of attacking commercial vessels? The affirmative answer rests on the same arguments that apply to submarines; one must attack commerce by every possible means, this one and all others. What is astonishing is that recent polemics have generally avoided the point as if the problem ought not to exist. The Root Resolutions, fiercely dogmatic in proscribing the use of the submarine in commercial war, said not a word about the airplane even though, from the humanitarian point of view, the question of rescue of personnel is even more insolvable for the latter than for the former. . . .

The results obtained by the airplane against communications will vary completely depending on whether they act against convoys or against isolated ships. Escorted convoys can be attacked without hesitation, as military formations, because they leave no uncertainty as to their nationality. Even supposing the worst case for the attackers, that the aircraft were forced to stay at high altitude to avoid the antiaircraft fire of the convoy and the escorts, their bombs could still inflict grave losses. Slow and unmaneuverable, deficient in antiaircraft protection, and usually of high displacement, the merchant vessels would have no way to resist such an attack.

The situation will be very different for isolated vessels. Unable to force a ship to stop and identify itself, an airplane

31. Pages 317–25, a narrative history of "irrational" efforts to ban submarine warfare against commerce, are omitted.

can easily be deceived by false signals, false flags, and camouflage. Moving in for a closer look exposes the airplane to enemy action, while an attack without establishing the victim's identity risks hitting a neutral with all of the attendant diplomatic consequences. Perhaps, in certain particular wars, like that of 1914, one can attack as blindly as the Germans did, but such is a very rare exception upon which one cannot construct a general theory.[32] It would be otherwise if one could make the neutrals accept certain regions as "war zones" where aircraft can act against any merchant ship found there . . . but a thoroughly blacked-out ship would still have a good chance of escaping the airplane at night.

Airplanes can also further the attack on communications by scouting on behalf of raiding vessels, locating distant targets for them and warning of the approach of enemy forces. During the 1914 war, the *Wolf* employed a small seaplane for these purposes. Aircraft are doubtless very useful for dealing with convoys or warships but less so for isolated ships whose nationality would have to be determined. The *Wolf* operated far from the supposed theater of war,[33] where the great majority of ships were enemy and none bothered with camouflage.

Finally, the airplane can attack sea lines of communications via their endpoints on land, that is, by bombing commercial ports. Effectively implemented in the past by shore bombardment, this process now receives from the airplane a more powerful means against which the adversary is less well defended. Such attacks constitute a much greater novelty than air attacks on commerce at sea. Imagine what could be achieved by an enemy who, unconcerned with in-

32. Oddly, Castex uses the impossibility of identifying neutrals as an argument against air, but not submarine, attacks on unidentified shipping.
33. Off East Africa.

ternational considerations, were to attack a bottleneck like the Suez Canal in the hope of plugging it with sunken ships. Of course, political concerns render the field less open than one would think. Commercial ports contain neutral vessels, upon whose destruction governments look with disfavor. Formerly, in the case of offshore bombardment, time was allowed for evacuation. It is impossible to give such warning before air bombardment, although one might give a general warning at the beginning of the war if all of the parties not involved in the conflict were willing to recognize it. Here again, the solution may be the establishment of "zones of war," in which the commercial ports of belligerents would be included.

From the point of view of defending communications against aircraft, the new conditions are not favorable to modern, weakly escorted convoys. This kind of convoy is extremely vulnerable because it is easily identified either by attack aircraft or airplanes scouting for a surface ship. Against a threat from the air alone, solo navigation is much preferable to travel in convoy because of the problem it introduces for aircraft.[34]

If they must be used, convoys require strong air cover. . . . Sufficient resources do not exist, however, to provide all of our many convoys with the necessary protection, and convoys must therefore be consolidated to minimize the aircraft required. A system of huge and infrequent convoys is not unworkable, and the necessary concentration of air escorts can be managed if one has the initiative of operations. There does not seem to be any compromise between large convoys and individual sailings. . . .

34. Assuming, again, that aircraft exercise a restraint in dealing with unidentified shipping that Castex does not expect of submarines. In other contexts, Castex is a strong advocate of convoys.

THE INTERMEDIATE CASE IN OUR DAY

Examples of the attack on and defense of communications have come almost entirely from wars in which there was a great disparity of strength between the organized forces of the belligerents and where the weaker had to resort to the attack on communications as a "minor counterattack. . . ." In all of these conflicts, attacks against communications were generally carried out only by weak vessels against which relatively little protection was necessary.[35] In particular, the last war has exercised an excessive influence and brought us to believe the defense of transports to involve responding only to attacks by submarines and feeble surface elements and to make only rare references to enemy aircraft. Thus, we have arrived at the satisfying concept that we can defend our communications by employing large numbers of convoys guarded by small numbers of weak escort vessels that will suffice to ward off the weak attack we expect to meet in the next war. We assume, with little effort of imagination, that the flow of commerce will take place almost normally, as it did from 1914 to 1918.[36]

To disabuse ourselves of these false ideas, we must assume the middle case, likely to be our situation in a future war, in which the struggle is between adversaries with fleets equally able to dispute the mastery of the sea. The equivalence of strength will translate into the reappearance in the war for communications of significant surface forces capable of delivering not merely minor counterattacks but powerful, concentrated major attacks.[37]

35. "The theory of the convoy system is that ships are normally exposed only to sporadic attack," Corbett, *Principles*, 265 (author's note).

36. An understatement of the efficacy of commerce war from 1914 to 1918.

37. Pages 232–38 are omitted.

But the surface fleet will participate in the attack on communications with all the help that modern technology can offer. For example, although the effectiveness of the surface raider is generally denigrated with references to its limited range of action and frequent need to refuel, the new diesel engine gives it a range of 10,000 miles or more. Since raiders can stay at sea for a much longer time and the relative effectiveness of each ship is much increased, powers formerly disadvantaged by their geographical situations can make themselves felt over a much broader field of action than before. Had the German cruisers of 1914 had a range of action of 15,000 miles, they would have been much more troublesome. The later actions of the *Moewe* and *Wolf* give a picture of the new conditions; in fact, we find ourselves back in the days of the *Alabama*. . . .

In the past, our commerce war was against submarines—slow, short-sighted, and unwilling to face enemy cannon. But everything has now changed, and we face an entirely different adversary. He does not fear gun battle but rather seeks it out as his normal mode of action and cannot be stopped by the third-rate escorts whose weak guns sufficed to frighten submarines. Like all surface ships, he is fast. He sees clearly and far, and his range of vision is further extended by cooperation with airplanes to a distance that one can estimate as being not less than one hundred miles in every direction. . . .

The surface ship is enormously more likely than the submarine to find its target. The danger area of which it is the center is not the small neighborhood threatened by enemy submarines but a vast circle measuring a hundred miles in radius and capable of rapid shifts of position once the ship has seen its prey. Under these conditions, slipping through the mesh is very difficult. The principal benefit of the convoys of former times, the possibility of avoiding submarines by choosing one's route and by changing one's course, has largely vanished.

Isolated travel regains its advantages because of the difficulties that aircraft have in reconnaissance. If one retains the convoy system, it will also be necessary to employ aircraft, either from land or from aircraft carriers, as distant scouts so as to discover the threatening raider in time and to deprive him of the advantage of first contact. It will also be very important to cross certain zones at night when aircraft are out of action. Finally, whatever happens, escorts must be strengthened until they are adequate to meet threats both on the surface and in the air.

Adequacy is relative, proportional to the power of the expected adversary. Since these matters are always somewhat uncertain, a seemingly sufficient protecting force may prove to be deficient in the case of a particularly strong attack. The past offers many examples of this sort, and this consideration leads us gradually to the integral solution that we must still address.

The modern middle case is characterized by the possibility of intervention in the attack on communications by major surface or air units, acting separately or together, and even, at certain moments, by the entry upon the scene of a whole enemy fleet or air force or even both together.[38] To protect commerce in these conditions there seems be no intermediate solution between very dispersed steaming by individual ships or the constitution of *large, very heavily escorted convoys* protected not only by surface ships but by numerous

---

38. The only case in which these eventualities would have little chance of coming to pass would be the very rare one in which the defender has such an aerial preponderance in the disputed zone that the assailant would dare risk only weak surface vessels in attacking communications (author's note).

aircraft. . . . It is, if you like, an improved version of the method in the war of 1914–1918. With large convoys, one puts all of one's eggs in the same basket, ensuring, however, in so doing the solidarity of the basket.[39]

Naturally, the increase in the size of convoys implies a reduction in their number, which is one reason that the method has not been thoroughly applied. The desirable rhythm of foreign trade does not always accommodate itself to large but infrequent sailings. Still, such is the system towards which we are evolving. Large convoys certainly do not confer an absolute immunity upon communications. While they cannot completely ensure that no transport ever suffers a blow from a shell, a submarine's torpedo, or an airplane's bomb, they are an effort to do everything possible to provide the maximum protection. . . .

Necessarily, if one expects the enemy's main fleet to intervene in the attack on communications, there is no course but to form a very large convoy that will be escorted *by one's own fleet* and the largest possible air contingent. There will be no other method than to oppose mass to mass, as did Jean Bon Saint-André,[40] the Japanese in 1904, and ourselves in 1914.

Moreover, it happens that this means of defending communications, large convoys escorted by all possible forces,

39. This question of convoys is one of those that most clearly demonstrate the evolution of methods over time. During the age of sail, weakly escorted convoys gave satisfactory results. With the appearance of the steamship, the convoy's virtues became less decisive, but they proved excellent against the German submarine campaign. Nowadays, faced with surface and air threats alike, it is hardly defensible and must be seriously modified (author's note). Castex's new caution about the convoys he advocated in *Synthèse* (1920) illustrates the effect of material changes on his historically derived theories.

40. A member of the Committee of Public Safety, Jean Bon Saint-André interested himself in naval matters to the extent of sailing on Villaret-Joyeuse's flagship, Jenkins, 206–9, 215.

can admirably serve the *manoeuvre* of the fleet by drawing the enemy to battle. This is especially true for the air force and offers a fruitful method of ambushing the slippery aerial foe.[41] Perhaps there will be air battles over convoys like the surface battles around them.

Because the entire main fleet participates in the attack on and defense of communications, the link between these two forms of action and the *manoeuvre* of the fleet becomes tighter than ever. Here is a tentative sketch of the possible *manoeuvre*. The fleet mounts a major attack against the enemy communications. Whatever the outcome, it moves quickly in another direction: let us say, to escort a large convoy to a major port. After accomplishing this operation, if it has not yet met the enemy, the fleet shifts to another enterprise, for example, mounting a show of force or an attack against the hostile coast, and returns from that mission to escort another convoy and so on. Since this series of operations will be interrupted whenever resupply is necessary, vessels with a satisfactory range of operation will prove invaluable.

The air force will necessarily accompany the principal surface and submarine force, and its activities will be dictated by what takes place below. It will shift its point of concentration depending on which sector is the most important at any given time and participate at the appropriate moment in the offensive or pseudo-defensive in the hopes of thereby sooner or later bringing about an encounter with the enemy counterpart. Because of its great mobility, the air force will, if the geographical conditions allow, experience no difficulty in cooperating with naval forces and will even have more respite than the latter during the intervals between periods of activity.

---

41. Thus, the Allied bombing of Germany in World War II caused the *Luftwaffe* to commit, and lose, its fighter aircraft.

This whole method of conducting operations appears as a series of operations strategically linked by a steadfast will that selects the successive objectives to correspond with an overall intent. One project at a time is accomplished with one's entire force before moving on to the next. At a given moment, one directs all of one's possible forces in the same direction and towards the same objects. . . .

This plan, in spite of inevitable difficulties of execution, appears efficacious and even genuinely artistic. It displays everything that, from the military point of view, contributes to artistry. It involves *manoeuvre*, the offensive, liaison of arms, continual activity, the thoughtful search for battle, consistent initiative of operations, and finally, a most important corollary, it provides the best method of attacking and defending communications.

PART V

THE SEA VERSUS THE LAND

CHAPTER 18

COMBINED OPERATIONS IN STRATEGY[1]

ALL OF the operations described above, blockade, mining, raids, bombardments, "*coups de main*," seem to touch only lightly upon the land.[2] However harsh, their impact is superficial. The sea appears unable to reach the land's vital organs.[3] Is this really true? Are what we have called "skirmishes" not of more importance than they appear? Are they capable of terminating resistance on land, that is, of achieving a decision? To answer these questions, it is necessary to consider the defender's situation, to find his weak points, or, better, the vital points where one can bring about his defeat. In this way, the proper route to a decision will be clear.

Whether or not one can attack the enemy's maritime communications and territory by sea or defend one's own depends upon whether one commands the sea. Moreover, while offensive success can be very profitable and affirms one's superiority, only defensive success, though negative

1. Raoul Castex, *Théories stratégiques,* vol. 5 (Paris: Société d'Editions Géographiques, Maritimes et Coloniales, 1935): 95–115.

2. These operations, assembled under the rubric "*escarmouches*," are the subject of Castex, *Théories,* vol. 5, part 1.

3. Written, of course, before the capabilities of the aircraft carrier, let alone ship- and submarine-launched missiles, had been demonstrated.

and conservative, is genuinely vital. Before killing one's enemy, it is necessary not to be killed by him.[4]

Let us take a hypothetical land power, possessed of inferior maritime forces. Let us refuse him the advantages of a successful defense and suppose him to be incapable of maintaining his maritime communications or of preventing the enemy from attacking his territory by sea. His situation will be incontestably serious, but how serious depends on the geographical situation.[5]

Let us begin with an island, an essentially maritime nation like Britain. Her power, as everyone knows, is a complex edifice that rests not only on the territory of the home state but also on an extended network of commercial, financial, colonial, political, banking, and agricultural concerns, of which maritime communications constitute the soul, the nervous system, and the arterial circulation. The center of gravity of the system, to use a mechanical analogy, is not in the "old country" but elsewhere at some mysterious point situated in the immensity of the oceans. For such a nation, the two equally vital objectives are the maintenance of maritime communications and the protection of territory. Both are satisfied by domination of the sea. Terrestrial superiority alone, however, will only save the territory and, by ignoring the fundamentally important maritime communications, allow the island to perish. Navy superiority is for her a matter of life and death, and represents both a necessary and sufficient condition for survival.[6]

Very different is the more common intermediate case of a continental nation having both land and sea frontiers. For

---

4. This is why Corbett is haunted by the defensive aspect of the problem and correctly envisages the offensive as following after the defensive (author's note). See Corbett, *Principles*, 231–61.

5. Repetition of typology in chapters 2 and 17.

6. The argument for necessity is clear, but that for sufficiency is not.

such a nation, maritime communications, through extremely useful, are not vital. The country relies at least in part on neutrals to act as its lifelines on land or at sea. Such was the situation of Germany and Austria, who managed during the 1914–1918 war to remain undefeated by the Allied naval blockade. . . . The Central Powers, however, were noticeably worse situated than normal for a continental nation of the "intermediate case." Surrounded on three-quarters of their periphery by hostile states, they had only a half-open window on the outside world. Though benefiting in this instance from unusually advantageous conditions, the Allies proved unable to strangle the enemy. If Britain were at war *alone* against Germany, however, the latter's maritime communications would not be subject to interruption because her resources would include the ports of her European neighbors.[7]

The power base of the terrestrial nation is, above all, at home.[8] Its colonies are often nothing more than appendages, distant satellites, which can be lost without extreme peril. Only France, through her relations with her African bloc, can be considered to be, for political reasons, in a position vaguely recalling that of Britain. The vital defensive objective is to safeguard the territory, which one can expect to achieve through possession of superior forces on land. Since naval superiority is ineffective against a danger on land, a continental nation will find land superiority the

7. Neutrals greatly affect the ability of the master of the sea to impose economic pressure. Sea mastery is most effective in the great conflagrations (like the Wars of the French Revolution and Empire and the 1914–1918 war), in which there were few or no neutrals concerned. It is less so in wars of limited scope where there are few belligerents and many powerful neutrals requiring careful treatment (author's note).

8. Castex vacillates between arguing that mobilization for total war has led to autarchy and that the industrial revolution created a world of economic interdependence.

necessary and sufficient condition for facing every eventuality.[9]

All of these characteristics are maximized when the land power is an immense whole, richly endowed with resources, virtually independent of the sea and capable of survival in isolation for an indefinite period of time. Examples of this extreme case, the opposite to the British, are the French First Empire at its apogee in 1810 and contemporary Russia, the giant between Europe and Asia.[10] The position of the United States, having a continent to herself, is entirely parallel. For these colossi, maritime communications have had and will have only insignificant value, and their disappearance would not even be noticed. . . .[11]

Let us digress. With an obscure and sure instinct, the *vox populi* of various nations has always discerned the vital objective. It makes a cult of whatever constitutes the necessary and sufficient condition of power, venerating it and deifying it. Public opinion in an island nation considers the navy as the essential instrument of its security and of its existence; the army is only a complement, valuable but unable to achieve by itself the primary goal of complete defense. Such is the current view in Britain, where the navy holds the high ground and Trafalgar is deemed a necessary and sufficient national event; not only did it save the territory of Britain, but, equally important, it and only it could save her maritime communications.

9. This explains, for example, why Britain and France ended their long struggles without radical revision of their respective positions. One remained superior on sea, the other on land, which were the necessary and sufficient conditions for their respective survivals (author's note). Again, a dramatic leap from necessity to sufficiency.

10. Castex, *Théories*, chapter 3 (author's note).

11. This is undoubtedly why Soviet military writers dismiss mastery of the sea as a "bourgeois idea" (author's note).

In a continental nation, however, public opinion regards the army as the principal tool and makes the navy no more than an important satellite. Before 1914, it took an artificial agitation to bring about the birth of a German navy,[12] and its activities were unnoticed by Germany's military leaders in 1914, who turned their attention to it only later, when they thought it capable of introducing into the game a decisive trump, the submarine war, or when it was a matter of supporting army operations in the Baltic. In France, sea power was seen as facilitating the organization and equipment of the armies of National Defense in 1870–1871. . . .

Consider popular impressions of the great Anglo-French duel of the past centuries. In Britain, the national heroes are the Drakes, the Hawkes, the Nelsons—saviors of the national territory, certainly, but, also and especially, exploiters of sea power to safeguard maritime communications.[13] In France, the great war hero remains Joan of Arc, liberator of territory through land power alone. . . .

We French sailors, nautical servants of a land power, must not be surprised by this attitude. Neither saddened nor complaining, we must accept the situation and concern ourselves with land war because of its importance to the country and the major role that we ourselves must play in it. Though strategically subordinate, our role is nonetheless vast and fundamental. Soldiers of the air must think the same way.

Let us now treat these diverse cases from the offensive point of view, keeping in mind the vulnerability of the land

12. See Holger H. Herwig, *Luxury Fleet: The Imperial German Navy 1888–1918* (London and Boston, 1980), and Berghahn.

13. For a discussion of the importance of the navy in British national consciousness, see Cynthia Fansler Behrman, *Victorian Myths of the Sea* (Athens, OH, 1977), especially pages 111–35.

to attack from the sea. One can only reduce an island state like Britain through naval superiority, which we will assume to have been attained. This superiority allows the invasion of territory and the interception of communications. But the first operation is not indispensable; the second is sufficient in itself against an island or semi-island belligerent. The sea can thus limit itself to "skirmishes" because one of these, the blockade, promises a rapid decision. . . . Peninsular nations can also be vulnerable, though less so, to this sort of operation. Italy, for example, would suffer significantly from the loss of sea routes and, in particular, from interruption of her coastal trade.

If the sea faces a continental nation, the problem is generally very different. Such an adversary being insensitive to interruptions of communications, one must attack his territory itself. Naval superiority proves to be only an intermediary that must be exploited through larger operations. Sea power is valuable only to the extent that it contributes to victory on land, and the sea will support the armies' operations or, better still, participate in them by landing forces from elsewhere. . . .

Britain herself, imbued as her people are with naval prejudices and the excessive conviction that mastery of the sea suffices to handle any contingency, has come to understand the limitations of sea power. Nelson, who found himself in the Gulf of Genoa during Bonaparte's stunning victories in Italy in 1796, lamented his own helplessness. In our day, Corbett acknowledges the situation in the following terms: "Because men live on the land and not at sea, the outcomes of great wars among nations have always resulted, except in very rare cases, either from what one army managed to do to the territory or national life of the enemy or from fear of the possibilities which a fleet could give to the army against the same territory or national life." [14] Thus, in spite of their reluctance, the British were forced to participate vigorously in the land conflicts of the wars of the Revolution and Empire and the 1914–1918 war. The necessity of waging war on land is even clearer in the third case, when the belligerent is not merely a continental nation but a continent in itself. . . .

In the second and third cases, achievement of mastery of the sea, acquisition and domination of maritime communications, however offensive they may be from the naval point of view, are only defensive actions within the framework of the war as a whole. If naval action goes no farther than this, it can neither strike the death blow nor obtain a decision.

If navies would do more, they must conduct combined operations, enterprises of vast scope that transcend the limitations on the sea's ability to operate against the land, which are described above. They are the centerpiece of what the British call "amphibious strategy." In these operations troops transported and protected by naval forces attack enemy territory either to obtain a decision or to contribute strongly to one. Amphibious operations can reinforce the existing effort on the main front, create a new front in distant and hitherto virgin territory, or do both at once.

Although the term *combined operations* ordinarily implies a contested landing of troops on a beach, which obviously requires a "combination" of the actions of the army and the navy, and even of the air force, though the latter's collaboration is a more strictly tactical one, an unopposed landing of troops in neutral, friendly, or allied country is also a combined operation. Thus, Wellington's landing in Portugal, the Allies in Turkey during the Crimean War, and the British and French in Salonika and Egypt were all combined opera-

14. Corbett, *Principles*, 16, quoted above, 44.

tions. . . .[15] Such operations belong to general strategy, which transcends land strategy, naval strategy, and air strategy and coordinates all three, uniting under a higher plan the actions of armies, navies, and air forces whenever the three find themselves simultaneously in play.

Perhaps the operations that concern us might best be described by the all-encompassing expression "overseas operation," which would include all operations involving crossing the sea and therefore requiring mastery of it. They come about through sea power, and they ought to be treated as part of the sea's offensive against the land.

This rapid overview of the nature of the subject leads us to scale our examination proportionately to the present study. We will address only what concerns strategy, excluding everything having to do with execution or tactics. We will treat only the intentions behind these operations, the inspirations that give them birth, their place in the general conduct of war, the needs that bring them into being—in a word, the elements of the general idea of *manoeuvre*. As the following will demonstrate, this conceptual area is already immense.

Overseas operations have on occasion had their confirmed detractors. An oft-cited condemnation from von der Goltz's *Nation Armée* argues that contemporary European nations are so well organized militarily that, even if all active and reserve troops were engaged on the frontiers, they could still rapidly amass superior numbers to counter a landing. Troops would always be available from depots and fortress garrisons, while the telegraph and railway would facilitate movement from the most distant provinces. Thus, amphibi-

15. During the 1914–1918 war, the only major overseas operation involving a contested debarkation with all of its difficulties was the Dardanelles expedition (author's note).

ous landings would suffer great difficulties and promise only poor results. For a populous state with a good military organization, they will prove an opportunity *for victory* rather than a serious threat.

All of this is true—if the sea commits the stupidity of attacking the land under such eminently unfavorable conditions. But there are more inviting possibilities. The landing force can intervene to reinforce the principal theater. It can attack at a distant point where poor communications hamper the defender's response. It can seize territory in a region where the adversary will be forced to guard extended lines of communications and that is very far from his other responsibilities. All these methods will improve the value of the attack because they will diminish the defender's strength in the landing theater to the point where the situation described by von der Goltz is entirely reversed.

This is the element of combined operations that constitutes the finesse in the strategic game. Everything rests on the *choice of point of application* of the new effort, on avoiding the bad point and on choosing the good. And here one should meditate upon Bernhardi's admirable definition of strategy as "the art of leading troops to combat in the decisive direction and *in the most favorable conditions.*"

In the course of history, several nations have made the mistake of launching their combined operations in the mistaken direction indicated by von der Goltz, and they have regretted it. But others who have avoided the error have prospered. It is clear, to illustrate the point, that the project sketched by Admiral Fisher during the last war for a landing on the coast of Pomerania in imitation of the Russians of 1761 was a very chancy one. After reflection, the British renounced it and other plans for landings in Schleswig or the Frisian Archipelago. The terrain being strategically deplorable, every advantage would have accrued to the defender. . . .

Von der Goltz's observations are valid only for enterprises that are so blatantly ill-conceived as to deserve no further attention. His horizon is far too narrow, and one can read between the lines of his work a sole concern with a Franco-German war.[16] He has not looked further, not acknowledged the possibility of future wars other than one that will pit France and Germany alone along the line from Luxembourg to Basel. He did not foresee the magnitude of the 1914 war, its half-land, half-sea form, the multiple theaters of operation, the role of the sea, the stabilization and continuousness of the main front, in brief, everything that should have made combined operations both possible and necessary. He did not think that the Germans, confirmed land animals who shared his world view, would themselves undertake combined operations in the Baltic Islands in 1917 and in the Aland Islands in 1918.

Other theoreticians of the same school and active commanders have criticized overseas operations as diverting troops from the principal front, but this point of view depends on the case. . . . True, perhaps, for the Franco-German situation in 1870, when the Germans were pleased by the prospect of seeing French troops scattered in pursuit of objectives in the north or south of Germany, but it is far

16. This narrow method of reasoning was von der Goltz's system. As he said in his famous aphorism, "He who writes about strategy and tactics ought to teach only a national strategy and national tactics, the only ones profiting the nation for whom he writes." Often repeated by others, this creed combines the true, the disputable, and the false. Undeniably one ought not live entirely in the realm of abstract strategy but must focus on one's own situation because it affects the destiny of the country. Such narrow inquiries cannot, however, produce a complete theoretical or doctrinal work, which must rest on analysis of the most varied possible range of circumstances. A work like von der Goltz's offers as general truth conclusions that are only valid for the particular situation and, when it neglects to make its assumptions explicit, entirely deceives the reader (author's note).

less so in other situations. It suggests a hypnotism by the current situation and lack of general understanding and lends legitimacy to Corbett's antipathy for the ideas of the continental strategists![17]

The situation will often be utterly different from that of 1870. It is possible that the struggle on the principal front will reach such a condition of stalemate that any major offensive would have to take place overseas. It is even possible to have such an abundance of force that not all can usefully be employed on the principal front. Fortifications there may allow troops to be withdrawn for use elsewhere without granting the enemy an opportunity to act. An ally may enter upon the scene with new forces and open a new front because he lacks political or geographical concerns on the initial one. All of these circumstances create possibilities and demands for new combinations through operations overseas. The 1914–1918 war provides apt lessons, and comparison with the 1870 war reinforces our understanding of the general principles.

It remains to add a few words about the realization of combined operations in the domain of strategy. The first question, whether creation of an overseas theater is possible and necessary, involves an infinite complex of conflicting political, military, naval, economic, psychological, and other factors. Since it concerns the overall conduct of the war, it must be handled by the government or, often, by the government working within the framework of a coalition.

Next comes the problem of choosing the region where the combined operation will take place. This decision, too, pertains to general strategy, but it is notably influenced

17. See Corbett, *Principles*, 75–76, for the argument that von der Goltz's emphasis on complete destruction of the enemy army "tends to turn the art of war into mere bludgeon play."

by land strategy, because its final objective is to put the army into action with the best chance of success. Land requirements dominate the situation and override maritime ones.

Only after the theater of future action has been determined do military and naval points of view return to a position of near equality. Each will have his own valid concerns in the debate over the choice of the landing point. The army commander naturally seeks a position where he can achieve superiority, establish a large bridgehead, and achieve easy access by land to his final strategic objective. The naval commander concerns himself with hydrographic and meteorological conditions, with the need for an anchorage protected against bad weather and enemy attacks, water deep enough for the navy to support the landing close inshore, etc. Because army and navy requirements will often be contradictory, planning will require compromise. But this is the domain of tactics. . . .[18]

It would be vain to deny that the technical instruments of our day render the execution of combined operations, and especially the contested landing, much more difficult than before. The speed of enemy warships has increased much more rapidly than that of the convoyed merchantmen, which are also vulnerable to mines, submarines, and aircraft. Surprise has become infinitely more elusive as the abundance of intelligence and speedy propagation of news make secrets hard to keep. Enemy reconnaissance aircraft sweep the skies in constant search for expeditions while radio alerts a defender capable of much more rapid response than in the past. His aircraft will quickly mass over the landing area. Defending troops will arrive by railway and truck, while the attacker's forces will be impeded by the vast encumbrances a modern army brings with it. The infantry

18. Pages 111–12 are omitted.

now carries an immeasurably greater weight of weapons and equipment, while the number of combat and transport vehicles has greatly increased. Some of these, tanks and heavy artillery in particular, even require special landing vessels. All of these details immensely complicate the task of the attackers. One may admire the landings at Old Fort or Sidi Ferruch[19] but must remember that the obstacles overcome on those occasions were trivial compared with those facing belligerents today.[20]

All of these difficulties naturally increase with the size of the landing and reach their maximum with the great combined expeditions that are of the most interest. Corbett, who rightly gave a very large place to overseas operations, wrongly limited them to the rubric of "limited war," a favorite idea of his that he treated as uniquely British. Corbett saw combined operations as intended to seize a minor piece of territory and hold it against all attempts at dislodgement. Colonial wars and certain European wars seemed appropriate for the practice of what he himself called "an inferior form of war." But Corbett looked only at indecisive examples, while we are concerned with combined operations on a grand scale, decisive attacks by the sea against the land, manifestations of amphibious strategy intended to obtain a victory directly, or, by unhinging the enemy on another

19. The bay west of Algiers where the French expedition landed in June 1830.

20. Some have deduced from these facts that landings will be impossible in the future, but this view is too extreme. Like the offensive against a fortified front, the problem simply requires the right equipment. Even now, solutions like an amphibious tank are being devised (author's note). For evidence of the contemporary French navy's skepticism about amphibious operations, see "Note sur le fonctionnement de l'Ecole de Guerre Navale et des Centres d'Etudes dans le cadre de la Défense Nationale," n.d., 1, Service Historique de L'Armée de Terre, Paris, Carton 2N20/3 (Dossier for C.P.D.N. meeting of 29 July 1936).

front, indirectly. In this fashion these vast enterprises, hardly "limited," have intervened and will intervene again in numerous wars, especially in the colossal perturbations that our old European world has experienced and will experience again.

CHAPTER 19

THE THEORY OF PERTURBATION[1]

I<small>T IS</small> strange—but it is a fact—that in the course of every century of modern times, with an almost astronomic periodicity, the tranquility of Europe has been disturbed by a nation or political group aspiring to hegemony.[2] Each of these attempts results in a fight to the death between that nation and the others, a struggle that has shaken our old continent to its very foundations and beside which all other contests appear minor. Many powers have successively held this threatening role: the empire of Charles V[3] in the sixteenth and early seventeenth centuries, France under Louis XIV in the seventeenth and eighteenth centuries, France again during the Revolution and Napoleon, and, more recently, the German empire of the twentieth century. At present, the peril is double-sided—Hitlerian and Fascist—and Soviet Russia will undoubtedly become a threat once she has

1. Raoul Castex, *Théories stratégiques*, vol. 5 (Paris: Société d'Editions Géographiques, Maritimes et Coloniales, 1935): 116–42.
2. I shall limit this discussion to Europe, but one will easily find hegemonies in Asia that support the conclusions drawn from the study of Europe (author's note).
3. Charles V (1500–1558) of the House of Hapsburg inherited Aragon and Castile (1516), Burgundy and Austria (1519), and became Holy Roman Emperor in 1520. His reign was a period of continuous struggle against France, the Protestant Reformation, and the Turks.

put her affairs in order and concentrated her power.[4] Thus, every century has its *perturbateur*.[5]

One flourishing nation, bounding with energy and thirsting with ambition, hopes to dominate all. Its essential characteristic is youth, vitality, and the possession of an untapped storehouse of human energy, and this characteristic explains everything because it implies brilliant activity in every direction. The *perturbateur*, powerful in manpower, in resources, in policy, and in arms, overtly manifests the intention of absorbing and erasing its neighbors.

One would like to live and work in peace. One would like to enjoy a little calm, the rare honest and peaceful pleasures of ephemeral earthly existence, the tranquility of a future that no storm threatens. One would like a little taste of happiness, of a blue sky, of a soft breeze, of the charm of nature, of a moment of repose in the midst of one's taxing daily labors. Impossible! Destiny is written, the destiny of eternal competition, of battle unceasingly renewed. In the presence of a monstrous ambition, one must, on pain of perishing, abandon the pen or the tool for the gun and the plot for the cannon, set aside productive tasks for bloody but indispensable ones in order to quell the enraged beast who disturbs the general tranquility.

The defeat of the *perturbateur* comes only after long and painful efforts. To put down the ambitions of the houses of Austria and Spain required an interminable conflict beginning with the Italian Wars[6] and ending with the Thirty Years War and the Peace of Westphalia.[7] Europe had to struggle for a long time against the power of Louis XIV.

4. Castex almost always employs the assymetrical labels, "Hitlerian" and "Fascist" for the German and Italian regimes.

5. Castex employs without further introduction this term borrowed from Darrieus.

6. France and Spain contested Italy from 1496 until 1559.

7. 1648.

She fought the Wars of the Revolution and Empire for twenty years. The Allies required four years, without the respites common in earlier wars, to put down the Germany of 1914. The future will be entirely similar. Every century has seen and will see a coalition war fought to dissolve a hegemony.

The struggle against one aggressor leads to the rise of the next in a kind of rotation. The reestablished equilibrium is transitory and unstable, and continues to manifest biology's perpetual evolutionary struggle. It is the "aggressive restlessness" dear to Mahan and to Izoulet. Even when fought in defense of a public good, fighting strengthens the muscles, hardens the soul, sharpens the teeth, and whets the appetite. Undertaken to combat one imperialist, it stimulates imperialism among the victors. Growing strong in the course of struggling for its own unity or against a dominating power, an unaggressive nation or race becomes a threat in its own right.

France was the champion of the European equilibrium against Charles V, against Philip II,[8] and then against the house of Austria. Her power increased in the process, and she herself became the aggressor under Louis XIV and, because inadequately subdued, again under the Revolution and Napoleon.

Prussia fought vigorously against the French danger, especially against Napoleon. The most intelligent and most energetic member of the coalition, her victory brought her military strength. Later Prussia, having become Germany, inherited the functions of *perturbateur,* which she continues

---

8. Philip II (1527–1598) marshaled the Catholic forces of Europe against the spread of Protestantism. In 1585 he allied with the Holy League of France in an effort to prevent the accession of the Protestant claimant to the French throne, Henry of Navarre.

to have today with, one fears, reinforcement from Fascist Italy, her erstwhile foe.[9] Russia, at one moment at our side against Germany, will perhaps one day take up in her turn the gauntlet seized from German or Fascist hands.[10]

In sum, over the course of the modern epoch, the trouble-maker has been displaced from west to east. In politics as in meteorology, one easily follows the center of the cyclone.

And in the unceasing cycle of struggle, yesterday's *perturbateur* is often called upon to fight today's or tomorrow's. Austria and Spain fought against the France of Louis XIV and Napoleon. At the Congress of Vienna, France was sought as an ally against Prussian and Russian threats. Nearer to us, France played a capital role in the war against Germany. Finally, it is possible that the civilized west will have future need of Germany as a barrier against Soviet Russia should the latter be driven by anti-European imperialism.

Although their final characteristics are strangely similar, two kinds of *perturbateur* must be distinguished. The "regular" *perturbateur*, though driven by a desire for hegemony, retains its normal internal regime and directs its energies solely to the outside. Charles V's Austria, Philip II's Spain, France under Louis XIV, and Germany in 1914 were all regular *perturbateurs*. The "irregular" one undergoes a revolutionary political and social change; examples include revolutionary France, Fascist Germany and Italy, and Soviet Russia.

The mentality of the irregular type is the more difficult to understand and demands more analysis. It is perhaps the more dangerous because, unsurprisingly, it tends to be more

9. A drastic oversimplification of the rise of Prussia.

10. The theory of perturbation leads to this conclusion, but the schema of east-west relations in chapter 20 supports another.

energetic. The revolutions and civil wars that give rise to the irregular *perturbateur* are effective indices of a level of combativeness so elevated that it directs itself inward before exploding outward. Civil unrest is the most vivid expression and surest symptom of an overflowing vitality, a herald of imperialistic energy. The *perturbateur* very often begins with cannibalism before unleashing himself on the world. The butchery of the Inquisition, the Terror, Hitlerian and Fascist persecution, and Soviet shootings and hangings all manifest variations of the same spirit; all are preludes to or accompaniments of military expansionism and demonstrate the force of the irregular *perturbateur*. Older peoples—calm, reduced in energy, inoffensive towards their neighbors—rarely make revolution.

The *perturbateur* is a mystic. His mysticism is at the same time a cause and a consequence. Leading him to use his power, mysticism is also a reaction of power on the spirit. He attaches his feelings of power to a super-human idea, to an allegedly superior principle—religious, social, or political—that he both serves and exploits. Philip II of Spain, Charles V, and Ferdinand II were religious mystics who put temporal power at the service of the Catholic ideal. Behind the thoughts and acts of Louis XIV lay the inspiration of divine right. The mysticism of the men of the French Revolution was philosophical and libertarian. In a proselytizing spirit similar to that of Philip II, they saw themselves as charged with spreading the formula of "liberty, equality, and fraternity" for the benefit of humanity. The notes of the *"Chant du Départ"*[11] broadcast this mysticism: "The sovereign people advances . . . death to the tyrants. . . . " Germany of 1914 fed on an intellectual and scientific myth—a conviction of the primacy of German culture. Now

11. A marching song written during wars of the French Revolution.

we have a Fascist mysticism, German and Italian, while Soviet Russia bestirs herself in the name of a new virus, that of communism. Communism, the world revolution, the emancipation and dictatorship of the proletariat, these are, at least apparently, the articles of faith that raise the masses, the elements of the modern Slav mysticism. The Russians claim these in the *"Internationale,"* the new *"Chant du Départ,"* which is not theirs but has been appropriated for their cause. The state of soul of the Russian revolutionaries, their willingness to suffer and die for a higher ideal, deceives one into finding in them, as they are described by Dostoevsky, the sentiments of the first Christians.

Mysticism extinguishes all freedom of thought. Penetrating into the domains of reason and the imagination, of science and art, it exploits them for its own ends, deprives them of all neutrality, and colors them in its own image. . . .

National mystics do not allow for abstract science, independent art, or other manifestations of disinterested intellectualism. Science and art are important only for their services to the cause. For the *perturbateurs,* reason is only a tool governed by ideology. . . .

The mysticism of the *perturbateur* takes its natural course in fanaticism, violence, and terrorism. Stemming from the overflow of the spiritual forces that support the national ambition and multiply its material force, these manifestations are dangerous to neighboring states.

The national idea allows anything and forgives everything. Murder, arson, theft, and rape at home and abroad become works of piety accomplished for the triumph of one's faith. The use of force is permitted and even recommended because it imposes the new religion on unbelievers.

The Spanish behaved this way in Flanders, in the New

World, and in Spain.[12] The Terror in the French Revolution resulted directly from this psychosis. Transported by confidence in future success, the Germans perpetrated many reprehensible acts of this type in the first months of the 1914 war. Hitlerian and Fascist persecutions derive from the same state of mind. The Bolsheviks take as their inspiration Nechaev's famous *Revolutionary Catechism* written at the end of the last century, which sacrifices to the success of the world revolution every rule of civilized morality.[13] Their fanatical and inhuman persecutions resemble the *auto-da-fés* of Philip II and might have been arranged by the dreaded master of the *Escorial*[14] himself.

The *perturbateur*'s fanaticism lends itself to rapid military organization in the service of mysticism's aspirations. It has its praetorian guard, its shock troops, its devoted militia. For example, the Jesuits of the sixteenth century, though they worked for religious ends rather than to further the power of the Spanish or Austrian aggressors, became surrogate soldiers because their own objectives paralleled the religious policies pursued by those governments.

The Bolshevik party, center and brain of the Russian fanatic, has also taken on the form of a militant religious order. The initiates isolate themselves from society, devote themselves to the central myth, take a vow of relative pov-

12. In fighting heresy through the Inquisition.

13. For a deeper knowledge of the Bolshevik question, I refer the reader to the excellent work on the subject of my comrade retired naval officer Henry Rollin (*La revolution russe. Ses origines. Ses résultats.* 3 vols., Delagrave, 1931) (author's note). Castex's politics incline him to see in Bolshevik behavior the reification of Nechaev's insistence that revolutionaries must cut "every tie with the civil order, with the educated world, and with all law," quoted in James H. Billington, *Fire in the Minds of Men: Origins of the Revolutionary Faith* (New York, 1980): 65.

14. Spanish royal palace.

erty (to the extent compatible with Russian venality), and undergo constant party surveillance of their private lives. Without seeking to force the analogy, one finds in the Bolshevik party, as among the Jesuits, rigorous discipline, absolute obedience, a militaristic spirit, and acceptance of the principle that the greatness of the goal justifies some degree of morally disputable action, that the ends, in a word, justify the means. Bakunin himself advocated imitating the Society of Jesus, while Marx and Engels objected violently to this tendency among their Russian political co-religists. One can make similar observations about the Italian Fascist and German Hitlerian parties.

The *perturbateur* coerces and persecutes through a political and judicial organization operating entirely outside of accepted principles and laws. The Inquisition, the Revolutionary Tribunal of 1793, the special Hitlerian or Fascist courts, the Tcheka, and the G.P.U. are all varying reflections of the same mentality. One burns while the others decapitate or shoot, but the inspiration remains the same. Not even the "pure" are safe. Ignacius Loyola was a target of the Inquisition, which held Archbishop Carranza of Toledo[15] in prison for seven years. Many French revolutionaries died on the scaffold. Notorious Russian Communists, Trotsky and company for example, were exiled or deported.[16]

The *perturbateur* allows neither equality nor freedom of thought, and this political and social amorality gives it a considerable advantage over societies that do. The state dominates everything, annihilating the individual.

Fanaticism's victims may flee from internal persecution.

15. Archbishop Carrenza de Miranda (1503–1576) was an adviser to Charles V. Imprisoned for heresy in 1559, he was only exonerated in 1576, a few months before his death.

16. Castex could have made a stronger statement had he included the purges of the 1930s.

Every perturbation produces its *emigrés*: the Moors of
Spain, the refugees from the Edict of Nantes,[17] today's anti-
Fascists and White Russians, and the Jews persecuted by
Hitler. But the fanatic's foes cannot count on aid from *emigrés*, who are cautious because the fall of the defunct regime
often resulted from their own mistakes and moral weakness.
Moreover, they are often at heart sympathetic to the aggressor in its conflict against the other powers. To the great
scandal of their foreign hosts, many of the French *emigrés*
during the Revolution applauded the exploits of the republican soldiers. The Jews expelled by Hitler's Germany continue to venerate German strength. The anti-Fascists have a
certain obscure tenderness for the national work of Mussolini. The White Russians, the Russian Orthodox, morally
support the Bolsheviks in their secular diplomatic struggle
against Britain and various Asian powers,[18] and some, like
their French precursors, would end up rallying to their new
masters.[19]

Thus, in the struggle against the *perturbateur* it is generally fruitless to attempt to distinguish war against the state
from war against the nation. The allies wanted to play this
game, to separate France from Napoleon in 1814–1815.
Another coalition dreamed of removing the Hohenzollerns
from Germany in 1818 and the Bolsheviks from Russia in

17. Moslems who refused to convert were expelled from Spain after a
failed rebellion in 1502, and Louis XIV's revocation of the Edict of
Nantes in 1685 led to a migration of the French Protestants who had
thereby lost the protections granted them by Henry IV in 1598; "*emigré*"
most often refers, however, to the royalists who left France during the
Revolution.

18. Such is the state of mind among Russian emigrants regarding a
possible conflict between the Soviets and Japan (author's note).

19. Nelson did not distinguish loyal Frenchmen from *emigrés*. "I hate
all the French," he said, "whether they be royalist or republican," and,
for his purposes, he was right (author's note).

1919. These were wasted efforts that the enemy peoples did not understand. For them, hostility to the foreign overrode everything. . . .

Mystic and fanatic, the *perturbateur* nation reveals an ardent nationalism. This is natural and comprehensible for a regular *perturbateur*. Since the normal power structure always has the task of satisfying the national aspirations and defending the country against foreigners, it is hardly astonishing if it fulfills this function unusually well during a period of perturbation.

But this tendency is much stronger in the irregular case. Even though the latter regime overthrows the power that had personified the country and represented its interests against those of foreigners, often making its revolution in the name of international and anti-patriotic concepts, the result is not what one would expect. In its nationalism, the irregular fanatic matches and even surpasses the regular. Nationalism quickly conquers the nation's soul; a new stimulant makes it even more potent than before.

Inspired by nationalism, the new aggressor nation considers itself to be superior to others, to be the repository of truth, the bearer of a torch capable of illuminating humanity. It is the son of God, or close to it. Comprised of the chosen people, the *perturbateur* reifies superior principles that justify its claims to hegemony. It must spread those principles for the good of humanity and conquer other peoples for the captives' happiness. These political ambitions are avowed with a candid cynicism. Thus, the *perturbateur* is led to imperialism.[20]

Nationalism and imperialism offer the key to still another observable phenomenon, the tendency of the irregular *per-*

20. Pages 128–30 are omitted.

turbateur to follow, but with increased vehemence, the foreign policy of the old regime. The old ideas seem to acquire extra energy. Rejuvenated and enlivened, they behave like a bacillus in a particularly effective growth medium. For example, the French Convention vigorously revived the foreign policy of the old monarchy by negotiating the Treaty of Basel while brandishing that of Westphalia and invoking the ghost of Richelieu. By pursuing the policy of the tsars, the Soviets demonstrate that Bolsheviks and royalists share the goal of pan-Slavism and the aegis of its patron Dostoevsky.

Foreign policy sometimes sharply contradicts principles cherished internally. As the treatment of Prussia and the Batavian Republic in the Treaty of Basel suggests, the Convention and the Directory were not especially kind to certain republics and showed a strange weakness for monarchies. The diplomacies of Communist Russia and Fascist Italy lend themselves to ironic humor. But nationalism and imperialism command; internal policy is one matter and foreign affairs quite another.

Of course, in the name of foreign policy, the *perturbateur* frequently intervenes in the internal affairs of other nations by supporting whichever faction leans towards its own ten dencies, thus pursuing its own interest under the cover of a religious, political, or social ideal. Philip II supported and financed the Catholic League. Our First Republic put all of its power behind the republican parties of other countries. Germany inspires and guides the Nazi movement abroad.[21] The Soviets, directly or indirectly, by themselves or under the camouflage of the Third International, aid the Communist parties of various nations, at least whenever Soviet foreign policy does not object, and hold them to a rigid discipline. . . . In every case, the supported party is

21. "Nazi" rather than "Hitlerian" because outside Germany.

413

the instrument of the imperialist policy of the protecting nation.

Nationalist and imperialist, the *perturbateur* can only be militarist. The conclusion is not at all surprising for the regular one. Thanks to the existence of a normal, stable, ordered, competently led regime, the military institutions of a regular aggressor state can develop to the highest level of effectiveness. They naturally receive benevolent attention from the state to whose projects they are indispensable. Here, militarism is a speciality of the house. Nations like Philip II's Spain, Austria under Charles V, Louis XIV's France, and Germany in 1914 were essentially militarist.

Militarism is less obviously natural to the irregular type. Its internal cataclysm demolishes the institutions of the ancient state, and its destructive passions hardly seem a suitable basis for the reconstruction of a powerful army. The new regime appears to have neither the penchant nor the aptitude for military growth. Militarism, however, is the result. Revolutions have the effect of stimulating military valor, which is one element of the passionate spirit that fills the community. The ambiance of struggle, the constant effort, the general exaltation maximize the qualities from which military institutions draw their strength. Cromwell's revolution turned England into an absolutely militarist state, first on land and then at sea, and gave her a hitherto unknown degree of force. Under the Revolution, one could see in the republican armies the gradual development of a fanatical military spirit driven by a vision of armed world revolution that had been completely absent from the mercenary troops of Louis XIV.

Hitler's Germany and Fascist Italy flaunt a dramatic renewal of military vigor, and the Russian *perturbateur*-to-be has not failed to follow their example. The latter's faith in the utility of military force has found plenty of encouragement within the Communist revolutionary tradition. Marx, who believed conflict a perfect means of assuring the progress of humanity and that the army was an excellent school, hated pacifists. Engels had a frenetic interest in military questions.[22] Lenin studied the subject with passion and believed that the oppressed class had to acquire military skills. Profoundly influenced by Clausewitz, he studied with equal attention the writings of Rossel and Cluseret,[23] the war ministers during the War of the Commune of 1871. Having achieved power, he was haunted by the desire to protect his revolution and his country from repetition of the defeats of 1904–1905, 1914–1915, and 1920 and put military questions at the top of his agenda.

Since Lenin, the Soviets have nurtured militarism in their party and their nation to the point of obsession. While other nations lack sufficient martial spirit even during war itself, the Soviets cultivate it in peacetime. War must inevitably follow the revolution, of which it is the continuation by other means, so the cult of force is practiced and honored. . . .

The martial spirit of the irregular *perturbateur* is naturally furthered by another natural product of revolution—dictatorship. The inevitable movement towards despotism, represented by Cromwell, Robespierre, Bonaparte, Lenin, Stalin, Hitler, and Mussolini, reflects the imperative to eliminate anarchy so as to defend the new regime and the country against foreign threats. Autocracy reinforces militarism because the dictator cherishes war both as a vehicle for fame and a justification for his unconstitutional regime. Such is

22. See Sigmund Neumann and Mark van Hagen, "Engels and Marx on Revolution, War, and the Army in Society," in P. Paret, ed., *Makers of Modern Strategy*, 3rd ed. (Princeton, 1986): 262–80.

23. Paul Cluseret was the Commune's minister of war for four weeks in April 1871, was charged with treason on 1 May, and was replaced by his deputy, Louis Rossel.

the logical process linking mysticism, fanaticism, nationalism, imperialism, and militarism.

The *perturbateur* does not generally shine at diplomacy.
Blundering along, committing every sort of serious error, it
offers its adversaries unexpected resources for salvation.
Psychological principles explain that the powerful suffer
from fantasies of unconstrained pride. The belief that everything is possible blinds reason and foresight and leads the
dictator to stir up new enemies at home and abroad. The
same pride leads to megalomania, to the unreasoning expansion of political and military projects. Soon it becomes impossible to pursue everything at once, and the aggressor per-
ishes in the quest for the impossible.

In its conduct, it disconcertingly juxtaposes genius and colossal mistakes, ideas of great combative value and political
blunders that a child would not have committed and that
stem directly from the sin of pride. . . . [24]

While military power is the trump card of the *perturbateur,* the opposing coalition is usually, in the beginning at
least, anything but militarily impressive. This is hardly surprising since coalitions generally band together to achieve
numerical advantage as compensation for deficiencies in
quality. The coalitions that fought against Charles V, Louis
XIV, Napoleon, and Wilhelmine Germany were all groups
of militarily weak states, and their difficulties in achieving
unified command aggravated the situation to produce weakness and impotence. . . .

Happily, however, the inferiority of coalitions is usually
only temporary. As a general rule, their value gradually increases to match that of the aggressor. Early reverses prove
instructive and, learning from their mistakes, the allies remedy what they can and copy the enemy's methods so as to

24. Pages 136–37 are omitted.

416

acquire a martial attitude. Once quality has become equal, the coalition's superior quantity becomes decisive. . . .

The national revival is largely moral, and it constitutes the good side—if there is one—of these huge conflicts. Renewed creative faculties and virility are the reward for spilled blood and have their impact on other domains of human activity after the return of peace. War reminds us of the need for work, for science, for energy; it is no accident that beet sugar appeared after Jena and synthetic nitrates after the Marne. . . .

Only painful effort gives birth to such important results, but the penalty for sloth is death. The *perturbateur* is a redoubtable adversary. Employing every new and unexpected weapon or method, it keeps its foe constantly disconcerted. The continental blockade and the Boulogne Flotilla, the submarine and gas warfare, the propaganda war and economic attacks, all forced their victims to scramble to find solutions through will and ingenuity. Against the *perturbateur,* the game is always truly interesting; not for a minute is one bored.

Eventually, after bloody sacrifices, long years of battle, vast expenditures of energy, the monster is vanquished. Dawn comes after a seemingly endless night. After such torment, how well one understands the intoxication of those, more fortunate than their dead comrades, who administered to the troublemaker the last, delivering blows! How easily one can imagine the enthusiasm of the British cavalry as it descended from the plateau of Mont Saint Jean in the last phase of Waterloo[25] or Gneisenau's furious pursuit in the

25. Wellington exploited the Old Guard's retreat with a final charge by the 40,000 troops of the allied center, but Castex romantically exaggerates the role of cavalry in an advance largely of infantry; see Chandler, *The Campaigns of Napoleon,* 1089.

course of the following night.[26] These feverish spirits avenged the memory of a long period of defeats, of slavery, and of humiliation. Theirs was a radiant, superhuman vision, which would be experienced in their turn by those who imposed upon their enemy the Armistice of Rethondes.[27]

Happy are those whose destiny is to do battle, so often painful and unhappy, finally victorious, always glorious, against the power unleashed against the rights of man and the liberty of the world! What finer and grander role than that of savior of peoples? How can one not envy the lot of leaders like Tacitus,[28] Marlborough,[29] Prince Eugene,[30] Nelson, Archduke Charles, Blücher,[31] Wellington, Joffre,[32] Foch, Pitt, Clemenceau,[33] of all those to whom fate confided the sacred mission of raising an unbreakable barrier against the *perturbateur* for the general good? Who will be the leaders of the future, who will defend our independence and per-

26. Prussian General Count August Gneisenau (1760–1831) conducted the retreat after Blücher's defeat at Ligny and the pursuit of Napoleon after Waterloo.

27. The Armistice of 11 November 1918.

28. Marcus Claudius Tacitus, Roman Emperor from 275 to 276, who defeated the Goths and the Alani during his brief reign before being murdered by his own soldiers.

29. John Churchill, First Duke of Marlborough (1650–1722), commanded the British forces in the War of the Spanish Succession.

30. Most famous for his collaboration with Marlborough against the French during the War of the Spanish Succession, Prince Eugene of Savoy (1663–1736) also earns a place on this list for victories over the Turks leading to the Peaces of Carlowitz (1699) and Passarowitz (1718).

31. Field Marshal Gebhard Leberecht von Blücher, Prince of Wahlstadt (1742–1819), commanded the Prussian army, which defeated by Napoleon at Ligny on 16 June 1815, determined the outcome of the battle of Waterloo two days later.

32. Joseph Jacques Césaire Joffre (1852–1931) was French commander in chief from August 1914 until December 1916.

33. Georges Clemenceau (1841–1929) was Premier of France from 1917 to 1920.

haps our civilization against the new threats that arise? In spite of their heavy cares and responsibilities, the leaders of the past and of the future are privileged because their actions had or will have the best possible moral support in their conviction that they fight for a great and altruistic cause. The noble task creates an ambiance of force, of passion, and of excitement. Generating courage and endurance, exalting talent, stimulating creativity, it offers the firmest reinforcement of the actions of the statesman and the military leader.

CHAPTER 20

THE *PERTURBATEUR* AND THE SEA[1]

M ENACING FIRST on land, the *perturbateur* then extends its activities to the naval and commercial realm to threaten nations beyond its reach. Maritime expansion is another necessary consequence of its aggressive drive because such a power cannot but push at once in every direction: military, scientific, political, commercial, industrial, maritime, colonial, demographic. . . .[2]

Thanks to fortunate circumstances and, especially, to the mastery of the sea, our continent has managed to escape domination by any single power. Supposing, however, that one of the troublemakers of the past had succeeded in bending Europe to its yoke, power would at least have remained in the hands of those members of the human family best suited by their superior culture and mentality to exercise it.

We have seen worse possibilities. We have seen attempts to overwhelm the white Western world by Asian or African barbarism. Our race, humanity's leaders, has several times

1. Raoul Castex, *Théories stratégiques,* vol. 5 (Paris: Société d'Editions Géographiques, Maritimes et Coloniales, 1935): 143–92.
2. The element of inevitability stems from Castex's definition. Pages 143–72, on the importance of the sea for the expansion of the *perturbateur* and the resistance by the defenders, are omitted.

420

been on the verge of engulfment by huge waves that would drown all civilization and progress. . . .

With a persistent regularity the invader from the East has approached by sea and exploited it for combined operations. Only the battle of Salamis stopped the Persian and, by denying him possession of the sea, prevented future invasions. Actium assured the unity of the Roman Empire and stopped the rise of a separate eastern state. The eastern wave pushed again against Europe with the Arabs. After conquering North Africa, the Orientals,[3] masters of the sea and holders of Crete, Sicily, Sardinia, and the Balearics, conquered Spain. They crossed the Pyrenees, and the West of Charles Martel and of Roland at Roncesvalles barely was saved at Poitiers.[4] Always dominating the sea, the Saracens made constant descents upon the civilized coast, wrenching tears from the eyes of Charlemagne.

With the Crusades, the West recovered a temporary superiority in the Mediterranean and went on the offensive for a time. It was the West that, supported by the sea, invaded the enemy's homeland. King Louis IX, at Al-Mansūra and at Tunis, temporarily shifted the ancient threat from one bank to another of the great lake.[5]

The first two Mongol empires did not move permanently into Central Europe nor reach the Mediterranean, but the

3. Castex refers to the Moslems, whose eastward offensive against China he ignores.

4. Charles Martel, founder of the Carolingian house, defeated the Saracens in 732 in a battle between Tours and Poitiers and known by both names. Medieval romance asserts that Charlemagne's knight Roland died with the rear guard of his king's army defending the Pass of Roncesvalles against the Saracens in 778.

5. For a more accurate view of the near disaster at Al-Mansūra on 8 February 1250, after which King Louis IX of France was captured and had to be ransomed, and the unsuccessful attack on Tunis, where Louis died in 1270, see Hans Eberhard Mayer, *The Crusades*, 2nd ed. (Oxford, 1991): 263, 282.

Turkish menace of the sixteenth century was more serious than any preceding one. . . . The Turkish effort was largely a naval one; their defeat at Lepanto in 1571, a memorable date in the history of civilization and for the moral destiny of the universe, allowed the West to breathe again. . . . In the seventeenth century, the West began an offensive in the Mediterranean culminating at length in the colonization of North Africa, expansion into Egypt, and the Crimean expedition. . . . The 1914 war finished the process by establishing the West's benevolent tutelage over Syria, Palestine, and Iraq. As during the Roman Empire, Europe again reigned unchallenged in this maritime zone. . . .

Salamis, Actium, Poitiers, Al-Mansūra, Lepanto, Navarino, Algiers, the Riff[6] are all acts in a single drama lasting more than two thousand years. The West survived by regaining control of the Mediterranean and undertaking combined operations there. Preemptive conquest and the imposition of civilization dammed the barbarian flood.

Admiral Mahan appears to have felt these truths strongly and to have particularly well perceived the maritime side of the eternal struggle for the destiny of Western humanity. He deserves special credit because this aspect of the question has gone completely unnoticed by most observers, and he set forth his views on the subject when no one examined either the past or the future from the point of view of competition between great racial families.

An expression of his thought, of his political system, can be found in a series of rather heavy essays or journal articles appearing from 1893 to 1904 and collected in a work called *America's Present and Future Interest in Sea Power*. Certain of the essays, "The Possibility of an Anglo-American Re-

6. French peacekeeping operations in her Moroccan colony 1925–1926.

union" (1904) and "The Perspective of the Twentieth Century" (1897), are a powerful evocation of the West's future in relationship to the sea. Mahan included the Americans among the Westerners, as part of Europe psychologically if not geographically. America and Europe ought to be intimately linked, and the American admiral's dream was to see the United States form a tight friendship with Britain and thereby complete the moral aggregation formed by the Dominions and their mother country. For Mahan, this ensemble, Christian in its tradition and mentality, constituted "the oasis of civilization in the barbarian desert," and the great issue of the twentieth century was which of two civilizations, oriental or occidental, would possess the planet and govern its future. . . . While not hating Asia, its customs, or its teachings, he instinctively rejected the prospect of a West destroyed or dominated by an invader and saw that only force could save civilization. . . .

Since the beginning of the twentieth century, we have been spectators of a veritable reawakening of Asia engendered by various causes. Japan's victory over the Russians in 1904–1905 had a profound impact on the entire yellow continent. Then came the 1914–1918 war, which not only generally shook the world but drained Europe militarily and financially. Finally and most important, Russia, changing camps after her defeat and revolution, turned towards Asia and, during the whole first phase of the Soviet regime, deliberately used Asia as a counterweight to Europe. The Soviet activity has been the most serious. Acting as a leavening agent, this half-Asian but part Western power has stimulated Asia to action. During this entire period Russia has clearly taken on the role of *perturbateur* of the future and has done so in fiercely anti-European style.[7]

7. Pages 181–86, on the Soviet threat and the West's civilizing mission, are omitted.

In view of the inexorable threat, the West must keep up its defenses and strengthen its military institutions and warrior virtues at whatever inconvenience to personal ease. It is bizarre and shocking to observe countries tormented by future uncertainties, countries like the United States and Britain and her Dominions, recoiling before necessary military sacrifices, especially military conscription. It is no less strange that nations like France strive further to lighten their military burdens. What can one say about the enterprise under way in Geneva, which happily produces more fuss than success, when the West faces so many serious menaces? Is it blindness and deafness or suicidal madness?[8]

On the military side, it is particularly and absolutely indispensable that the West remain master of the sea as it has been during the last four centuries.[9] Also, we will require mastery of the air, without which it is impossible to control war successfully on land or at sea. Superiority in these two domains will count for little against an aggressor who exploits command of the air to its limits without regard for neutrals.

From the military point of view, the political competitions that divide Europe at present render the greatest service by forcing all parties to retain respectable armed forces. Once the threat is clear, all can turn to the common defense. Were we disarmed, we could unite only our impotence.

8. And we touch here on a malady of exclusively psychological origin that struck a great majority of the West after the war. A mystique of peace, disarmament, renunciation of military things, horror of effort, loss of spirit of struggle, desire for pleasure, laziness, desire for material advantage in the form of allocations and pensions, financial waste, an unbalanced budget, etc. The examples crowd the mind (author's note).

9. And we must have warships built and equipped so as to have little to fear from the submarine and aerial counterattacks that the aggressor will not fail to employ (author's note).

If one looks at the present situation in Europe from the point of view of the eventual defense of the West against the eventualities we have mentioned, it is certain that many present questions will reveal themselves to have unexpected resolutions. One comes to hope that awareness of shared danger will lead European rivals to erase the many past and present hatreds through appeasements, reconciliations, or, at least, compromises without, however, sacrificing the existing military force. For example, if Germany agrees to live on good terms with its neighbors, who are members of the same civilization, one cannot see what interest others would have in keeping her weak socially, politically, or militarily. Rather, she would have to take her place in the system of Western solidarity and will constitute an important piece in the general defensive armature. From this point of view, we can only look with satisfaction at the domestic cleansing process that freed her from Communism and certain undesirable elements. The rearmament of Germany will not disturb us if we undertake a parallel rearmament in France and consequently augment the military potential of all of Western Europe.

Moreover, one can rightly deplore the disappearance of Austria-Hungary. An important component of Europe's protective shield, it will have to be reinvented in the form of some kind of Danubian confederation. It is equally essential that Poland be reconciled with Germany after the latter has been satisfied by the concessions mentioned above. The question is terribly complicated and bristling with difficulties but must be resolved. As for Italy, the Fascist regime is a major inconvenience for us, but it is incontestable that we are better off with the black shirts in power than seeing our neighbors delivered over to anarchy, militarily impotent, and with Communism at our gates. If Fascism understands its place in a defensive union with its Western neighbors, then one can only commend its birth and prosperity.

Only Japan does not have its place marked in the Western plan as a factor of order in the presence of the Asiatic disorder. It is still indispensable, always in the name of the same concerns, that the West follow towards the people of Asia, from Turkey to China, a wise and peaceful line of conduct, skillful and benevolent, and avoiding any reinforcement of the hostile bloc.

Finally, the Western nations ought to conform in all colonial actions to a clear notion of white solidarity in the presence of other races.

Unhappily, present realities are far from the hopes and vows. At the center of Europe, new aggressors have arisen in Hitlero-Fascist Germany and Italy that, forgetting their properly European duties, threaten the peace and tranquility of the continent. They have created for other nations, France among them, a much more immediate peril than the distant and hypothetical clash between Russia and the West. Concurrently, Britain has failed in her task of preserving the equilibrium, taking refuge since the war in a too-splendid isolation from continental affairs, manifesting indifference and incomprehension of the dangers all around us. With the Western union broken, the menacing elements have reacted and sought support in other non-Western or even anti-Western elements. And there is only an instinctive and logical conservative reaction.

France, head to head with Fascism and desiring to avoid any reverses for her Polish and Danubian allies, has made approaches to Russia, which is also disquieted by the ambitions of German Hitlerism. France works, as always, to find an eastern counterweight that would also make her independent from the Anglo-Saxons in matters of security. She finds herself led towards Slavism. An anti-Western solution?

"*Lys and Croissant.*"[10] What to do? Necessity commands. Poland has reasoned similarly. Her reviving concerns with Germany led her to turn towards the Soviet Union for support. Will she later act as the Soviets' advance guard against the West following the plan that Prince Czartoryski offered to Tsar Alexander I?[11] Is Asia already installed at Posen? One can fear for the future, but present circumstances demand this rapprochement of Poland and Russia.[12]

France is still forced to seek military reinforcement from her colonial troops, again to throw men of color against other white men in the latter's fratricidal struggle. Regrettable from the point of view expressed above, it is necessary for our security. And, once again, the choice is not ours but is forced upon us by the aggressor.

It is certainly desirable to resolve today's problems in line with those of tomorrow and the day after, but it is not always possible. Today's threat is the most immediate. If we are to survive, the rest must wait. The solutions imagined, however, are as ephemeral as the problems to which they correspond, and one must keep the permanent problems in view and prepare to focus in their direction when they again impose themselves.

This political and moral digression appears to have diverted us from our principal subject: the action of the sea against the land in combined operations. But this diversion is only apparent, for when one studies any form of war, one is infallibly led to consider the conditions in which it was

10. *Fleur de Lys* and Crescent—an unlikely amalgamation of the Bourbon and Turkish flags.
11. Adam Jerzy Kaiaze Czartoryski (1770–1861) worked to restore the dismembered Poland as a liberal state under the Romanov crown.
12. Written before the recent Polish volte-face (1934) (author's note).

fought and to investigate whether these conditions will exist in the future. Thus one slides unsurprisingly from the military domain to the political.

We see clearly now the characteristics of the amphibious enterprises that have occurred in the great conflicts that have embroiled humanity and determined its fate, characteristics having a great and poignant interest, past, present, and future, and deserving our passionate attention.

One can then see by what sort of mysterious connection of fate, of providential fixation of destinies, of superhuman determinism, mastery of the sea has played the decisive role in the combat against the powers of destruction, against the agents of Evil, against the immoral ambitions focused on the enslavement of others. Every time, with an implacable rigor, it has prevented the insanity of a man or a people from changing the face of the earth. It has regularly saved the freedom of the world and of civilization, and it will save them again if complemented by the aerial superiority that is now its indispensable component. Sea mastery has intervened to ameliorate the lowest moments by permitting defensive islands to survive. In happier times it has increased the available means of attacking and overthrowing the *perturbateur*. In both cases, its effects were revealed largely through combined operations. Depending on the circumstances, maritime power has been either the multiplier or the divisor of land power, reinforcing or weakening the decisive effort by the land armies who protect or conquer territory. . . .

MAJOR PUBLICATIONS BY ADMIRAL CASTEX[1]

1903

"Le nouveau port de Saigon." *Revue maritime* (June 1903): 1377–1402 (Chapter 2, *Les Rivages indo-chinois*).

1904

Les Rivages indo-chinois. Etude économique et maritime.

Le péril japonais en Indo-Chine. Réflexions politiques et militaires.

"Le pavillon national en extrême-Orient." *Revue maritime* (March 1904): 367–430 (Chapter 8, *Les Rivages indo-chinois*).

1905

Jaunes contre Blancs. Le problème militaire indo-chinois.

1907

"Note sur un cas particulier de la méthode des hauteurs égales d'étoiles." *Revue maritime* (June 1907): 517–44.

1908

"De l'essence propre et du rôle d'un état-major naval." *Revue maritime* (May 1908): 259–90 (Chapter 2, *Le Grand état-major naval*).

---

1. Includes only books and journal articles. All French works are published in Paris. For the more extensive list from which this is drawn, see Coutau-Bégarie, *Castex*, 228–45.

1909

Le Grand état-major naval. Question militaire d'actualité.

1911

Les Idées militaires de la marine au XVIIIe siècle. De Ruyter à Suffren.

"Les traces de l'oeuvre de Suffren." *Revue maritime* (February 1911): 259–311.

1912

L'envers de la guerre de course. La vérité sur l'enlèvement du convoi de Saint-Eustache par Lamotte-Picquet.

"Unité de doctrine sur terre et sur mer." *Revue militaire générale* (July 1912): 95–97. Summary of *Les Idées militaires de la marine au XVIIIe siècle.*

1913

La manoeuvre de la Praya (16 avril 1781). Etude politique, stratégique et tactique.

1914

La bataille du XVIe siècle. Lepante, et ses enseignements d'actualité. Lecture at the Ligue maritime française, 13 December 1913.

"La liaison des armes sur mer au XVIIe siècle." *Revue maritime* (February 1914): 145–71; (March 1914): 289–319; (April 1914): 5–16. *Revue militaire générale* (December 1913): 750–82; (January 1914): 17–51. *Journal of the Royal United Services Institution* (February 1914): 211–36; (March 1914): 359–85.

1920

Synthèse de la guerre sous-marine. De Pontchartrain à Tirpitz.

Chapters 1–4 also published in *Revue maritime* as:

"Charactéristiques de la guerre sous-marine allemande" (January 1920): 1–29; "Parades et ripostes" (February 1920): 101–84; "Particularités diverses" (March 1920): 305–26; "Le rôle des flottes cuirassées. La liaison des armes" (April 1920): 478–503.

1921

"Functions of the Office of Naval Operations." *Proceedings* of the U. S. Naval Institute (December 1920): 1987–99. Chapters 1–4 of *Questions d'état-major* prepublished in *Revue maritime* as: "Principes d'organisation" (January 1921): 12–30; "Les renseignements" (February 1921): 161–184; "Les ordres" (March 1921): 301–23; "Exemples d'ordres" (April 1921): 462–82.

1922

"La conduite de la guerre. Le G.Q.G. maritime." *Revue maritime* (August 1922): 160–87.

1923–1924

Questions d'état-major. Principes. —Organisation. —Fonctionnement. 2 vols.

"Von Spee's Strategy at the Outbreak of War." *Proceedings* of the U. S. Naval Institute (November 1924): 1876–78. Reprint of article in the *Baltimore Sun*, 2 September 1924.

1925

"Effect of Aircraft on Future Warships." *Proceedings* of the U. S. Naval Institute (January 1925): 154–56. Reprint of article in the *Baltimore Sun*, 3 November 1924.

"End of Giant Dreadnoughts." *Proceedings* of the U. S. Naval Institute (March 1925): 467. Reprint of article in the *Baltimore Sun*, 23 December 1924.

1926

"Réflexion sur la conduite des opérations combinées." *Revue maritime* (May 1926): 594–626; (June 1926): 734–67; (July 1926): 62–79.

"Les noms de bateaux." *Le moniteur de la flotte* (14 August 1926): 1.

1927

"Les idées militaires contemporaines et la formation de l'officier." *Revue de Paris* (1 May 1927): 93–113; (15 May 1927): 328–49 (Chapter 7, *Mélanges*).

1928

"La modernisation de l'éperon." *Revue maritime* (January 1928): 1–21; (February 1928): 191–222 (Chapter 5, *La Liaison des armes sur mer*).

1929

Théories stratégiques, vol. 1: *Géneralités sur la stratégie.*

1930

Théories stratégiques, vol. 2: *La manoeuvre stratégique.*
"La guerre sous-marine allemande." *Revue de Paris* (15 September 1930): 344–66.

1931

Théories stratégiques, vol. 3: *Les facteurs externes de la stratégie.*

1932

"The Weapon of the Weak. A French View." *Journal of the Royal United Services Institution* (November 1932): 737–43.

1933

Théories stratégiques, vol. 4: *Les facteurs internes de la stratégie.*

1934

"Le blocus." *Revue maritime* (May 1934): 289–322 (vol. 5, part 1, *Théories stratégiques*).

1934

"Devait-on attaquer les Dardanelles?" *Revue maritime* (July 1934): 1–37 (vol. 5, part 4, chapter 3, *Théories stratégiques*).
"La campagne de Salonique." *Revue maritime* (November 1934): 577–98; (December 1934): 739–64 (vol. 5, part 4, chapter 5, *Théories stratégiques*).

1935

Théories stratégiques, vol. 5: *La mer contre la terre.*

1937

De Gengis Khan à Staline, ou les vicissitudes d'une manoeuvre stratégique (1205–1935).
"Mer-terre-air." *Revue militaire générale* (July 1937): 13–28.

("Importance variable de la maîtrise de la mer," vol. 1, 118–28, *Théories stratégiques*, 2nd ed.).

Théories stratégiques, vol. 1: *Géneralités sur la stratégie*, revised and expanded second edition.

"Les servitudes de la stratégie." *Revue militaire générale* (August 1937): 209–24.

"Réflexions sur le danger aérien." *Revue militaire générale* (October 1937): 403–32. ("Le facteur aérien," vol. 1, 418–44, *Théories stratégiques*, 2nd ed.).

1939

Théories stratégiques, vol. 2: *La manoeuvre stratégique*. Revised and expanded second edition.

"Les liens des diverse stratégies (Un cas concret)." *Revue des questions de Défense Nationale* (May 1939): 45–73 (Chapter 1, *Mélanges*).

1942

"L'Afrique française ou la revanche de la terre." *Mers et colonies* (April–May 1942): 3–5.

1945

"Les liens des stratégies." *Revue de défense nationale* (July 1945): 6–22.

"Aperçus sur la bombe atomique." *Revue de défense nationale* (October 1945): 466–73.

1946

"De quelques aspects militaires de la géographie." *Revue de défense nationale* (February 1946): 147–61; (July 1946): 3–16 (Chapter 2, 32–51, *Mélanges*).

1947

"Océans et mers étroites." *Revue de défense nationale* (February 1947): 159–71 (Chapter 2, 89–112, 121–24, *Mélanges*).

"Du déterminisme géographique." *Forces aériennes françaises* (February 1947): 591–603 (Chapter 2, 64–75, *Mélanges*).

"Marine et nation." *Revue maritime* (April 1947): 410–33 (Chapter 9, first version of *Mélanges*).

1948

"Les arrières." *Revue de défense nationale* (January 1948): 3–20;
(January 1949): 3–20 (Chapter 4, *Mélanges*).

"La mer et la liberté du monde." *Recueil de l'Academie des jeux
floraux* (1948): 139–62.

"La pure doctrine." *Forces aériennes françaises* (December
1948): 307–31.

1949

"Le haut enseignement militaire." *Forces aériennes françaises*
(March 1949): 755–76.

1950

La manoeuvre au plan défense nationale." *Revue de défense nationale* (January 1950): 3–17.

1951

"Toujours la revanche du barême." *Revue de défense nationale*
(June 1951): 696–99.

1952

"L'Afrique et la stratégie française." *Revue de défense nationale*
(May 1952): 523–34 (Chapter 4, 184–200, *Mélanges*).

1953

"En Méditerranée avec le Pentagone." *Revue de défense nationale*
(August–September 1953): 123–34.

1954

"La Russie et la mer." *Revue maritime* (July 1954): 843–56.

1955

"Moscou, rempart de l'Occident." *Revue de défense nationale*
(February 1955): 129–43. Partial republication, *Revue de défense nationale* (April 1967): 585–89.

"Quelques aspects stratégiques de la guerre d'Indochine." *Revue
de défense nationale* (December 1955): 523–38.

1959

"Sa majesté la surface." *Revue de défense nationale* (April 1959):
604–15. Partial republication in Chapter 2, 42–47, *Mélanges*.

1970

"Marine et nation." *Revue maritime* (May 1970): 581–94. (Chapter 9, 401–13, *Mélanges*).

"Le cas géostratique français." *Revue de défense nationale* (October 1970): 1526–38. Extract from Chapter 9, *Mélanges*.

1976

Mélanges stratégiques (Théories stratégiques, vol. 6). Preface by Rear Admiral Lepotier.

1991

La Liaison des armes sur mer. Edited by Hervé Coutau-Bégarie.

INDEX